DECLINING TO
DECLINE

Age Studies

Series Editor

Anne M. Wyatt-Brown,
University of Florida

Anne M. Wyatt-Brown and Janice Rossen, eds. *Aging and Gender in Literature: Studies in Creativity*

Margaret Morganroth Gullette. *Declining to Decline: Cultural Combat and the Politics of the Midlife*

DECLINING TO DECLINE

CULTURAL COMBAT AND THE

POLITICS OF THE MIDLIFE

Margaret Morganroth Gullette

UNIVERSITY PRESS OF VIRGINIA

Charlottesville and London

The University Press of Virginia
© 1997 by Margaret Morganroth Gullette
Printed in the United States of America

First published 1997

⊗ The paper used in this publication meets the minimum requirements of the American National Standard for Information Sciences—Permanence of Paper for Printed Library Materials, ANSI Z39.48-1984.

Library of Congress Cataloging-in-Publication Data

Gullette, Margaret Morganroth.
    Declining to decline : cultural combat and the politics of the midlife / Margaret Morganroth Gullette.
        p.   cm.—(Age studies)
    Includes bibliographical references and index.
    ISBN 0-8139-1721-2 (cloth : alk. paper)
    1. Middle age.   2. Middle aged persons—Social conditions.   3. Ageism.
    I. Title.   II. Series.
    HQ1059.4.G85   1997
    305.244—dc21   96-37520
                                                                                   CIP

To my mother, Betty Eisner Morganroth,

my father, Martin Morganroth (1905–1974),

my brother, Lewis Neil Morganroth (1943–1966),

my husband, David George Gullette,

our son, Sean Morganroth Gullette,

and the generations we represent.

Contents

Acknowledgments

"WRITER AND INDEPENDENT SCHOLAR"—these precious titles can also be a cover for occupational homelessness and loneliness. But over the past decade I have felt rich in friends, and the project rich in allies. Mark Halliday's response to the chapter of *Safe at Last in the Middle Years* on the power of decline narrative gave the initial impetus to *Declining to Decline*. In my attempts to write essays—sublime contemporary form of freedom—that mixed autobiography, literary and cultural commentary, musings and theory, politics and passion, and (of course) the midlife, age, and aging, Alix Kates Shulman has aided and abetted. Her own writing too gives me courage to believe there is an audience waiting at that unorthodox intersection. Werner Sollors was the first person in the humanities to see the theoretical potential of my work on the midlife; reading him, I came to believe that I should work toward an intervention in culture. He came upon me floundering out of the morass of positivism and offered me a timely pull out onto dryer, higher ground. Mike Brown saved me from theory terror: his wise special blend of phenomenology, existentialism, postmodernism, left politics, and tolerance for my own idiosyncratic mental structures let me hope that room could be made for them on the big globe of cultural studies. After many years, my precarious hope for a community in the humanities that cared about the issues has begun to be realized by the far-flung and valiant age-studies posse—especially Thomas Cole, Kathleen Woodward, and Anne Marbury Wyatt-Brown.

My midlife adventure under my two brave new rubrics started in 1986–87 at the Bunting Institute of Racliffe, then directed by Elizabeth McKinsey. Only that nurturing place could have pumped me up enough to leave my day job and strike out transversely across the disciplines and the genres. The following year the Murray Center allies read my first efforts at mainstream prose with enthusiasm: the late Rose Coser, Evelyn Nakano Glenn, Debra Kaufman, Eileen McDonough, Virginia O'Leary, Ellen Rosen, and Mac Runyon. Paul Hernadi at Santa Barbara picked out this relative unknown and let her launch her social constructionism of the midlife at his 1990 conference on "Aging and Dying." A fellowship from the National Endowment for the Humanities for a historical study gave this contemporary one the grounding it needed. That work in progress, as well as *Declining to Decline, Safe at Last in the Middle Years,* and my other projects are to me all parts of a series called *Midlife Fictions.*

Editors at different kinds of publications paid me to practice turning age critique and theory into readable bite-sized bits. Audreen Ballard, editor at *Lear's* in its brief glory days, when it actually thought it could reform the midlife of women, printed such audacious concepts as "age ideology" and "system" long before anyone in the theory journals did. At the *New York Times Magazine,* Nancy Newhouse helped turn that first awkward piece into comely prose. Laurence Goldstein at the *Michigan Quarterly Review* wrote tough-minded fascinating letters. And Robley Wilson at the august *North American Review* published my very first midlife essay in 1978 and offered me the key-note address at the *NAR*'s 175th anniversary party for my attempt to unthink the midlife. Marcia Ann Gillespie at *Ms.* simultaneously cut and improved and cheered, a rare feat. Nancy Essig at the University Press of Virginia saw the manuscript of *Declining to Decline* whole and steered me toward clearer versions. Gerald Trett regularized the manuscript with delicacy and precision. I have had the best editors in the business.

Many Boston-area institutions have given me a temporary home, collegial-ity, and a chance to present my work (even when it crossed their disciplinary lines): the Schlesinger Library at Radcliffe, the Wellesley Center for Research on Women, Women's Studies at Northeastern, the Women's Studies Commit-tee at Harvard, and the English department at Simmons College. My thanks to the late Pat King, Barbara Haber, Susan Bailey, Debra Kaufman, Susan Su-leiman, and David Gullette respectively for their invitations. The reference staffs at the Schlesinger and at Widener Library at Harvard have been cordial and indispensable colleagues. Mary Berg made the Society of Institute Fel-lows, the postgraduate body of the Bunting Institute of Radcliffe, a platform. Through many of these years, Warner Berthoff has generously shared his per-manency of desks and shelves.

For a long time, the only midlife work akin to mine was that of people in the social sciences, many of whom were gracious about my own parallel work: Janet Z. Giele, Margie Lachman, Jackie James, Judith Brown. Bert Brim, the head of the MacArthur Research Foundation on Successful Midlife Develop-ment, held out a helping hand across the border.

Since 1978 I've tried out many new ideas in small discussion courses I've given at the Radcliffe Seminars, with the strong support of then-director Nancy Downey. I might not have had the chutzpah to think "age autobiogra-phy" could be a genre of interest if the participants hadn't been producing it along with me in verbal accounts that needed only the label to become self-conscious. Over the past fifteen years, my women's group—whose members now span from thirty-nine to sixty-six—also helped me develop faith that, in the midst of a hostile culture, there can be mental liberation from the desperate trials of middle-ageism.

Being "marginal" has a good rep among progressive intellectuals and activists these days. I don't doubt the benefits, for me, of looking sideways at our culture, or up, askance, or down. And the project might have been unthinkable if I had been climbing the ladder of a traditional academic career as I once planned. But marginality can also impede. David Gullette has been my main support in every way; he has kept me going through periods of discouragement, and has been my first and last editor. Sean Gullette, from the generation in training to be rivalrous, shows that there can be mental liberation from youthism and helps me deconstruct the most painful of all binaries, that between parents and children.

For leads about how to extend the freedom marginality provides, I want to thank Frinde Maher, John McDermott, Inez Hedges, Victor Wallis, and the others in my study group. One branch, of course, is action. As a delegate from my Sister City Project, I visit San Juan del Sur, Nicaragua, every year to work on education, nutrition, and health projects; as I write, my husband and I are just back from our eighth trip. Here in the North, marginality has allowed me to speak as a public intellectual about crucial questions hidden by the terms of current social debate.

That the condition of the middle years is such a moral and political issue should become clear in this book—perhaps even by the end of the first chapter. In holding such a belief, I have found increasing support over the years. All the friends who have lived lives parallel to mine since college and have granted me intense glimpses within, have also given the concept of age identity dense reality. Along with the friends the project has brought me, I rejoice in Caroline Cross Chinlund, Stephen Chinlund, Penelope Sales Cordish, Cornelia Wilson Higginson, Coppélia Kahn, Andrea Petersen, Judith Morganroth Schneider, Suzy Scarff Webster. They, along with those I have named and others in my thoughts, constitute the affinity group for whom I initially write. *Declining to Decline* could not have come into being without those elective affinities.

Some of these chapters, or parts of them, have been excerpted in different versions in mainstream magazines, literary quarterlies, and academic journals.

Versions of "A Good Girl" and "Ordinary Pain" appeared under those titles in *North American Review,* in September 1990 and May/June 1993, respectively.

Two short sections of "Face-Off" appeared under different titles in *Lear's:* "Autumnal Face" in January 1990 and "Face Lift Con" in March 1991; a third section appeared in the "Hers" column of the *New York Times Magazine* on January 29, 1989.

"Midlife Heroines, 'Older and Freer'" appeared under that title in *Kenyon Review,* Summer 1996.

A short excerpt from "Menopause as Magic Marker" appeared first in *Ms.* in Summer 1993; the entire chapter appeared in the fall 1994 issue of *Discourse.*

A short excerpt from "My Mother at Midlife" will appear in *Ms.* in February 1997.

"The New Gender Politics of Midlife Bodies" appeared under a slightly different title, in *Michigan Quarterly Review* in fall 1993. It has been reprinted in *The Male Body,* edited by Laurence Goldstein (Ann Arbor: Univ. of Michigan Press, 1995).

An excerpt from "The Politics of Middle-Ageism in a Postmodern Economy" appeared under a different title in *Dissent* in fall 1995.

The cartoons from the *New Yorker* are reprinted by permission: "Well, There's Mid-Life," drawing by Koren; © 1985 The New Yorker Magazine, Inc.; "In the last few months . . . signs of aging," drawing by Koren; © 1990 The New Yorker Magazine, Inc. *Doonesbury,* © August 17, 1992; reprinted with permission of Universal Press Syndicate. All rights reserved.

1

Vulnerability and Resistance

Vulnerability

WHEN I WAS almost as young as Dante Alighieri at the time he found himself in his dark wood, I realized I was having perplexing inner conversations with myself about aging. A voice would say sharply, "It's too late to think of starting this new career." Then another voice said, "But you're not even in your prime." Then the first would list all the reasons I should feel belated, and the other would argue back.

These jagged episodes of self-appraisal occurred unexpectedly, first thing in the morning or at 2:00 A.M., startled into activity by some slight cue: a dour sensation, a twinge of sadness when a former movie idol appeared in an older "character" part, a pang when the radio played a high-school tune I loved by, even though I wouldn't be seventeen again for anything. Etcetera. As if the external world were an enormous, comprehensive file of age-related cue cards. An almost automatic soliloquy, at first it was too brief, or perhaps too well repressed, to become conscious: it felt like a sudden drop in blood sugar or realizing an old friend had snubbed me. But I got more proficient, so to speak. Without volition, as if I had been drilled, my mind could scroll through a ready-made list of what I took to be age deficiencies. The contrast of my youthful past with my depleted present could transpire in a second or go on for an unhappy hour, color the night and the day, threaten the accomplishments of the years. Swinging back and forth between these poles—decline or progress?—I couldn't decide who I was in order to end them. "My first person pronoun was ? / instead of I," as poet Fanny Howe puts it.[1]

These anxious soliloquies didn't stop as my thirties went on. Something in me kept saying that it didn't make sense. I was too young to feel like a has-been: healthy, happily married, with a young child; I was solving my career problems. My father had died a few years before, but grieving didn't seem to figure in these secret conversations. They were about *aging*. I was too embarrassed or perhaps too depressed to tell anyone about them. But I started listening to people about my age with pointed attention, and, reticent as they might be, I felt they must be enduring similar premature, shifty self-assessments. I began to find hints of them in print. Say a man was relishing a self-congratulatory plus ("I still have most of my hair"); quick as a flash the rebuttal comes, "I only have so much life left . . . I'm on the downhill part." Or it could go the other way around. "My brain cells are withering . . . but I learned French at fifty. But why can't I remember that name?" In the 1970s and 1980s the few who noticed such feelings of loss (in high-status men) were astonished.[2] I was far from being alone. Nor was this a *woman's* problem.

Warily, I started to look out at the culture for explanations of the midlife soliloquy of age anxiety. I didn't find anything that satisfied me. The experts are divided—just like the soliloquy. To them too aging-into-the-middle-years is a toss-up between a curse or a "growth experience." Sociologists and developmental psychologists and their pop epigones tell us that most informants believe we're getting better in middle life—more compassionate, better able to cope with problems, more sensitive to others.[3] Looking at my friends, I can only agree. I could even add to the progress side: "we" grow more resilient, assimilate new concepts faster, stretch our moral ambitions, invent new pleasure for ourselves, control envy and malice better. Some people (including me) make breakthroughs that go way beyond earlier narrow expectations of "the middle years of life." Whether we know it or not, we are in the process of developing that substantial sense of self-over-time that I call age identity. Midlife could be a name for that long rich time of life when we possess both knowledge of the workings of the world and maximum power to make change. This view could lead us to question the other experts and eyewitnesses—the ones who say the opposite. "There seems to be a remarkable consensus of opinion among researchers and adult development theorists that entrance [*sic*] into middle age is frequently stormy and stressful." Common sense is on this side: at some point, feeling that we are declining is supposed to be "natural."[4] Who can deny it?

If "we" are doing as well as some tell us—and even believe it—why are we so vulnerable to age-related grief? If midlife decline is natural, why can we feel so disappointed or angry? And if bittersweet "ambivalence" were the answer—a tad of decline, a jot of progress—why would we keep oscillating between the extremes? Is there a way past these slippery, contradictory "truths"?

If *Declining to Decline*—and age studies more generally—cannot explain these conundrums, among others, those reaching midlife are liable to exhaust themselves in repetition and self-doubt. Although it may appear merely personal, the phenomenon of midlife aging also has immense ethical, economic, and political consequences—far beyond those the discourse usually permits us to consider. Explaining "the midlife" is not boring, petty, or depressing, as we may have been led to feel. It's urgent; and the better we get at it, the more exhilarating it will be. If we can demystify midlife aging, we can begin to imagine, experience, and share a more vital, fair, bearable vision of the entire life course. To do this, individuals must see themselves not as isolated bodies but as collective stakeholders capable of resisting the culture and transforming it.

Aged by Culture

The basic idea we need to absorb is that whatever happens in the body, human beings are aged by culture first of all. This is social constructionism.[5] *Declining to Decline* applies the principle to age. Everything we know of as culture in the broadest sense—discourses, feelings, practices, institutions, material conditions—is saturated with concepts of age and aging. The particular beliefs and feelings about the life course that North Americans internalize and the narratives we happen to tell at midlife compose a set of effects with a discernible history and devious, well-supported, interlocking maintenance strategies. *Age ideology* is my shorthand term for the system that regulates it all.[6]

"The midlife" is a cultural fiction. (I always put it in imaginary quotation marks, like "aging.") The new age category serves as my decisive case first because, young as I was when all this started, that was what I had to call the time of life when all the contradictions came home to me. Second, because it is through analyzing the middle years that I can push the principle to its inevitable, radical conclusion: even with "aging"—now the most unabashedly bodily of all the supposedly body-based conditions—we should look first and hardest for constructedness.

Ageism is an ancient prejudice, but middle-ageism is our own local twentieth-century toxin. We can trace it in its current forms to an explosion of midlife discourse that began in the early 1970s. A cultural inquirer in a hard hat cannot help but observe that this boom is creating its own audience. A columnist declares, "Technically, you are now known as an aging baby boomer . . . one of you will turn 50 every 7.5 seconds." The group in question, regularly labeled "aging" (as if it were part of the name) in fact includes people born before 1945; and those born after 1964 are overhearing the same discourses. This enormous audience is being constructed to pay anxious attention as the discourse shouts, *"Middle Age: The Magazine for You—Yeah You!"*[7] When we listen and identify, the overriding fact of our identity becomes our location in the life course. Midlife discourse takes for granted a commonality that overrides, class, race, national origin, sexual orientation, region, personal psychology, politics, historical experience, state of health—even, often, gender. "We" are the audience—the age class, the anxious ones—being constructed.[8] *Declining to Decline* is intended for those, of whatever age, who want instead to pay attention to how that "we" is being constructed.

This book is not about old age. (Since people tend only to hear "old" when the words *age* or *aging* are spoken, it is worth saying this slowly). Nor does *aging* best describe what happens to my age peers; privatized into narcissism, it's about what happens to ME. I dread *my* birthday, I celebrate yours. (After all, *you* may be getting wiser, more compassionate, more competent with age.) Pundit Joseph Epstein intones his version of the doleful lore. "By the time one has reached forty, unless one is a very great fool, one realizes that one is no longer playing with a fully loaded shot-clock. . . . By fifty, despite all the cheerful talk about expanded life spans, it is better to assume that one is already playing in overtime."[9] Doom shrouds the crystal ball. Decadism makes visible and collective what might be evanescent moments of panic. One of these public birthdays may even trigger the requisite feelings. "Fear of fifty" is being standardized.

What is historically noteworthy is that aging-as-inward-anxiety has become a quintessentially *midlife* problem. People ask when the middle years "begin." In chapter 9, "From the Master Narrative of the Life Course," I argue that this is a defeatist question, revealing belief in the truth of decline. Midlife progress-thumpers, with the trendy middle class in mind, answer brightly, "The midlife used to begin at forty. Now it's fifty. What a success!" But in fact decline starts saying, "It's downhill all the way" much earlier. A birthday card prophesies, "You'll be hearing a lot of comments and wisecracks about the end of your youth, the waning of your powers, the unmistakable signs of advancing age and so on. DON'T PAY ANY ATTENTION. 30 IS A GREAT AGE!"[10] Through the blue smoke, age ideology has moved the "problem" of aging backwards—from old age into the middle years and toward even younger ages. Despite the longevity revolution that began a century ago, we are being aged by culture younger all the time.

Once "the midlife" exists within the orderly sequence of all the other named age classes (childhood, adolescence), it becomes preposterous for anyone raised as part of this audience to deny its existence. It has ontological status. (Every time I use the term, the mere mention lends midlife an effect of reality. An example of age ideology contaminating attempts to evade it.) Serious consequences flow from simply accepting the category as real and universal in this way. Perhaps the most serious is accepting decline at midlife as natural.

Showing how our dominant culture teaches us to feel bad about aging and just how to feel bad and how early to start is one main aim of this book. The system that maintains the decline meanings of midlife aging depends on an enormous range of subtle and blatant coercive discourses: we inhale this atmosphere every day from breakfast to the late news, thinking it's normal air. It's a phenomenon of everyday life.[11] Doses of variable toxicity waft in on cartoons, billboards, and birthday cards, MTV and coffee mugs, conversation, canonical poetry, newspaper articles, fiction, movies—the kinds of available evidence this book most depends on. The system is busy at whatever level of literacy or orality or visual impressionability the acculturated subject is comfortable with. Because progress and decline are posed as a competition between equal and opposite truths in the soliloquy and because progress is presented as truer truth by many midlife experts, it was important for me to discover how vast—unequal—the power of decline is. It is the "play of coercion, both as actually experienced and as anticipated," in the words of William Earnest, that any critique of age ideology must begin to reveal.[12]

Declining to Decline tries to expose the decline system bit by bit and repudiate it whole. I want us to be able to identify it, whether produced by commerce, politicians, the media, the medical/pharmaceutical world, sexology, academic or pop experts, loved ones and friends, or from within the self. Socialized into knowing what is normal and human, we learn about midlife aging somewhat the way we learn about our gender or our race. In adolescence we learn, narcissistically, the values upholding the cult of youth. Even children are exposed, learning the attributes of "middle age." This lore passes for truth. Young, we hear the human future confidently described—the only part of the "unknown future" that everyone seems sure of.

In time we join the group of those debating within ourselves whether or not we already belong in the unhappy age class.[13] The age at which this occurs remains undetermined. That is the crucial moment that I discovered through my soliloquies—the moment when midlife aging was being made into a relentless topic of introspection. As early as you begin to apply the attributes to your own self, you are being aged by culture. Although this transition deserves to be called *resocialization*, the process is lived as a seamless experience. Sometimes, retrospectively, it appears to have happened in a moment, like walking through a door: the "Entrance" into Midlife Aging.

The ideology's cult of youth has thus fixed "youth" as a name for fun, energy, sexuality, intensity, hope—all the cultural goods now alleged, despite all evidence to the contrary, to have a short shelf life. Syndicated columnist Ellen Goodman slides swiftly from truism to decline. "The 'youth generation' is middle-aged. . . . Losing touch with youth, it's easy to lose touch with youthfulness, with the eager sense of possibilities."[14] Belief that aging is a midlife phenomenon, the interpretive practice of reading our own body and mind for signs of decay that have always been identified abstractly beforehand, telling a life-course narrative constrained by the gross plot options of the system (peak, entrance, decline)—these are major features of the curriculum. Even our *feelings* are learned, starting with anticipatory fear of midlife aging, including envy of or anger at the currently young, nostalgic reminiscence that amounts to envying oneself when young, sorrow or even shame about "losses," and premature fear of dying.[15] Middle-ageism is a set of stereotypical meanings pumped out over the age class. Hyping special clothes, foods, interests, exercises, attitudes to sex, children, and death, in thousands of ways both superficially and deeply it governs the "experience" of approaching the midlife or living it. The ideology wizens the middle years.

None of this is natural.

Nor is it just a problem for people in so-called *midlife crises.* That term marginalizes and privatizes pain, singles out and extravagantly labels certain sufferers, exculpates the behavior of others, and denies cultural commonalities.[16] I believe that being forced to deal with midlife aging, in our culture, on the culture's terms, itself constitutes a crisis. Aging-into-the-middle-years is actually a socially constructed disease with an adolescent or childhood exposure and a midlife onset. Starting from there, *Declining to Decline* disentangles some of the major confusions. In this chapter I suggest the utmost reach and then the limits of decline ideology over self and society.

Most serious of all for the self is the threat to *age identity,* the complex autobiography that we could be building up as an incremental achievement over the course of our adult lives. Through being resocialized, somewhere in these vague stretches of the middle years people are pressured to abandon their subjective sense of themselves, shedding precious stores of self-esteem, losing not only cumulative selfhood—*being*—but the prospect of becoming. The belief in midlife aging strips this away. Many chapters show how *identity-stripping* works.[17] The second half of chapter 11, "Doing Age Theory," fits midlife decline into a theory about the priority and potential of age identity. Some readers may want to start there.

Fortunately, we are not static automatons but self-preserving consciousnesses—selves with memories, projects, interpretive powers. Feelings of decline and confusion at midlife may feel "spontaneous"—they hurt for real—but they are products of specific conditions: historical, not inevitable. Understanding this, we can conceive of changing our feelings—not as a miraculous conversion, but as a liberatory outcome of learning to think about age and aging in a novel way.

We think we age by nature; we are insistently and precociously being aged by culture. But *how* we are aged by culture—*that* we need to know much more about.

Telling Decline

Intimate as it may seem, the soliloquy of age anxiety can make plausible to the most skeptical how a shared cultural script can be internalized. Now I know that no matter what happened to me, those moments came (and still sometimes come) from a universal script that I made into "my" experience. I was just another good student taught how to improvise from dictation.

In the emergency people react differently, of course. Some find in decline a kind of identity, rueful pleasures and bitter meaningfulness. Some ask in panic: "Am I winning or losing?" Others succeed in calming their anxiety only to find the whole experience soon repeated. Others object that it's not so bad "to be on the downward slope." Bobby Lee, a character in McMurtry's *Texasville*, responds with typical contradictions: "I ain't, and besides I've got my brakes on." Some call on religion. Drawing on their achieved identity, others test their belief in personal "progress" under these bleak and inauspicious conditions. And there are certainly some for whom life-course optimism is a solid and relatively unshakable given. Yet I suspect that even the luckier and more optimistic also fall willy-nilly, from time to time, into the form of "midlife crisis" I have been showcasing here. In any event, however functional our intuitive survival mechanisms may be personally, we fail to see the situation as an ideological dilemma.[18]

The oscillations operate in any subjective or social realm that individuals learn to connect with the midlife. Tutored into taking a bad part for the whole, we begin to multiply losses in all the realms of value: creativity, beauty, sexuality, health, friendship, parenting, mental functioning, earning power, right to judgment. The cloud of allegedly age-specific miseries can engulf politics, the nation, the earth; decline becomes a global metaphor. The habit of conflating losses produces deeper internalization.

Aging-into-the middle-years can be felt as a deep discouragement whose source is believed to be internal, bodily—an unimprovable entity at both the surface and the core of the self. If midlife men and women are passively sad, the privatization of decline has a lot to do with it. Psychologically, this may drive a person inward to dwell on implacable deterioration, sometimes to the point of despair. Not yet fifty-five, philosopher Jean Améry felt (as his translator summarizes his book) that the terror of his experience at Auschwitz had been, "incredible to say, less filled with internal *horror* and *anguish* than the experience of aging."[19]

Most of us have dealt with some of the unbendable iron of life: pain that does not go away when we reconceptualize it, unemployment, the death of a child. Sometimes these things happen in the long middle of the course of life. If we were not crippled by decline thinking, fewer of them would appear to have any necessary connection to the midlife or aging. Decline replaces all other sources—accident, history, economics, politics—with a body-based narrative that permits only one meaning: personal declineoldageanddeath. Morally, it undermines the "optimism of the will" that Antonio Gramsci memorably told us we need to sustain. Decline can make losing seem like the only form of life—irresistible.

Can anyone escape the crisis of midlife identity-stripping? Possibly: people who never received mainstream ideological training, immigrants who came to the United States in adulthood, groups like the Amish, non-English speakers unless they read in translation.[20] Alternative midlives—and nonrecognition of the midlife—remain unwritten as long as "the midlife" rules. And of those brought up within the toxic zones? Resisters—feminists, antiracists, and other activists—may have acquired some limited immunity. Age autobiography, survey data, reports from the therapeutic community, may eventually confirm that there are important differences in the ways in which individuals or groups defend themselves against decline ideology, but until this kind of inquiry is under way we can only speculate about factors that may limit internalization.[21]

There's a cliché that *men* don't suffer from midlife aging. (Many men know otherwise.) In fact, although gendered differences remain, some of the familiar binaries and hierarchies of the midlife are breaking down. If men once had immunity as a group, the group is losing it. Chapter 8, "The New Gender Politics of Midlife Bodies," shows how the commercial exploitation of male bodies is reducing "older" men to the status "older" women used to have. Even the top 10 percent of economic winners, mostly white men of a certain age, living on unearned income and government welfare to the rich, may find their identity undermined by the equation that "masculinity equals youth." "From the Master Narrative of the Life Course" shows that men tell stories about entry into midlife aging at ages as young as or younger than those women are led to use.

Women's resistance, when strengthened by feminist precedent, may actually be readier than men's. Women novelists have a superior record disputing parts of decline narrative on behalf of women, as chapter 5 suggests. Yet, without a movement to help them as the culture turns on them, men flood mainstream writing with their unexamined sense of decline, and many women still experience the midlife through the mainstream. The waning of the double standard at midlife clinches the hold of decline ideology over women too. As each of us is urged into telling some version of the collective plot, midlife decline narrative is becoming an overriding, inclusive narrative—a "master" narrative.

For all who stage them in the home theater of the mind, male or female, then, telling decline narrative can take place in the absence of illness, in the presence of material well-being, in lives marked by achievement, in periods otherwise uneventful, in a country and century in which at forty significant numbers of people have lived less than half their adult lives. The richer, male or female, become vulnerable to decline arguments that have purchases built into them. The sick, the impoverished, the overworked, the victims of bias, can only be further confused by universalizing discourses that make *aging* their problem at midlife. They may know better, but can't make their alternative knowledge swing dominant common sense around.[22] In some contexts, we need to underline strongly how different one forty-five-year-old is from another: middle-ageism overlays and exacerbates sexism, classism, racism, homophobia. Yet tactically we also need to be able to emphasize what we share. Being aged by culture in the Nineties can be treated as a plausible *minimal* level of vulnerability. If *Declining to Decline* treats even middle-class white men as becoming increasingly victims of midlife decline and as perpetrators of the system, it also considers men as moral agents and potential allies. The enforced bond of contemporaneity might come to be considered a collective problem. For everyone who can understand how, solidarity becomes more likely.

To hold on to this, we have to see through the most compelling of the false universals. The dread of aging is alleged to be "human," connected with fear of "mortality." In Bernard Malamud's *Dubin's Lives,* a midlife man stationed in the staving-off position says, "One learns where life goes. . . . When you know the end the rest moves up only too quickly."[23] We find this rapid slither from midlife to dying in poetry, in popular speech, in "serious" fiction— mainly by men about midlife men—and in uncritical social science and philosophy. Since people at midlife are relatively healthy, death comes to us discursively. Rare is the writer who does in a protagonist as young as fifty-seven, as John Updike killed off weak-hearted Harry Angstrom in *Rabbit at Rest.* But younger and older people are represented as dying around us to sadden our survival. "Realism" is supposed to lead us to "accept" death fears as fundamental and natural.[24] But suppose the realists are teaching us instead that somewhere in the midlife is right on schedule for fearing mortality?

This, in a prefatory way, is what age ideology does to produce at midlife a solitary individual in an "aging" body who cannot imagine resistance.

Resistance

Combat

If *Declining to Decline* did no more than convincingly point to an inescapable system that now attacks us at ever younger ages, horror or acquiescence could still remain the likeliest responses—the same emotional attitudes that I criticize the current positivism for producing. The first challenge for those who identify with the cause is whether we can rally energy, power, and cultural space to combat the severe internalization of "aging" that, colonizing far beyond the body, now distorts economic and human relations across so much of the life course. *Declining to Decline* argues that we should try. We need, to begin with, a better concept of hope, uncoupled from private fantasies of midlife upgrade. This requires not only firm concepts of social construction but plausible belief that collective resistance is possible.

A hint that there is a way out from within lies, paradoxically, in the very oscillations of the obsessive soliloquy. My seasick indecisiveness did not come from perfect belief; stubbornly, it never ended once and for all on the side of decline. Although many repeat decline discourse, this is not incompatible with possessing a latent healthy will to oppose it. Far from being "denial," this is akin to the adversarial will that preserves slaves and other captives from wholly internalizing the master ideology even before they have a movement to support them.

This book is the report of my attempts to understand the ideology, to try to breathe freely. I was slow to recognize that there was an enemy diffused through the culture—the biggest, vaguest enemy, the enemy out there and inside. When I did, it made me angry—as if I had found out that a corporation had filled my house with toxic fumes; and even angrier when I figured out the fumes had to be everywhere. The metaphor of combat initially felt alien. But "combat" has come to feel right. This kind of resistance isn't literal fighting; it's psychological and conceptual. Everyone not reduced to total abjection has practiced it in one form or another.

Calling it "fighting" means you recognize that you are angry-with-cause. But even with justice on its side, fighting may at first mean fear of deadly force, fright and hyperventilation. You think the enemy has no weak places, that it is monstrously hegemonic and shape-shifting. But you learn the struggle won't kill you. You get up groggy, but when your head clears it's clearer than before.

Age theory saved me. The idea I slowly came to understand—that age had to be socially constructed—pulled me in good time away from the bodily solipsism and bone-deep resignation that I've described as a midlife threat. It explained phenomena that I had been studying for years (if studying is the right word in reference to a system that keeps depriving you of breath) with poor comprehension. It was like finding an oxygen mask during a tear-gas attack. To me theory has to be practical, plain-speaking, personal, poetic, speculative, passionate—theory for all of us. (It can also be winsome, dismissive, haughty, down-and-dirty—whatever works.) It needs to be everywhere. Underneath even the earliest chapters of *Declining to Decline* the autobiographical ones that may seem least conceptual, there's a healthy whiff of saving theory.[25] It's in the quotations, hiding in the jokes, the riddle, the suspense of the form, the unruly mix of genres.

It isn't only writers who tell narratives of their life course; each of us is granted a normal right to practice telling it, starting early on in life.[26] The danger is that we rely on blunt decline or progress conventions. I told myself my first decline story at about age eight, shortly after I started going to grade school. I could have gone on in the same pitiful unreflective way forever. Yet despite many reasons not to, I developed a potentially powerful progress myth. How this happened I describe in the next chapter, "A Good Girl." I could have gone on to tell progress narrative too in an unreflective way, jogging forever between the poles. Progress versus decline turns out to be another one of those clashing binaries that theorists warn us against because the system it maintains is so compelling.

My true resistance began when I started writing autobiographical essays about my own midlife that consciously countered decline. Through this writing I discovered the combat positions of a self being aged by culture and resisting, at first intuitively, and then with critical intent. "A narrator can become aware of narrative conventions as problematic. In our culture racist and sexist language are commonly experienced that way."[27] Starting as young as possible, the narrative of the life course can be retold with deliberate resolve to attack the age binary young/old and the narrative binary progress/decline. Throughout this book, I point out how—starting in part 1, "My Private Midlife."

Using the personal essay for the sake of cultural critique has a distinguished tradition that includes W.E.B. Du Bois, Emma Goldman, and George Orwell, and an immense contemporary proliferation, which includes Rigoberta Menchú, Patricia Williams, Omar Cabezas. Age critique is only beginning to get such a lineage.[28] *Declining to Decline* takes age as seriously as these writers do their causes. This specific critical emphasis produces a new form—*age autobiography.* "My Private Midlife" confronts some of the most devastating emotions midlife people are taught. "A Good Girl" and "Face-Off" trace my struggle out of nostalgia, mental and physical; "Ordinary Pain" unlinks my middle years from fear of the decaying body. "The Other End of the Fashion Cycle," in part 4, links our learning of age-related loss to getting sucked into the shopping cycle. Collectively, all the fragments might be called "Annals of a Developing Age Identity."

I wanted these annals to record not only processes but little victories in the long war I eventually discovered myself waging—to decide what aging means to *me* at midlife, beyond decline ideology, and to explain this so that it could be properly heard. The emphasis falls different ways: on my first night-blind struggles, to show the might of the culture; on the strategies that I stumbled upon and then, when I found them working for me, practiced and modified. I had a lot of luck that allowed me to evade some of the worst effects of the system; the dedication page of this book and its acknowledgments put my gratitude up front. I skimp on my failures, not to deny they occurred, but because some failures are not useful to other people, and reciting them may be harmful. There *is* an ethics of narrating age. In these early days, as narrative struggles to get free from automatized tropes, rough guidelines I have developed prompt me to be extremely careful.

Every chapter looks beyond myself to reveal standard ways of being aged by culture. Getting arthritis, remembering childhood, dealing with youthism and rejuvenation propaganda, relating to older and younger generations ("My Mother at Midlife"), having menstruation terminate ("Menopause as Magic Marker"), being pushed down the economic slide ("The Politics of Middle-Ageism in a Postmodern Economy")—all of these and more are ideological cruxes, situations when subjects must obey or the system fails. Part 2, "Women with Attitude," shows what can happen when a whole collective refuses to obey.

I do not assume that even a dominant culture confronts everyone with the same particular problems. Nor do I think it right, at this early point in anti-middle-ageism, to warn away readers who may think they are sociologically or psychologically unlike me. The accounts are meant to work like fiction, to absorb and provoke a reader, to jiggle into action certain passions and motives and mechanisms. I want to make fighting against age ideology seem both important and doable. Indeed, I'd like to make it feel like something you do already, that only needs more consciousness to move it into a higher gear.

Organizing one's own resistance may be the most imaginative and soul-searching thing a self can do. It's hard work. People may respond at first by resisting the apparent implications. "Does this mean I must give up my cherished identification with 'youth'?" "How (much more) oppositional do you expect me to be against this culture?" Feminists may not realize how much more there is to be done. Men may ask, "Why should I give up the claim that

I age less in the middle years?" Some women might say, like the character in Alta's prose poem "Pretty," "Can you imagine the bottom of that horrible fear? that each year I could only become more afraid. . . . a horrible fear that drove me to a plastic surgeon, that drove me . . . drove me . . . drove me, tell me i'm not oppressed. ask me what i want. tell me you don't like my methods. listen to my life & see that it has been intolerable and leave me the fuck alone."[29]

Some of the victims are likely to start screaming, fearful of being touched. We have to understand this. Age ideology doesn't just provide the toxic atmosphere we breathe; it puts a nose on your face that in the mirror you can't tell from your own; it puts ugly interpretations into your head that your eyes then seem to see; it calls these distortions nature. As Raymond Williams remarked (in another connection), "A structure of feeling as deep as this enacts a world, as well as interpreting it, so that we learn it from experience as well as from ideology."[30] Decline is strong, in part, because some people also get psychological and cognitive benefits from endorsing aspects of the ideology. For some, achieving progress primarily means countering decline: we buy the products out of *personal choice, elite consumers* making *informed decisions* on the basis of cutting-edge medical/endocrinological advice; we *take individual control over the aging "process."* We get the cachet of sharing the wisdom of decline writers, the bitter pride of feeling able to bear the truths.

Given how much there is to undo, *Declining to Decline* has to tweak that false nose. This may hurt—at first the nose feels like *self.* The woman in the poem says angrily, "Tell me you don't like *my* methods," as if she had invented plastic surgery all by herself and feminism were going to blame her for it.

But maybe those who have intense objections to the deconstruction of midlife aging can see their reaction as a sign that they are approaching a point of crisis. In the realm of culture, Patrick Brantlinger argues, crisis occurs when an ideology is challenged by increasing numbers of people as *not* representing or as "*mis*representing" important aspects of social experience.[31] And a sense of crisis, bitter as it may be, helps: it makes answers imperative. Emotional resistance makes equally good use of irritation, cold determination not to be a dupe, curiosity about what the self might feel like less cumbered with ideology, excitement at hearing oneself utter counterdiscourses, *believing them.* You detach scraps of pseudoidentity pasted on by middle-ageism: you shout, "It's a *false* nose." That's externalization, and any bit of it is a relief. Sometimes, startled by the sheer repetitive monotony of received opinion, resistance breaks out in healthy laughter.

The will to resist has already produced novels, mostly featuring women in their middle years, that teach readers about the empowering dimensions of time in circumstances of grave difficulty (chapter 5, "Midlife Heroines, 'Older and Freer'"). The culture doesn't yet call *these* uses of time "aging." But it could. Once people begin telling stories about their ageist conditioning, we can expect more to gush out in relief, the way the stories of racism and male chauvinism and masculinity training and homophobia gushed out as soon as there was an audience for them. Then there can be truly new accounts of midlife being and becoming. Fuller speech is also narrative—nothing that comes into discourse is plain vanilla truth. Age autobiography nevertheless provides solid evidence against the mainstream connotations of "aging" as a natural, biological, prenarrativized, ahistorical, universal decline. We can begin to blow the ideology away with our breath. Counternarrative is the speech of *pneuma; pneuma,* the long-repressed voice of age identity.

Toward a Politics of the Midlife

In the long run, hope needs a collective critical project that will go on the offensive against the system. Internal resistance, once articulated and theorized, could become collective. Not easily, since so little attention is paid to theorizing age, even by people who interrogate everything else. Because age has been the neglected dimension of theory, we lack wise retorts, common assumptions, a basic critical vocabulary. Not easily, because we have to understand how decline works interactively, and that involves our own complicity in maintaining the system. Not easily, because decline is shored up by other systems. Not easily, because anti-middle-ageists (including me) have been relying on weak strategies. I want to introduce these imbricated problems briefly.

Although the learning process goes on privately, the politics of midlife aging carries decline way beyond the self. By confessing details of our decline, we share public stories of bad aging with one another and our children, as if each of us were all by ourself the center of a pervasive advertising network blaming the midlife for almost any problem that occurs, singling it out from all the tangled, overdetermined, preventable or reversible sources of human misery. In the same grand national collaboration, doing the work of the commerce in aging, too often we sell one another "hopes," such as passing as young. As long as middle-ageism goes unchallenged, such remedies (aside from being expensive, synthetic, and masochistic) are useless. Even our bulky numbers may now work against us: The entire 76 million born between 1946 and 1964 may also learn to keep entropic notions circulating.

Decline has become the default content of our age discourses. When the clichés get repeated, nobody has a firm, rapid, consensually valid response. In many groups, if anyone demurs, the crowd smiles and sings out "Denial." In a *New Yorker* story by Lorrie Moore, a fifty-year-old man thinks that the idea that we become "wiser, better," is "a myth concocted to keep the young from learning what we really are and despising and murdering us" when really there is only "regret and decrepitude up ahead."[32] Feminists too sometimes speak as if "progress" were only suspect as empty hype, which leaves decline the only "honest" narrative about the life course. Each of us gets positioned so that the best we can do is struggle to assert that midlife is, for some, personally, not primarily a decline. As long as decline is permitted to take the high ground, we will have tremendous difficulty making our opposition feel real enough to ourselves for it to become a permanent, stable part of the self. If ignorance is innocence, and vulnerability an excuse, then up to now we have been innocent. No one thinks there might be an *ethics* of discourse about the midlife.

Victims of age ideology, we become perpetrators in our turn. If a person can be made to feel truly inadequate by virtue of age—not exactly guilty but somehow worthy of punishment, destined to lose (a lover, a job, a promotion)—then he or she may identify with whatever powers remain. Reasserting maleness in midlife may involve homophobia as well as age-graded sexism. Homomasculinity makes the aging of gay men start even younger and carry more severe penalties. In general, the mental strategies promoted by midlife decline magnify success in the sexual realm as well as failure. In heterosexual life under the double standard of aging, midlife men can use their relative power to mock midlife women, ignore them, tell jokes about the monotony of long-term marriage, and, like *puer eternus,* "attempt to preserve something of the atmosphere of the stag night well into middle age."[33] And women at midlife are not deprived of weapons against men: the feminine weapons of flirting, alluding to a man's decline in looks or sexual power, and the newer ones of feminist-inspired self-esteem. In an era of artificial scarcities, anyone can feel obscurely threatened—by the very source, age, that might assure power. Turned outward, decline thinking becomes middle-ageism.

In response, age theory asks people first of all to practice a radical skepticism about all cultural means of naturalizing the middle years. To begin with—but this alone would involve a tremendous revision—people need to disentangle their own intimate experience and its real causes from whatever they are offered as their "experience" of aging. Theory relocates under the cultural umbrella several kinds of drastic change that are perniciously confused with "natural" aging. First, there are physical alterations and diseases that derive from discriminatory socioeconomic practices, environmental depredations, lack of access to information and to health care—circumstances heavily determined by class, gender, race, sexual orientation, ethnicity. Socially induced illnesses often take decades to manifest themselves and appear at "midlife," but they are not natural concomitants of aging. If tomorrow biologists discovered antioxidants that could be eaten at breakfast and promised us 120 healthy years of life, the secret agents that age us at midlife would still be at work tomorrow afternoon.[34]

The second kind of drastic change is the drop in economic level that so many people now fear and experience at midlife. Life-income curves rise with age but they peak in the decade after thirty-five for women and forty-five for men and earlier for each class. Income disparities between groups widen at midlife. In 1991, the median income for African-American men forty to forty-four was 79 percent of the median for white men; in the next older cohort, it drops to 64 percent; in the fifty to fifty-four cohort, down to 54 percent. For all women, the median income in the thirty-five to thirty-nine group was 52 percent of that for men; in the next older cohort, 50 percent; in forty-five to forty-nine-year-olds, 48 percent.[35] Work is actually a gigantic age/class competition that judges victors at midlife, the peak, on measures like income, security, deference—"seniority."

Seniority at midlife, never very stable in the twentieth century, has come increasingly under attack even in the middle class over the last twenty years. Midlife Americans compete for the lessening number of good jobs, forced into early "retirement," part-time "flexible" work without benefits, or unemployment.[36] In all classes, "thousands of Americans with years of experience are experiencing the vicissitudes of MAAD—middle-aged and downward."[37] If adult children are learning to "despise" us, it's not because they're learning "*what we really are.*" It's because they are being used to undercut our midlife salaries. The political-economic system, going about its business, has no objection to having all these effects lumped together as "aging."

Decline is getting stronger because it leans on growing economic insecurity at midlife. Midlife age-discrimination threatens to reduce the earnings and the power of the entire workforce, curtailing the American Dream and embittering our image of the life course. My final chapter, "The Politics of Middle-Ageism in the Postmodern Economy," connects the hostile economic facts of the midlife with the hostile representations that cloud our minds.

Decline ideology invisibly diminishes the life chances of everyone who moves into the midlife age class, isolating individuals from one another and other age groups and undermining the influence that people might wield on behalf of the age class and its causes. Once aging has been administered at midlife, we never do regain the powers that we are unable to exercise. Disempowered, embittered, some people withdraw from action, hedge their politics—mysteriously turning into the midlife caricature we were taught to deride and anticipate. While blaming aging, a population clinging to a decline view in a period of actual economic decline may also pick other scapegoats. Age ideology tends to make such a population more self-involved, atomized, and subdued. A nation demoralized in such ways is dangerous—likely to be mean-spirited to "losers" domestically; paranoid, hostile and belligerent abroad.

Decline narrative actually does register something real. Not in its comic or ambivalent forms: these are effectively denials that a grave collective problem exists. But even its despairing forms are misleading. By locating "aging" as our sorrowful essence, they prevent us from looking for meaning elsewhere.

Nothing gives a better idea of the power and nature of decline ideology than trying to resist it and failing. It should be clear by now why it is not adequate merely to add to the number of positive midlife discourses.[38] They already abound in our culture and are increasing. Allegedly, Boomers are rich—*The $800 Billion Over Fifty Market*—courted by advertisers, writ large in national politics. The new name writers currently use—"the midlife" rather than "middle age"—also suggests that we are winning.[39] But these facts miss the story. We do not need more peppy messages, tactics that don't admit our own awful internal corroborations of the culture's middle-ageism, that offer private solutions and ignore systemic problems. What all the right tools might be to unlock the collective will to resist, we cannot know yet. But surely it is worth trying next to bind midlife phenomena tightly to age ideology, material conditions, and a serious politics of liberation.

One issue for this book is why the existing midlife counterdiscourses have so slippery a grip on our hearts and minds and make so little impression on dominant discourse. It's not their fault, of course, that they don't come from "everywhere," but from motley local and special sources: self-help guides, the positive-aging movement, certain "soft" fields of academe, women's fiction, and the traditional cultures of respect for old age. Feminism, although admirably assisting women to deal with sexist ageism, has ignored the male midlife decline story and thus missed the linchpin of hegemony. We don't yet have effective age theory or an antiageist movement for the middle years. Age scholars have not succeeded in making age a recognized concept for cultural analysis, not to mention a great life-course theme. Nothing reduces decline's ontological necessity: that the midlife *exist* so that it can have harsh "truths" said about it.

Like gender and race, age ideology is another "body"-based system of categorization. Like sexism and racism, middle-ageism hurts and discriminates. There is much to learn from feminism and antiracism about undoing it. But age theory cannot develop merely by trying to match age to models of gender or race; in some ways age is sui generis.[40] Racism and sexism rely on characteristics the subjects are allegedly born with, and this birth story is part of their ideological power. Being middle-aged is not congenital. In the Nineties, midlife aging too needs to be denaturalized and estranged by activism and age studies.

Age studies names the interdisciplinary movement that wants to disrupt the current age system in theory and practice.[41] It is inspired, like this book, by feminist fiction and theory, critical social science, cultural studies and postmodernism, taking what's conceptually or politically relevant from each and projecting those big lights onto the "middle years" and the rest of the life course. In a culture so strikingly naive about age, the benefits are all ahead of us. Once we begin to interrogate age ideology consistently, the work should be psychologically liberating, intellectually energizing, politically empowering. In my most progressive and progress-oriented moments, I envision the anti-middle-ageist movement crossing boundaries—racial-ethnic, male/female, gay/straight, privileged/immiserated, left/right—uniting people by presenting them with credibly self-interested causes for forming coalitions. It could cross the ever more rigid boundaries of the age classes because the benefits will flow also to the now-deluded young and the yet-more-vulnerable old. Within this framework, I see *Declining to Decline* as a survival manual and guide to resistance.

If we find after serious inner investigations that the midlife is not naturally dominated by (bad) aging, could we teach ourselves how to say, neither boastfully nor defensively, that its script is not universal? If enough of us did so, what would be left of the midlife as an "object of study"? What would be left of midlife "aging"?[42]

The idea that we might escape being aged by culture is breathtaking. And breathgiving. We can barely begin to imagine living in such a future. Certainly, the complex ordinary pains of life would remain, and the great world's troubles. People would still get laugh-lines, swaths of gray, a natural weight set higher.[43] But we'd wear such changes with a difference. Discarding standard social meanings, each of us would be able to defend and thus hold tight to a complex idiosyncratic narrative of age identity. Your story would be yours; mine, mine—diverse, unroutinized. Published, such stories would strike with bold explicitness or subtextual power at decline's infuriating certainty. Simultaneously, we would be evolving a vision of the age culture we want to live in: deciding what values such a culture would nurture among the generations, and what altered structures of relationships, practices, institutions, and material conditions would be needed to support these values. This is a vast agenda to which I return at the end of the book. As a byproduct, the private scenes of age anxiety would erupt less often and would be confronted by a firmer mind. It seems safe to say that by knowing a little age theory and applying it to that questionable invention, the middle years, more of us would age more happily, more meaningfully—that is, in current terminology, *less*.

This moment in the Nineties will eventually seem an early phase of combat. This book offers an outline of overall strategy, examples of tactics that have proved valuable so far, a reckoning of possible future guerrilla maneuvers. A lot of the writing started because something a friend or relative said opened up the pain of a general problem or suggested a more effective taunt, a more balanced stance. There were tête-à-têtes in which each of us built up so complex an age identity that the binaries collapsed beneath the weight. Over the years of my attentiveness, I picked up material for this precious hoard not only from long-term friends but from students, from men and women I'd just met who confided in me at conferences or supper parties or over coffee, strangers overheard in the supermarket, at the bus stop. Conversation—that overlooked resource in a world of texts, that Pandora's box of cultural debris, enraging incomprehension, and admirable wisdom—has probably been my main source and motive for this book. One problem of writing it was how to reconcile what people were reciting with what I was discovering. Terry Eagleton, a humane theorist, rightly believes that, "in the critique of ideology, only those interventions will work which make sense to the mystified subject itself."[44] Despite the life time I've put into this project, the books I've written, the good luck I had and the good allies I found, I remain—none of us can help but remain—close to that "mystified subject," only partly escaped. To fail less, we need more company. Everything else follows from that: public counternarrative, a movement, public policy, a moral vision of a different society, an age revolution. This book extends an invitation to raise your voice, join the struggle, invent more tactics. Until we are all freer, none of us can be very free.

Part One

My Private Midlife

2

A Good Girl

CHILDHOOD gradually dwindles from memory with a kind of alarming fatality—one of the sad and apparently irreversible effects of moving forward in the life course, another curse (some people would say, the worst) of aging. What appears to be left of childhood is a set of simplified tales of events and sensations. Sometimes I doubt whether what I am repeating is even an actual memory, so much does it feel like the simple memorized version of an earlier telling.

What we have *read* remains, of course, but in a bare, hollow way. Most people can tell you the names of a few books they adored as children, when the alleged "pleasure of the text" was no pseudoerotic rhetoric, because reading was our prime resource for delight. As people name their books, their gaze mists over with a kind of empty nostalgia; it becomes clear that they have forgotten why they loved those pages, just as they can no longer recall the powerful neediness with which they clutched a favorite blanket or rubbed a ribbon of satin against their face.

I ran through the usual: the Bobbsey Twins, *Little Women* and *Jo's Boys,* Nancy Drew, *Cherry Ames, Student Nurse.* But some books I read the way children do, and as literate adults almost never do: closing the novel only to start it again, and reading it through in the same highly selective way again. I mean that within these books I had favorite parts that continued to draw me in and rivet me and I think shock me no matter how many times I read them. Until recently, if asked about these rivets, I would have replied that I must have "needed" those sections at the time, and those particular plots. But what plots they were, and why they served me, had mostly disappeared from my memory. Latterly, even those long hours of reading alone in my room had become abstract and legendary. Disconnected from the particular powerful emotions they had evoked, they provided only tedious information: "I had always been a reader." "Even at age ten my dream was to spend my life buried in a book." It is true that my adult career was in some general sense set by the solitary inclinations of that grave child—captured in braids, with folded hands, in a school photo taken in the fourth grade at P.S. 208 in Brooklyn.

With the passage of time, not the origins of the career but the inner person behind that still, inexpressive face became fascinating to me. The child I was from ten until the age of fourteen or so, with the direct but unrevealing gaze and the severe mouth, conceals a secret I now want to know for my present sake. Proust says that old selves, like vases, contain the aromas of far-off years, and he longed to "open the vase" to become a child again, not in nostalgia's vague blur but exactly as was.

Since I like being an adult, I never invented Proust's belief that the power to feel intensely weakens after a certain age; I don't need to open the vase for the same reason he did, to find a better way of being. Far from it. But I became curious about my child self, with a cause of curiosity (or two or three) that is of our time and, as Foucault would say, our "episteme." Many people, among whom I include myself, believe that growth and change are possible all along the life course, and others (among them conservatives and genetic determinists) say no. Some theorists of the self now claim that there is no "core" or true self. The components of what we call identity are given to us willy-nilly: gender, nationality, ethnicity, or race; roles as daughter, sister, student, wife. We are a bundle of influences—think of onions, artichokes, or bales of hand-me-downs.

This might be merely a strongly worded alternative description of the social construction many of us already live with. And that is such an important idea that we should never quite forget it. But from their totally different viewpoints, the determinists and some identity theorists seem to want to rub it in that we are products rather than, say, people with some freedom and responsibility to discard old mental clothes and change our story. Aside from the tone in which our "givenness" is impressed upon us, I find the idea objectionable—politically and ethically, to begin with. It cannot be *proved* wrong—most of the things we believe are not susceptible of proof or disproof—but it is turning out to be objectionable on too many grounds to too many cultural critics.

One of the subjective ways of judging, it occurred to me, would be to relearn what it was like to be that obscure and irretrievable ten-year-old child, and compare her with myself at midlife. Autobiography is "alluring," says one critic, because "all 'I's are sites where generalized operations of power press ineluctably on the subject."[1] Had she had a self? Had she had "agency"? If I could decide such things, I might know better who I am now—always a mystery when an important point of comparison has been lost. But that early "text" was, I thought sorrowfully, no longer inside me; it had hidden behind the face in the photo.

What I remembered about her, with one significant exception, was pretty much just what the rag-and-bone dealers might expect me to find: the banality—the normality—of a child not yet hurried into adolescence: quiet, diligent, conventional. The grandchild of immigrants, with a mother who was longing to become a schoolteacher, and a father whose radical politics, lack of education, and stubborn individualism left him no choice but onerous self-employment, she was early labeled as having "exceptional intelligence," as they used to say in those narrow, coercive days, when only getting A's counted. By the fourth grade she was inevitably a scholar-drudge. A good girl.

That's what she looks like in the picture that charmed and intimidated me for so long. The serenity of achievement—that's what I see on her face. The calm—the admirable, wonderful calm—of knowing what is required and knowing that one can produce it. Sweet-natured, compliant, bookish—that was the reputation in the teachers' room. By the time that child was ten, she was the principal's pet. And the principal was the awesome Miss Elsa Ebeling, who commanded that world of upwardly mobile Jewish children and their mostly Gentile, mainly Irish, teachers. Seven feet tall, bony as a witch, distant as a god, was my frightened view.

This image of little Margaret compares favorably, of course with the anxiety I felt at so many times in my later career as a scholar-drudge. Indeed, in later feminist days, I often used to think of her at that age as wonderfully free of gender anxiety in that remarkable female-dominated institution, P.S. 208. It never occurred to that girl then, as it was to occur to her seven years later, when she started college, that she would have been better off born a boy. In the eyes of her world, she was securely A+. Moreover, she had been the first-born; after the birth of a brother two years later she continued to be special. She was loved by both parents: if her mother read her work aloud and kept the extended family informed about her achievements, her father taught her baseball and stilt-walking and let her ride on his truck. No wonder she didn't need to smile for the camera.

Now it seems like pure chance that I discovered who she *really* was. At a dinner party in the late Seventies, an old college friend, the novelist Bart Gerald, happened to ask me what my favorite children's book had been. At a hazard, as it seemed, I offered the title of *The Count of Monte Cristo*. When he asked why, it was easy to fling out a casual answer. "The private adult education," I said first; and then, with a laugh, "Revenge." I had said better than I knew.

For those unacquainted with Dumas's novel, the private education takes place in the prison of the Château d'If after Edmond Dantès, in young manhood and about to marry the love of his life, has been portrayed as an active Bonapartist, is unjustifiably sentenced by the newly restored Bourbon regime, and then is forgotten in prison. His tutor there is the aged Abbé Faria, supposedly mad but in truth astonishingly learned, who over the course of their long imprisonment together—close to twenty years—gives Dantès everything the ignorant sailor needs to become a gentleman and a learned man. And to effect his revenge. Faria gives him an explanation for his incarceration (he was betrayed by three friends), esoteric knowledge, the means of escape, inconceivable wealth, and the calm to plot and wait and reveal nothing.

In the photo, that ten-year-old, who would soon chance upon the novel, already had the glance of impermeability that Dantès acquired over frozen decades of suffering and expectation, and that, as Dumas describes him, conferred the terrible personal power of intimidation.

Dantès's revenge occupies most of the novel: in my brown-paged edition, whose edges break in little fingertip-shaped sections every time I eagerly turn a page, it requires the end of volume 1 and the whole of volume 2. At forty, with all that an adult could want in the way of material and social and intellectual possessions, he dedicates himself entirely to destroying his three enemies. Years pass before Dantès has worked out the extent of, and set limits to, his just anger. But these adult meanings and the notion that this was a midlife plot, and a most peculiar one, occurred to me only later (long after that dinner party)—when I was myself over forty and had more than *I* had ever expected in the way of material and social and intellectual possessions, and was in fact investigating the literary category, which I had discovered and named, of "midlife fiction." I was considerably estranged from the child-self that had selected that peculiar plot for her own when I began puzzling about the way revenge attracted her.

The puzzle arose because of the image in the photo. What was that privileged child doing memorizing a revenge fantasy? But as soon as I said the word *revenge* to Bart, even before I reread Dantès's story, I knew that it provided a genuine key; it clicked in the lock, if it didn't quite open the door. Of course, I had suffered from premature success, a condition hard to recover from. Despite having girlfriends—Merry Stachenfeld, Fausta Price, Nan Zeichner—and a fourth-grade boyfriend, I had felt lonely and isolated. What about that decline story I had concocted out of my one scant decade of life? I dated my Fall from the time I started school: my Eden had been the preschool years, before I had needed to be perfect. "It's better never to be older than five," my eleven-year-old self perversely warned my littler cousins. But when in midlife I recalled telling them that horror story about aging-by-eleven (!) it seemed like a joke. The idea of looking deeper to discover why that impassive child had been so very "sad" (if that is what she was) didn't seem necessary.

Some years later, at another dinner party, I recognized what had to have been the second crucial book in my most private library. The conversation became general after someone asked who our favorite fictional heroines were. "Mrs. Ramsay," someone ventured. My husband, an early male feminist, said instantly, "I leapt from Stuart Little to Dorothea Brooke." "Jane Eyre," said some others. "But which Jane Eyre?" "The one who loves Rochester, of course." "No," I found myself saying, "The Jane Eyre of the Red Room, the one who denies St. John Rivers." (Whoever says conversations at dinner parties are barren, has not had my luck.) Mine was a minority view, as it happened: the others had all read Charlotte Brontë's novel later, in adolescence, and inevitably as a marriage plot. By the chance of having read the novel before being inculcated with romance conventions, I had managed not to notice that it was a romance. I scarcely remembered Rochester, except once disguised as an old woman.

Shortly after, I looked up the passages that my memory had so fervently recalled from many years before. Like the _Monte Cristo,_ I have the actual material object of childhood in my library still, with pages very brittle now; like many of the books left behind by one of our tenants, it has a navy cloth wrapper.

It was a curious accident that I had not read _Jane Eyre_ (or _The Count of Monte Cristo_) since childhood: I had become a teacher of literature, and especially of novels, but had never taught either. This was to be another fortunate accident, because if I had read them in order to teach them before I knew _how_ to be interested in them, my childhood values would have been obscured and permanently overridden by my pedagogical necessities. Or if I had read _Jane Eyre_ in the Seventies, a standard reading might have twisted my attention to the Jane-Rochester couple (and Rochester's maiming), away from Jane's confrontations with Mrs. Reed and the minister Rivers, whom she refuses to marry. As it was, in the Eighties nothing prevented me from picking out the sections I had once prized in the book as unerringly as if that preteen had once crayoned the passages that mattered to her.

I had paid no mind to Jane's first mentor, the gentle Helen Burns, except as a person who needed the example of Jane's rebelliousness. Someone looking at that photo might suggest that I had absorbed Helen's religious submissiveness—and maybe I _had_ borrowed some of my demeanor from Helen Burns. But in my early teens, the natural sister I chose was shy, charmless, bitter, outspoken, orphaned Jane. Turning the pages at forty, I quickly found the incident in which her wicked stepmother wrongly imprisons her in the room they all believe is haunted. This had been one section I drank from: "'Unjust! unjust!' said my reason, forced by the agonizing stimulus into precocious though transitory power: and Resolve instigated some strange expedient to achieve escape from insupportable oppression—as running away, or, if that could not be effected, never eating or drinking more, and letting myself die."

When released from the cruel dungeon, Jane turns on Mrs. Reed with astonishing bravery—like a snake:

> *Speak* I must—I had been trodden on severely, and *must* turn—but how? What strength had I to dart a retaliation at my antagonist? I gathered my energies and launched them in this blunt sentence,—[At forty-something I reread these lines with the same thrill some people experience as the cavalry comes over the hill.] "I am not deceitful. If I were, I should say I loved *you*. . . . if anyone asks me . . . I will say the very thought of you makes me sick, and that you treated me with miserable cruelty."
>
> "How dare you affirm that, Jane Eyre?"
>
> "How dare I, Mrs. Reed? How dare I? Because it is the truth. . . ."
>
> Ere I had finished this reply, my soul began to expand, to exult, with the strangest sense of freedom, of triumph, I ever felt. It seemed as if an invisible bond had burst, and that I had struggled out into unhoped-for liberty. Not without cause was this sentiment: Mrs. Reed looked frightened. . . . I was left there alone—winner of the field. It was the hardest battle I had fought, and the first victory I had gained.

Those familiar with psychoanalytic thought will instantly suspect that Jane's rebellion against Mrs. Reed represents, but diverts attention from, any child's ambivalence toward her mother, who thus gets divided into two people, the good mother and the bad—sometimes a guardian or a wicked stepmother. Perhaps. I remember my mother as kind and patient (she still is), but no doubt she incurred my wrath in late childhood by relatively minor limitations on my freedom, and of course in radical and, as I saw it, life-denying ways, by coercing (encouraging) me to use up my time in doing schoolwork rather than reading novels.

But if this were all I had discovered—this banal application of analytic theory to my own life—this excavation and mining and reconstruction of the past would scarcely have been worth the effort. Rather, I want to point out what rereading taught me that was truly new. A child's "hardest battle" and "first victory," may well be over a mother figure. Over whom would we have our first triumph, and in what other circumstances, if not over our primary caretaker? What happens to those children who are never loved enough to experience a victory in resisting their mothers? For me to be bold enough to enjoy that passage, however tremulously, my real mother must have made it safe for me to resist her, by giving me, in Jessica Benjamin's words, both "appropriate mirroring of autonomous activity and secure confirmation of connection and closeness."[2] Although Jane is feared rather than loved, that first victory provides her with the experience of victory that will enable her to fend off the much more seductive coercions of St. John Rivers, who is a more powerful antagonist than Mrs. Reed by dint of being male and self-righteous and rhetorically facile at a time when Jane is vulnerable to being stirred by a confused mix of submission and mission. Later (with the book in my fortyish hand, I saw this with dreadful clarity), being able to conceive of opposition to male will was to be a source of strength and trouble to me.

What I took originally from Jane and kept as a weapon was the form of her resistance: language, which Brontë describes as the first power of the weak. "What strength had I?" Jane asks; well, look for strength and you find it: a language that is at first self-descriptive and then turns accusatory and then becomes exultant rhetoric. I must have craved the feeling that she calls "un-hoped-for liberty": the eruption that has been long suppressed but long prepared, so that it emerges in devastating and unanswerable paragraphs. The snake has deep lungs and a tongue. Already, all my future expansions—and inhibitions—most visible in political life, were written in invisible ink across that page.

This is the place to mention a humiliating political failure that occurred in the third grade, a failure that I recognized instantly as such, and for years was ashamed to recount. The assistant principal, no doting Ebeling but a martinet named Murray, one day kept the whole student body in after school, forcing us to repeat her favorite song, the revolting "Mockingbird Hill," and making me sick with anxiety that my mother would worry because I would arrive home late. To be blamed for anything, even something I could argue was out of my control, was intolerable to the obsessive perfectionist of nine. As it turned out (to my surprise) my mother was not especially worried, but I decided to take revenge on Mrs. Murray by typing up little slips of paper—many many slips, as if the whole school had joined me at the one Royal—expressing our outrage at her injustice in punishing us all for the infraction of a few. All afternoon I typed variations of the strict truth: "Mrs. Murray is a tyrant." That would teach her to suffer as I had suffered! Then, strategizing in a pained, nightmarish way about where to leave them so that she would find them without learning who had dropped them there kept me awake and tormented late that night. No criminal ever planned a murder with more agonizing forethought. The one ideal location was the stairwell, sheltered behind two swinging doors, right across from her office on the second floor. The next day I climbed the stairs in a purposeful way, as if intent on an errand. I stood there for a terrifying instant with my hands in my pockets, clutching the neatly cut and typed bundles. But the fear of discovery and retaliation won out. The good girl didn't drop the slips, any of them.

The third and last of the books I came to identify as crucial to me was Richard Wright's *Black Boy*. I believe I read it at a slightly older age, also many times. I reclaimed it as one of "my" special chosen books only in 1987, when an African-American scholar told me (it was at a lunch party this time) how much Wright had been influenced in writing by a Chicago-based school of sociology; the professor said Wright had tailored his memories to the sociologists' notions of the black culture of poverty. "Curious," I burst out (with one of those flashes of outspokenness that ruins my self-image as a woman of the world), "how when I used to read it, it seemed like my own life."

Saying that sentence—the fact that it might have seemed odd to anyone merely looking at me—summoned me to justify it. At twelve I was not male, not black, not a devotee of any school of sociology; nor did I then have a sense—which became quite strong when I arrived at college—that in the Radcliffe scheme of things my family was relatively poor. Nor was I beaten by relatives, nor had I had (or considered having) sexual intercourse, nor did I know what gonorrhea was. These differences I could recall, and sitting beside my brilliant table companion, I fell rudely silent, stupefied by the discovery that this story of deprivation too had once been a favored representation of my experience.

When I reread *Black Boy* shortly after that lunch, the same weird ecstatic sensation came over me as when I had reread the important fragments of *Jane Eyre* and *The Count of Monte Cristo*. I could read it as I had once read it and only as I had then read it, when I had memorized whole dialogues and scenes by dint of identification with that other child. Once again, I became the Richard, so vulnerable and confused and defiant, that Wright had described. The early-morning scene where his uncle asks him the time, and his answer unwittingly puts his uncle in a fury of exasperation and vituperation, left me just as blank and bewildered as it once had. Even as an adult I had to read it twice, and only then was the adult critic finally able to conclude that Wright had deliberately omitted any explanation of his uncle's anger: he had left it (as he had felt it) as an aporia. But in the first rereading, I became an uncomprehending child, who cannot even under duress understand what makes grown-ups so fierce, or what she has done wrong.

It was a sort of ecstasy to be out of my mind in that way—out of my present mind—so completely. But after the brief ecstatic time warp, and the recognition of it, my adult self did something that only *it* could do: it saw without fear of projective mistake the kinds of passages that child had needed decades and decades before: it understood truths about the child that she could not have known. It couldn't help cherishing her too, with a little pathos that she would empathetically have repudiated. And the adult self was able to make rapid connections and dismiss false interpretations with authority, in the discoveries of that moment and those that followed. *Black Boy* turned out to be more shockingly violent than I had remembered, but the scenes that had bound me to Richard uncannily resembled the one in *Jane Eyre*. Wright included many of the same form—fables of adult injustice and childish vulnerability—but one in particular I had made mine: an earlier scene where his aunt gets into a towering rage over an obvious pretext, beats him once publicly and then tries to beat him again at home even when she knows he's innocent.

> I did not want to be violent with her, and yet I did not want to be beaten for a wrong I had not committed.
>
> "You're just mad at me for something!" I said.
>
> "Don't tell me I'm mad!"
>
> "You're too mad to believe anything I say. [But] . . . you're not going to beat me! I didn't do it."
>
> "I'm going to beat you for lying!"
>
> "Don't, don't hit me! If you hit me I'll fight you."
>
> . . . I grabbed up a knife and held it ready for her. (119)

He doesn't use the knife, but he won't let it go. His mother and grandmother intervene, and he needs to say again, "I'm not going to let her beat me; I don't care what happens!" His grandfather tries to take control, and he says again, twice, "But I don't want to be beaten! . . . I'm not going to let her beat me." And then, finally, "Aunt Addie took her defeat hard."

The same setting, injustice; the same reaction: resistance and the accusation of adult wrongdoing; the same result, the wilting of the power of the dominator. But that reading child must have known before she came upon Wright that there were some cases where language was purely insufficient. I had caught the good girl. The language of resistance was not (or was no longer) enough for her, she wanted knives.

The Taste of the Past

She was emotionally an alien, but I saw her, to my amazement, plain. Yes, I had stumbled on three precious old vases, I had cracked them and put a wet fingertip inside each jar. The taste was intense but bitter. I suspected I would never be able to recover it again by reading these same books, and indeed, when I rechecked the passages to quote them, they had lost their savor. But, by knowing the girl at last, I could make sense of the changes the woman had undergone since then. Access to the child had been thrilling but brief; access to the development of my life story was to be—I felt this at the time and know it now—a permanent acquisition. Fragments of my adulthood clung around my new knowledge in radiant order. My hesitant steps toward activism: Vietnam, the teaching fellows' union, the feminist movement, that first visit to Nicaragua. A huddle of mere facts—odd detached scenes—hatreds—certain writings, some of which had never seen publication—frustration—leaps of faith. She and I were not wholly discontinuous—these things were the trails between us. Something of deep emotional interest to my adult self was thus revealed.

I saw that the three life stories, with their overlapping passions and brave hopes and resistances, had not first molded me in their image. Something in me *chose* them first. Of course those parts fitted me exactly, like those children's blocks that come in two pieces: when the correct two are pressed together, they wedge into each other firmly and make a whole. But I had made the books fit, by discarding parts that didn't. In those far-off years, something I felt met three forms of discourse and bonded to them and became a more solid, definite construction as a result. Rediscovering these one after another, I had half solved the psycholiterary detective story that I am telling.

Until I read *Black Boy* again, I did not have quite enough material to understand who were my child self's elective affinities, what plots mated her desires. As in fairy tales, there have to be three repetitions before meaning coheres. And then, with three, I suddenly had too much material. I could not see what the prize pupil in the close-knit Jewish family had to do with the nineteenth-century French male political prisoner, the Victorian girl-orphan, the impoverished black boy in the pre–World War II South.

Some of my readers may smile at my naïveté. And perhaps I could more readily have seen the pattern if it had not been partially occluded by a then-unchallenged aspect of literary theory, now distanced by the name "essentialism." It took me a while to figure out that the good girl had not yet learned to read as white, a girl, a bourgeoise-in-the-making, a modern. Between the ages of ten and fourteen, she hadn't picked up those social identifications. Or if she did, they were weak. She slipped into fictional spaces that were coded "male," "French," "southern black" "poverty-stricken." And what matched her then proved absurdly compelling; it endured decades of forgetfulness, the overlaps of later life, a professional career that involved reading perhaps thousands of novels.

So I was slow to recover Margaret's meanings from our three books. If I yielded momentarily to the suggestion that the good girl _must_ have found all that difference alienating, it was because I was reluctant to conclude that my vision had been so dark in childhood. I couldn't miss the common patterns. All those "orphans" deprived of goods that kids never get enough of—attention, love, protection? Literal incarceration—brief in _Jane Eyre_, prolonged in _Monte Cristo_, and more like her own, without walls, in _Black Boy_—must have meant to her imprisonment in institutions. Which? The family, the school, the larger sociopolitical world? She had a self all right, and it was not the self she was known to have in P.S. 208 and at family parties. The first thing that self knew about itself was that it had so little agency. She suffered the stress of opposing the influences, and weaknesses she couldn't name or cure. She searched out descriptions of the conditions of the dispossessed. She only read as _young_.

Those heroic moments in the novel were to her the worst moments of life. There was no oppression without resentment, a sullen tapeworm; no cry of "injustice" without a dangerous judgment of someone in power; no revenge without heart-stopping images of retaliation; no resistance without agonizing conflict; no hope without the threat of failure; no escape without loneliness. The books gave her weapons too, or sharpened them, and seemed to urge them on her, but they were all double-edged: loud voice and high vocabulary, vicarious triumph, models of patience, persistence, solitary stalwartness. They made it all so hard, when all she wanted (_wasn't_ it?) was to be calm, calm, like the coward in the photograph.

The dispossessed you always have in you. When I stopped being a child, I became a woman, a junior adult in the hierarchies of academe, a novice writer; a political dissenter in the era of Vietnam and the civil rights movements and the Contra war; a human struggling against what she wanted to reject of her own conditionings. At every moment in history, most people in the world confront similar external powers, some far more overwhelming. Many don't understand their condition: they believe it to be eternal, and the thought of resistance never occurs to them. In terms of enlightenment and empowerment, I was lucky to have found certain progressive fictions and considered them my own.

Getting the dispossessed into fiction is a relatively recent literary phenomenon. Their being represented as *struggling* against their oppression is even more rare. The revolutions of the late eighteenth century, military and intellectual and poetic, had given writers who wanted them—always a minority—language for understanding previously unacknowledged forms of oppression. Each of my three novels was to Margaret a cry of personal suffering ("Me, me")—and what use would they have been to me or any other reader otherwise? It isn't likely that I intuited, however obscurely, that they were part of *my* psychopolitical formation.

Brontë published *Jane Eyre* in 1847, at the end of a decade of social agitation that was ending in revolutions. Dumas wrote *The Count of Monte Cristo* in the same decade, but cannily laid it in an earlier period (of failed resistance!), the restoration of the Bourbons. Wright published *Black Boy* in 1945, after African-Americans had experienced the rising expectations and rising frustrations of the war years. It was Wright's preface to his conversion to activism through the Communist Party, *American Hunger*. Wright truncated the book into its present shape, as critic Janice Thaddeus notes in a fascinating article, at the urging of judges at the Book of the Month Club.[3] In its form as published, it is akin in spirit to the American and English and French individualist liberalism of the first half of the nineteenth century.

I've spoken in passing of hope. All three of my books, two intentionally and one by the lures of publishing history, are progress novels, and one is a midlife progress novel. Progress novels construct hope as a reasonable emotion. The characters suffer, but they don't succumb. Afterwards, the novels decree—they provide—some kind of reward. Richard heads north to emancipation, Jane marries her loved one, and Edmond goes off at midlife with his doting protégée, Haidée, and his countless millions. In effect then, I had collected three bildunsgromane. The German term usually refers to novels about the education of young people, but of course the educations described in my books, with the exception of Edmond Dantès's deeply desired, Rousseauistic tutorial at Faria's feet, are irregular, rough, imperceptible to their victims. And they keep going for Edmond into later life. *Education* would simply be a fancy word for experience that couldn't be evaded. There's a reward for all the protagonists, but it's not cognitive. From my midlife concern with the passionate issue of whether we can abandon emotions that do not serve us, one reward looks like entrée into a new form of being. Wright says in the last pages, "The face of the South that I had known was hostile and forbidding, and yet out of all the conflicts and the curses, the blows and the anger, the tension and the terror, I had somehow gotten the idea that life could be different, could be lived in a fuller and richer manner" (281). The good girl made a few eliminations and in place of "the South" read "childhood," and it was her story.

These books, then, contained curious implications. (They may look contradictory, but need not be.) They definitely hyped anger, fed scenarios of revenge, but they also insidiously undid my learned childhood pessimism about the life course; they taught me, without my having the slightest suspicion of what I was learning, that power came from being older. (When, much later, I taught a course in midlife progress novels, I tried to show how narratives could do that.)

I could not have failed to note their endings, although through the intermediate years I'm sure they could not have figured in my descriptions of the books. When I sought to go away to college, in the back of my head was Richard on a northward-bound train. I know I clung to the dreams Dumas enshrined. The fantasy of discovering buried jewels stayed in my mind long, long after I should have known that I could earn my own living. But overall, what I chose to believe in was progress, the coming by some means of better days.

The Last Taste

The revenge fantasy turned out to be a stupid weapon in adulthood. The powers-that-be weren't feeble like Mrs. Reed or Aunt Addie. Naming their injustice to them failed: I became tongue-tied out of fear of being too angry and then impotently angry at having been silent, or I said some shred of what I meant but they shrugged off the description. Perhaps all this sounds childish, but many activists, I imagine, have experienced such reactions in political confrontations. Failing in those ways fed more revenge fantasies, all impossible to execute. Failure wasn't an argument for giving up the struggle, but (as I initially perceived only dimly) for changing weapons. Then I stumbled upon other weapons. (Writing was one. Writing last was better than revenge.) Jane and Edmond and Richard used escape, and I did too, but it threw me back to the little kid behind the swinging doors. It isn't an easy thing to change your weapons, when you got them in childhood and clung to them in bitter imagination. Edmond, I discovered when I reread the book, also gave up revenge— after he had coldly enjoyed a sufficiency. But I would never have consoling millions. I have only my own opinion to support me here, but replacing revenge fantasies was one of the wisest and hardest things I did in early midlife.

The last time I chewed vengefulness marked a stage in my coming into adulthood. I was in graduate school—belatedly getting the advanced degree that was supposed to assure me of the kind of modest security my mother had had all her working life as a public schoolteacher—when the postwar academic job market collapsed. Even at the top schools, using the old-boy network, faculty began to find they couldn't place even their best students. The chair of my department was married at that time to one of the richest women in the country (not long afterwards she divorced him). Lunching with the graduate liaison committee, this man said to us, "Some of you will wind up driving cabs." He was the last person I "hated"—not personally, but as the mean, ignorant, plutocratic representative of all the haves. "He knows not what he says," I would remind myself. I was still naive about the triumphalism of power.

As the market collapsed, my university—Harvard—tightened its belt around our necks. A group of us formed a union. Hundreds of people I had never known from all departments attended the first meeting; our oratory was witty, angry, scathing. Over the year, sitting on living room floors, standing up in kitchens sharing cokes and chips, we practiced arguing and educated one another in economic analysis and political systems. Slowly it began to make sense to me that for the miseries of national scope that befall you, you don't blame yourself. And you don't go it alone.

When we organized department by department, a graduate student asked me with aggressive defeatism at a public meeting, "But what if we fail?" Although I had no conscious knowledge of my three novels, I must have cherished their harsh meliorism. Edmond does not despair either when he's tunneling with a teaspoon or marking off the lustrums on his prison wall. (The *Shawcross Conversion* is a similar fable of midlife male patience followed by victory.) Jane goes out into the snow to follow a voice. Richard endures unendurable repetitions of incomprehension and meanness. Resistance acts not knowing for sure whether it will defeat the oppressor. The dream of progress—the dignity of resistance—must have stayed in my mind. Far from legitimating the status quo, the plot of progress was reinvented with the revolutionary collective impulse and is related to it. Perhaps, as Camus and others believe, none of the oppressed would ever fight who did not possess that dream. And no child—no person—would ever grow.

In small groups people met to draw posters, invent slogans, lobby the press, design strategy, elect representatives. I was one. By spring we had eleven hundred members. Marginalized, underpaid preprofessionals at the bottom of an infantilizing hierarchy, with the help of sympathetic undergraduates we brought one of the powerful universities to a halt with two successful one-day strikes. And something happened—was happening—to my "nature." At night, I ground my fantasies between my teeth until my jaw ached; but in the daytime, for the first time in my life, I organized. When I became an activist, I ate and slept union. By the spring, my jaw had healed. Vengefulness was slipping away.

Even as children, unwillingly subdued to the desires of others, something in us craves to grow into power, and tilts toward what it senses to be right for growth. What a child loves to reread, as Bruno Bettelheim argues in _The Uses of Enchantment,_ is a clue to her developmental needs. Even the child self has a sense of justice and truth. It resists; it says, "You lie." It rebukes power, as when Richard says to his uncle, "You are not an example to me. . . . You're a _warning._" Jane wills truth-telling and becomes the brusque, "savage" self that rejects Rivers's offer of martyrdom and sexual teasing. And Richard wills independence, not to be a chair-bottom weaver but a writer. If one part of the earliest core self is sheerly negative, a matter of pure resistance, the counterbalancing part is desire. Would anyone argue, in face of poor Margaret's fear of conflict, that her desire to resist was imposed externally?

What saves children (and grownups too) is that what gives pain from the self need not remain a fixed part of the self, as I found to my astonishment had happened soon after I said the word _revenge_ out loud. I was able to accept revenge as "my" main motive as readily as I did (after the hesitations I've described) because in my thirties I had finished with it. I never would be omnipotent, but I didn't need to perform all resistance alone.

Thinking about the midlife, as I did quite a lot in the late Seventies and Eighties, and of course my own relationship to it, gave me a startling new mode of understanding my childhood. When I started to teach adult students and bring the midlife into cultural studies, I was suddenly able to think of my parents in the Fifties not as adjuncts of my life but as persons with their own absorbing life history and development. My contexts must have included my parents' desires, not just for me, but for _themselves._ My father's left politics were being stymied by the Cold War (why was Wright in our small library?). Over the dinner table my parents talked often about family friends who were losing their jobs in McCarthyite purges. My friend Joey from 52d Street, too pudgy to be a good ballplayer, had a father who lost his job, and nobody would give him another. My parents were tense and abstracted. At the kitchenette table my stomach knotted; mashed potatoes went down okay but I cut my little meat portion into smaller and smaller morsels, so fork-and-knife action looked as if it continued. But my mother was beginning her career as a schoolteacher about then. All at once, she obtained a career, economic and emotional independence, freedom from housewifery. With two incomes they made a broader front against the world.

These facts offer much and withhold more. Obviously, adult emotions were surging around, but I don't know exactly what emotions they were. Perhaps through my solitary reading I embraced passions they were feeling during the long Cold War terror. If my father suppressed his anger, turned sour with exasperated hope, while my mother lived out a buoyant progress plot, that would certainly furnish the good girl with a tidy origin myth. But I remember my father's voice raised loud in attack and assertion (nothing was more exciting than family parties where grownups argued politics) and I was proud of him for standing up against the whole family. My mother was a progressive too, but quieter and more certain that pessimism brought no good conclusion closer. Those were also the same years when my father bought a small business and was finally able to get out of heavy lifting. Who can say what waves of anger the girl of twelve, the woman of thirty-nine, the man of forty-seven were exchanging? What banners of liberation? These are not rhetorical questions. If I cannot be sure what all the influences were during a period I have suddenly been able to probe so deeply, how can anyone without such access speak confidently about the creation of early selfhood?

One thing I surely knew is that my parents had more power than I did. My mother in particular gave me an example of adult willing and getting. But Margaret could not *be* thirty-nine at once. Ten . . . twelve . . . fourteen is impoverished, helpless in choices. No wonder Margaret identified with outcasts, wanted to drop poisoned notes, stumble on a bag of jewels, leave a blade in an enemy's heart. The only thing my parents unquestionably determined— and that was merely by begetting her—was that she had to be, for a while, a child.

At moments, her life seems scarcely tolerable, regarding it as I do from later and stronger days. And yet I'm reluctant to say she was peculiar; and I can't imagine the kind of therapists I admire reading this story to conclude that she was particularly neurotic. On the contrary, the thought cannot escape us that there must be many children in the same fix. Perhaps all children? If she, so privileged, so distinguished within the precincts of the young, can have been so wrought up, so muddled and needy, for so long (without even the excuse of puberty), what of children without her resources?

The self some theorists wanted us to acknowledge until recently might be described as a mixed bag of imposed, assumed, and fairly rigid identities. I can now partly recognize that as the self the good girl was saddled with. Now that I know her better, however, I can confidently add that the bag was not a static container; it included both loathed and desired identities. Her given conditions were powerful; why else would she have needed knives? While I don't. And this leads me to an unexpected but inescapable conclusion. Suppose the self that is being theorized today is not a lifelong self but merely, by some colossal mistake, childhood's self. (I won't stop here to inquire how that mistake could occur.) But in that case, giving it up couldn't be much of a loss. The old-clothes dealers can have it. Particularly if they'll consider letting all of us have a midlife self. And if they'll let everyone invent about it more engaging metaphors that take into account the sense so many adults get from their age identity that it is at once full of necessary and precious and intimate pieces of self. Something like the box of jewels I looked for in the fields. But not inanimate. Ready to defend itself from intrusion but flexible and playful, open enough to expel trashed pieces and collect or create new material at the same time. A friend.

At this point I find in myself a lassitude about investigating further the girl in braids. I won't get better access; a little further and I'd be inventing. In any case, given my present inclinations, backward seems a silly direction to be aimed in—it makes more sense to look forward, to keep my eyes open for what will happen next.

In an earlier era, too, this whole story of childhood concealment, adult forgetting, and midlife rediscovery and liberation might have seemed trivial. Or it would have been rejected in different ways—utilizing either the older Freudian line that is skeptical about adult change or the Proustian line that emphasizes loss and decline from childhood being. Now I think we can see that these attitudes toward the life course, though apparently contradictory, were not merely simultaneous but related, with deep roots in turn-of-the-century reactions to the newly invented "middle years" of life, the construction of midlife decline narrative, and the simultaneous cult of youth. "Given . . . nostalgia's source in the threat of identity discontinuity," as sociologist Fred Davis writes, and the obscurity of the threats, many people reaching their middle years in that period responded by disliking midlife aging.[4] Proust and Freud were unwilling to relinquish links to past life periods; each in his way expressed a deep longing for childhood and its intense family-centered traumas. One of them wishfully theorizes that the links never disappear however much one wants them to, and the other that under certain unforseeable circumstances the links can be miraculously reclaimed.

These are touching myths, at some level. Saying this suggests that their enormous power is fading. (This is happening, in part, because "human beings [are no longer seen] as essentially conservative, unwilling to give up old satisfactions for new.")[5] What touches me is that so many people needed decline for so long. Many still do. Even George Orwell, after unsparingly recalling the weakness, credulity, and dread from which children suffer, ends his essay "Such, Such Were the Joys. . ." by announcing "what one invariably feels in revisiting any scene of childhood: How small everything has grown, and how terrible is the deterioration in myself!"[6]

To me the middle of life no longer seems a priori dreadful. It's possible to see it as bringing relief, if not from childhood, then from adolescence or young adulthood—or from all at once. And—whatever we think in depressed moments—adult powerlessness can never be as complete and oppressive as childhood powerlessness. Perhaps other readers will be as surprised as I once was that what the older theories of the life course touch most closely is each other, and not us at all.

The motive for telling this story deepened recently when I woke up in pain and excitement knowing I had just had a movielike dream left over from childhood. The main persona in the movie was invisible: I, its eyes, saw only its legs and hands. This ungendered bodiless self was mounted bounding on an exhausting but invisible apparatus that impeded forward motion by forcing it first up and then down—as if something trying to fly was compelled to touch ground at every step. Around this self rose and fell a vast hilly city. At first it (the self) bounced easily, as if in play. Then a moment came when it became "late" "very late"; the family was momentarily leaving or had already left, in a car; somehow the self knew they would be traveling down a steep main street. The self had to get up that hill because there was no other way to intersect with the tall ones in the car; had to get back rapidly, before they left or got too far. Had to keep going downhill, though, and farther away, before rushing and turning right back and up, because huge fenced-in blocks like prisons or handball courts forced a detour. In this emergency, the apparatus turned villainous, a pogo-stick demon. Finally, an elevated subway smoothed swifly alongside, but the bounding body could never keep up, always reached the rare stations where the subway stopped, too late. Then panting furiously, extenuated, lungs collapsing, the self found itself stymied in a cul-de-sac, barred by a gate. Looking through the bars was like looking through a muzzle. Past the bars, the subway fled uptown.

Obviously, one part of the dream resurrects a time of my inexperience when I still thought "downtown" was *down*. The last time this dream invaded me in force was I think in my teens, in college. It was much more of a nightmare then, more breathless and endless and exhausting. Now, possibly some powerlessness during my day had revived it (although it's possible that a mere sensation of breathlessness had summoned it). For whatever reason, now it was more curious than frightening—like checking out a videotape of an old horror film. The action is the same, but one's feelings don't recur. Probably I'll never understand where that terrified child self thought she ought to be and what she feared constituted the obstacles in her way. I do know, gratefully, one thing: adulthood opened the gate.

Coda: The March in Pienza

Weeping at parades can be a moment in a trajectory.

For a long time, I thought my occasions of weeping resulted from martial music operating on a sentimental sap; only a fascist would let trumpets and drums massage her stupid heart valves. One day in Pienza in central Italy, though, tears came as a small straggling parade without music passed by me. Down the Renaissance cobbled street appeared the vanguard. They hoisted banners carrying in two words their good wish (PEACE) and their earnest timetable (NOW). Another banner sang out, "Si vuoi la pace, prepara la pace" (If you want peace, prepare for peace). Some of the children carried factory-made pennants printed with the hammer and sickle; the party of Gramsci must have organized the event. A few people carried discreet homemade cardboard signs bearing the letters D.C. (Democristiani, a conservative party) or a socialist red carnation. It was the Eighties, the papers hadn't discovered Party corruption. A woman whose five-year-old carried a pennant in his grubby fist chatted with a man whose somewhat older daughter carried a D.C. placard solemnly. Most people didn't carry anything. Yes, we said to one another, this is a peace demonstration.

First came a group of women wheeling carriages with their babies inside, and then some pushing strollers, with some men holding toddlers by the hands, and then women and more men with school-age children, who winked at friends on the sidewalk and waved to friends cheering out the windows of the painted houses. The adolescents sauntered by and the twenty-somethings, jostling each other in groups, or occasionally two by two. Girlfriends marched with linked arms in twos or threes or chains of seven whose ends had to curve forward or back to avoid hitting the housewalls. A few boys walked arm in arm. There were men in the heavy blue shirts that farmers wear, and some farm couples on their tractors, spotlessly cleaned for the occasion. There were other midlife men in provincial dark suits with vests—lawyers and notaries, we thought—and women wearing gold chains and designer sweaters and those comfortable walking shoes that are the signature of chic matronhood. Three midlife women walked together, one carrying a paper fan. Then came the elders. Two men in wheelchairs, one smoking. A young woman and her mother arm in arm. Groups of two and three couples, friends. Two remarkably handsome old men, one with a cane, came by with two men who were clearly their sons but perhaps not quite as fine looking. The marchers went by for a long time. Pienza is not a big town: over the heads of the marchers one block away I could see the dark conifers that held back the fields and made a background for their procession. It seemed as if the whole town and the surrounding country had turned up to participate or encourage; and the tourists turned out of the papal palaces to watch them go by. Yes, we said, this is a peace march.

There was a hubbub of talk as everybody walked at the sedate pace set by the leaders with the baby carriages and the toddlers and the idea that the elderly were walking behind. "The young mothers aren't with their own age cohort," I said crossly to our son, so that at fifteen, he wouldn't pick up the notion that women should be subordinated to their babies. People were greeting neighbors they passed and switching places to talk to others in the line of march. While it was something like a *passeggiata,* the evening promenade that takes place in small cities in Italy in the cooling summer nights, this was noisier, more theatrical, sociable, and purposeful. For a political demonstration it was like a vast extended family speaking out; it was a genealogy come to vigorous life on an urban frieze. All over the country that day people in communities were marching together, with a declared, practical, feasible, limited, utopian agenda little of which was likely to be fulfilled any time soon.

My chest filled; impatience gripped me, longing—to join and shout, know all marchers, strut all walks, hold six banners, drive all vehicles, quicken the pace, bring the change remake the world do it now. And there I was, an outsider tethered teetering on the curb, the frieze blurring from time to time because my heart and mind were with them; but they passed, they passed us by, by my husband, by our son, by me as I stood in place, wishing I was one of them, wishing we were three of them—sharing what they had in common, knowing clear-eyed solidarity is the answer to the questions never stated, but not yet in the street.

3

Ordinary Pain

A Few New Twists

SOME PEOPLE might say I got a head start on middle age when I got arthritis over a decade ago. My first back trouble had come upon me even earlier.
I was trying to raise a double-hung window that I had painted shut, and being
too lazy to move the potted jade plant underneath it, I was standing to the
left of the window shoving my muscular arms sideways and up against the
resistance. The window suddenly shot free of its glue of latex, and the top half
of my torso propelled itself upwards as if saying goodbye to the bottom at the
waist. The next two weeks are a blur.

In some ways, the next few *years* are a blur. The muscle I pulled never
seemed to heal entirely, or perhaps I kept reinjuring it. (It took years before I
got a diagnosis of arthritis—osteoarthritis.) My back shouted for attention. I
spent an unfair amount of time at the office pressing up against a wall with a
knee raised, or lying on the floor with both knees raised, and I held conferences with my boss standing in the stork position. My word processor was
decorated with a hand-printed sign that ordered, Rise and stretch every
twenty minutes. I needed a special ergonomic chair; my boss ordered them
for all of us. Friends suggested unappealing and contradictory exercises: pull-
ing the bathroom sink out of the wall was the action of one of them. At one
point I was convinced that the trouble came from the bed: my husband said
his back hurt too (like one of those primitive spouses who act out parturition
with their wives, complete with groans). We bought, at enormous expense,
an orthopedically approved bed. I have a deep distaste for drugs (I'm the only
person I know who got through the seventies on three tokes), but when I had
to, I took painkillers. From time to time I wheedled deep-heat treatments out
of my prepaid managed-care medical plan, each of which gave me a full hour
of normal pain-free activity—a memory of what life had been like all those
years before the jade plant intersected with the double-hung window.

Pain is harder to describe than remedies. I could almost always feel it from inside on the right side of the spine just below the waist—more when I woke up in the morning, expecting to feel well rested, but also more coming home slumped in the car at night, or after reading for an hour or two upright in a chair in the evening. The 90 percent of Americans who have had back trouble can tell, from that last sentence, all the things I was doing wrong. We all know that I sat still to read because all movement is painful, and surcease from pain is worth almost anything, even (later) worse pain.

What no one talks about convincingly, even in the many recent discourses on terminal illness, is how your identity tries to change when your body changes. I had been a strong active woman. What a wonderful thing to be. I was proud of my strength, and the things it enabled me to do gave me a lot of pleasure. When I was mixing concrete, I could carry the fifty-pound sacks of cement. When I decided that the new hedge needed to be planted on a mound of earth a foot higher than the surrounding terrain, and the topsoil arrived, I shoveled, ported, dumped, and packed tons of it myself in not much more than a long morning. I have never weighed more than 128, but I could put my back (sigh) into nailing and lifting. I used to arm wrestle. I had good endurance: if I couldn't work as fast as a bigger person on a lot of jobs, I could hang in there as long. When my husband and I built our summer house in 1979, just a few years before my first trouble, we got up at seven and worked until seven, and though we were both eager, I pushed the pace.

That is what I lost.

Maybe not every woman has gotten this kind of work out of her body, or loved it so much for this particular reason. But when you can't do what you once liked to do, whatever that was, you fear you're becoming a different person. In my case, the case of a small woman who liked doing manual labor around the house and grounds, fearing I'd be a different person was almost entirely an *internal* process, in the sense that it was private, almost without witnesses. Few people knew about my construction projects. I work ordinarily in various sedentary communities—writers, teachers, educational administrators, activists—and the sedentary are rarely competent at manual labor and scarcely notice it or know how to value it properly. (Once I carried an eight-foot wooden curtain rod across Manhattan for a friend who had just moved into a new apartment and couldn't get to the hardware store herself: she was impressed out of all proportion to the feat. The rod was light, and it was larky balancing it on my shoulder through the uptown streets. It was my one public performance as a strong woman.)

So when I stopped being able to carry cement and lug the potted plants outside in the summer, nobody but my husband knew or cared. It wasn't like being a man with the same avocations—known for being a strong man—

who had gotten less capacitated. Nobody thought less of me for it. *They* didn't think I was a different person—a "declining body." If I was being wedged into a decline story, only I had the power to impose it on myself. That's what I mean by saying it felt almost entirely like an internal loss. And that's how I know that what has to be dealt with, even more than the pain, is the internal pressure to administer to yourself a label like "failing."

People who know me only as the author of a book with the title *Safe at Last in the Middle Years* might think that no arthritis victim could have written it—that no one with a chronic illness could sport that title. For me, it's the other way around. Wear-and-tear arthritis, as they told me it was called, appears to be one of those ailments that you earn by living. Having one of those gives me a right to talk about "midlife" adjustments. More than a right: something like a responsibility.

The personal psychological issue is what to do with an acknowledged loss, a daily degree of pain, a potential for acute distress. A given and named condition is not thereby *your* condition. Your condition is your reaction, your living with your changed body, and the new state you and it make together. It's really a narrative issue: how do I want to fit this into my life story? If you are lucky enough to have no idea offhand what I mean by this, think hard about what it's been like for you to be sick.

Learning to Be Sick

How do we learn to be sick? This may seem a curious question. But it has an obvious answer, if we ask first, "*When* do we learn to be sick?" These days, you might think "the midlife" was the answer, what with all the notice given to men getting heart attacks and women breast cancer at forty or fifty. (It's often said that this is tougher on men, as they've never been sick before.) Old age is the other quick answer. One eminent psychologist says, "It is the occurrence of illness which makes the need for compensation most salient, and such events are more likely to happen in old age than at earlier periods of the life span."[1] These answers, although popular and encouraged, seem wrong to me. The fact is that illness is likely to strike first in childhood, and frequently. Surely most people learn what it means to be sick, with a set of compensations and physical, psychological, philosophical, and verbal correlates, when they are very young. Conceivably some of this learning goes on before a child learns how to speak. As with many things we acquire, then, maternal mediation sets the tone of our experience.

When I was sick as a child, my mother set the tone *piano* and *alegre*. She came in and out frequently and cheerfully, tidying my room and the bed and my nightclothes and me. She came in bearing soup with a napkin and dry crackers; she came in announcing new books from the library; she came in balancing the humidifier, or to read her mail, or just to say a friendly word— to ask how my book was, or to say that Marsha Weiss from across the street had asked when I could come out to play, or to say that Bobbie Bush had brought the homework assignments. (Although I wasn't allowed to do the homework yet, it was a relief to have all the assignments.) If I had a fever, she gave me alcohol rubs. I remember the first chill of exposure to the air, and then the greater chill and trembling as the alcohol evaporated, and then, finally dressed and covered, the sensation (however brief) of having my own skin back again, warm without sweatiness, smooth without slickness, my damp hair combed up off my forehead, my head sinking limply into the grateful support of the pillow. Looking at the child in the beautiful colored illustration to "The Land of Counterpane," I felt no interest in manipulating sharp metal objects or making a world out my rough, disordered, woolly blanket. I rested my eyes on the wallpaper, and traced the shallow curves of its basket of flowers.

For illness, everything became special. *I* was special. My little brother had to be more quiet. My father made evening visits to my room as if I were a dignitary. Marsha-my-best-friend—whose mother was afraid of germs— came to the window and tapped, and made funny shapes with her face and did her best mime, of taking her eyes out and swallowing them accidentally and having them peer up at her. The dry crackers were to avoid upsetting my stomach. The expensive medicine was to make me well quickly. The trips to the library, the tissues, the thermometer, the humidifier all lined up on my vanity table together, were for me. Much was permitted when a person was sick. You could drop your snotty tissue on the floor and it would be picked up while you slept. You left your dirty dishes on a tray, your wet towel knotted up in a ball, your sweaty pajamas in a heap—you were supposed to. Once, when I was eleven, I was hospitalized for an operation (the removal of a thyroglossal cyst); and a nurse came in during lunch a few days later and stopped to watch me inefficiently spooning up the last of my soup. When I asked, in my polite good-girl way, "May I lift the bowl and drink the rest?" I received exactly the tolerant, amused approbation I had expected. Really, the world was very kind when you were sick.

Convalescence (that lovely word) was an even more special, carefully graded experience. Convalescence lasted for days after the fever had gone: there was a day or two of "dangling" legs over the bed: no going out yet, no real walking around. I found those days so tedious that I usually finished my homework, all too quickly. During that time toast appeared, and then toast with butter, and then pieces of moist chicken cut up small, and rice with gravy, and rice pudding with raisins, and then other delicacies to tempt the appetite. Then, if the weather was fine, there was a day partially spent out-side—not of course playing, but getting used to the sunshine and smelling the brackish air from the sea and noticing, when I dropped my book on my stomach, the way the yew bristles clustered in V-shaped formations like the wings of birds.

My mother provided the order and cleanness and good smells that a sick person needs so much more than a well one. Most of all, she was _present_. She didn't shun me for being sick. I didn't learn until years later, in adulthood, from the haphazard and evasive ministrations of other people, how much some people hate or dread and avoid the sick. I had experienced none of that in childhood. On the contrary, I had been taught that the person—the sick body—was to be cared for, cosseted. Its limitation didn't matter. It was loved _more_, it deserved to be. Maybe it's in sickness more than in health that a child learns what being loved-for-oneself is all about. Once you have learned this, it's a lifetime possession. Or it could be, if those who got it could hold on to it.

I like to think that most mothers pass this possession on to their children in some degree, and that if sons exercised caring as much as daughters do, men could more frequently be good caregivers, and also (not coincidentally) better patients at midlife and after. As it is, women seem to benefit most in preparing for being patients.

The Two Doctors

For years I had stayed out of the reach of the doctors. So far the MDs had done nothing for me but provide a diagnostic label and occasional painkillers. Early in 1991, however, I took the rash step of asking for a specialist's opinion, with all the risk that involves of encountering ignorance dressed in authority. It seemed like a good idea at the time. I had had bad nights for three weeks during a trip to my sister city in Nicaragua, getting out of a sagging mattress every morning almost unable to walk. I could scarcely do my stretches. My muscles seemed to have shriveled.

Back in the States, my specialist stalked into the consulting room with the unhurried vigor of a sixty-year-old privileged male; he was attended by an admiring young female subaltern. "You've lost a disk," he boomed out, in a voice made to carry to the back of a theater. I felt as if he took me for many more than one person, which made a bewildering start to the interview. "Gone!" he said dramatically, cheerfully, and forcefully, as if I would try to deny it. "Completely gone." He steered me out to see the X-ray. No space between the disks, one bone grinding against another, he pointed out; the nerve compressed. He had a toy model: wooden vertebra, rubber disks, plastic nerve tubes. In shock I watched him manipulate the toy. I'd seen an X-ray and a toy; which was my back?

Back in the consulting room, he watched me walk, bend, twist. "Astonishing mobility," he commented. My heart sank further: why should it be astonishing that I could do what I worked so hard to go on doing? He asked severely what I had been up to in Nicaragua. I had been enjoying some shoveling at a preschool site. (To be honest, I'd felt anxious about it at the time.) That was bad. Shoveling was out. Almost anything I did or liked to do was dangerous. He implied that I had had control over my back—my pain, my life—that I had regularly abused. "I'm an old man," he said, with the proud relish of hypocrisy. He was thinking of his powerful tennis game, I was sure. "You're not an old woman, but you have to be careful. You can't do the things you did when you were young." *Act* like a not-young woman, was what he meant to say. *Think* not-young. Caution. Why, a whole picture of the midlife mindset was conveyed by his tone.

"Let's try to keep fault out of this," I said coldly. "I don't see what age has to do with it; I had an accident in my thirties." He knew this already.

On the other hand, he had no idea why I wasn't in more pain. "We used to think these things were wholly mechanical, but they're not. You're doing something right, but we don't know what it is," he said, denying me control in the same cheerful tone in which he'd blamed me for misusing it.

Bravely I ventured, as he and the still-silent acolyte appeared to be on the way out the door without having left time for my questions. "What's the prognosis?" Who can say? was the gist of his answer. Chivalric male, he was trying to protect me from my awful future. It took me only a few hours to figure out that I had just gotten the worst news of my personal life.

Scared and helpless, I looked as steadily as I could at my prospects. Of course I tried to dissociate the "news" he had given me from his personal baggage about aging and disability and my gender and his authority. But even after subtracting his psychocultural problems, insofar as I could, the "facts" looked no better for me. He hadn't mentioned any alleviation. I extrapolated from the nerve pain I had been feeling: whenever that began to worsen, my work day would gradually shorten, I would slowly become disabled and dependent. How long would that take? Ten years? Five years? Two? Two would mean I wouldn't see my next book through the press. I'm a slow worker, I might not finish it. I was now so distracted that I could scarcely concentrate on work at all. At first, when I thought about all this in the middle of the night (pain woke me, and fear kept me awake), I just cried—quietly, so my husband wouldn't wake up.

But being a feminist activist, a former administrator, a midlife woman, and a mother has some effects on mental habits. "What can you *do?*" is the question you train yourself to ask. I could commit suicide to avoid the worst of it. I've always believed in suicide as an option for the sane suffering from incurable degenerative diseases. But suicide, which should be a private issue, is now becoming public, and bound to become more difficult to encompass without interference. To try to decide how best to commit suicide in 1991, with the media full of news about the arrests and trials of those who tried to assist, was to march ever more rapidly over the abyss into self-pity. I looked with hollow eyes at my dear husband; my son, whose wedding I might never attend; my mother, who would survive me.

All that saved me from despair is that my pain slowly, inexplicably, withdrew. It dropped below pre-Nicaragua levels. I stopped taking the medication. My mobility returned; my extensions were as good as I could remember them being. In grief over my lost future, I had gone to a psychologist. The first time, I wept and told her about my fear of disability. The second time, just two weeks later, almost free of pain, I felt almost embarrassed to be taking up her time; I thanked her for her help, which had been precious. I didn't go back a third time. Pain dominates or absence of pain dominates the mind. It may have been irrational to stop worrying about disability and impediments to dying, but I couldn't hold on to my fear. All I had left was resentment against the jolly terrifying orthopedist, and a kind of sullen resistance to the idea of inevitable physical decline and accommodation that his tone and silences had promised.

It was almost an accident that I subsequently talked to another doctor about my back: I went to see this one, an internist I've known for fifteen years, about something else altogether. He is about five years younger than I am; very fit but not superior about it. He presents himself as a bare-facts man; he likes to repeat lecture material from med school. He appeared to be doing that now. After the accident, the original trauma, he said, the disk had obtruded into the muscle, the muscle had inflamed; ergo, pain. It was fortunate that no one had induced me to have the fusion operation, which used to be given too quickly. Thousands of people had slipped disks. By now, mine, left alone over the years, had "resorbed"—vanished indeed. But it hadn't vanished entirely; a sliver was left that kept bone from grinding bone. The body had, in one way, healed itself. Pain might recur, from doing almost nothing: shaking hands, or lifting a cup of coffee. I still had arthritis, of course.

This felt like a completely new story. It was curious and wonderful and acceptable and liberating. One, it was not my fault. And (big two) it was a *progress story.* The details remained stable and familiar, but the whole tendency of the narrative—that I had lost my pain by losing my disk—spun the orthopedist's narrative around on its ear. My internist told grim facts about the operation that I would need if/when the sliver too resorbed; he laid out a possible prognosis in more detail. But I left clutching my progress story, and eventually laughing to tears.

Thus I learned a lesson that most doctors never learn sufficiently, and that cannot be repeated too often to patients. This is a warning about listening and believing. Doctors believe they're telling facts. Instead, they possess their tiny factoids, as well as their age and social conditioning, and also—most important of all—their private inclinations to tell progress or decline stories in relation to the patient before them. Gender, race, class, and all other biases may or may not play into a particular doctor's story. But age certainly does. Why did my sixty-year-old orthopedist lead me to believe the decline version of my story, and my same-age internist tell me the progress version? Aside from everything else I've hinted, I think the orthopedist was used to talking to "old" people, who are cautioned to give up mobility because it's assumed (wrongly) that they have no choice; they'll take the advice docilely; they're prepared for that decline story. Now that story can be told to people at midlife. And as for not revealing the prognosis: well, doctors like that lie to "older" people, thinking that they expect the worst anyway, but aren't strong enough to bear it said straight out. Doctors like that praise themselves for not being able to deliver painful truths, sensitive souls that they are, when actually what they can't do is be intelligent enough to recognize that they have options about how to tell a story about the future.

The two doctors did not contradict each other technically. Each of them told a story about an X-ray and a history that began around the jade plant. But the consequences of the stories they told . . . The consequence of hinting that it was too late for me to avert my destiny, even if I changed all my sleeping and waking behaviors, was that I was plunged into planning my suicide. The consequence of hinting to me that my body had healed itself as bodies often can do, and that I was likely to have less pain for a while except from accidents that cannot be avoided, is that I have been leading a normal life, and just this afternoon rowed my husband strongly around a lake, using a powerful deep-plunging stroke I never knew I had.

Of course they always tell you to get a second opinion. This would be good advice only if the two opinions could be guaranteed to diverge when it mattered that they diverge. But you might get two decline storytellers in a row, especially if you're female or "old"; and old now means, in our culture, very young indeed. Sensible practitioners unafraid of "aging" are probably hard to find. It's true for many people, that _your_ midlife aging may anticipate their own, trigger their own fears. But when it's a question of the docs and what they'll tell you . . . If only we could stay out of the hands of the living gods altogether. But this evasion is often impossible, so my default would have to be: _Distrust._ Distrust bad news. Not because bad things don't happen. They do and will. But the person who announces them as such, in these contexts where interpretation makes so much difference, probably does not have your welfare at heart. Knowing what we know about the role that mind plays in illness—all illnesses, even the worst—a story well told could lengthen, or at least gladden, your one and only life.

Bodily Continuity

Arthritis—being a chronic condition with rare (in my case) acute phases—scarcely alters my day-to-day reality. The main problem is that every time I experience pain in that telltale place I worry—I think rationally—that it's the disk announcing its disappearance, which would usher in a whole new world of interminable pain, wasted time, and difficult decisions. Except for that very first time, I've never been totally incapacitated. For a while out of habit I continued to lay tile floors and nail up ceilings with a partner (one summer's chores when my husband and I put in an extra bathroom), but I don't take such risks any more. I can do other projects that don't use the back stressfully if I don't mind working only a few hours at a time and being rather wiped out the next day. I can't do manual labor two full days in a row. Work that used to be thoughtless now takes precautions: I stretch more, heft a weight before I try to lift it, avoid jumping from heights. I can't be reckless. I felt how lucky I was yet again when I read about Sully's bad knee in Richard Russo's _Nobody's Fool_ (1993); there is also a movie version with Paul Newman. Like me, Sully had an accident _and_ got arthritis, but instead of healing, his knee is hideously worsening. He's a sixty-year-old carpenter on disability who wants to earn money under the table. Russo shows him thinking about saving himself from a daily cycle of pain that affects every physical act from putting on his boots to chasing a ninety-year-old runaway down the street, that involves him in the law's delay and the connivances of insurers and tests lifelong character traits. Nevertheless, Sully doesn't waste an extra thought or an extra metaphor on his too too sullied knee. It's a remarkable portrayal of making bodily problem-solving habitual, efficient. By not writing himself off, Sully is free unexpectedly to fill up his lonely life, heal childhood wounds, reconcile with those he hurt in his young adulthood—Russo lets him script himself a nice little male midlife progress novel. That sounds right to me.

I've become a weaker active person, which is rather different from being an ex-active person. I haven't let my identity change drastically. From my point of view, I have continued. This is standard practice for some people who wind down through aging, like the farmer Bert Brim tells about, who, approaching 100, continued to be assiduous at the plot contained by his windowbox.[2] And I have a backlog of accomplishments that I see every day. I changed my built environment. I *earned* my wear-and-tear label.

Day to day, my disability, like my manual skills, is almost invisible. No swelling, no very obvious lack of mobility, some lack of flexibility. From the point of view of other people, it's like having, say, a stiff neck. Unless I tell people—even if I inadvertently groan at some physical overextension—they won't know. They don't label me as middle-aged, although at midlife the mere mention of words like *arthritis* or *tendonitis* or even *tennis elbow* can stimulate endless monologues by people who have decided that this announces their "entrance" into midlife aging. Free of the age label, I could truthfully tell any story I wanted that was my own. And that free storytelling was the luck that saved me from decline ideology. I had suffered a loss, not a metaphor for decline. Once I had escaped from the spray of synecdoche, I could estimate that loss accurately. That's what I am doing here. As my story continues to unfold, although I now know the risks of toxic bombardment, I am fairly confident I'll be able to keep it accurate.

As long as middle-ageism lasts, freedom lies only in private interpretation. This is not enough.

Kept secret, my chronic condition cannot of course stimulate other people to compassionate sickroom behavior. I don't expect it. I don't miss it. The extraordinary tending I got when I was a child—optimal tending—did not "spoil" me. It didn't make me "like being sick." It doesn't make me prolong staying in bed—I find bed rest boring, even though when I need it I do what I always did: read without stopping. No, the loving care I got simply internalized some beliefs about the body in illness (not mine alone) that are, as far as I'm concerned, truths.

They're rather hard to put into words. But they have nothing to do with "middle age" as a separated and distinctly different and diminished part of life. If anything, they have to do with life-course continuities that bind me to myself, whether as child or adult, presumably until death does me part. Do I still think that I'm special? Perhaps that's what it is, in some qualified way. It's not because I have *this* condition ("arthritis"). It's not because I "suffer" from a condition. I never considered that I was "suffering" when I was sick as a child, even though children don't know how long sickness will last, and I try not to feel sorry for myself now. It's a quite impersonal reflex. I simply treat myself when I hurt the way I'd treat somebody else I liked who was sick. I think people are entitled to good health care, from their friends and, ideally, from the state. Where I myself am concerned, I make myself more present, I care more, I cosset more; I smile with sympathetic ruefulness. It's true that from time to time I curse my body as an alien and rail against its fate. But that doesn't seem to undermine my kindliness to myself, unwillingly attached to that body. I might have preferred to be spared this extra occasional measure of self-tenderness. Not being masochistic in health, I didn't need to create an excuse for caring for myself. I would prefer that my normal in-no-pain relationship to my body were a constant. But I have no choice about it, and I'll probably have less sometime in the future. My reflex will be tested in more extreme ways. Until then, I can't complain.

Disability and Culture

The kinds of pain and disability and loss of prior power that I am familiar with fill recent male midlife novels. In David Lodge's *Therapy*, for example, the narrator's bad knee is supposed to have destroyed his self-esteem, his sex life, and his marriage. Overnight he starts taking acupuncture, aromatherapy, psychotherapy. Of course, he can afford them. (The richer you are, the sicker.) Over the course of John Updike's tetralogy about Rabbit/Harry Angstrom, Harry finds his golf swing has gone down the tubes; a heavenly pleasure connected with youth has been lost. Martin Amis's Richard Tull in *The Information,* after a long decline in his status and moral nature, loses at tennis, snooker, and chess to a competitor he has always previously beaten. Only in *Nobody's Fool,* where the protagonist is a carpenter, is his knee injury treated as a constant, invasive, material condition of his life. In the middle-class novels, male midlife disabilities are petty but *telling.* In other words, a reader can find the symbolism ludicrous and nevertheless conclude that the midlife is drearily predictable and his own physique deteriorating. And he may share the conclusion I have many times heard men say and never understood. "Downhill all the way."

During my years of suffering I was spared misplaced metaphor and all that self-pity. When I finally tell the story now, one "moral" in fact can be that this is *not* a midlife decline story. Chronic disability is not "naturally" a trope for midlife decline. Incapacity or chronic illness at midlife may have nothing to do with "aging"—it may derive from an accident, or a gene, or a workplace injury. And then there are the socially constructed impairments that take a long time to manifest themselves and begin to appear in middle life: some high percentage of the heart disease that kills African-Americans disproportionately and prematurely, the breast cancers that have become the scourge of postwar women, the hypertension caused by work structured to strain the body's responses, and all the other diseases historically wrought by twentieth-century technologies, environmental and pharmaceutical toxins, commercial exploitations. The victims, unlike me, cannot be blamed for carelessness or anything else. Over a lifetime they have been denied adequate access to such things as clean air and water, good diet, information about prevention, work that permits them control or relief, government regulation on their behalf, medical care. The *poorer* you are, the sicker. Increasing chronological age, as social epidemiologist Peter Schnall says, "can be a proxy for exposure—exposure to abuse, disuse, and misuse."[3] In such a formula what the biomedical model would have us call "use" is residual. Age theory must bear this in mind. The man of forty who is being overmedicated for high blood pressure, the woman of thirty-five who has acquired carpal tunnel syndrome from sitting all day in front of her company's visual display terminal—in what sense is this their "aging"? They are being injured by those in authority over them. And they are simultaneously being aged by culture.

Not all of these new "social diseases" are curable, but they are all preventable.

Chronic disease is also a trope for loss of control, almost a midlife axiom. Yet, as my cousin the epidemiologist also tells me, in illnesses like high blood pressure, often you're likely to have *more* control as you age. People get savvy about protecting themselves. We can exert power over symptoms whether we know it or not.

All of these new interpretations and attitudes come with new responsibilities. And to begin with, we must tell these stories properly.

The Genre of My Complaint

The tones I've used here for talking about my trouble come from none of the current discourses about "the body": the philosophical/abstract, the midlife hyperbolical/symbolic, or, finally, the semitragic in fiction and autobiography, the tone of the victims of a sudden onslaught (car crash, heart attack, stroke, rape, animal attack). Ills like arthritis or slipped disks or chronic fatigue syndrome—chronic ills that people live with for a long time, sometimes for decades—need to be told in new tones. The tones I find appropriate have this in common: they're not dramatic, and they refuse collocation beside the thrilling, the scenic. There's no blood, no ambulance, no high-speed ride, no critical intervention, no high-tech excitement, no drastic cure. There's no rapid response from the world at all. *There's no movie version.* In general, violence, suddenness, panic, terror, justify the stylistics appropriated by the type of pain that finally must acknowledge itself as an episode, however long-term its consequences may be.

Back pain has its spasms, but it's the type of a different kind of pain: daily, cumulative, possibly "progressively" worsening, about-to-affect life at every level: economic, sexual, social, mental. Most people don't recover; they live with it. Sometimes the predicted happens; when it does, it is partly what we knew all along was on its way. Perhaps I should have made more of this here: magnified it, dramatized it to fit our cultural expectations about "inexorabil-ity." Not only have I not done so, I've eschewed the temptation. It would have risked another fall into automatic writing. Midlife decline snakes into our language in thousands of ways.

Chronic suffering takes different forms; if we ever begin to listen, the sufferers will have a lot of alternative stories to tell.[4] Inexorability doesn't ex-press the way our waves of knowledge come to us, the way we discover our private response at the same time we endure what feels like bodily injustice. The people in the still-untold stories suffer, but they don't display gritted teeth. (How could one grit one's teeth for a quarter century? And still take nourishment?) Abstraction doesn't come readily when the twinge is always there. But despite the twinge, the real story is not the body. It never is. The real story is the story itself: what you make of it. Up to now, our stories have been unwritable, or maybe just unacceptable. But why? For the culture, the problem lies with what they inevitably refer to. Ordinary pain.

4

Face-Off

"Autumnal Face"

A WOMAN doesn't need a mirror to find herself having a moment of regret for her passing—or, if she's in a really foul state of mind, her past—"beauty." The day I started writing this, such a moment was triggered for me when I caught out of the corner of my eye a certain cut of garment popular with women of college age and those who emulate them. "Not for you," said a sinister automatic voice. Out of fugitive visions, sudden sadness.

What should we think of this common phenomenon of painful self-deprecation in an era when semifeminists pointing to Gloria Steinem, Candice Bergen, Cybill Shepherd, and Jane Fonda are trying to convince us that midlife is a "wonderful" epoch for women, physically? Agree with them, of course, and work to make it true for the rest of us. But what shall we do with that moment of sadness?

Let's give that sadness its due, because feelings that aren't given full due never die: they lurch out of the murk, claiming they're authentic because they're so intense. Which part is falsely true, and what is the whole story? It seems that almost everyone remembers and some want to dwell upon better skin, better muscle tone, a stronger profile at some earlier period. Nostalgia is built into this exercise. Dangerous—intense, tempting, anxiety-producing, masochistic—life-course nostalgia.[1] My own "beauty" was certified in college—since certification is where this topic often begins—by the fact that a dishy male photographer put my picture, in black turtleneck, into a college magazine. I, the high school "Brain," the girl with the highest grade point average, was suddenly propelled into the impossible empyrean of the Beauty Market (Desirability, Sex, Marriage, Upward Mobility). This is the moment for women when the cult of youth becomes real, because *you* are the cult figure. You are perfectly sure it can't last, and you're right (but not for the reasons you think). At a slightly later than traditional time I married, leaving the market with relief and never looking back. But male heterosexual attention that was supposed to be considered flattering didn't end. A decade or so later it began to taper off, though, except for a few older men who freshened up their sense of masculinity by chasing women around tables.

Most women have such trophies. There can be a certain sour pleasure in the nostalgia about them. It implies that though we aren't beautiful anymore we once were. This is untrue in more ways than I can deal with here. It does imply something true about hetero men on the make: that younger men often employed shameless flattery and vulgar importunity and other obvious techniques and that the older men they have become usually don't. Some women deeply mourn the tapering off of this treatment and others think it's one of the marvelous advantages of getting older, but the important thing for all women to notice is that men's behavior is an index of nothing but men's training, needs, and strategies. If you concluded from the last paragraph that I was and am one of those rare gorgeous women whose advice is therefore irrelevant to you, think again. I went to a college where they admitted one woman for every eight men. It was like the Old West. Although the boys' scramble for a girl allowed me to believe I was precious goods, being in that market never made me happy enough to mystify my own "youth." Since nostalgia depends in part on how people gild their youth as it recedes, I was saved from _that_ part of nostalgia, and from the equivalent amount of effort it would have taken to shake it off.

The more I think about it, the more dangerous I think untheorized nostalgia is for women _or_ men in this culture, now. Even apparently innocent items from the past can lead to unhappiness greater than any joy possible from self-congratulatory recollection.

A lot of women, like me, whose sad remarks imply that they remember being "more beautiful once" are lying. We're verbally passing as older people—a cultural compulsion about which I shall have a lot more to say. We may once have been more attractive from someone else's point of view—usually some male's—but we have failed to remember how little personal pleasure that opinion gave us. I have not forgotten and no longer let myself forget to state my anguish about my pimples, my nose, my chin, my hair (my hips, knees, elbows, etc.) at the very same age when I hoped my classmates were noticing my perfection in the college magazine. Or how it took forty-five excruciating minutes to rouge my cheeks and darken my eyes to the required standard. Freshman year in college, at their request I gave a makeup demonstration in the communal bathroom to the backward: the non–New Yorkers, the sheltered girls who had gone to single-sex preparatory schools, the less avid, the less anxious, the less skillful, the not-yet-fully-trained. I was their model.

And all that time I never smiled at myself in the mirror. I sucked in my healthy cheeks, took a three-quarters profile, and tried to look gaunt. (That was a period when models weighed fifteen to twenty pounds *more* than they are allowed to weigh now.) At seventeen I pulled up the slack skin at my temples to make my eyes look more exotic. Although I've said that young people didn't then have to pass as young, I did. I did speeded-up movement—spun on my heel, whirled my skirt, flung myself into attitudes. These were tableaux, movie moments, being seen as youthful. Others did too; I had learned some of this mimicry from a high school boyfriend who wanted to be a model. I was too short, which I took as tragic even though I didn't want to *be* a model. I was never beautiful to myself.

At every period of my life but one (*now,* over the past ten years or so, in despised midlife) I have wished to be younger. As early as ten I wanted to get back to the age of five, before the trials of school began. I mention that again because it was the last time for a long time that I told a life-course narrative directly out of experience, unadulterated by ideology. After my teens the first reasons I had for wishing to be younger were confused with beauty's alleged location in the life course: beauty was possible only in youth, and youth was always passing or already past. At eighteen I started on the script of nostalgic lamentation—the loss of the perfect skin I'd had at twelve. When I was twenty-five I discovered I had a pot and mourned the flat stomach I'd had at eighteen. Actually, in college I already hated my pot, but at twenty-five I saw the ridiculous error of that juvenile self-criticism (telling a little progress tale of increased wisdom that perversely justified nostalgia and self-criticism at twenty-five. I hadn't yet discovered all the bad kinds of progress narratives there are). At twenty-seven, having had a baby in the interval, I grieved over the flat stomach of twenty-five. As far as I was concerned, at every age I lived through I was never lovely at the time, I was always flawed. Although I had never been "beautiful," I had always been *more* beautiful once.

Every woman I know goes through some version of this age-graded dissatisfaction, learning the life-weariness of nostalgia as she goes. Accepting the formulas of nostalgia means learning that you are not beautiful or not sexy or not something, any more. Men learn this too, because young men have sexual freedom and attractiveness, bodily strength as well as other powers that they lose through being aged by culture. They too were more beautiful once. They too exaggerate the amount of face they have lost. Midlife men have not been eager to say how ageism works against them; and feminism, concentrating on women's losses, has perhaps helped to silence men's. But, as we used to proclaim when these men were boys, there will be no full liberation without men's liberation. Men who are no longer boys may recognize themselves in my account. They should tell these stories of sadness, not as simple declines but to work out their own salvation from nostalgia. And men my son's age should tell how "looksism" is stalking their youth. Getting trained in "the brief perfections of youth" is the first and the solidest foundation of masochistic nostalgia.

Partly insulated by my intellectual's scorn of the media, I was nevertheless deeply affected by precocious middle-ageism. Exactly how early the culture teaches girls or boys this lore of decline we don't know. But by fourteen my best friend and I (she _was_ a beauty, and her sister looked like a model) knew astonishing things. I remember clearly one summer day when we were at Brighton Beach: one of us noticed that a shapely woman had slight sloping thickenings above her waist on both sides in back, and we each said, in turn, "That will never happen to _me_." What we then thought could be done about it I cannot imagine. The woman was probably thirty. Girls of fourteen—both those who are mediocre students and those who get top marks—can learn with absolute conviction that beauty matters enormously, has a single standard, is going to tail off with age, and that choosing for that not to happen is a matter of individual decision and effort. Our one-liner summarizes all the female age lore a girl needs in order to grow up—soon afterward—into being an "aging" woman. At fourteen she is already culture's female fool.

If we look at this dispassionately, it's a shocking comment on the culture. In college I was already so brainwashed that I read as a satire Donne's poem that begins, so dramatically, "No spring, nor summer beauty hath such grace / As I have seen in one autumnal face." My professor, a Renaissance scholar, said it was a praise poem. I said Donne had to be kidding. Actually I think now I was partly right. Donne's poem sponsors its opening assertion with some effort, but he too was embedded in a middle-ageist culture that discriminated more against women that men.

In general, I remember well what it felt like being me, all through those years called young. I was sad. Not pitiable from the outside. Who would have pitied a young, well-educated, middle-class, married white woman, particularly in the phase when I was encumbered with only one child, working on an advanced degree, with excellent child care and a husband who helped? Even when I got my degree at the bottom of a recession, couldn't find a job I'd been trained for, and took the second choice that seems so far down from the first, few people would have cared to pity me. But nobody lives her life from the outside. I knew well enough that I should count myself among the lucky ones. But then why did I feel so little and mean and washed up? Why was I so shy, easily intimidated, starved for recognition, anxious about my future? My face still loomed large in my self-image, but differently, with the academic work context thrown into the mix. Now, although not beautiful enough to get by on beauty (as some were said to do), I was still too striking to be taken seriously. From time to time I said to myself, not sure whether to believe it, "I'll be listened to [by men] when I'm 'older.'" Why was I so concerned about my face?

Midlife Exhilaration

How could I understand until I started feeling different? I know a lot of women who revalued themselves and their lives just at the moment when the culture was trying to convince us we were no-longer-young. We gave forty the back of our hands. And forty-five and so on; it got to be a habit. We started striding around doing our work, giving the world a head-on look. We started flinging off the old labels that masked us. When you've got it, we felt, there comes a time to flaunt it. The feminist midlife quietly came into being over the course of the Eighties. It was not yet widely noticed as a cultural phenomenon, partly because feminist theory scarcely talked about "age" and partly because younger women crowded us out of mainstream visuals: the thirty-something "Superwoman," the teen mother, the twenty-something seeking either an abortion or the perfect romance.[2] I for one didn't then mind this media anonymity. As in a tempered greenhouse whose lights have been whitewashed against glare, it made for denser and more spontaneous growth.

Like so many women my age, at about forty I started feeling better. It was like convalescence, a slow, midlife cure—as if we were taking tiny homeopathic pills marked Energy, Enlightenment, Self-Delight. They took about ten years to work. Over that time, a friend I shall call Frances disentangled herself from her marriage, got a degree in law, fell in love, married again, and had her first child. Gillian also became a midlife mother, by dint of falling in love and moving in with a woman who had a teenage daughter. Sheila, hetero and single, started acting and writing plays. Barbara had been divorced; she got an M.B.A. and a series of high-powered jobs and single-handedly raised her two children. Judy separated from her husband painfully and with self-doubt, started on Prozac, raised three children, and made a career in academe. Elaine's bulimia ceased; married, with one child, she got her credentials as a therapist.

After years of congenial work that was not where my heart was, I accumulated the courage and money to start doing what I wanted—a life of independent study and writing. I redid my identities as "woman," and "steady earner," and that complex self-adjustment left me open to the broadest ideas of change—free, eventually, to embrace activism and believe in resistance. The "midlife," as I started to call it, felt like a new beginning, but not from the bottom; rather, from some solid base higher up. After many delays and false starts, I began to become who I am. I'm still at that work.

Forces inside and outside helped many women age in this unexpected, exhilarating way. Young, many of us were undervalued and underemployed; dithering or uncertain, punching our time cards until midlife self-discovery. The social movements of the Sixties and Seventies have to get a big share of our gratitude: antiwar resistance, black civil rights, women's and gay liberation. For me, it was primarily feminism. Feminism, like a good therapist, envisioned a Next Self. Like a tough coach, she counseled, "No pain, no gain." Like Mother Time, she lured us forward, cajoling, "Have patience, it will come." The pressures of the movements on education, law, and the workplace also meant that those who sought better-paying jobs—even in nontraditional fields like law, finance, medicine, entrepreneurship—sometimes found them. For a time affirmative action was able to keep lifting our feet above the sticky floor. The social movements explained why "success" didn't come to all, or argued that social justice was preferable. Even where they did not focus on specific obstacles—like "midlife aging"—some taught women to value whatever women had, whatever women accomplished. In general, they taught women the operations necessary to value what culture throws away. We had almost all been culture's throwaways. It was later in life that we learned to look at "trash" twice, the second time with political questions.

And other things linked to aging also freed us: practices like mothering and other forms of teaching, surviving the capitalist workforce, making long-term friends, loving and being loved, doing volunteer work for important causes. What they have in common is that through our own efforts we solved problems and became better people. Without receiving degrees for it, we convinced ourselves that we were constant learners and strivers, failures who could try again, self-improvers. This is part of the healthy narcissism that Heinz Kohut and my mother believe is necessary throughout life. Social scientists and educators call this "value added." The process can give people going through midlife a view of life as Bildung (like that I acquired from novels very young)—a view that experience is a set of acquisitions. Even if you are stuck with the same bad job whose real wages never rise, your story must be a *becoming*. All this becomes part of your age identity—at first tentatively, and then, if reinforced conceptually, more solidly.

Individually, we reappropriated our lives, and they look like fine possessions. For a time after I first discovered all this, I was infatuated with mine in a postobsessive midlife way. I was giddy about subverting middle-ageist culture so *easily*. (I didn't yet realize how hard it was going to be to hold on to;

I didn't expect middle-ageism to get worse again.) Well, that headiness mellowed into a more solid enduring relationship to self. The Nineties are testing this further—aging us all faster. Despite everything, I take credit for half creating what I manage to like about this life of mine, wait without fussy scrutiny to see how it grows, and regularly braid age and history into all my life stories. Although I'm now irritated by the "Women and Aging" rubric and think it does disservice by implying that only women age, it was good to use new power to enhance the idea of female aging-into-the-midlife. We look good to one another. We earned these wise smiles, these capable hands, this air of competence. Against the strong currents in our culture that deplore aging, we're admiring our age because it's a part of us, whom we like so much better than we ever thought possible in the bad old days.

Face-Work

In this thick context, my midlife face ceased to be a problem in the old young way. Face altogether assumed a lesser place. This turns out to have been, as so often, a matter of rearranging the proportions.

I had been too young, that was my trouble. *Youth* is a word so dazzling that its meanings can be both dominant and invisible. People use it as a trope not just for beauty, energy, and sex, but for "power" and "self-confidence" and "self-delight." Values for which, in my bravura mode, I just used the word *midlife*. So, it follows that in "Face-Off," *young* means what it felt like to me all those years ago: thin, poor in resources, pathetically vulnerable to dominant cultural scripts, torn by feeble longings to resist, individualized and isolated from others, powerless to formulate—not to mention execute—resistances. Is it any better for women who are young now? Very likely, for those who call themselves feminists. But it will take them twenty or thirty years before they will be able to say whether they agree about the meaning of the word *young* for them. Yes, they may decide in midlife that good looks are wasted on them now. As they were on me. I do better with the smaller share (as an observer might see it) that I "have" now.

Only at midlife did I become a little bit safer from all the sexist and protoageist pressures. Along the way I undid the bad side of physical narcissism—that is, the part that was dependent on social notice of my "femaleness" as young—young body and form and movement and gesture. On the whole, I like the corpus. In fact, one of the odd pleasures I get now from looking at old photo albums is surprise at how unchic I used to look, in every era. Also I looked, well, young—blurry as to identity, banally pretty, uncertain, even frightened; and when not frightened, foolish. Symbolically, early in midlife I developed a new public walk; I dropped the youthful "female" swivel and mastered a purposeful rapid stride. I took the pace from a friend in business, but it looks so different on each of us that she probably hasn't noticed. I was one of the first to wear a body-purse—the kind with a long strap that slips over the head and leaves the arms swinging free. None of this development was "work." It didn't take consciousness; I noticed it only after the fact. I see others acquiring similar signs of changed age identity. This is what some of us seem to me to be "flaunting."

I accomplished work on my face too. I don't spend forty-five minutes of my precious day on my makeup. I don't spend three. And I don't worry about that three.

Experience and decisiveness have made the daily public appearances easier. I have a hairstyle I like for the first time in my life: almost carefree, and the gray springs out in curls. (It's a perm, which some feminists disapprove.) All the previous hairstyles I've had now look like mistakes. When my photo is taken, I don't pose. In public work settings with men, I no longer smile as constantly. I please for other reasons than the abstract esthetic qualities of my face or the sexual signals it appeared to send (to those prepared to read them). I see people smiling when I walk into a room, out of long acquaintanceship or in anticipation of conversation. In other words, without knowing what I was doing, as I came into my middle years I developed a way of being a woman that struck a better balance between representing femaleness and "me-ness." I had felt foolish aping the category "young female"; as critic Susan Douglas has said, almost every woman who aged during the feminist wave came to feel embarrassed about the girl she had been.[3] That too liberated us into midlife selfhood.

Perhaps anyone who is older-than-young now can reconstruct a progress narrative of the life course using even the most intractable material age ideology provides us: face.

The faces of others look different too. I don't seem able to give up the concept "beautiful," although I argue later that that's a good direction to go in. Nor does it seem possible to eradicate looksism at large, although we could certainly interrogate it harder. Thanks be, I'm not eighteen, to be content with the narrow definition of beauty borrowed from TV and fashion magazines. With my more eclectic esthetic vision, I include many more kinds of faces. I'll admire a handsome jawline or beautiful eyes without requiring that the rest of the face meet some uniform standard. I gave up unconscious white-skin prejudice without a struggle during the years of "Black is beautiful." I always knew that not all the young are beautiful. Everyone can see that's a false association—obviously twenty-five-year-olds can be plain, with bad skin and lackluster hair. And we also know, if we let ourselves know it, that women who are not-young can be gorgeous.

Once in thrall to the classist motto "No one can be too thin or too rich," I am reworking my relationship to fat and to capital. Inspired by a cousin active in the Fat Acceptance movement, I think it's stupid not to be able to see beauty in strong or big or fleshy women. (Fat *men,* I admit, I have more trouble with. It's a prejudice, and I'm working on it.) In the sauna in my mother's Florida apartment complex, where retired European, South American, French Canadian, and North American women take off their clothes, I learned to like the heft of their bodies, the pugnacity of letting the body be, the softness of skin and flesh. Softness summons up relaxation, languorous sexuality, or energy devoted to comforting, caring. It's easy to like metaphorically.

Mulling over these associations, I see the younger women in the gym, in training as junior Cyborgs, differently. Isolated and dedicated, they signal that they are economically competitive and athletically sexual, even potentially warriorlike—that is, "young." They believe they will be more desirable to management and to men who want a financial supplement and an energetic lay in one person. It makes me unhappy to think of the pressures that produce those goals. Both capitalism and heterosexist patriarchy have an increasing interest in detaching the young from the "soft" values of childhood, and in preventing us from afterwards reattaching "softness" positively to midlife and older bodies. By liking softness, I find a tiny way of opposing those values.[4]

Character, which takes longer to recognize, matters more in my contemplation of my peers. I find myself seeking out the interesting faces among people more or less my age and calling many of them handsome. In passing I may note the striking elegance of some young people, but the few expressions possible to youthful beauty often make me impatient, and the self-consciousness makes me sigh, "Well, they'll get over it in time." What holds my gaze are well-defined features marked by intelligence and experience. I can bear to look upon the changes made by confrontation with the world. Why shouldn't facial lines be as highly valued as the fine cracks in older paintings, but with the added benefit of having meaning? As if we were revolutionary painters, women over—currently, I probably have to say—*thirty-five,* have to decide that we are as beautiful as we need to be. Or that we can live with whatever looks we happen to have wound up with, without bothering to characterize their quality on a universal scale. There ain't no such scale. A woman has only to settle on her attitude and hold it with conviction.

Beauty has been a trap because it was both hyperimportant and hyperexclusive. Spread more democratically, it becomes an innocent (and less important) pleasure. There is actually far *more* beauty around than there used to be.

Some of my friends provided a tough test of my championship of our midlife faces, because I remembered them well from an era when they seemed flawless, when I had guessed nothing about their inner qualms and dejections. Yet the fact is that it is their contemporary visages, with their contemporary expressions, that I discovered I love. Their spring beauty was banal in comparison, and marred by competitiveness (mine, ours, women's in general). I have nothing to say to those faces in the photographs, and wonder what we found to talk about. How could I come to love them better over the years and not learn to think that aging—which got us here—is positive? Whatever the sniping of the culture, I think they look *wonderful.* And how could I find myself genuinely loving their looks and not grow into better liking with my own?

Brushing my teeth is a test of the Mirror Scene of Aging. I have cold-eyed days, but I can report that I regularly gaze at this familiar spectacle with something like the steady affection I might give to a friend's face. I can admire it for the same complex of reasons—a mixture of esthetic appreciation, tolerance for imperfections, ethical approval, and long sisterly association. Finally, without posing in three-quarters view, I can smile directly at me.

Possessing an Age Identity

I'm not *finding* my identity. I never mislaid it; it wasn't something fixed early that could be mislaid in adulthood, as if through carelessness. That metaphor of "finding" is not trivially wrong; it is powerfully ageist. A pop encapsulation of Freud's master narrative of decline, it implies that everything important happened in childhood and that as adults we have no role in producing a self except to correct early mistakes. It also implies that once we "find" identity, like a found object, it will stay essentially the same. On the contrary, mine maintains itself and grows, doing all its inevitable things: discarding unwanted identities, building onto older ones accretively, producing diverting interactions, anthologizing its stories. If it seems to be telling me the meaning of time passing, actually I've been constructing it. It is always mine to remake, but it wasn't truly "mine" until I had actually done some remaking and knew that I had.

By being human and living long enough, everyone acquires an age identity. But they don't know about this possession in a way that would be useful inside our sinister culture. My colleague Sabine Sielke said, "I expect certain things [related to aging] to happen, but they do not; and when they don't, I take note of that contradiction." Good sense is a will to assert one's knowledge of one's own life course as truer than the received truths of middle-ageism. But the master narrative of aging prevents people from knowing their own life course in detail, disabling them from recognizing such contradictions. They automatically fill the slot where "age meanings" should go with "decline"; they silence other more accurate and nuanced narratives. To fortify the good sense of age identity, we need deepening self-reflexiveness about autobiography, and suspicion of feelings (like nostalgia and self-hatred), however "intense," that may stand in the way of identifying what we have internalized. Then the kind of personal recollection and introspective contrasts I've been recording are free to appear.

As for recognizing the resistant value of age theory, feminists might latch on sooner than nonfeminists; people aware of social construction sooner than those who are not; male scholars of masculinity sooner than men in general; gerontologists sooner than people afraid of thinking about age; philosophers of time and identity sooner than others without such interests; activists in any field sooner than those who think consciousness is enough; skeptics and unravelers of power sooner than true believers. But people shouldn't be discouraged even if they have a history with their face as complicated as mine.

Let There Be a Gap

My old bad habit from my teenage years, of wincing when I come upon my face accidentally in a mirror, I lost for a long time. But I have had a harder time than I once thought possible not to reacquire it. In other words, step by step I undid patriarchal sexism, emerging at around forty as a woman satisfied with her face for the first time in her postpubescent life. But as I emerged jaunty and flaunting, priding myself on coming into womanhood in my middle years whole, middle-ageism was trying to knock me down *again*.

So I live a mental moment when I can see that "sexism" and "ageism" have some separable features; or can be used to name two different cultural operations that operate at different ages. Both use the face as one register of merit. Both reduce self-esteem in ways that weaken the self in every power relationship. Sexism works on the young female self, socialized to have pretensions to narrow definitions of youthful "beauty" and unforgiving about ugliness. Looksism could name the effects on the young of both genders, who are too young to rely on age identity and are under pressure to count on nothing but youth. In the Mirror Scene of Youth, looksism shows the self as unavoidably less perfect than a same-age other.

Middle-ageism works in the Nineties on the feminist self who has solved _those_ problems, or—if _solved_ seems too ambitious a word—diluted them with lifetime accomplishments. Women who have become adult since 1970 have all surmounted quite a lot of sexism. Even those who consider themselves not-feminist have experienced some mental liberation. When the decline narrative takes on the midlife woman, it takes on a much _tougher_ target. Even a woman without much in the way of external buttresses may have much more inner structural support than she had in her youth.

I once said to a good friend, "Feminists don't age. The others do." She liked it. "A bumper sticker!" she laughed. But if we had given the idea a minute's more talk, we'd have come out of it on the other side of exhilaration. How does middle-ageism work on feminists? What of feminists who haven't undone youthful self-hatred? What do we do next to resist?

For the purposes of revising the master narrative, one critical opening might be the discovery of some gap between the scripts and one's own friendly relationship to the self that has been lived with over time. The Scene of the Gap is never anecdotalized, so I want to represent one. It starts with the Mirror Scene of Midlife Aging: "Possessing my precious age identity, when I look in a mirror I expect to see the familiar, expressive, benign face that has grown on me. Since I overcame female adolescent insecurity about it, it has represented my normal ground, waking-up-as-me. But suppose one day I don't see that look? Suppose the gaze from my no longer native face reveals self-disgust? Middle-ageism shows me a self less perfect than my own younger self used to be. The Mirror is asking me to ask, 'Am I ugly yet?'"

Until now one main response has been to rely on the "progress" aspects of one's age identity. When the culture holds up its mad Mirror, some midlife women can retort, "I look fine now, naturally." Thinking positively has been the advice of women's magazines, some pro-female novelists, even some feminist theory. It probably represents a lot of actually practiced age work.

It's not enough. Not because "progress" is an untrue story. Many other people at midlife could no doubt recount how, by their own different paths, their personal relationship to their looks has improved over time. But when I choose "I look fine," I open myself to the middle-ageist retort, "You don't." (And this retort still comes too easily to me. The age gaze is always the gaze of a hostile Stranger. And the Stranger is not always or even often young, but keeps forever at all ages the culture's ideal of youth.) Repeating "I look fine" creates an impasse, as if two children were screaming at each other, "Do so." "Do not." Setting "progress" against "decline" constitutes a terrible, isolated, oscillating, emotional impasse—it's another example of the impasse _Declining_ to Decline opens with, the classic binary of age ideology. The more devastated we feel when "progress" narrative has been attempted and fails us, the more heartfelt will be our desire to get beyond positive aging, out of the binary.

There is a way out.

At that panicky moment, age theory (bolstered by feminism) reminds me that I have no reason to speak the script automatically and name my trouble "aging." My trouble is actually the culture's funhouse Mirror, reflecting what I have internalized of its hostile age gaze. True, something I take as "personal" triggered the Mirror Scene—but my task will be to find out what the cultural causes were, not let "my" "aging" be the scapegoat. Then, in a ferocious movement of liberation, I am able to regain my age identity and criticize the culture of disgust. Soon I can see both looks, one after another—the smile and the grimace, the grimace and the smile. A curious emotional experience, proving that I was moved without will or conscious notice from my own story of my face to the false narrative provided by the ideology. *Now,* if I choose to say "I look fine," I see, as it were, both my physical features and the smile that is seeing them.

Through developing age theory out of personal history and social criticism, a subject comes to understand the construction of the impasse, including its personal, interpersonal, group, and universal dynamics. I had to write parts of "Face-Off" separately and then most of this book before I could make this understanding meaningful with regard to "face," that inevitable object to which midlife decline ideology forces our inevitable return.

And what of the midlife woman who has never felt her face as benign, the midlife man who thinks of himself as increasingly repulsive? The shock that leads people toward age theory may come from seeing that they actually have a *choice* of gazes and a choice of narratives—between the dominant one that wars against their own best interests and an as-yet-to-be-written one that serves them. It's only in a context like this that something helpful can be said about practices that feminism has made controversial but that go on nonetheless, like face-"lifting."

Under the Knife of the System

An unmarried twenty-one-year-old college student tells me that she is saving up her money in order to buy facial surgery. A thirty-two-year-old mother of one calls in to a talk show I'm on to inquire nonchalantly about the feasibility of breast augmentation. Actresses say, "I've had no plastic surgery yet, but it's a possibility in my future. Isn't it in everyone's." Women of all ages are paying thousands of dollars to have slits cut in their lower eyelids or in the ridge behind the ear or in the soft places of the body. Girls undergo sexist training to become "women" who will in turn undergo sexist-ageist training to become "older" women. The typical face-lift candidate is between forty-five and sixty.[5] Many women regard going under the knife not as a doom but as an opportunity.

Sometimes I feel as alien in America as if I had arrived from another century or another planet, and contemplating facial surgery as an antiageist tactic is one of those times. But instead of staring in fascination at our anomalies, I'm wringing my hands. I wouldn't be so distressed, of course, if there were only four women in the country, of enormous wealth (or four men), who treated their bodies so recklessly, who so misunderstood the psychology behind drastic self-alteration, who feel so driven that they override the psychic and ethical implications of their decision.

But there are thousands dropping into the anesthesia. Boomers have allowed themselves to be redescribed as an "aging" cohort. And in the mainstream cultural binary, "against" aging there is only one practical response: "progress" here means simulating youth. Even some of my friends are contemplating facial surgery: feminists, handsome women, women who have— or appear to me to have—many sources of identity and self-esteem. Even I, despite my readiness to smash the mirror, can idly surmise for an instant in front of it that I'd look better with a little tuck _there._ (Not one of my smiling instants. Not an idle moment.) I see all of us, including men, as potential victims of a system that has gone dangerously out of control. It has, in fact, no self-correcting mechanisms—unless we intervene collectively. It's middle-ageism, more and more often cutting its ideological imperatives into living flesh.[6]

It's not a good argument against facial surgery, apparently, that the flesh benefits from its shocking restyling, if at all, only briefly. Medical dangers arise. Lawsuits become necessary. And styles change. Twenty years later the bobbed noses of the past are no longer girlish or cute—or rather, no one wants to look "cute" in that particular way. The large breasts that silicone provided are not only daunting health risks, they're also no longer "voluptuous"—they interfere with jogging and dancing. Today's decisions would not guarantee tomorrow's "beauty" even if they lasted.

But they don't last. Fixed noses show the shine of scar tissue; the implants may heave even if they don't trigger illness or immunological damage. Even the short-term isn't promising. The chin and the under-eye area begin to respond to gravity again before the scars have healed. It takes weeks or months before the face loses its bruised and injured look. How soon afterward does a woman look in the mirror and murmur "for nothing" and perhaps steel herself again in preparation for the next round of operations?

I don't repeat these sad facts to add yet another layer of doom to midlife aging. Women believe all too easily that the midlife is a doom for them. They say (ever more articulately since feminism began to explain the system) that men control the system, that men buy youth and beauty, that the market rules, that the job hunt has replaced—or added to—the pressures of the husband hunt. Women repeat the media's versions of the doom story to one another. And while they may talk calmly, some are desperate, ready for anything. How would a woman bring herself to run all the risks of major surgery, including the risk of damaging the face she's lived in and looked at and touched with some degree of kindness all her life, if she weren't made desperate? With all the feminist literature available, she can know all the risks she cares to know. She shudders with revulsion, but she says the operation is what she "wants."

Such wants are constructed deviously. The system creates a woman's desire for surgery by undermining her confidence in herself and then manages to make her say that this is *her* desire. Having sold the midlife to her as a decline that can't be compensated for, the system sells her certain remedies. Having gotten her to take lipstick, etc., for granted, it tries to convince her that surgery is in the same league. Sociologist Kathy Davis believes that women do it to be "ordinary," to "take [their] life into [their] own hands," to determine for themselves "how much suffering is fair."[7] This is the best statement women can make for themselves when wishing to speak of their "agency," because they don't have access to the level of analysis that would enable them to recognize themselves as objects of niche marketing in a middle-ageist system. Getting people to call the suffering of surgical overhaul "fair" is possible only because the suffering from aging-into-the-midlife has escalated so high. Calling the recourse to surgery "agency" is a new twist, made necessary by the success of feminism. No self-respecting woman in her middle years can now afford not to represent herself as an agent. Even determining to suffer the lesser evil can be presented as agency.

Men are being poisoned too, and in the same ways. "All Together Now" shows them as the fastest-growing group of consumers of cosmetic surgery. This was inevitable. They were sitting there complacently, an untapped market. All that was needed was to raise their anxiety level. Thus the next escalation begins. The system is getting more inclusive, and inclusiveness tightens the system around everyone. Women who hesitated to get a face-lift before, when it was a "woman's thing," can get rid of feminist guilt by saying it's a unisex operation. And if other men are doing it, a man can more easily stifle his hesitations.

Anyone who thinks I'm insensitive to the plight of the girls and women and men who go into these doctors' offices has misread me.[8] It's the system that makes me angry. But in utilizing anger we need to aim it also at human agents who act on behalf of the system and benefit from it financially. The surgeons make my gorge rise, and the editors of women's magazines who shill for them by uncritically publishing the doctors' self-endorsements and the victims' self-justifications and brief moment of self-celebration. The typical plastic surgeon says, "I see [patients] months later when they're healed up. They're different people. That's wonderful. That's what cosmetic surgery can do in a positive way." All victims are supposed to improve through "difference" from themselves, in the name of "feeling good about themselves."

Surgical patients *are* "different," of course, if not for long on the face, then inside. They are confirmed in their age identity as the self that did that to itself. In saying this, I don't mean to hold above a woman's or a man's head the prospect of later self-hatred, as a final argument against practices like cosmetic surgery. Practices in themselves are rarely damnable, or for that matter, laudable. I don't deserve praise for spending only three minutes on my makeup now. And only I have the right to condemn myself for those forty-five minutes lost daily during my misspent youth. But anyone should be able to see, and judge harmful, as I do now, that in the communal bathroom Margaret trained other young women to brood over their inadequate faces, to yearn for an impossibly static form of beauty, to submit themselves in the long run to the age ideology that would lead them to shudder away from mirrors. This ability to condemn one's past obedience to the system is not self-hatred. It wasn't "me" who did that. It wasn't the same self.

What the controversy over face-lifts (or victimage in general) omits is— once again—time. Process. In a word, aging. Over time, I change, and looking backward see the process starkly. An earlier (younger, weaker, more stupid) self partly vanishes. A newer self (older, more independent of the ideology, more ethically capable) replaces it. Proust described these "deaths," as he called them, as powerfully as anyone ever has, because he thought that stupid self was enchanted. But aging-into-the-midlife can break that enchantment. I don't regret losing the young self I have described. No one would. What we want age studies to do is to help the midlife person who is suffering—not by threats but by reminding her of her precious age identity, shoring up her

critical faculties, complicating simple nostalgia, channeling her anger outward, making resistance operational.

If there's a counterstory, a better truth, how does it raise its small clear
voice? "Only resist." That is its frail imperative. It goes along with the progressive injunction (in E. M. Forster's words) "Only connect." Every woman who
looks her friend in the face and says, "You're beautiful as you are," resists
and connects. But only if this comes not out of lying "kindness" but out of
understanding both the hostile age gaze and the resistant smile. Every man
who knowingly looks his friend in the face and says, "You're beautiful as you
are," resists and connects. The sons and daughters who say, "Don't do it, Mom
(Dad)" also fortify their own resistance. Every woman who looks her boss in
the face and says, "I didn't do it, Mac, I'm fine as I am," strengthens that man
for himself, against the day when his boss might say, "We need a younger man
in Mac's chair." And she also empowers him to work for her, against the day
when they'll say, "Don't we need a younger woman, Mac?" Every person who
does this for someone amplifies the counterstory for everyone else whose social and psychological lives they touch. Every woman who looks at her mother
and says "I like the way you look" ("the way I may look a generation hence")
batters the system in one of the places where it feels most reinforced. Insofar
as the system's massive structure is upheld by our beliefs and utterances and
practices in private life, we can weaken it.

If anyone still has doubts about whether the personal is political, rehears-
ing these scenarios might settle them. But do the scenarios have the pathos of
mere private resistance—the fragility of a truth that hasn't received network
notice? In the Nineties the Baby Boomers are seeing the ideology's walls rise
even higher around them. Before the turn of the new century even new midlife women could find themselves turning to their sisters and brothers saying,
"I loathe the idea of surgery, but it's a business necessity." As job discrimination against people at midlife strengthens, all of us will be at risk in this way.
Of course I am fighting for myself too. We could be enlightened but *still* vulnerable.

Only collectively can we attack the system. Those ready to resist can get
help from several sources: from feminists, from men outraged by the perception that they're no longer exempt, and in general from the vast midlife generation as it discovers critical age studies. The cohort could choose to actively
ride the advance crest of its demographic wave, utilizing the equivocal power
of its numbers. If we decide not be a passive market bred for narcissistic
consumption, we can use our tastes, our feelings, and our dollars to make
changes. We wouldn't just put the plastic doctors out of business. We wouldn't
only boycott the media that deprecate us and ignore the loss of our life

chances. We would practice age theory sweepingly. We would educate the young about what's coming next to them. All together we could be a power—economic, social, political, and cultural. This is the real face-off.

I intend to be there, openly graying and wrinkling and exulting at every victory.

Part Two

Women with Attitude

5

Midlife Heroines, "Older and Freer": Constructing the Female Midlife in Contemporary Fiction

> I think that in almost any culture the older women really begin
> to have a certain power. So, I'm getting older, so I really feel
> freer than I ever felt. I probably will feel even more so. I think
> some of it comes from being part of a movement but some of
> it comes really from just getting older and also making my
> own living.
>
> —Grace Paley, *Women Writers Talking*

PALEY, interviewed at the age of fifty-eight, was providing a miniature history of a major social trend in late twentieth-century North America. Her interviewer, Ruth Perry, coming back to fiction, responded, "And yet there aren't many writers [in 1983]—I can only think of you—who have given us images of older, freer women." And Paley said, in her simple gnomic way, "Well, it's just because that's where I am and I seem to always be where I am."[1]

Even in 1983 Anglo-American literature already had a few novelists representing heroines who became older and freer, and by now the culture can boast of a splendid new liberatory genre—the midlife women's progress novel. What progress means in fiction, and doesn't mean, will become clearer. In 1988 I wrote a book that described Margaret Drabble's and Anne Tyler's separate inventions of the form. At that time it felt like an occasion for celebration to have any depictions of women's—or, for that matter, men's—aging into the middle years that were not based on a plot of decline and loss. I also described John Updike's and Saul Bellow's approaches to progress novels about midlife men. In the euphoria of the discoveries, and in homage to life-course development and countercultural narrative, I called my book *Safe at Last in the Middle Years*. In *Safe at Last* I didn't attempt to consider the universe of midlife heroines being represented in fiction or the psychological implications and ideological effects of so widespread a revisionist genre. With regard to women characters, it's time to begin to do this. (There are more male midlife progress protagonists than there used to be, but they are not easily comparable.)[2] Since midlife progress fiction can be a force for cultural combat, we need to be asking hard questions about the conditions under which it is currently produced.

Until the second wave of feminism, only isolated novels—like Mary Austin's *Woman of Genius* (1912), Willa Cather's *Song of the Lark* (1915), Robert Herrick's *Homely Lilla* (1921), Virginia Woolf's *Mrs. Dalloway* (1925) and *To the Lighthouse* (1927), Zora Neale Hurston's *Their Eyes Were Watching God* (1938), E. H. Young's *Chatterton Square* (1947)—had disturbed a mainstream male culture of stereotypes laced with malice. At a bad period for the midlife, F. Scott Fitzgerald famously said, "There are no second acts in American lives." But there were in fact at the time some ugly second acts, and midlife women got bad parts in them: the overbearing mother-in-law, the wretched sexual has-been, the maternal nag.

Since the mid-Seventies, however, we have been blessed with conditions favorable to the representation of midlife female protagonists. A broad conversation has gone on among major women writers who have been aging within a more pro-female environment. They made available, and women readers eagerly bought, more positive narratives and more varied tones of voice about the middle years of women.[3] Not enough tones of voice, but enough so that anyone who wants to can see the energy, subjective diversity, range of possibility. Drabble's narrator in *The Middle Ground* repudiates the dogma that only exceptional women have interesting midlives. "How had she managed to acquire the deadly notion that everything she did or thought had to be *exemplary,* had to *mean something,* not only for herself, but also for that vast quaking seething tenuous mass of otherness, for other people. WOMAN APPOINTED AMBASSADOR. WOMAN FLIES TO MOON. WOMAN KILLED IN BANK RAID. WOMAN OF FORTY-SIX HAS TWINS. Well, no wonder, of course, one couldn't be all those women at once, nor was there any possible way of being all the things that women might be, in one lifetime."[4] In Anglo-American representation, the novel has been democratically constructing a plethora of lifetimes, quietly characterizing as ordinary heroines women who are straight and gay, of many classes and regions, racial and ethnic backgrounds, across a very wide swath of mid-adulthood.

Although not yet clearly recognized as a genre, the female midlife progress novel boasts other popular and influential producers: Nadine Gordimer, Doris Lessing, Paule Marshall, Toni Morrison, May Sarton, Alice Walker. They have invented not just heroines but plausible narratives of psychological and ethical success, ignoring both male patterns of success and stereotypical female midlife patterns of decline.[5] The popular midlife romance _Bridges of Madison County_ suggests that even romance, that impervious tradition, can be slightly altered by the cultural proximity of the midlife progress novel.) Movies like _Fried Green Tomatoes, Breathing Lessons,_ and _Foreign Affairs_ (the last two from novels by Tyler and Alison Lurie, respectively), fighting conventions within the far more ageist visual media, suggest that the large female audience also has some power to redirect the representations of television and film in a way more favorable to midlife women. The progress novel is changing the midlife cultural imaginary. Of all the media it still provides the most effective strategies for antisexist and antiageist resistance. I want to treat these novels as a genre, emphasizing common features and the limits within which divergences operate.

Collectively, I believe, the genre constructs a new female midlife character and thus helps its readers construct their own midlife subjectivity. In the postwar period critics have seen this psychocultural process at work via novels about Jews, African-Americans, gays and lesbians, Native Americans, Chinese, Chicanas/os. Now it's the turn of the "middle aged." When a previously misrepresented group acquires enough convincing fictional protagonists—diverse, compelling, counterstereotypical—people in that group can undertake transforming processes, using the fictions interactively.

Most readers of novels still read as if fiction were mimetic: Teresa Ebert says it is "_read_, in other words accepted [at a particular historical moment] as an accurate and 'true' representation of the experience it refers to." This trust allows narrative (including decline narrative) to work on us. As theorist Nancy Armstrong puts it, narrative works not by "mere reflection, effect, reproduction, or distortion of some more primary terrain of events, but rather as the very stuff by which we come to be whoever we are." We do not slavishly imitate fictional "models"; we choose some elements of the model intuitively and use them creatively. "At stake in all imaginative activity," Charles Altieri proposes, "is the question of who we become by virtue of the roles we try on and the struggles we enter."[6] When my seminars' course participants praised _Beloved_, it was because they had found in its acutely painful story of loss and slow trajectory of recovery some allegory of their own roles and struggles and plots. Midlife progress novels permit readers to compare the values and options of protagonists, stabilizing, expanding, and overthrowing (parts of) their own sense of self; developing ambitions, altering decisions; revising and renaming their very feelings; finally, renarrativizing their life course. The operations that readers can perform on liberatory fictions have become more possible than ever before for midlife women.

Genres are always in process. I describe the achievements of this genre first; then its possible—desirable—next moves. This sequence enables me to bring curious evolving news from the culture front.

A Different Kind of Progress

How progress novels treat "loss of beauty" displays the genre's strategies of resistance. None of the novels I refer to treats this in women's-magazine fashion, as the single most dreadful problem for "older" women: at worst, the protagonist's preoccupation with her body takes up a small place in the text (no protagonist contemplates getting a face-lift). And they all eschew the romance approach, which is to pretend aging has no negative effects. The progress novel is too hardheaded and too knowledgeable about the culture's sexist ageism to fall into that silly trap. There may not be a "beautiful" woman in the whole canon, but there's an amazing range of appreciations of the midlife face and body. Doris Lessing's Jane Somers declares in *If the Old Could,* "I saw in the looking-glass this rather good-looking woman, not badly made, solid rather than slim, with a face redeemed from ordinariness by the great grey eyes, and the pretty silvery chunks of hair that make people look: Is she grey, or is it a dye?" Refusing to use an early photograph to provoke a Mirror Scene, Jane at fifty-five concludes, "I saw something else as I stood there, looking from the photograph to *me*—it was me as I must seem to [a younger woman]. The unreachable accomplishment of it, this woman standing there so firm on the pile of her energetic and successful years. What a challenge, what a burden, the middle-aged, the elderly, are to the young."[7]

Liz Headleand, a psychiatrist in Drabble's *Natural Curiosity,* notices that she is "withering." To her, "it is an interesting process, and she watches it with an amused fascination." Liz is fifty. In Drabble's *Radiant Way* Alix Bowen, kissed by a married man she loves, thinks "Ridiculous . . . a grey-haired, middle-aged woman in an apron. But she knew she was not ridiculous, it was not ridiculous; extraordinarily handsome she knew herself to be, as she stood there in Caroline's blue striped butcher's apron." Alix is about forty-five. Middle-aged Celie, in Alice Walker's *The Color Purple,* having been told all her life that she is "ugly," sums up, "Nothing special here for nobody to love. No honey colored curly hair, no cuteness. Nothing young and fresh. My heart must be young and fresh though, it feel like it blooming blood."[8] And the woman she loves comes back to her, observing jealously how "fine" she looks.

Harriet Hatfield, in a novel by May Sarton, explains why she's better looking than before: "At sixty one comes into one's own face at last. I was, you have to admit, a rather plain person in the old days." Alison Lurie's Vinnie Miner is another who has benefited from aging. "But just as she was resigning herself to total defeat, the odds began to alter in Vinnie's favor. Within the last couple of years she has in a sense caught up with, even passed, some of her better equipped contemporaries. . . . She is no better looking than she ever was, but they have lost more ground. . . . Her features have not taken on the injured, strained expression of the former beauty. . . . She is not consumed with rage and grief at the cessation of attentions that were in any case moderate, undependable, and intermittent."[9] Sixty-one-year-old Alice, in Barbara Kingsolver's *Pigs in Heaven,* observes that "even her body is mostly unchanged. Her breasts are of a small, sound architecture and her waist is limber and strong; she feels like one of those California buildings designed for an earthquake."[10]

In midlife progress novels, the face and body are never used as the sinister index of aging that the culture teaches us to read. Alice feels the same; continuity matters more than change. Harriet Hatfield, Vinnie Miner, and Celie are handsomer than they used to be. In an earlier Jane Somers novel, Jane's losing an obsessive interest in the cleanliness of her body—giving up her long, self-absorbed hot baths—is a sign of maturity and involvement in the lives of less fortunate women. Loss of some beauty doesn't entail other losses—doesn't, for example, mean that a woman will never be loved (although Vinnie waits a long time) or not be able to work. Attractiveness, if that's the right word, or self-approval, has nothing to do with age: it's a question of life energy, or well-being, or a history of shared love. Or something that might be labeled ugly doesn't repel. In general, appearance simply looms less large in midlife progress novels than it does in novels written in anxious young adulthood about (and by) younger women. This technique, changing the ratios, may be the most convincing strategy of all.

These fictions provide an array of enlightenments for dealing with the-body-as-the-dial-of-time. All together (because proliferation matters), they teach women to look at one another with new eyes. This is the first psychocultural effect I want to notice. Any midlife progress novel revises the norm that we might call "pathetically or despicably aging." All weaken the effects of the corrosive, powerful ideology of aging we grow up submerged in. It's as if all these women writers give midlife women a chance to compare notes about what we have been up to over the past twenty, thirty, forty or more years, and to say to one another, as if we were at one vast cohort reunion, "How have *you* come through?" You don't have to have gone to college to participate in this reunion. You join in the conversation simply by reading the right books. In an era in which fewer people read books, and in which few films provide countercultural images, the novels of the midlife women's progress genre ought somehow to be required reading.

The genre doesn't ignore the bitter iron of life; its toughness about the world is one way it avoids producing a simple dogma of implacable or pastel progress that would be the mirror of decline ideology. Heroines are not born again, instantaneously rescued. But the plots do show them rescuing themselves from situations of radical depletion. One of the unspoken psychological, ethical, and cultural functions of progress fiction is to redefine heroism at midlife to include self-rescue. Ordinary heroines are not heroic in a fatal classical way, like Antigone or Cleopatra, who defy state power. (The genre does contain space for resisting the state.) They do survive, cope with, or resist whatever batters them. The authors choose their vicissitudes from the massive private and social array: tragic accident; financial hardship; discrimination; loss of partner, child, friends; psychic self-ravaging that has gone on a long time. Middle-ageism is the hidden vicissitude they are all subjected to. Not necessarily in the text. It is buried in the reader's own thought: "How can she overcome this, now, *at her age*?" The genre answers the culture's reiterated motto, "No second chances," with plots that are nothing if not new starts.

In *The Realms of Gold* (1975) Drabble chose a famous archeologist who thinks her depressiveness comes from a family curse. In *Foreign Affairs* (1984), Lurie built her version of the genre around a self-pitying middle-aged New England female academic who doesn't believe in her own lovableness. In *The Color Purple* (1982) Alice Walker restored a homely, poor, southern black woman whose childhood and young adulthood have been a series of losses and degradations.

One difficult set of novels—the most spare in terms of recovery—deal with women who have lost children. Yet progress novels don't leave us in calamity; they lead us by the hand through the psychological processes of survival and at least the early stages of recovery.[11] One necessary stage in recovery is self-trust, believing we are worthy to survive after such a blow. As a therapist, Hannah Burke in *Other Women* argues most wryly and explicitly for the value of time. "What about her own despair? It didn't seem to be around much anymore. . . . The older she got, the less anything could upset her for very long. Maybe the only real cure for her clients was the aging process. But that could take years."[12] So midlife progress plots often cover years.

Midlife heroines have emerging strengths they haven't needed or known how to use; in some plots they can do much more than cope. The word *coping* itself implies that we are in a world of low expectations, forcibly held down. But the genre suggests that a woman may have been holding expectations down too low, misled by a faulty estimate of her power to oppose hostile circumstances. She might miss a good thing by assuming it's too good for her. "Merely coping" wouldn't be a moral fault and couldn't prove to be a fatal characterological trait, but it could turn out to be an inadequate tactic. The genre rings danger signals about the passivity and self-mistrust of merely coping.

To evaluate the genre fully, we need to ask the more positive question, "How much can she attain?" Even at midlife protagonists sooner or later make good wishes for themselves. Readers dope out these wishes and these dreads, however implicit; and we judge outcomes by what the protagonist obtains, avoids, or suffers. Heroines do not always get everything they want, or everything we could think of to want for them; nor do they always keep what they obtain. But however close the genre edges toward decline, it shies away from the fictional punishments that feel like comeuppance. It can mete out reward because it creates and depends on ethically interesting characters whose worst acts are justifiable or whose best ones are commendable. The genre by definition disowns a story of time balanced more toward loss than gain. It's a male forty-four-year-old narrator in Richard Ford's *Independence Day*, Frank Bascombe, who judges that "fixing one in six [crises] is a damn good average and the rest you have to let go—a useful coping skill of the Existence Period." Balanced, at times precariously, astride judgments of "crises," "averages," and "skills," progress novels tilt in subtle ways toward granting characters better odds.[13] The genre rewards making a good wish for the self.

Such plots resist the middle-ageism of fictional conventions. Take the privilege of "making love." "In books, plays, films, advertisements, only the young and beautiful are portrayed as making love. That the relatively old and plain do so too, often with passion, is a well-kept secret," Lurie's narrator reveals (213), as Vinnie starts doing so with passion. Hannah Burke, long married and having hot flashes, is propositioned by a "charming" young male colleague; she's surprised, "now that she was into the heavy maintenance decades," but uninterested (7, 25). Mutual love as a plot conclusion also used to be reserved in fiction for the young (straight or gay, male or female) alone. Sometimes real love comes for the first time in midlife, as it does to Vinnie and to Celie in *The Color Purple*. Sometimes it's the best of all loves that comes then, as in *The Realms of Gold*: when Frances Wingate marries the love of her life, both her reasons for doing it and the prognosis for happiness are better than they were the first time around. If love can come after divorce, it can also surprise a widow. Midlife fiction can give a second chance even to that most dubious and derided of heterosexual conditions, the long-term marriage. Justine Peck, the wispy seeker of Anne Tyler's *Searching for Caleb*, discovers late in a long marriage that it has been the right situation for her, not just one she wanted desperately for the wrong reasons when she was young. When the partners are male, these midlife men usually have good qualities and feel multidimensional. (In treating the opposite gender, the genre is hands-down superior to most midlife progress fiction written by men.) In Tyler's *Breathing Lessons,* despite the husband's ruinous depressiveness, the incorrigibly optimistic wife finds a bare margin of benefit in continuing the relationship.

The romance plot, ending in marriage, used to be obligatory for young women even in "high" fiction; then, in feminist fiction of the Seventies, abandoning her marriage became a semiobligatory plot for a young-adult woman who had walked naively into the romance. Midlife plots break both age-graded molds. Heroines can be free of heterosexual mystification or the related belief (which lesbians might hold as well) that a woman is not complete except in a couple. Harriet Hatfield, the widow in a lesbian relationship that lasted twenty-five years, feels without regret that the coupled part of her life is over. In *The Middle Ground,* Kate Armstrong at forty-plus says this explicitly at the very end of the novel. The man who loves her asks,

> "Do you think you will ever fall in love again, Katie?"
> "I doubt it. Why should I?"
> "Why should you indeed."
> "I've done all that. Once or twice too often, in fact." (259)

Many Drabble heroines come to this conclusion. Liz Headland goes through a divorce in *The Radiant Way,* and in its sequel, *A Natural Curiosity,* she seems to have no inclination to begin a sexual life again. It is Liz who congratulates herself that

> having given up sex and contraception, her bodily existence had been of an exemplary calm and regularity. Odd to think of, almost impossible to remember, the tormenting anxieties of those earlier decades: whether one was or was not pregnant . . . whether or not one was bleeding irregularly, whether the pill was masking real illnesses, whether or not one's partner was losing interest, was too interested, was inadequate, was faithless. Tempestuous times. So much anxiety, about one's reproductive system. (*Radiant Way,* 244)

If novels begin to give accounts of menopause more frequently, they won't be able to improve much on this vision of the transition to a less anxious time in the life of the body. Of course, given the pro-sex features of our culture, there are plenty of signs of exciting, loving sexuality (occurring, presumably, perimenopausally): Celie. Vinnie Miner. Hannah Burke (although there could certainly be more information about what it's like). Another difference made by being older is that sexuality doesn't oblige a woman to be dependent; she maintains her autonomous life, achievements, pleasures, selfhood.

At midlife a heroine has many tracks to her life. The more general difference is that she can get what she wants _then_ even if it's quite different from what she wanted earlier. In Paule Marshall's _Praisesong for the Widow_, Avey Johnson, sixty-four, whose family fought hard to get into the middle class, has a visionary ritual experience in which she renounces her dry, bloated, prosperous life of excess in White Plains; her plan at the end is to return to the South Carolina island she used to visit as a child, to spread to another generation her great-aunt's grandmother's story of how the Ibo slaves walked away over the water to freedom. In _None to Accompany Me_ (1994), Nadine Gordimer's Vera Stark, married for forty years to a man she had loved passionately, finds that she needs him very much less than he needs her, and lets him learn this and slip out of her life. These recognitions have consequences for theories that depend heavily, and often implicitly, on continuity. Continuity has meant holding on to values or wants, and is itself valued as fidelity or promise-keeping. But narratives that include both midlife time and ethically approvable characters may force some modifications in ideas about both identity and moral behavior.

What some midlife heroines can also attain, it turns out, is work attuned to their talents and interests, sometimes for a cause. Harriet Hatfield will be able to make a (modest) living for the first time, from her women's/lesbian bookstore. There's some room for fantasy in midlife, or, put better, there's enough achievement that isn't fantasy for readers to relish work successfully when represented in fiction. Celie had been a housewife until she left for Memphis with her lover, Shug. She makes a pair of pants for Shug, beautiful and comfortable; then she makes a man's pair; then she goes into business and opens a factory for unisex "Folkspants." Jane Somers, befriending a very old lady, listens carefully to her stories of young-adult gaiety and poverty, and starts writing historical romances and then sociology of women, giving up her full-time job as a women's magazine editor to do so.

Novelists do not represent economic anxiety at midlife—or its causes— enough. A grave lapse, becoming graver. But _The Middle Ground_'s Kate Armstrong, a working journalist, is shown unable to afford the time to upgrade her scholarly skills. _Beloved_'s Sethe will still be a cook, _Breathing Lesson_'s Maggie will still tend the elderly. These characters are not judged as failures, nor are their lives measured by status and wages.

Midlife progress novels find a way to let the heroine live where she is. That may mean downgrading young adulthood, not a difficult task for this genre. In many of these novels heroines recall their pasts as younger women, or the novels tell their stories starting them young, as if giving their biographies. (Only meaningful lives—representative lives—deserve such long biographies. And unlike film flashbacks, which tend to glamorize at least the looks of youth, fictional flashbacks can't privilege the bodily past unconsciously.) By this means, we have depictions of the social history of women in England and America as life was lived by women who moved through the decades mainly since the late Sixties. When female characters look back in midlife or as the novelist tells their story, we see early adulthood, on the whole, as a dangerous age. We learn of fear of pregnancy in the pre-pill days, homemade abortion, dreadful marriages; the wearing responsibility of raising very young children, sometimes alone and in economic deprivation; the coming of sexual liberation, and then walking away from "sexual liberation" (putting it into quotation marks); the divorce revolution; male infidelity and inadequacy and meanness; the long-term effects of having been neglected or abused in childhood. It wasn't much fun being young.

For many reasons, memory is important to midlife fiction. The memory of youth was a discovery that could be made only by midlife narratives. Virginia Woolf said she didn't know—or really like—Mrs. Dalloway until she invented her memories. Current novelists have another reason for wanting to write about their characters' recollections of their thirties, forties, and fifties. This is where the untold stories are. (With midlife fictions as models, many writers must be asking themselves why they tell a story from eighteen to thirty and call it quits just when it's getting interesting.) Memories thicken a character's life, justify it, explain her identities. The main effect is to provide a contrast between youth then and "where I am" now. These novels are not nostalgic; after a certain point, nostalgia would be a suspect emotion. As urgent cases like *The Color Purple* or *Beloved* or *Other Women* show, a woman must be able to get free of the bulk of her past. She has survived it, living on into the present. The past has been borne in order that the present might be different. In progress narratives, recalling being younger is a way of expressing gratitude for having moved on in the life course. If these are development stories—which risk naive optimism—a skeptical feminist slant can ward off sentimental, too-easy resolutions. The "progress" such novels convincingly model is that it feels better to be older than younger.

Implicitly, any narrative tells a story of life-over-time. The story that mainstream culture harps on is that midlife aging is a disaster to be feared and warded off. The version of progress offered in mainstream women's magazines and self-help books is too blandly uncritical to win more than superficial acquiescence and too lacking in social context to function oppositionally. Midlife women's progress novels give time meaning in altogether different ways. They can be read as encounters between grave risk and brave response. Life in the middle is rich and complicated, dense and perplexed, situated in particular specific conditions of income, status, relationships, psychic history. The midlife for heroines is risky, like any other part of life, and more danger- ous because of middle-ageism. But it is also "safer" than youth because the heroine is herself a site of comparative power, intelligence, understanding, pleasure, expectation, intention. Name any good thing (except for mere youth-in-itself) and it pertains to the midlife. The moment for being aston- ished about this is over. How is it, though, that growing numbers of women's novels can resist the dominant culture and model this complex kind of progress?

Credit has to go first to the social revolutions of our time—feminist, racial-ethnic, class-focused, and lesbian movements in law and culture. These movements have been making legal gains and winning discursive market share in the same decades in which these heroines came into being. Many women derived strength directly from the movements. In general, change and choice and enlightenment—one definition of "progress"—have been much- theorized values of the last three decades, promoted not just by the civil rights movements but by therapeutic communities, life-span development theorists, popularizers of stage theory, gerontologists; and implicitly, to some extent, by liberals and people on the left. Some who work in development in urban areas or the "Third World," as I do, angered by worsening conditions wrought in the name of "progress," may argue against the glib use of the word in histori- cal and political discourse.[14] Generationally too, "progress" can be used to dismiss older people, supposed to represent the passé, and their experiences, values, and versions of history. But severally, each of these fields requires some version of the same idea: that the life span of an individual must contain at least some potential for "progress." Even if personal progress or later-life happiness could be proved to be an illusion (which I doubt), it would be a necessary illusion. The AIDS Foundation of San Francisco has produced a brochure showing affectionate midlife men enjoying "golden years," in an at- tempt to depathologize the gay image, get younger men to imagine a future, and recreate a public progress narrative.[15] No politics is possible without the hope of individual development to support the idea of communities that need and intend change. Despite their diverse agendas and some indifference to or contempt for the rationales of the others, the overlap of the "progressive" subtexts must have affected everyone in the culture listening to them.

Economic independence probably enabled some women to read them- selves into progress narratives. Even though on average women's wages peak earlier in the life course than men's, women's have grown slightly over the past twenty years while men's have dropped considerably. Through social movements, working-class women can experience themselves as having become more "active and reactive."[16] For middle-class women, the curve of wages rises through at least the early middle years, and many freedoms now linked with the midlife have become possible: reeducation, changes in jobs and careers, renunciations of hated kinds of work, adventures in postponed areas (travel, social service). Each of the women who have written progress novels must have a complicated relationship to the opportunities of the postwar era.

But many women are less touched by economic advances or the discourses of empowerment. Upgraded work at midlife is a fantasy; they may be working two jobs, facing underemployment, or losing a job. Such women are more vulnerable to applying to themselves a midlife female decline narrative, having fewer reasons not to and fewer sources of resistance to them. The danger of decline narratives, with their own powerful claim to mimesis, is that they foreclose the future, expunging hope, making effort seem superfluous, and too often confusing "aging" with bad men, bad children, bad government policies, and bad luck. The danger is that disadvantage could be imagined by the disadvantaged as an implacable bar to living or telling any kind of progress story.

The basic contribution of the midlife women's progress genre has been to broaden the possible definitions of life-course "progress" and make these outcomes seem *accessible* and *plausible* in a way that theory, or exhortation to change, or psychotherapy, or even a decent job with a future, each by itself or all together, may not. The assumption is that survival or recovery comes first; then the sense of expanded value—new psychic ambitions—growth in the sense of one's usefulness, spiritual redemption. Without humbug, the genre teaches that a woman can make a good wish for herself and get it and dare to call it good. For two decades, apparently, many readers have needed this balm.

In print, heroines also model resistance, make abstract theory make sense. The straight-talking Shug Avery of *The Color Purple* retorts, to a man advocating submission to the conventions, "Albert. Try to think like you got some sense. Why any woman give a shit what people think is a mystery to me" (171). Only a woman sheltered by a solid subgroup, and trusting the genre, could read that without trembling for Shug's future. Although the fierce Sophia pays a hideous penalty for speaking freely in a racist subculture, she too recovers. Once a reader learns she needn't tremble, she can pick up a new tone of voice. Every free speech invented for a novel's scenes of private life could ultimately be uttered in real life and have an impact on the whole social text.

Like other heroines, Drabble's Esther Breuer in *A Natural Curiosity* brings the news to women who might not have formulated it for themselves. "One would think . . . that options would have diminished to nothingness. Instead of opening up. As they do. Odd, isn't it, the way new prospects continue to offer themselves?" (306). In tones from mild surprise to wild exhilaration to cautious belief, women who read fiction or have other access to a plausible progress narrative can be led to wonder why they used to think that life would close down into the old cul-de-sac of middle age. Women have found many ways to read midlife progress narratives as allegories of their own life-course experience.

Men, unfortunately, have had fewer and weaker messages of this kind addressed to them, and many more messages about midlife male decline, failure, and loss. While women have been following heroines for decades, midlife men have had the "death of the hero" dinned into them. Like the antihero of Martin Amis's *The Information* (1995), they can recite *The History of Increasing Humiliation,* the descent from gods to "failed kings, failed heroes," to the middle class and "social realism" to "*them.* Lowlife. Villains" to "us."[17] This begins to explain why women sometimes feel that they are living in some other decade than the men in their lives, or that the men are acting as if they were years older than their chronological age. And why some men feel jealous of their female partners, uncertain about how to benefit from a revived midlife. We need a parallel study of midlife men in fiction, to ascertain how age, gender, class, and sexuality have intersected for men over the same twenty-year-period. Men do read the midlife women's progress novel; and I suspect they also benefit, insofar as they can apply personally the genre's generic message that aging need not be a decline.[18]

The greatest gift of the genre is that—most of the time, only implicitly—it appreciates aging into the middle years. (The uppermost age of the progressive heroine, now in the mid-sixties, should continue to rise.) Every progress plot uses its time to move the protagonist toward a greater degree of empowerment. *Empowerment* can be a vague and empty word. Narrative, though, makes real what it *feels like* to move toward achieving some more desired state. A particular novel might move the evolving protagonist from a miserable childhood or young adulthood to a richer midlife, from bewilderment, conflict, despair, pain, defect, toward some degree of meaningfulness, resolution, hope, serenity, fulfillment, freedom. As an older adult, a reader can note that her desire for a "post-gendered world of greater equality, in which the traits and privileges now assigned to men and women on a dichotomous and unequal basis would circulate more freely" is likelier to come true at midlife.[19] America's slow growth toward circulating "white" and "straight" privilege more freely also informs many midlife novels. These are central values of any progressive vision. Life-course progress—for an overwhelming majority—depends on social change.

My classes at the Radcliffe Seminars read a group of these novels. We focused on age in fictional and mainstream media texts with the same close attention that other courses give only to gender, race, class, sexual orientation. We made the midlife subtexts explicit. By the end of those seminars I felt certain that a midlife woman aficionada of such novels can testify better than a nonreader of her own age, or a reader who lacked our communal intellectual/emotional experience, to the powers of the midlife and the significance of progress narrative.

But I wouldn't draw too sharp a distinction between my seminars' participants and other readers. I suspect that the average woman in her middle years has evolved. She is at least an "applied feminist," by which I mean that if she doesn't call herself a feminist, she has still been influenced and changed by progressive ideas and ideals.[20] In the same way, she is becoming an applied antiageist—a *life-course* progressive. Like a fictional heroine, she can make bigger claims in the real world to achieve her goals. "I used to be a different person," a woman will say, with impatience and pride. And without disowning her young self, she means that she likes herself better, as worker or mother, lover or friend, speaker or thinker, now. Asked whether she'd rather be a midlife woman now or at some previous era, even during a rough patch of life she might answer, "Unquestionably, now."

The evolved Midlife Woman is less impressed than she used to be by generalized markers that divide life into stages in order to impose decline narrative on her. Her life is marked by self-identified events and continuities: stopping smoking, making a new friend, walking the pro-choice march in Washington with her daughter and son, having a vision on the beach, joining an affinity group. And the most tragic things that happen to her don't automatically certify decline: they have to receive her own interpretation. In our best moments, many of us live like this.

The progress novel, at least implicitly, has made change and choice and enlightenment seem accessible *via*—not in spite of—aging. The very length of a heroine's time line and the techniques she has mastered to solve her younger problems seem to the New Midlife Woman assurances that she (heroine? reader? both?) is a substantial person. Watching heroines recover from earlier traumas, readers are reminded of psychological strategies, reinforce them, or pick up new life skills. Such a reader has been trained—in the way that living with characters in fiction trains us—to construct life stories as ameliorative sequences, starting with her own. In such a woman's thinking, any evolution over time can be generalized as aging-enhanced. A critic might say that this generalization is irrational. Without ignoring history, I see no reason not to praise many of these empowering effects as effects of time. It would be good for everyone in the culture to call them "aging" and link them to life-after-youth.

In my Utopian agenda people *would* consider the midlife progress novel required reading. (In that future, if the word *progress* initially hampered an impartial assessment of the genre, existing midlife progress novels and the critical literature around them would disarm the critique.) Men would be deconstructing their own midlife genres, following their own diverse lines of development, and writers would be re-representing midlife aging in nonfiction as well. Critical age studies would be taught everywhere—in continuing education, to undergraduates, in high school. Age consciousness-raising would be developed and taught at home and in the schools. Valuing the empowering dimensions of aging, and seeing its links to social change, feminists, cultural critics, and narratologists would be the first theorists in the humanities to include age as a vital category. Historians and critics would be discovering how crucial the concept of "the middle years" is to any understanding of the twentieth century.

Although there are many causes for worrying whether in the future midlife heroines can go on being produced, the midlife progress novel has been proliferating even in our troubled era. Literary critics one hundred years hence, reading the genre to date without any context, might conclude that midlife women had come so far by the late twentieth century that they had become a special, prized age-and-gender category.

The Freer Heroine Combating Middle-Ageism

"Not far enough."[21] This could be the motto of fiction operating within a generic tradition. The novels I've talked about have done important work devising, reflecting, and modeling a new midlife female subjectivity. But all of it, massive an achievement as it is, only cleared the ground. Inevitably. A writer moves beyond what she and others have already accomplished, either because she has been compelled to solve emerging problems in her own life course, because she is aware of competing representations of problem-solving (fictional or nonfictional), or because the culture churns up new challenges. It is hard to define a task before a number of writers have accomplished it— and some would say, futile and presumptuous. On the other hand, the power of utopian thinking lies in its lack of respect for givens, its urgent insistence that certain things must change.[22]

At best we are not uncontaminated by middle-ageism. Even feminists who do age studies stumble upon clots of self-hatred that come from untheorized internalizations. *We are all recovering ageists.* One evolved Midlife Woman had a nightmare after seeing *Death Becomes Her.* Another doesn't know why *The First Wives' Club* obscurely let her down. The "Year of the (Midlife) Woman" having passed on, many have noticed that women aren't on the front pages as much any more.[23] Even an optimist has dismayed moments of feeling "There's not a lot of good time left," but she doesn't connect this with the hostile atmosphere she has been living in: menopause discourse (discussed in the next chapter), Glenn Close *already* playing Norma Desmond; reviving *Sunset Boulevard* at all; TV shows in which cold, inarticulate midlife jerks are adored by young women who outclass them twenty ways; books with titles like *How Did I Get to Be Forty, and Other Atrocities.* (I got to be forty by not dying beforehand, and damn if I'm going to consider that an atrocity.) The real atrocity is cultural and economic depreciation of women (or men) for being "past" youth. As a Fay Weldon character says, at a little over fifty five, is "this my punishment? To believe that I am still alive, and live as a useless old woman in a Western industrialized society?"[24]

This is a bitter but wised-up remark. It takes for granted that "uselessness" and "aging" are not things that befall me because I don't exercise enough or buy skin creams or get a face-lift. Our problem is not primarily biological— not for many more years, if ever—but out there in historical processes. The only problem is that it's just a remark. It's not a depiction of a situation, it's not an analysis of institutions or discourses. Progress novels have been slow to recognize and reveal the mechanisms behind midlife aging.

Case in point: the grim socioeconomic facts. The wonderful woman doesn't always get the job—and sometimes she loses it—because of her age. As my final chapter explains, superannuation is one way the postindustrial transnational job market junks excessed workers. Nor does the wonderful woman's job success matter if she dies prematurely of one of the socially-induced diseases of the twentieth century.

How should midlife progress fiction respond to culturally constructed superannuation and midlife cancers and heart attacks, the internalizations of aging and middle-ageist propaganda—the full range of problems specific to the contemporary midlife? The temptation for mainstream representation will be to portray midlife women (and men) as emotionally weak, intellectually mediocre, morally inadequate, repeatedly failing in the workforce, unlucky in love—declining. (This is the way much male fiction portrays men at midlife.) Run on corporate money, mainstream popular culture is likely to become saturated with victims guilty of being "too old."

In such circumstances, midlife fiction should not fall into the trap of eschewing the progress plot. The midlife is currently the best "place" in the life course to examine how we are aged by culture, and midlife fiction is an excellent "place" to grapple with it. The heroine capable of learning so much can *discover* that midlife aging is a set of personal fears that society teaches us to internalize, a set of material conditions it inflicts unevenly, and a set of attitudes toward the age-gender class. The basic problem of unemployment could be part of a plot. Particularly if the heroine finds the energy to continue job hunting and finds a decent job, she might answer, "The *character* and entitlement and skills and hope and trust in community that progress novels help to build may be more important, in terms of facing future evils, than whether past heroines faced exactly the kinds of discrimination that we now want to see some face." It would be useful to have a character collecting unemployment insurance, maybe getting knocked off the rolls after twenty-six weeks, finding out whether her state will give her food stamps.

Locating middle-ageism in discourse and economics, while an enormous achievement, opens up yet more challenging problems. As the same Fay Weldon character says, "In the middle portion of my life . . . I was prepared to believe, how I wanted to believe, that I had to cure myself to cure the world. Now I believe I have to cure the world to cure myself. It is an impossible task. I am bowed down by it" (48). Without counting on cures, we need to move from psychological survival into age politics, and from individual salvation (such as it is) to collective understandings and action. Eventually age theory will provide fuller deconstructions of the sources of midlife aging. But even then we will need literature—fiction and nonfiction—to show what deconstructions feel like as they slowly become mental habits and practices.

There is much more that writers of progress fiction can do once they can demystify and destroy what they themselves have internalized of decline. One of the subtle weaknesses of the genre is that it often inadvertently fetishizes young-womanhood ("being young"). Having invented memory, and needing the past to be there to be recovered from, the midlife novel sometimes can't seem to give up the retrospective mood. Heroines often have too much past. It may be deplorable and deplored, but it takes up room that could be used for present-tense activities. Out of a related bias, the heroine's future can seem skimpy—an effect produced by *Praisesong for the Widow*, by *Breathing Lessons* (perhaps intentionally), by Toni Morrison's *Jazz*. Prolepsis—the technique of letting the reader know what the character's future is likely to be—needs to be animated by the writer's knowledge that for readers "the future" always means "being older yet." In the ending of every novel there's a further implied narrative about aging.

Some midlife fictions are beginning to try to "cure" the world—that part of the world that produces ageist stereotypes and midlife misery. The first baby step was to thematize fear of aging, as Doris Lessing does in the intense *Diary of a Good Neighbor*. The heroine, Jane Somers, starts off as a woman who has failed her husband and her mother as they lay dying, and sets out to "learn something else": how to "behave like a human being and not like a little girl." Her development is told as a story of her learning to care for an old woman: initially "an old crooked witch," then a very poor, frail, dirty, smelly, sordid being of ninety; then a woman with her own stories, a present sense of self, intentions: Maudie Fowler. Initially, it's hard for Jane even to be with her, feeling "so trapped"; she has to force herself to visit, help, come close, feel empathy.[25] By the end, as a friend, she accompanies Maudie to the hospital, holds her, helps her die. Jane Somers undergoes an initiation with complicated stages, from selfishness to empathy, from aversion to connection. By making Somers fifty rather than young, Lessing went way beyond those sentimental fictions in which an old woman is treated by a young one as a being of uncomplicated beauty, wisdom, and power—a genre that might be called the romance of old age.

But in making Maudie Fowler at ninety the object that we must learn to love because she is us, Lessing misled us about the sources of fear of aging. In our culture everyone's relation to "old age" is also constructed; middle-ageism cements it into place more solidly. If we dread old age as early as our thirties or forties, it is not because "revulsion" is innate. The old age of many women has been actively immiserated by gendered and racialized and ageist inequalities throughout the life course, by inadequate pensions, bias in social security, and the like. Partly because of this, old age in general can be represented as lonely, terrified, boring, sickly, and costly to society. But it is midlife aging that repels women first. Fear of fifty intensifies fear of ninety.[26]

Alison Lurie's *Foreign Affairs* took the next steps. Lurie saw midlife aging as a question not of natural dreads but of settled unexpectation, habits of self-demeaning. She placed the blame where it belongs: with men who carry the virus of sexist ageism, with literature and the media, with internalization. The heroine, Vinnie Miner, is "fifty-four years old, small, plain and unmarried—the sort of person that no one ever notices" (3). "Even today there are disproportionately few older characters in fiction," Lurie wrote editorially (ignoring Lessing, Drabble, Tyler, et al., but making a general point that still holds good a decade later). "Vinnie has accepted the convention; she has tried for years to accustom herself to the idea that the rest of her life will be a mere epilogue to what was never, it has to be admitted, a very exciting novel" (207).

If only the convention that "people over forty have no life" were widely recognized as middle-ageism, Vinnie might have used her twist of resentment to combat it. As it is, she accepts the convention, and her self-pampering, kleptomania, self-pity, and fantasies of revenge (the methods that Lurie, a sympathetic moralist, gives her at the beginning of the novel) reinforce her isolation. Her rigidities show the reader how stereotypes may almost become "true." Self-pity, to which all human beings are prone at times, can be a culturally constructed disease at midlife. Self-pity prevents Vinnie from noticing that the unsuitable man who courts her is actually in love with her; prevents her from seeing that she loves him; and thus prevents her from relishing (except for sex) the one true love affair of her life. The experience is slowly changing her, however: she acts unselfishly and he tells her she's a good woman, "and for the first time Vinnie almost believed him" (270). She has one moment alone on a park bench when she "not only feels happy but curiously free" (206). After her lover dies of a heart attack, though, she can convince herself only by logic that he has loved her.

But the novel may have a cultural effect that is quite different from what happens on the last page to its main character; this often happens. Reading _Foreign Affairs_ could convince a reader that the world "is full of people over fifty who will be around and in fairly good shape for the next quarter-century; plenty of time for adventure and change, even for heroism and transformation" (207).

Fear of midlife aging has been given a particular focus in a cluster of inter-reverberating novels. These describe what I call the "postmaternal" years.[27] A heroine's children, so central for so long, are seen to need less care or even to have grown up and left home. _Realms of Gold, The Middle Ground,_ Tyler's _Searching for Caleb_ and _Breathing Lessons, Beloved,_ all "answer" the twentieth-century's middle-ageist/sexist question. Can a woman bear to release her children? So much for the old ornithological metaphor: all the novels but _Breathing Lessons_ show that life doesn't empty out like a nest, because it has become cluttered with accumulations. Drabble puts the heroine of _Middle Ground_ (1980) explicitly in a "draughty space" to begin with, but shows how her busy life engages and enriches her; by the end she's holding a huge ragtag party, which her almost-adult children help her prepare for. She has a man in the wings who wants to marry her; she takes in strays. Kate anticipates the future explicitly. "Anything is possible, it is all undecided. Everything or nothing. It is all in the future. Excitement fills her, excitement, joy, anticipation, apprehension. Something will happen. . . . It is unplanned, unpredicted. Nothing binds her, nothing holds her. . . . She hears her house living. She rises" (277). Reaching midlife, the genre tells us, a woman is still and always central to her own life.

But we dare not second-guess the ways of being that progress novels will valorize, because their countercultural waywardness can lead anywhere. In *None to Accompany Me,* Vera Stark actually sheds many other accumulations—responsibility for grandchildren, for a house that always felt borrowed. Unlike almost all other favored midlife heroines, she has "less" by the end. But what she has is hers by choice. Gordimer makes Vera's politics active; politics is her life-work, not a new start; and it's law, which can alter nation-states as well as individual lives. Vera's desires may puzzle and disappoint readers who expect the rich possessiveness of the ends of *The Middle Ground* or *The Color Purple.* But Gordimer has opened up midlife possibilities once again.

Far from weakening its sense of midlife possibility if the socioeconomic/ cultural situation for midlife women worsens, the genre needs to become more inventive about its heroines' ambitions, more political about their choices, and less timid about their actions. The trick works when writers invent heroines who are smarter sooner, more outspoken. Can a heroine decide to disseminate antiageist rhetoric on a picket line without taking a whole novel to come to this decision? Can she work on a "psychological" problem and discover how it was set off by age cues? If one can, another can take part in a federal sting operation designed to test whether retailers are rejecting women applicants over forty without reading their résumés. Or six friends can redesign a major American city by spraypainting "AVENGE AGEISM" or "GUERRILLA MATRONS" on ad billboards that promote anorexia in thirteen-year-old girls.

Why not? Readers of the genre are prepared for a gamut of worldly obstacles and a gamut of initiatives. Trusting what the midlife woman reader has already become, writers of the genre could become braver in their representations. Deeds will have dense histories; a heroine will be given an age-conscious biography: exposure to ageism, resistance, growth of age identity. Adolescence could include the time midlife Mom edited her first college paper on cyberporn. Childhood, the time when Aunt Lydia looked at her niece's small face and sighed, "Downhill all the way," and Dad said briskly, "Bullshit."

To achieve the radical genre that the culture needs now, writers may need to editorialize more explicitly about midlife ageism than fiction usually sees its way to doing. They may need a central character or narrative voice positioned a little more in the vanguard of the culture, a teacher rather than the slow learner who is often the subject of feminist fiction. They may need to foreground fear of aging, as in the following excerpt from a memoir by Alix Kates Shulman. *Drinking the Rain* doesn't feel the need to provide much in the way of flashback. Present-minded without nostalgia, it treats hectic youth in a few pages, rushing to get the heroine to midlife.

I had long expected—indeed, had promised myself—to be reborn at fifty. For a number of years I had been noticing that here and there in our youth-focused culture some defiant one embraced fifty not as doom or disaster but as an opportunity, a staging area from which to begin an ascent. At fifty Mother Jones, after losing her entire family to the yellow fever epidemic of 1867, was reborn as a union organizer; at fifty Emma Goldman was deported in the Red Scare of 1919 to the Soviet Union where she hoped to create the New Society; [and] after one life Scott Nearing, knocked off balance by the Depression, moved to Vermont to begin his great homesteading experiment. . . .

Why not me?[28]

Contemporary Anglo-American fiction has made clear that the "middle years" do not have the same connotations for all. Under the frown of the culture, some will find them years of "heavy maintenance"; they'll be swept away by painful feelings, buy decline fiction for the miserable comfort of knowing that others are suffering as they think all must suffer; critique the progress narrative for the wrong reasons and shut themselves off from its wisdom. Obviously, I want both women and men to resist that frown, and use fiction, and friendship, and feminism, and any other aids, to help them do it. Changing the way we ordinarily talk about these matters is itself a massive cultural task. Think: when a friend does something adventurous, how long it might be—if ever—before we hear, as the admiring response, "How middle-aged of you!" Every gain will have to be fought for against powerful interests as well as ingrained habits of thought. Yet for the age-conscious and culturally resistant, with luck the middle years can be "so peaceful and exciting, as Gertrude Stein once said of Paris."[29] Midlife progress fiction has its work cut out for it.

6

Menopause as Magic Marker

WOMEN in their middle years are living through the aftermath of the early Nineties, the years of the horrific menopause anecdote. We were inundated with menopause discourse: all the loss, misery, humiliation, and despair supposedly in store for us unless we took the pharmaceutical exit from female midlife aging. Daily press stories, women's magazine articles, talk-show discussions, major magazine essays, two books for popular consumption by well-known women writers (both achieved bestseller status, for a while simultaneously), obligatory reviews of the bestsellers, a menopause anthology. Merging and overlapping and reinforcing at the overlaps, the discourses made menopause as public as fame can, leading (since men overhear everything) around back again into private life. The circulation/dissemination was remarkably thorough, in a mainstream culture based on repetition passing for the new. (Readers feel they are getting important new news, without being able to say what distinguishes it from the old.) As the menoboom tails off, it will already have done its job on the relevant generation of women.[1] Within our age/sex system it will have produced for "menopause" a *cultural consolidation,* a discursive phenomenon in which for a space of time—which can last decades—a set of beliefs and issues and verbal formulas and tropes and binaries become fixed as the only terms in which talk on a particular subject makes sense to the speakers.

There was next to no news about menopause in 1991–94, certainly nothing that kicked off this particular discursive exfoliation. What happened in fact constitutes a *re*consolidation of an older age-graded narrative about women's lives. This life-course decline narrative requires as its pivot a critical moment, an event. The event crudely divides all women's lives into two parts, the better Before and the worse After, with menopause as the magic marker of decline. "What, *this* menopause again?" was my reaction when the first article in what was to be the menoboom appeared.[2] Whatever else it did, the current reconsolidation managed to reestablish menopause as a major life event. It crowds out midlife women's other diverse contexts, by writing MENOPAUSE across the social text in large thick quasi-indelible strokes.

The menoboom provides a case of culture impinging on the midlife—a clear case of women being aged by culture. Why are the mainstream media producing this *now?* How do midlife men fit in? Do women endure the consolidation without resistance? If we can propose answers to these questions, we may yet be able to intervene to ameliorate the cultural situation of the midlife woman—the situation for which the word *menopause* now more often reductively stands.

In the Year of the Midlife Woman

Why now? The stock answer makes this a feminist epistemological issue: the Baby Boomers want to know! "Sexual enlightenment has gone so far that it's time to tackle the last taboo subject"—this view presents menopause discourse as a triumph of feminism, like taking sexual harassment public or shaming TV talk shows into finding more experts in economics and international politics who are women. Silence implies taboo, feminism breaks silences; ergo, women need to "speak menopause." Let me break into this artifact of a syllogism at every point.

Women in general, and Baby Boomers in general, are always at risk of being told what they "want to know." How can it be a taboo subject when the word appears everywhere you look? How can it be taboo when women are signing the books? When there are more items for a bibliography than a scholar can easily keep up with? Women can be told by a woman writer that other women are talking about "it" at dinner parties. (The implied taunt, "Do *you* dare?" keeps alive the implication that speech about menopause has been cruelly repressed.) Far from being taboo, it's in real danger of becoming obligatory. And what it obliges us to do is "prepare" ourselves early for the marker event as a disaster foretold.

The timing of the menoboom was determined by demography, marketing considerations, and the need for a backlash. Historically, backlash occurs when a subordinated group has made enough progress to be viewed as a threat. Menopause discourse flourishes at a moment when (some) women are seen to be powerful, rich, and attractive. (Some) men start worrying that women are getting too much of the good things of life: they assume men must be losing out. These worries center on midlife women, because now—in the Nineties—it's in their middle years, if ever, that women get power. As with fiction, the historical basis for this once-preposterous sentence is that America is twenty-plus years into the ongoing feminist revolution. One vast branch of American feminism from the beginning supported and produced women's desire for education, ambition, upward mobility, and political power; and it and they have kept cracking open the ceilings.

As at previous historical moments of progress, "Wonderful Women of Forty" emerge into textuality.[3] This happened in the wave of Anglo-American feminism between 1900 and World War I, and it's happening now. Today the wonderful women can be fifty and up; they are getting the broadest array of cultural goods that midlife women have ever gotten; the goods are more widespread—and they seem more of an encroachment on male power.

Publicity follows success the way a dog follows a bone that's being dragged away. The year 1992, a presidential election year, was nicknamed in the press "The Year of the Woman," although there was no woman at the top of any of the major-party tickets, the Senate's gender composition could change only very slightly, and so on. In many mouths, it was a wistful, hypocritical, or envious label. Yet it was the year of the (Midlife) Woman. A few did get big titles: senator, congresswoman, attorney general, secretary, and the power and influence that go with them. Behind Senators Braun and Feinstein and Boxer stand mayors, prosecutors, CEOs. In the glamour classes, midlife women are now seen to get money, prestige, fame, and the related perks: gorgeous clothes, fit bodies, handsome postures, level undistracted eyes, and sexual partners. About the other classes, we have midlife progress novels. Most striking of all, at all levels midlife women have become verbally more assertive, psychologically more self-reliant than they were when young. Many have made it their business to unlearn the silly, flirty, self-defeating mannerisms they were taught. In short, they have produced themselves and can be represented in midlife as competent, energetic, nurturing, tireless. "Ageless." This vast re-representation has historically subversive salience: the midlife cohort of women is aging in such a way that *aging* need not be the major fact to know about them. Menopause as a marker event is an anachronism. It could have disappeared. Without the reconsolidation, it probably would have.

In everyday life, in an era long enough marked by feminist advances, at every class level there will be female heroes out there for the men of that class and below to envy. All midlife men know some women like this. If they haven't divorced them earlier, they're likely to be married to one. Their sisters have changed before their eyes, once negligible fluff, now with real weight at the family table, heads of households, survivors of unemployment, or, it may be, makers of breathtaking deals in seven figures. Some women have real money and power, and more have psychological power—but it's never been the reality that counted. Unless they are invested in equality, men imagine more power transferred to women than women ever feel they possess.

What woman, sniffing the stale sweat of male alarm, can't recognize the backlash? Gender backlash by definition targets women, but as far as age is concerned, it's different strokes for different folks. Younger women get hit in the canonical ways, with sexual harassment and rape, abortion limits, pornography, battering and murder; and, at the level of representation, images of themselves being tortured and murdered on TV and film. These techniques have been amply documented and their mechanism seen for what it is: cultural control over women's inner lives. Where they can't control the social reality entirely, they can still try to control the imagery. And—back to us now—midlife women get hit with middle-ageism in the form of widespread public menopause discourse, male science that assumes we've all got a "deficiency disease," and male commerce that sells us the supposed remedies. The imagery and "information" fueling the backlash are published by men who would deny their envy or alarm or even their interest in control, and written, too often, by women who (I like to think) would not do it if they understood that they were being aged by culture.

"Only Women Age"

Before I describe how the current consolidation of menopause discourse (when unresisted) age-grades women, diminishing them and producing "aging" as a midlife decline, we need to hear again in a minimalist sentence what menopause means in the local biology of North America. In the order of menstruation, it's the end of menstruation.[4] As such, it's an absence (as existentialists might say), or (anthropologically) the *end* of a gender marker. Making an invisible absence into huge social graffiti and keeping the ink fresh in the public view requires an immense textualizing apparatus.

Everything else women are told is not universal, and cannot be an attribute or (as the media and gynecologists and now women unreflectively say, using the language of disease) a "symptom." This is true even of the perspiration that has been given a special signifier because it's midlife women who are perspiring. (Nota bene: some women, not all. "We do not know why only some women flush after the menopause.") Medico-sociological surveys sometimes assert what percentage of sampled women say they blush and perspire. The production of such statistics (and being made to use the special term) have negative effects, making skin-temperature change seem important, even dominant, in the lives of women of a certain age. What is being created is a common emotion: fear of "flushing"—of being *seen* to be a-midlife-woman-in-a-sweat. That fear, along with a host of other interrelated, age-graded, inextricable emotions, was part of the consolidation. Women should be wary of all the scare statistics produced by dominant discourse. Mine are explicitly part of a project to disrupt it; I'm tweaking that false nose. Mary Poovey comments, "As a discourse that *claims* a transparent relation to the objects it represents, statistical representation masks the meanings it does produce at the same time that it puts these meanings into play."[5]

In fact, for most women who have stopped menstruating, it's probably safe to say that the incident doesn't loom large in their whole life story either at the time or in retrospect. (The vast majority of women finish having children long before, just when their husbands do. Not menopause but birth control ends their reproductive period.)[6] So much else is going on in the years between forty and sixty nowadays. Before this current consolidation, post-menstrual women were unlikely to want to spend much time in the beauty parlor, their women's group, or other female spaces talking about it. Women often rely on their mothers to provide prophecies about the life course; thus some women in my cohort have blamed mothers for not telling enough about menstruation and intercourse. Now they read their mothers' silences about menopause as prudishness. My mother didn't mention hers until I asked her, and then she said there wasn't anything to remember. Moreover, since what doctors said about menopause included "frigidity" and "insanity," what our mothers chose not to repeat may have represented tactical silence. But all the alternative meanings of maternal silence are obliterated by the theory of the "taboo."

If so, perhaps women today should be cautious about whatever they are repeating to their daughters, since it too comes from an antifemale consolidation. And perhaps, despite the enormous cultural pressure to tell and magnify and make this an EVENT, the marker that divides a younger woman from herself growing older and divides midlife men from same-age women, real cultural power might consist in *refusing* to join the public discourse and saying why.

Unfortunately, silence is now nearly useless as a resistance. Once mainstream discourse forces a public consolidation on an age/sex group, its members lose powerful weapons: privacy and private interpretation of bodily experience, and the luck never to learn stereotypes from media authorities. There are always pockets of culture that consolidations never reach and individuals who simply disregard the hell out of them.

Feminism can respond by interrogating the menoboom's negative effects and by trying to control mainstream discourse more effectively. One strategy I favor is to keep representations of menopause proportional to its place in a whole life story, or better yet, since women need to be reinscribed as indelibly diverse, in many different whole life stories. What we convey thereby is our sense of the *continuities* in our lives, or the discontinuities unrelated to menopause. Thus we discursively override both the biologism and the pessimism of the menoboom. Before the end of this chapter I hope I have made it clear why we need to override both at once. Feminist movements that attack only the pessimism—from Eliza Farnham in the antebellum period to the crone movement of today[7]—fail to disrupt either the young/old or the male/female difference on which inferiority is based. The "after-is-better" rhetoric and ceremony may elevate women who can identify with them. But the movement, like mainstream discourse, only reinforces the marker event, so the next wave of pessimism rides in on it yet again.

Our discourse should *use* that promising, speaking "silence" as a truth that on the whole nothing happens. Or that even if *something* does happen, our adult competence manages it handily. A recent anthology of menopause accounts was prefaced by one woman who said she had no story, the invaluable Grace Paley. "I seem to have forgotten those years or maybe that year."[8] But the rest of the book was inevitably eventfulness, since that's the only story that sounds like a story. "Nothing happened that I couldn't cope with" has to become more public—as well as becoming a bigger part of woman-to-woman conversations. One woman who had sweats and broken sleep for years, and vehemently refused hormone replacement, wanted to tell me only that she'd coped. She didn't tell horrifying anecdotes or represent herself as a menopause "survivor."

Cultural critics are not ignoring individual pain by querying how female suffering gets used discursively. In the mainstream, while women were being encouraged to tell all in the name of sisterhood, a selection of worst anecdotes was plucked like plums and reheated in the mainstream press in a stew of statistics. However poorly written an article, a dreadful anecdote will become memorable. Indeed, in poorly written articles, only a dreadful anecdote will be remembered. An Associated Press reporter who interviewed me about menopause asked me what my "menopause status" was. I explained that I preferred that this not be public, so that readers would be unable to reduce my life and work to my "status." Anecdotes imply that "menopause is hush-hush because it's too awful to talk about." And like statistics, such anecdotes also imply that "menopause dominates your life," that it's "cataclysmic," that, in another canonical term reintroduced by the menoboom, it's "*the* change."[9]

As has been the case since the 1890s when "sex" hormones were discovered and their source immediately called the "puberty gland," menopause-as-magic-marker instantly leads to rejuvenation drug as magic eraser. This is where science and marketing join the backlash in the Era of the Midlife Woman. The menoboom circulates the idea that midlife women without drugs are sick, aging, old, and obstinate. To construct endocrines as the way out, the marker event must be biologized for all its worth, its terrors must be magnified, and women's readiness to take pills must be deftly aligned with "other" midlife progress stories.

Hormone Replacement "Therapy" (HR"T") is the regimen of exogenous estrogen and progestin currently being offered, discursively and of course materially, to all "perimenopausal" women—including the female Baby Boomers, for up to thirty or more years of life. It's a drug with known risks and an annual market running over a billion dollars.[10] One implication of the reconsolidation is that "you" have to take it; another, that "everyone" already does. In fact, one statistic might for a while remain important rhetorically, for resistance: the indeterminate but rather small percentage of American women without hysterectomies who use HR"T." About 5.8 percent were on HR"T" in 1990, but the percentage had gone up by 1993. One study cited "recent physician surveys indicating 75–95 percent of gynecologists would prescribe estrogen to most of their patients."[11] But even a 9 to 1 ratio of users could still be meaningless to the women bent on cultural resistance. Whatever my menopause status, there's no way I'm going to start speaking as if menopause were my disease.

If the mainstream had a menoboom-resistant strain of writers, we could be hearing many voices talking out loud in public about the longed-for freedoms of being postmenstrual. Leaving behind cramps, fibroids, tampax, shields, the Pill. Wearing a white suit any time you want (unless you're on HR"T," which reproduces monthly bleeding). Having better sex without pregnancy fears. Journalists could write articles as long as they like about "Better Sex after Menopause," and "Carefree after Fifty." It's doubtful that they could publish them now in the mainstream. And if they could, the weakness of such articles tactically would still be that they make "postmenopausal" a narrow synonym for what might be the most original, unscripted years of our lives. Is it in our interest to talk about every quality of older womanhood in such terms? Witness the maddening overuse of "postmenopausal zest" in this consolidation: the dot of "reassurance" that asserts how fundamental menopause *must* be, the stain of biologism that reduces the powers of later life to an automatic mechanism. Is being postmenstrual what made Eleanor Roosevelt a great woman? We are asked to accept a kind of condescending praise as the explanation of the fact that most women (miraculously) do not succumb to midlife decline discourse and depression.

"I have a vast life elsewhere" could be the most effective recontextualization. It makes sense for our splendid new comprehensive genre, the midlife woman's progress novel, to deal with menopause this way. How much attention would Celie and Shug have paid to menopause in *The Color Purple?* How would a Fay Weldon heroine react to a gynecologist prescribing HR"T"? The wise psychiatrist in Lisa Alther's *Other Women* perspires intermittently without losing her place in her life. In appropriate circumstances and genres, women writers and public figures might place becoming postmenstrual in the context of their whole life narratives. In short, feminist age studies needs to break the medico-cultural grip of the anecdote (hypostasizing female dread of "symptoms") and of the master narrative (hypostasizing the female aging "event").

Finally, women need to talk in print as big as they can find about the gendering effects of having their supposed female-hormone deficiency diseases made so public. I've said the bad news was brought to us because of male envy, male medicine, male commerce in aging, and the complicity of some women in the process. Until recently men have had no movement of their own to buoy their self-confidence and proclaim that even in their forties and beyond they are a rare undiscovered species with virtues and powers that are truly human, thus deserving of a better break in the late-twentieth-century dog-eat-dog American Empire.

This is the other half of the backlash story. The fact is that, even as a commerce and literature in male midlife aging grows, until recently midlife men have managed to keep their own physical problems, fears of aging, and responses relatively secret. We can now see *how* they did it. Within the mainstream, silence is an achievement managed by a dominant age/sex class. The reconsolidation made female menopause the code word for midlife aging. Thus, in an ageist pro-sex society that fears old age and notes its despised signs even in thirty-year-olds, discursively speaking *only women* age.

The more there is in print about the female menopause, the more it reinforces—or, in the Era of the Midlife Woman, reinstates—a weird illusion of disparity. Midlife men benefit passively from the double standard of aging. Men who have no part in producing menopause discourse and get no income from the commerce, even men who worry about their prostate or Alzheimer's, or wonder whether to try testosterone shots, are led to think "Poor dears" and thank their chromosome that their plumbing is different. "A man" is that half of the nation that doesn't need to know the word *osteoporosis*.[12] On a late-night TV talk show, husbands discuss the topic "Her Menopause Is Driving Me Crazy," and the wives obediently confide their symptoms of difference. If living with a man who believes that his biology is superior is repulsive for a woman, it can also be dangerous—for him, and for both of them. "For a man who cannot come to terms with his own fears of inadequacy, aging, separation, and death, connection to the menopausal partner may be emotionally untenable," Suzanne Phillips observes.[13] Whether heterosexual or lesbian, women are more at risk from discourse that makes them out to be the "menopausal" gender than from menopause itself.

That men age is a truly taboo subject. There's a silence that needs to be broken.

Collapsing the Later Life Course

Many women believe that it is menopause (rather than menopause *discourse*) that ages women; they accept the culture's conclusion that it's a biological marker of decline. But how is this accomplished discursively, as a cultural power play (particularly when all the public evidence about wonderful women implicitly denies it)?

A surprising amount of so-called menopause discourse is actually not about what supposedly happens around ages forty-five to fifty-five, but about biological bad news that may or may not occur, to both men and women, at much older ages. The articles of consolidation tend to have a common structure. In the guise of telling readers not to worry, most medical and popular presentations tell women what there is to worry about, so that women are effectively briefed and prepped as medicalized subjects. I call these articles and books the "Reassurance, but . . ." texts. They din into our ears a monstrous muddled list that includes but is not limited to alleged losses of beauty, an asymptomatic condition that affects a minority (osteoporosis), sexual discomfort or pain (this too has its special name), accidents (bone fractures), diseases (heart disease), Alzheimer's and even death.[14] Costs are prominent. In a state turning away from universal health insurance, creating panic about rising health costs, and allied to powerful medical and insurance interests, a great deal of ageist culture goes to show that women never die, they just cost more.

HR"T" is then slipped in as a remedy. Many texts promote HR"T" in a sly, offhand way that suggests it's noncontroversial. The manual that used to be given out by my managed-care medical-and-insurance plan baldly asserted, "Women who do not use E.R.T. may lose 5–8 inches in overall height in the postmenopausal years."[15] "News" about osteoporosis almost always implies what I call the quick-step bone-mass sequence: osteoporosis leads to falls, falls to fractures, fractures to expense and death. It implies that the pill saves me all eight inches.

Counterfacts or counterattitudes that might disrupt the horror or the inevitability of the items in the list, or their scientific basis or the claims for HR"T," get blurred in mainstream discourse. So do the *risks* of estrogen. None of the items in the bone-mass sequence is in fact a quick-step from the next. Some items concern processes that take twenty, thirty, or more years to oc- cur—if they ever do occur. The image of female old age they construct is preposterously decrepit, particularly since some of these processes have little to do with age per se. Some medical researchers believe that reduction of bone mass needs to be clearly distinguished from its possible sequelae; and that the latter are determined by factors other than hormones or age, such as low weight, poor diet, smoking, drinking, lack of exercise, poverty. Some of the quick-step problems we hear about in an irrational disproportion to their likelihood of occurring, like dying of a fall. "Less than 2% of falls in the aging population result in fracture," one study reports, breaking the inevitability of the mystic bone-mass sequence. These writers point out that the institutional- ized have the highest incidence of fractures and the worst prognosis; pre- venting falls is important. "Reducing the number of risk factors might reduce the number of fractures more directly than estrogen."[16] These are social issues that we should concern ourselves with; they should not be used to terrorize midlife women, even if as old women—mostly by dint of living longer, outliv- ing same-age (male) caretakers, and being worse off economically than men—some of us are likely to be vulnerable.

Some researchers now believe that dietary supplements of vitamin D and calcium can not only prevent or reduce the loss of bone density but also re- duce the incidence of fractures in women as young as 69 and as old as 106.[17] This research discovery, in fact (untainted by commercial tie-ins), had the only title to being called the hot news in the menopause field. If reported widely it could have done something to counter the consolidation.

This discourse is carefully framed to be narrow, deterministic, demeaning, and terrifying. Via the uneasy agglomeration of scares and the complemen- tary silence about men, the culture has managed to make women fearful that midlife marks the fall into bad aging, and menopause means you wake up overnight an alarmingly diminished person. Menopause resonates for women as a *sudden* loss of bodily integrity, a loss that must involve an enormous "change" in self-concept. (This fear about discontinuing to be oneself is repre- sented as though it afflicted only women.) The relevant cohort is the new market vaguely styled "aging Baby Boomers." A woman may now begin to feel that this is an obligatory topic for her long before she nears the likely age—as early as thirty-five or forty. Menopause is on its way to becoming a *psychocultural* disease for the age class of women who haven't had it yet. And the whole cultural endeavor makes women in general hyperconscious of the ailments of old-old age and of "female" causes of death. Our whole last half of adulthood is collapsed into itself, mercilessly shortened. This is a form of cultural terrorism.

No other cohort, male or female, at any age, gets told a future-health-risk story like this. We do not tell girls of eleven, for example, that the childbirth that they will soon be physiologically ready for can involve miscarriage, edema, episiotomy and loss of sexual pleasure, caesarian sections, malformed or diseased children; magazine articles don't tell pregnant women all the things that might go wrong in labor. Although men are now told more often that they can suffer at midlife from sexual decline or impotence, there is, so far, less equivalent discourse striving to make men of forty-plus as anxious about their aging and self-concept. If a man breaks a bone at forty, people say, "Bad luck"; if a woman does, they tut-tut "osteoporosis." The culture fits *her* bone into a decline story. In the media, direct contrast—what men suffer at midlife, die of, how much younger, and what *it* costs—is limited or mitigated.[18]

By making women's problems so medical, so visible, so traumatic and so tied up with female "aging," the culture achieves mysterious and implausible effects. It's not only that it treats women as if they alone aged—bad as that would be in itself. It treats longevity, because it's female, as if it were solely a disaster. (Perhaps men should congratulate themselves on dying younger!) It treats the problems of illness in old age as if they modeled normal old age, relying on our ageist ignorance of normal old age. As women of all ages come to feel anxious and defensive and exposed, they are taught to buy products that then enable the press to dwell on women's "vanity" (a culturally constructed emotion if ever there was one). Men, imaged as exempt from anxiety about aging and heedless of vanity, become invisible as anxious agers and consumers of remedies. They don't let themselves be pressured into humbling disclosures. Prostate discourse, also widely disseminated in these years, does not include men talking about broken sleep and pain peeing.

In the middle years, then, the vast cultural imbalance between men and women should make women cautious about how they break their personal silence. We even need to consider a tactical talk-rule: not to mention anything alleged to be a "symptom" except in an unrecorded conversation with another woman or a man who loves you reciprocally. If a woman thinks she has a symptom, she need not share it around the water cooler. When her lover tells her that he *thinks* he's a trifle slower than he used to be, *then* she can tell him (her choice): "Women experience no clitoral changes however old they get," or, "Perhaps. But let's not begrudge the time." Even women with no anecdotes to share, however, will want to take the menoboom's effects seriously.

Unequal Power in the Discursive War

Although my ruling metaphor has been that of consolidation, a metaphor that might imply hegemony, there is actually a skirmish on, potentially a war, about representing menopause. Almost all the big guns are on the other side: the pharmaceutical industry (especially Wyeth-Ayerst, the company that produces Premarin, as well as menopause "information" that many clinicians rely on and repeat or reprint for their clientele), gynecologists, the producers of beauty products, and the media mediators who shill for the companies through articles that are "infomercials," especially the women chosen to write on the subject, who almost to a woman lack the feminist skepticism or indignation to find experts to counter hormone theory, detail estrogen's risks, or discuss the discursive effects. Although we learned in the very years of the menoboom that, because of the "known" protective effects of estrogen, doctors tend to *overlook* women's heart disease symptoms and misdiagnose their heart attacks, no article I saw deployed that savage irony.

On our side there are a small but increasing number of critically trained women and some men teaching readers how to think better about all this and pressuring the medical establishment to break out of its age-graded sexism. Plenty of feminist material is available in books, feminist journals, and specialized publications (and there may be private experiences, a subculture of resistant lore provided by mothers, older women, friends). The problem is that the antagonists are not (yet) getting read and authorized widely enough. They deconstruct concepts like "deficiency disease" that everyone should learn to suspect.[19] They remind us that "the health system has been forced to search for previously untapped markets of healthy people."[20] They have done skeptical research on the history of the medicalization of women's bodies and they describe the suffering *that* has entailed under the terrifying term *iatrogenic illness.* They attack specific defects in assumptions and research, which has been based mainly on heterosexual white women of some means who see gynecologists.[21]

A feminist antiageist agenda must be ambitious. By the millennium (and I can't say that I expect it by the year 2000) every woman—and not just feminists who read the fine print—and every man, should know that "midlife aging" like aging later on is a unisex dilemma with a powerful gendered component. If midlife women form groups, they won't be narrowly focused on "menopause"—they'll meet to teach one another cultural analysis and resistance to middle ageism.

We'll know more facts about men, and put them into critical relation with facts we know about women. Men get Alzheimer's. Men can have hot flashes. Men also lose bone mass as they age; it is estimated that 17 to 20 percent of those known to have osteoporosis are men. "Flushes in both sexes may relate to the absence of some (unidentified) substance secreted by both ovary and testis," conjectures one researcher who has overcome gendered thinking to this extent.[22] The "discovery" of a *gene* for osteoporosis, recently announced, could further weaken the reliance on gendered hormone theory.

Differences between groups of women, now largely neglected, will have to be explained. There's research arguing that most women lose bone mass normally—at about 1 percent a year in later life—while a much smaller group are "fast losers."[23] Some quite young (premenopausal) women get osteoporosis. Everyone with an interest in women's health knows how poorly researched other matters of intense importance to women are. Why don't we know more about arthritis or lupus (predominantly women's diseases, but ones that do not get connected with menopause)? The one thing the items on the muddled list of women's "postmenopausal" conditions and diseases appear to have in common (that separates them from, say, arthritis) is that they can now allegedly be prevented to some degree by HR"T". Perhaps even nonscientists can be suspicious of a process that isolates and groups an array of medical problems that affect diverse populations and calls them female, age-related, and menopausal. For a century medicine has relied on hormones to explain femaleness: ill-health, asexuality, aging. Those who know this history can't help but wonder to what degree the cult of estrogen may have distracted researchers from more diverse and fruitful paths.

HR"T" has to become enflamed as an issue. Even if it were not a controversial drug, its marketing would maintain the aging discourses that have such harmful effects. But it is extremely controversial. Every popular article should mention that the FDA requires the companies to include with the medication an insert listing its risks. Many women learn them that way, not from their gynecologists or the media.[24] HR"T" should be seen not as a standard prescription for our disease (de rigueur in the "medical model" of aging) but as a site of possible resistance to the medical model, to sexism and ageism in general, and to the unnecessary anxieties and psychological distress and confusion that they cause. According to Sonja McKinlay, a statistician and expert on menopause, letting it be known that you're on HR"T" may become a requirement for women in upper levels of management and government, to prove that you're "in control" of possible symptoms. Margaret Thatcher made it known that she was a user. In the current panicky climate about health care costs, insurance companies may pressure doctors to pressure women to go on HR"T," or employers may do so directly, on the premise that this will reduce illness and keep costs down.[25] If this occurs, even if HR"T" were to be proven safe and effective, women on it should keep quiet about it, so women's competence doesn't get confused with their medications. And all concerned should protest.

The entire issue of "risk" needs to be problematized. Midlife women who are not at risk for anything may take HR"T" primarily because they want to look "young," although no estrogen product now dares to claim that effect. The market's widely circulated fantasy of rejuvenation has made taking HR"T" a covert choice over whether to grow old or not. This is part of the endless cultural coercion on women to "pass." Some women choose to take HR"T" (as an interview study by Phoebe Cushman reports) specifically to avoid "loss of libido" or the "symptom" whose antifemale name is "vaginal atrophy."[26] These conditions were invented in the early twentieth century, by (I am convinced) older heterosexual men angry that they were supposed to be learning the new art-of-love, impatient with foreplay, proud of rapid ejaculation if they could still manage it, and careless about the feelings of midlife women and the desire of some to participate in the new sexual freedom.[27] Because some men still feel the same, and because mainstream discourse links sex problems at midlife to women and not their male partners,[28] some heterosexual women may fear vaginal dryness more than osteoporosis or heart disease. One sentence about it may do more to sweep them into internalization of age-related body-blaming than any other rhetorical feature of the "Reassurance, but . . ." texts. Yet current testimony from sexually active older women outside of clinical samples suggests that few experience symptoms and that symptoms can be relieved by noninvasive means (such as topical lubrication) without hormones. Other studies usefully report "little or no change in [women's] *subjective* sexual arousal."[29] One or more of these lines of rebuttal might dissipate the fears that lead women to elevate their sense of being "at risk" if they *don't* take HR"T."

Risk assessment seems quite primitive at the present time. My own gynecologist didn't try to discover whether I'm at risk for osteoporosis before she announced that I ought to start HR"T" as soon as I stopped menstruating. She didn't mention calcium or other alternatives, like calcitonin and exercise.[30] Not having done a baseline bone-mass test, she has no idea how much bone mass (if any) I've lost already, or whether I'm a fast loser. Some researchers doubt that any of the existing markers enable clinicians to decide who is most at risk. Although HR"T" is given to women with family histories of heart disease, even pro-HR"T" writers like Regine Sitruk-Ware and Wulf Utian admit the possibility that "cardiovascular risk will be increased, as some progestins would reverse partly the beneficial effects of estrogens." The greatest risk of HR"T" is now breast cancer, epidemic among American women: "There is more consistent evidence to suggest that the risk of breast cancer increases with longer durations of therapy," say Hunt and Vessey in the same volume. It's amazing that writers who notice such evidence can use the word *therapy* without quotation marks. Although Sitruk-Ware and Utian somehow find their way in the face of all this adverse evidence to see a "clear advantage for benefits" of HR"T," they conclude by conceding that prescribing over the long term for women rests on "a balance of risks and benefits, dependent on a number of unanswered questions."[31]

The recent failures of the medicalization of women's bodies ought to give women pause: the overuse of hysterectomies, the Dalkon Shield, DES, silicone breast implants, and most relevant of all, the reluctant response of the profession to the discovery that unopposed estrogen, the form taken by women in the Seventies, was linked to endometrial cancer. One response was that it was an easy cancer to cure.[32] Add to the possibility of iatrogenic illness patriarchy's history of updating the bad-news-about-menopause list as items like "involutional melancholia" drop out. Shouldn't that make women skeptical about any discourse that argues them into taking expensive and inadequately tested chemicals for half of their adult lives? Even after a woman has been told she specifically has a higher risk of something, skepticism should embolden her to get another opinion, or to plunge into the specialized monographs—particularly those that query reliance on estrogen as a cure-all. After so much ideology-driven malpractice, how much should we trust the "experts"? One current National Institute of Health study will be released in a few years; health-care feminists believe it will shed more unbiased light on terrible questions of risk.

Meanwhile, there can not even be a gain in knowledge from the vast unlabeled "experiment" that midlife women are being subjected to. One practical strategy would be to lobby the Food and Drug Administration to label HR"T" as "experimental" as it did in 1992 for silicone implants. This would force gynecologists now recommending it to strengthen their warnings about its risks (if only because of the possibility of malpractice suits if HR"T" turns out to cause cancers).[33] The effort would also bring medical ethicists into menopause discourse. Up until now, only some feminists have seen menopause treatment as a set of ethical problems. Rhetorically, it would be useful to call the issues around menopause "ethical" and "cultural" as well as "feminist" and "antiageist."

Preparing for Cultural Combat

Discourse is not just "talk," it's never just talk. That women feel forced to attend to this particular one, and what they are then exposed to reading, over and over again; what editors permit into print or prevent from appearing— all this affects our self-image, our human relations, our cultural identity, our mental health and quality of life, our attitude toward aging and our under- standing of old age and death. The average midlife woman relying on main- stream publications has little or no access to resistant discourses and an enormous amount to lose from listening to scare anecdotes and the master narrative of "change" disguised as "information," and from feeling she has no choice but to take them to heart, repeat them as truth, and rush off to get her steroid prescription. Even when well educated and curious , women may not be adequately trained to see how the discourse operates or too constrained by respect for current sexual science to see that women have a right and rea- sons to be dubious and to resist. Young, midlife, old—we are all more vul- nerable because of the way the consolidation of the early Nineties framed menopause discourse.

The most likely users of HR"T" are well-educated, higher-income women. The HR"T"-takers in Harris's California sample were not only whiter but thinner, did more aerobic exercise, had fewer children.[34] Virginia Olesen com- ments that "the social stratification system which denies lower- and working- class women this therapy also enables them to avoid its risks."[35] Higher socio- economic status makes expensive bodily interventions feasible; education opens women to the ideology of "expertise." Feminist education carries with it training in ideas of "entitlement" and "empowerment" and "control." In- deed, women who feel good about themselves—who fit the model of the "wonderful woman" of the Nineties (and this definition certainly can include feminists)—may be *more* vulnerable to menopause rhetoric about "taking control of their aging."[36] Instead of using HR"T" for a short term, as most women who take it have done, such women, living in the consolidation pe- riod, may decide never to stop. We don't yet know much about the specific, differential effects of the consolidation on women's anticipations of meno- pause or their practices. But in Cushman's 1994 interviews of twenty Radcliffe College alumnae aged forty-six to fifty-seven, five out of seven women using HR"T" started since 1991, and four others said they would like to take it but their doctors forbade it.[37] Cushman's interviews also uncovered women not using HR"T" happy with "feminist valorization" of menopause, who use lan- guage of "naturalness" and consider medicine an unnecessary or dangerous intervention. But such important information about how women resist the prescribed in a culturally defined moment is relatively inaccessible.

In conversation, and possibly in their own inner colloquies, women I know appear not to know that they may be ordering their beliefs and preparing to make their "choice" on the basis of information tainted by gender and age biases and marketing imperatives. Even feminists fall into ways of speaking that augment the consolidation. A theorist leading a mixed-gender meeting, reporting that she is having a hot flash, adds wryly, "For the next twenty years." This is a scenario so clinically exceptional that I had never before seen or heard it mentioned. A professor tells me blithely that she will need HR"T" because she is "small-boned," and another because of a family heart history. The latter's gynecologist hadn't mentioned how slight is the effect of estrogen in lowering rates of heart disease for women. "The current research focus on the cardioprotectivity of estrogens may require rethinking," writes John Mc-Kinley.[38]

And what of the gynecologists who have pervasive doubts about HR"T"? One tells me that she feels a medical and ethical obligation to present the anti-HR"T" argument in the strongest terms. But what will she do confronted by a woman without symptoms who asks for medication (which is now a frequent occurrence, as a result of the unpaid forms of propaganda for HR"T" that I have been considering all along)? The consolidation made the situations of such doctors much more difficult. Their cautions fall on ears deafened by the menoboom.

Even more depressingly, I meet women I consider feminists, who are aware of the ubiquitous presence of cultural mediation and skeptical of scientism, who respond to the menoboom as if they were personally helpless. They're performing the Mirror Scene more often, asking if the catastrophic "signs" have (yet) appeared on their faces or bodies that will identify them to an imagined gaze, or their own, as "postmenopausal." However able this or that woman might feel herself to be at midlife (producing important work, loving and being loved, healthy and asymptomatic), as a body-in-the-world she feels vulnerable to middle-ageism, unable to convince others (men?) of her true worth, drained of energy and confidence that might go into age politics. One way out is for her to will to believe in hormonal antiaging effects. In her self-dislike, she wishes for a face-lift, punishes her body in subtle ways, "trusts" her gynecologist, and, asymptomatic, takes magic medication. I say this on the basis of intimate conversations with a small sample representative only of highly educated, mostly academic (white) women from about forty-five to fifty-five. Most starkly put, menopause is close to being lived—even by relatively demystified women—as a descent into decline.

Some of these women are angry at me for talking about menopause as a socially constructed experience. Not that they're naive about other internalizations; many have fought successfully against their own erstwhile young-adult belief that men were intellectually superior to women, for example. But age-related difference works on a different, intrasubjective binary: it makes a woman less than her*self*, inferior to her (apparently biological) self at an earlier phase. By pitting her against her younger self, decline appears free of construction, as if there were not a hostile ageist world outside manipulating the comparison. (It's as if wrinkles were exempt from rules of signification.) This decline, she believes, she herself can *see*, in the signs that "others" see. And in her soliloquies of age anxiety she may whipsaw faster and farther: now seeing herself through an ever more critical, menoboom-sharpened gaze, now seeing herself as before the consolidation in her ungraded, private, continuous or progressive way—as (perhaps) one of the wonderful women.

As I found in front of my mirror, this terrible double consciousness need not go on forever. "There is frequent tension between the received interpretations and practical experience. . . . But the tension is as often an unease, a stress, a displacement, a latency: the moment of conscious comparison not yet come, often not even coming," as Raymond Williams has astutely pointed out.[39] Yet with "conscious comparison" can come critique of the age ideology. The disruptive potential has to be latent, and once a woman feels it, it needs to be welcomed—reflected and reinforced—by women's networks. What may make women willing to try to transcend the state of double consciousness, I suspect, is that they find it to be both intellectually suspect (too negative, naive, contradictory) and deeply fatiguing, distressing, and incapacitating. Out of this moment of psychological dilemma and apparent impasse, women might derive anger and resistance, and find the momentum for a new phase of feminism much more conscious of middle-ageism and active around age-related issues that surface in the media. High time too. At some point feminist theorists might want to ask themselves why feminism was not—I won't say better prepared for a menopause consolidation, because it came out of the blue—but more resistant in the face of it.

What of the culture beyond? Might the current menopause consolidation liquefy by itself? I'm not sanguine about this, but I can name some areas of potential meltdown. As a society the United States has been moving away from the mystique of pronatalism, as do all modernizing societies that need the work of women and a reduced birthrate. If these needs continue, in a gradual but more retarded way the cultural values connected with pronatalism should weaken, not disappear but become firmly subcultural. The claims that HR"T" can make may wither; or with the rise of genetic explanation, hormone-based science may subside. Losing marketing pressure on the culture might result in fewer descriptions of menopause as a disease state and short conduit to old age.

The situation of men may exert pressure on the consolidation also. Midlife men are becoming more vulnerable—trained to connect dysfunctions, physical losses, and pains with middle age. The same medical/commercial forces that have been bringing women their public menopause are on the verge of bringing men their public climacteric. Men too are being pressured to become anxious. They're beginning to buy rejuvenation, like women (see "All Together Now"). Driven by their own misery, encouraged by age theory, men might discover that they have their own reasons for rejecting "the change of life," aside from solidarity with same-age women.

What might happen when both genders learn that ageism internalized is a stressor, a depressant—what I want to call a psychocultural illness? Feeling "decrepit," assuming that no one will take a sexual interest in you henceforth, believing that your future ended yesterday are symptoms of middle-ageism, not aging. What might happen when men as well as women realize they share the Too Late Syndrome and want to discard it? When they know that it's not their looks or their climacteric "status" or anything else objective about them that produces the syndrome? "Midlife crisis," as I said initially, is a culturally constructed disease. Learning this could change male-female relations in the middle years for the better and lead to age-connected activism. This could be the right decade to learn how to fight the mutual enemies; together we could invent the new talk-strategies against the next reconsolidation. This future, if it were to come about, would leave intact only all the *other* sources of middle-ageism in our culture.

7

My Mother at Midlife

WHEN MY MOTHER was thirty-seven years old, married with two children, she went back into the workforce and permanently changed all our lives. She got a teaching job as a first-grader in the public elementary-school system of Brooklyn. Daily she came home haloed with the prestige of being a teacher, reveling in the pleasantness of the work. Her day ended at 3:00 P.M., unlike my father's, which began at 5:30 in the morning and ended at something like 8:00 at night. She could be home at the same time that my brother and I returned from our own more fraught engagements with the system. The part she didn't revel in openly was the part that most altered our family circumstances and relationships. The money. We stopped being poor and became, almost at a bound, rich. Or so I felt it. There was more meat on the table; new clothes for all of us, designer clothes from Loehmann's for her; over the years, elegant modern furniture in the living room. The kitchenette was renamed the dining area and a white Saarinen pedestal table arose from the new white tile floor like an altar. I was ten when she made that first leap, and my brother was eight. "I couldn't wait to get out of the house," she said to me years later. At first the idea that she had wanted to get away from us shocked me in my nursery narcissism. Now I understand it perfectly.

My mother led the way. A year or so after that, one of her sisters-in-law went to work as a teacher, and a few years after that, her sister became a librarian. In both those families also, many things were bettered: the housing, and the look and feel of the furnishing, and the kind of hospitality that was offered; and underneath, the power relations between the husbands and wives, and the good feelings that could develop out of a better balance. The man was released from the relentless grim pressure to be "the breadwinner" in a market where his level of education and skills and class went too cheap and couldn't be made to be worth more no matter how long the hours he worked and what he chose to work at. And with that burden a little released, the daily grudges and blaming dwindled: the lowered thin voices and the slammed doors, anger when a dish was broken, the soap ends saved and pressed together. In many families the Depression hung on long after the postwar boom.

Those women were lucky to be poor—or more exactly, lucky, since married, to be married to men who needed help under American capitalism and were not too conventional to accept it. In middle-class houses in the Fifties and Sixties, as we now know, desperate housewives with children underfoot were drinking, taking pills, feeling undercompensated and wasted and helpless; their lives were ruled by husbands who held all the desirable power and by a system that approved. Many, men and women alike, were living out the clichés that love ends after marriage and "real life" begins: middle-class anomie, the end of the Cinderella fantasy, the long joyless drudge of the middle years.

My mother, and then my aunts, were saved from that. They had no tradition of useless leisure, no lying myth of being a protected sex, no sense of transgression when they walked out of the house with the keys to their own car. My father had said to my mother, "You spend so much time at the children's school anyway; why don't you try teaching?" Wherever I looked, everyone worked. Women were no different. My aunt Olga's tiny mother, a widow, was still working, baking strudel. My father's mother had minded the store and five children while her husband the would-be scholar dreamed. Another aunt, who was divorced, sold for a fancy furrier. What was luck to my mother was having a job where you worked only 183 days a year and didn't stand on your feet all day, where you were surrounded by children who loved you and left your classroom every afternoon flushed with learning and praise. It was much easier than work had been cracked up to be. "The children taught themselves," she said, inadvertently explaining why her teaching was so successful. "What could be more wonderful than helping someone learn."

She moved out into a bigger world. Sometimes I tagged along with her. Once a month now she had her hair done, first in the little local place near Utica Avenue, reached on foot by walking past the pharmacy, the tiny grocery where mom-and-pop charged too much, the butcher's with sawdust on the floor, the shoemaker's with the row of iron shoe-shine chairs, to a shop sharply odorous with hairspray, with cafe curtains down to the radiator, on which the ladies' magazines were grouped invitingly. Later she went to a busier, worldlier place on Church Avenue where women smoked and drank cokes and talked in louder voices. There they dyed her hair mink-brown with glints of red.

Handsome, strong, energetic, she always had stories to tell while she did her lesson plans at the Saarinen table: what the "girls" said when they had lunch together (the first divorce, the first juvenile delinquency), the little girl in her class who didn't know what a *hammer* was, the way everyone in *her* first grade class could read by Christmas; how the principal described her imaginative classes to the other teachers, and what the lessons were. Soon the house was peopled with "my children." At first I rebutted, "But *we* are your children," after a while the other children didn't seem to detract from our importance. They were even in a curious way company. My own life at eleven and twelve was drab, intense, and, until I found my best friend, lonely. I was timid to the edge of mania, living over isolated slights in bed at night for years, remembering with shame how I had failed to confront Mrs. Murray with her injustice and bring her to tears and repentance.

My mother was "popular," that inescapable Fifties' accolade and requirement. Her lively reports were full of "Doris Danto" and "Claire Rothman" and "Esther Malament," the fascinating Other Women of my family-centered childhood. They were that distinguished thing, "colleagues." Later my mother had mentors, Miriam Fox and Evelyn Heller. Together they gave her that distinguished thing, a "social life," which was different from family parties, where the fathers argued politics and played poker for bobby pins and the cousins shrieked and ran into the kitchen for more cake. Her colleagues called my mother by her two names. "Betty Morganroth will be there," I heard one say, complacently. Right then, although I didn't know it until forty years later, I decided I had to figure in sentences like that or life would not be worth living.

Through the colleagues came glimpses of other ways of living ("apartments"), other children. Sometimes I visited their strange houses. Lil Rosenthal had a distracting mirror that went from side to side of one living room wall, hung just low enough to show my own pale round staring face, like an emerging moon, at the bottom. She was my mother's closest friend. For the first time I learned how much death mattered, when she died in an open-heart operation and my mother openly grieved for her.

Although almost all my mother's friends were married, there were few men visible in this world, or audible either. I rarely heard a man's two names said with that relish of familiarity that captured the women in a mouthful. The exceptions were "Uncle Harry" and "Max Shapiro." Uncle Harry was my own great-uncle, whose full name was always pronounced "Harry Eisner Principal of Franklin K. Lane High School." He who had arrived an immigrant without English praised my mother's A's and made anything but college seem a detestable ambition, at a time when my mother, in dumb adolescence, thought being a department-store salesgirl would be a blithe, prosperous life.

On rare occasions, one or two of the women came for coffee, and out came the crimson tablecloth otherwise never seen, its creases attesting to meticulous home ironing, and the Dansk pot and matching cups in dull black with glossy lining. Our apartment—the bottom of a two-story house with the tenants upstairs—not only contained a few well-designed objects, but it was also clean and well ordered. From my bedroom desk I heard the absorbed voices of the colleagues and at times a float of kind womanly laughter. My own life became reenchanted to a degree because it was reflected by all those alert ears and observant eyes. My mother's friends heard the stories about my perfect grades, my beautiful braided hair, uncut since birth, my creative compositions, my being invited to talk on the radio about colonial and ante-bellum houses in our neighborhood, Flatbush. My mother attended PTA meetings as an equal now, teachers in my school held her in esteem, my tall dismaying principal, Miss Ebeling, took her aside to talk about John Dewey and pedagogy.

At this time my mother was always cheerful. She opened pickle jars with large capable hands. She knew the meanings of words so I didn't have to look them up in the dictionary, and she put them in a sentence. She did mental arithmetic faster than anyone when she updated her checkbook. She recited poetry. "What care I how fair he be / If he be not fair to me?" She knew whole poems from her college courses. I wasn't sure she was "beautiful" because no one in the family said so (the word was reserved for a first-cousin-once-removed on my father's side), but I drew her picture and once made a water-color painting of her, wearing the mannish shingle that was stylish at the time. I have photographs from her thirties, wearing one of those coifs where the hair is rolled and tucked under, that we associate with her favorite stars, Bar-bara Stanwyck and Bette Davis and Kathryn Hepburn. She looks smart and charming and comfortable in her body. Wearing outfits with cummerbunds and boleros and Dolman sleeves, she stood in front of the camera with one foot poised a little in advance, the skirt held out just a bit, a smile of slightly self-conscious pleasure on her face.

Once when we came out of Honam's, our Chinese restaurant, my father and I were walking behind her and my brother Lewis, my mother's heels click-ing with characteristic vitality. "Doesn't Mommy have a good figure?" it sud-denly occurred to me to ask my father. "She certainly does," he answered, in an unexpectedly emphatic, proprietary way that took my observation away from me. But I was startled and in some way pleased that he had revealed something about himself and about them that I had vaguely surmised. From that one sentence I kept the impression that my parents had a satisfying sex life. (All I had learned, at most, was that my father did). His observation held me in reserved silence when later on my contemporaries implied that their parents never had sex. Later yet I had another thought that stayed with me. Money in the bank conveyed independence, a sort of challenge (noli-me-tangere against-my-will); it was sexy.

When I was twelve, my mother took a year's leave of absence to go to Bank Street and take an "Em Ay." That sounded rich in the ear, a new vocable; it started trains of thought that went anywhere in the world, like the IRT after the last stop I knew in Manhattan. The new great names appeared close at hand (the old ones, like Roosevelt and Paul Robeson and Helen Gehagan Douglas, were dead or very far away). The new ones were quoted daily. There was no place better than Bank Street; important things were happening there: she wrote papers and observed classes and learned so much. Bank Street ultimately meant a transfer to a different—and a better—school, with a dedicated progressive principal, "Max Shapiro," and assistant principal, "Miriam Erdos"—new characters in the vast endless play of my mother's biography, who valued her, and she them, more and more every year. Max Shapiro after the school day ended used to call his good teachers over the PA system after visiting their classes and say, "You made my day." Nobody made his day more splendidly than my mother. She knew to the dollar how much the Em Ay meant in salary. Every so often she went through the litany to me: the base pay, plus the extra for her years in-service, plus the extra for the extra degree. Every year the amounts grew, as reliably as time passed.

She kept her own bank account and checkbook. (I didn't know how unheard of that was, or how dangerous in some families it could be.) In my family my parents had an agreement about who paid for what: my father paid the mortgage and the heat, for example. The Knoll sofa came from her account, and the maple buffet that opened up long and pale, and the presents that would otherwise have been skimpy and unlovely. By my early teens we shopped regularly together, and she would let me play the Top Forty on the radio all the way there and all the way back. I was as ignorant about money then as any spoiled child could be. By this time we had a convertible whose top went down in good weather. My mother drove safely, both hands on the wheel, with her competent coin-profile, skirt neatly smoothed underneath like my own, perfect posture.

And then there was a crisis and her account mattered more. I was a straight-A student and I had set my heart on "going away" to college. My father wanted me to go to college, that was absolute. But he said no, a girl should live at home; "Margaret could go to Brooklyn College." That was obvious, as I passed it every day on my way to high school. In fact, I was already going to Brooklyn College, to take a course not taught at Midwood; it had no glamour or freedom, it would have been like going to high school for eight years—and I hated high school, it would have been like a sentence to the penitentiary. I think I must have been too astonished and dismayed to say anything in my defense; I, saw my whole dream ending right there in a minute in the kitchen. But my mother said to him firmly that I would go away and she would pay. And that was the end of it as far as I ever knew.

It was not a "scene," but it must have been part of the long difference made by their each having their own money and their own ideas about it. My parents did argue at times; I heard the tones of it from another room. Children who live in small houses hear this more. I hated their arguments, where my father might suddenly erupt in rage. That he did so rarely made the prospect more terrifying. Not to have occasioned an argument was an almost incredible relief. My mother won this one because my father ceased to object. The fact, unspoken, was in the air, that I had beat the odds by getting into the best college in the country, only the second girl from Midwood to do so, and with a scholarship that paid for tuition and some part of rooming expenses.

Readers expect a scene, perhaps (autobiography and fiction so often rely on scenes). But for normal life mostly we pray to escape them. It was my mother's income that really made the difference. Even if my father had been a different man, an angry overbearing man, that power might have subdued him. What could such a man do to thwart us? Money would put down the college deposit, carry my luggage out the door, buy my plane ticket away. Scenes arise from *unequal* power. Money equalizes power, money deflects scenes. I grasped the human sides of that syllogism instantly.

My mother also won because she cared, more than I knew. She had gone to Brooklyn College and was proud of the education (I still know the names of her great teachers, like Harry Slochower). It wasn't until years later that she told me—in a tone, for her, of surprising bitterness—that in those days the classroom buildings were all downtown and it "didn't have a campus or residence dorms." Obviously she knew what "going away" would have meant to her (slumber parties? more interesting men? other good things that were unimaginable to her who had not had them?) and wanted me to have them all. So there was no "scene," but that conversation over my head and my fate was the primal scene of my young life. It was as if my real life started from there.

My mother did pay the rest of my room and board, and she gave me an outfit that was like a trousseau, and a monthly allowance that (while half of what some of my roommates got) in those days when boys paid, I could get along on. All my younger girl cousins coming behind me benefited from my mother's historic decisiveness about her own wealth. Eventually, all who went to college went away.

My father, for reasons that were then incomprehensible to me, sent me nothing—nor did he explain why, not even later when we became so close. Rivalry over a child is supposed to be bad for the child, but perhaps not fighting is worse. Only recently did it occur to me that he might have been too proud to explain, or that he might have distrusted that elite university. And in the battle for me, he must have sensed not only that he lost but that he had lost inevitably. And it wasn't just money, or even class. As a man—at that time and with his background—once he couldn't teach me baseball and walking on stilts and carpentry, once I hit adolescence, he didn't have the right skills or training or instincts to deal with the "me" he could see—with my moodiness, my protointellectual's class arrogance, my terror of not making it, my intermittent ruthlessness, and (although I hid it) my reckless conviction that I should experiment with sex despite feeling emotionally unready. My mother might not have had the skills to deal with such a child either, but she didn't see this in the same way, or perhaps at all, because she trusted me.

Freshman year I started working Saturdays to add to my allowance. Few students at my college worked in those days. The coffee shop I bused was on the way to the football stadium, and although I never cared for football, cradling the spoons one behind another while my classmates sauntered past in pairs was bitter. I didn't cry, but I pitied myself intensely; the gulf between them and me seemed impassable. There was no one there to explain, cheerfully and grimly, what I would have said to my own child, "That's class, dear." But my mother must have heard something dark in my descriptions, because she raised my monthly check a little and told me I shouldn't work during the school year, I needed my rest when I wasn't studying.

My own private life had begun to crowd hers out, and college and then graduate school on the other side of the country nearly erased my whole family. I went forth under her aegis but then forgot in the midst of my own storm-productions who shielded me from the harder, higher, hailstones. In the first years of marriage, though, I occasionally took refuge with her mentally. I think of those years, for a young woman, as the Equality Wars. The wife fights to be treated as well as if she were a friend, and the husband is ripped out of his supercilious male teenage self-absorption. The negotiation was more unequal in the Sixties, even when both people started out as we did, committed to equality. Whenever I got close to giving up the struggle, I'd say to myself, through my teeth, "My mother would take me in. There is a world elsewhere." I probably could never have gone back home, even had I married a man I couldn't finally like. But every woman needs Coriolanus' concept of "a world elsewhere" to save her from desperation. I would bet that every woman who marries has walked out the door mentally—and some have nowhere to go. Well, I was lucky. I learned noncoercively that sometimes a world elsewhere doesn't matter. You just decide to stay and change the one there is. Her money made that deliberation possible too.

For a decade or so, I half lost her through not paying adequate attention. Forgetfulness was made easy for me. She never made a claim, never mentioned any of her gifts, never asked to be thanked in the myriad covert ways that other people—other mothers, fathers, lovers, friends, spouses—ask to be thanked. Nothing has diminished either her generosity or her verbal kindness, the like of which I have not come across in all the years since. By now, still (or again) observing her with the same love-kindled eye, I know what she would say about that. Why should she have asked for requital? She loved and trusted me, whatever was good and natural would follow. On my side, I see now what was invisible then, a woman growing into benign maturity. She wasn't needy in any of the familiar ways that women are led to be needy at midlife, and if she had private needs she still kept them to herself. She had a life she had never dreamed of having, not even when she was her father's darling, eating a latke in the window of a corner house above the grocery store, one flight up in East New York. The intervening Depression, the unreality of "keeping company," childbirth, the hardships of the war years, the anxieties of McCarthyism, were over. When I went off to college she had major human growing still to come. She was only forty-four, with many accomplishments, many affections, many heartaches of her own ahead of her—heroism and tragedy—her own embracing, self-made and unpredictable life. That was what I almost lost.

My Mother's Midlife and Mine

If women lose track of their parents at the start of their own independent lives, sometimes they find their mothers again when their own children are born, when they need to know what to do next and become curious about what their mothers did for them and to them. No one needs to be the first to open the door; two doors open simultaneously. Perhaps three, the father's too. These rapprochements began for me when my son was born. But I was still preoccupied with my own life, husband, baby, career—overwhelmed by the simultaneous demands of early adulthood. It took another six years before something happened that jerked my attention back to my parents. My father was diagnosed with amyotrophic lateral sclerosis, sometimes called Lou Gehrig's disease. It is a degenerative muscular disease whose course of decline is unpredictable; there can be slow onsets, blessed early releases. My father got neither. He lost speech first; the muscles in his strong legs and arms began to atrophy; slowly the power to eat diminished. My mother took a leave of absence to be with him. I was living in another city. From a distance at first, I learned the meaning of irrevocability. After five months of that, I moved back home with them and stayed until the end. He wanted to die at home and we helped him do that. This is not the place to tell about them—his stoicism and bravery, her patience and resilience. But a few outcomes have to be mentioned in this context. Since then, "decline" has not been a figure of speech I use lightly. Because my father died at sixty-nine before he had a chance at normal aging, I know how sharp the difference.

Because of that dreadful watch, my mother and I bonded in a way that few parents and adult children ever need to do. She asked me to come and help them, so I steeled myself and came, leaving David to take care of Sean for however long it would take. She made the decisions about my father's care. Quite properly: she was his age-peer and long-term companion; I started as a young, scared thirty-three, and she was a competent, mature woman just turned sixty. By the end, though, I had grown toward her. We entered (I, rather belatedly) the long middle span in which a parent and child have a chance to be equally adults together.

When my mother considered remarrying, it was I who was her confidante. When they eloped to the Caribbean, it was me she cabled. When she left her second husband, it was to come to our house. When she decided to live single, we started to have longer and more frequent phone conversations. Being equally adults together doesn't require being equal the way more or less same-age friends are. She didn't have the sense of me-in-my-context that they did, and I didn't have that sense of her. I don't have her resilience or sweetness, and no amount of contact will get them for me. I don't think I've ever read anything theoretical about achieving intergenerational equality, but it's high time to start talking about it.

Our reunion in turn prepared the way toward a series of interrelated liberations. Not all at once but over time I definitely stopped confusing my mother with the "psychic" mother of childhood—when Mother is all-powerful and child is all-dependent—although I could still gratefully recognize her as the woman who had nurtured little Margaret decades before. I got past the need-for-total-separation stage that psychoanalytic theorist Jessica Benjamin describes as "Mother does not need me, she is perfect; I will become perfect; cease to need her."[1] After age two-to-three, the phase of first separation, this is "the second individuation," the phase beginning in adolescence that supposedly makes a person—even a woman bonded to her mother—a separate adult. That lucidity enabled me to see "Mommy" as "Betty Morgan-roth." Because I listened better, she etched herself into my consciousness as the social and economic actor I have described—a self in her own right. This is an important cognitive and emotional development for any adult child. I had to learn not just that I was "different" from her (that, in adolescent arro-gance, I had already believed). I had to accept that *she* was different from me, an independent subject with her own unique age identity. Until I let my mother go free, I couldn't have conceived of the topic "My Mother at Midlife." (It's still a mother as seen by a daughter—the typical youth perspective—but the mother is the heroine.)[2]

Without that understanding of her, I might not have been able to regard "the middle years," as I began to do a few years later, with the analytic optic I have continued to sharpen. I probably could not have begun breaking free of the culture to define my private midlife. Without having done *that,* I could not have been much help to my husband as he negotiated the male gauntlet of "entry" into the middle years. I certainly could not have let our son go free with the same security that I would survive it, go on loving him, and see him becoming an adult equal in his turn. The ability to distinguish between the culture's age ideology and my own experience and my husband's made all my current age work possible. Perhaps most of all, I would never have been able to grasp for the concept of "being equally adults together."

Fifty Ways to Lose Your Midlife Mother

Women who have found their own ways to become equally adults beside their mothers may agree with me: in normal circumstances it is not an impos-sible life-course task, but getting it understood as a valuable one certainly seems daunting. It isn't set as a goal. Until recently, Benjamin says, psycho-analysis did not envision "the overcoming of narcissism, the possibility of recognition and mutuality occurring in the dyad."[3] In many cases, daughters may not befriend their mothers again for years. A number of my acquain-tances report it can take a decade—the lost decade. Sometimes a daughter does not look carefully in her mother's direction again until the poor woman is sick or weak enough so that even an eye blinded by infant imagos, child-hood injuries, or adolescent and young-adult disappointments has to see how unequal the contest has become. The mother seems to have been "old" for-ever. (And then there are daughters who care for their ailing mothers even though they could justify not doing so.) Sometimes the mother has to die before the daughter learns to regret the lost years.

Much of this is unnecessary, wasteful. The mother has lost forgiveness and love that might have sweetened life in ageist America. And the daughter has missed everything I was granted.[4] At the least, she has foregone the years when the two of them might have been most equal. Failing to observe her mother closely at midlife, she misses understanding one other same-gendered midlife both intimately and with detachment before she gets there herself. She has passed up advantages that she could transform into weapons when it is her turn to deal with being aged by culture.

Why don't women look harder at these tremendous losses? We would take them more seriously if we looked at them first personally, even self-servingly, as precious benefits that can't be recovered later on. It is a grave problem for our culture as well that women, and men too, so often are forced to deal with the dependency of one or both parents, probably the surviving mother, without having gone through a period of seeing her at least as a midlife center of self, if not a friend.[5]

And we have yet more to lose if we in our turn have children who are adult or nearly adult. Being equally adult together with them may be one of our secret dreams. It was certainly one of my cherished goals as our son tore his way through adolescence. We and our friends felt that we were egalitarian child-rearers: we treated our children fairly, speaking to them as little persons with centers of self as soon as they could understand speech. Many parents in our age class worked to the same antihierarchical ends. And I hope we all reap the reward—we don't lose those ten good years. Nevertheless, as we become "middle-aged" in the eyes of our children, we risk losing out again if *they* reenact acculturated estrangement from us. We could have been "ideal" parents (if there were such a thing) and still lose their love in *our* middle years. My own history with my good mother can make clear that this happens.

The loss of those years in my case is puzzling. It can't possibly be blamed on—dire word—*matrophobia,* the catchall term that muddles together factors I want to disaggregate.[6] If ever there was a tight mother-daughter bond that became only more solid at a crucial moment in adolescence, it was mine with my mother. If ever a mother gave a good example of a working woman's independence, that was my mother. Nor could I complain, in the Gen-X way, that my mother sacrificed her children to her "career."[7] No, because she not only manifested but enthusiastically talked up the benefits of her work, I had only positive ways of interpreting women/mothers working. So in my case the loss is not predictable from Chodorovian theories about the allegedly tight mother-daughter bonding effected by a culture of separate spheres in which even when women work, it's women who primarily raise children. The loss is also not predictable from feminist theories that women who joined the movement resented their nonworking mothers for not giving them adequate role models. And, as I've said, I'm pretty sure my mother had given me the two things psychoanalysis thinks of as the prerequisites for adulthood: permitted autonomy *and* secure connection. And still I "lost" her, comparatively, for many years. If that could happen to me—to us—powerful extrapersonal forces must be pressing in from all sides. Men as well as women I have talked to about "the lost decade" agree: They are puzzled that in their twenties and sometimes later they lost mothers they had been close to. I want to speculate about some common barriers erected by the culture. We may find that there is no essential reason why adult children should let them stand.

A person's late teens and twenties in American culture are hideously overburdened. But I now see becoming equally adults together with our parents not as an added task but as a relief, a help dealing with the burdens. Why did it take me all that time, from seventeen to thirty-three? The overall answer is that getting the balance right between autonomy and connection in relation to mothers at that time of life is made to be difficult. One known extrapersonal force is the cultural pressure to overindividuate. Malestream culture forces children to be "father"-identified—to accept authority and hierarchy. The child diminishes her own nurturing side, out of a need to differentiate from "the maternal"—her mother. Given sexist stereotyping, the consequence if she doesn't is to feel infantilized.[8]

Whatever the psychological "need" to differentiate, instrumental economic ends are also served. It just so happens that during the time of the second individuation the adult child also suffers the stress of joining the economy. Young women joining the workforce, like their brothers, fall under "the Law of the Father." Just as I did. People have to be "individuated" for the sake of work relationships under American capitalism—resocialized out of childlike trust and (in democratic families) collectivist habits, into a more isolated wariness, egoistic competititiveness, and acceptance of powerlessness. Sociologist Lynn Chancer looks at how this is effected: how bosses give "approval of an inconsistent nature," how certain workers are asked to position themselves to "look" strong while being submissive, how young workers are first cast into the masochist's role. Joseph Heller's narrator in *Something Happened* explains, "I have lost the power to upset things that I had as a child; I can no longer change my environment or even disturb it seriously. They would simply fire and forget me as soon as I tried."[9] He sees the connections between having formerly experienced parental tenderness, losing power on joining the workplace, and sensing that the life course will be a decline. The system pushes us toward rage and frustration (sometimes dismissed as "infantile"), and then into resignation and passivity, a.k.a. adulthood. The flat tone of Heller's novel expresses the deadening effect on the midlife psyche of having given up anger—and hope—out of "realism."

Did I blame my mother—crazily—for having to toughen up? Neither of my parents could protect me in the sense of mentoring or networking; they didn't have academic connections. On the other hand, my mother had everything: tenure, colleagues, a smooth routine, respect, fulfilling work—everything I didn't have and wasn't sure I'd ever get. I didn't know until now that I envied my mother her midlife acquisitions. However much I griped at senior faculty and employers, I didn't blame *them* for what I was undergoing; much less the system. A lot of psychic work was going on in my twenties and thirties, presumably some of it dirty displacement of this kind. I had useless years, refusing to join the system and feeling like a failure because I wasn't in it. Feeling failed and hardening myself in order to succeed seemed necessary at the time. Some of this training was "accomplished" and some of it never will be. I individuated, and I didn't rely on my mother.

Yet as adult children individuate for whatever muddy combination of psycho-economic ends, some may maintain an ongoing fantasy of maternal protection. (This serves the system, making it more bearable without threatening it with change.) Even when they know rationally that the psychic Mother of childhood cannot protect them, they may hold on to it as a symbol because in a heartless system that seems the only haven. In the crucial years when emerging adults adjust to the workforce and don't yet have a reliable partner, they are caught, able neither to utilize the sweet Mother for real protection nor abandon it. In these circumstances, people offered age equality would be likely to dismiss it as either impossible or, if possible, harmful—a loss. Living in age equality would involve admitting that, whatever their age-related differences in the workforce, parents and adult children are exposed to similar forces. It means moving on to the cross-generational acknowledgment that we are relatively helpless alone and need to be allies together. As beneficial as conscious generational solidarity would be psychologically and politically, it has been almost unthinkable ideologically.

Some adult children face the economic world apparently tough enough for anything—at least, the "Yuppie" represented this, and then the Cyborg. Having abandoned the psychic Mother, they separate from the real one in a self-centered way; having demystified their parents, they lose interest in them as people. They may continue to "love" them, but they don't necessarily move on to see them as individuals, midlife centers of self, potential equals, social and economic and moral actors. They couldn't tell a minibiography, "my mother at midlife," even in fragments like mine. In our culture even a loving adult child of a loving mother has to battle against some combination of permitted fantasy about the Mother and indifference toward the real woman.

To connect with my real particular mother, it turned out, I also needed to become more successful by the standards the economy set. Self-esteem is long in coming in our economic system, if it ever comes. That may be why, as psychologist Dorianne Lebe believes, the years between thirty and forty are "developmentally optimal for the resolution of separation and oedipal issues": that is, reconnection with the mother.[10] Looking back from midlife at our own young-adult years, and simultaneously seeing our own adult children confronting the workplace, many parents can suddenly see young adulthood clearly as a scary developmental/economic phase. Whatever the economic conditions of the era, anxiety is a given at that age. While those now at midlife were living through those years, many of us lacked the economic and psychological theory to understand this. As our adult children enter the workforce, many also believe that their economic future will be leaner and meaner than ours. Shouldn't we wonder whether they are being cast as masochists, feeling unsafe, losing the power to be angry (except at us), hardening into indifference, fading into passivity, and calling it all adulthood? And what theories, if any, are they using to understand their relationship to us?

All this is painfully overdetermined. Yet another force makes it hard for the child's twenties to seem a level playing field on which a young adult and a midlife adult might meet for reasons beneficial to both. This force is the enormous "difference" felt to be made by age. A particularly ugly middle-ageism was spawned in the Fifties and Sixties. An age difference of twenty or more years even in adulthood was already *supposed* to be a "gap" and was treated as a problem for the older person, not the younger. In the Eighties and Nineties, the gap has been widened by the alleged superiorities of youth, constructed through differences of style, class tastes, techno-knowledges, sexual behaviors, even biorhythms. (I dance, my mother doesn't.) The cult of youth is an insidious part of late twentieth-century middle-ageism.

Even when I was young the midlife decline story was expansively vicious. At my worst, in adolescence, I felt scornful; I refused to get on the life course with has-beens like Willy Loman or the mother in *The Glass Menagerie*. I really thought at times that I might well die before I reached twenty-one, which would definitely preclude aging-into-the-midlife. I was partly ashamed of the classist prejudices I was conscious of, but I couldn't undo my ideas about "middle age" because I thought they were "real" attributes. They didn't describe my actual parents very well, but I felt vaguely that *they* and not my parents would determine what my later life could become. There were many contradictions here (and an astonishing kernel of common sense), but I lived the future in dread. Middle-ageism, blown up over the past quarter-century like a Macy's parade balloon, further excuses youthful solipsism even when it drags on into the child's thirties and forties. Middle-ageism combines in strange ways with the fantasy that age equality would be harmful: of course it would, it could only mean declining like your mother. Midlife female decline is probably an idea some young people congratulate themselves on possessing, to prove they've gotten beyond maternal fantasy. If she ages, she's real. If she's superannuated, I'm autonomous.

Any of this enflames the relationship. Who has not been influenced in judging her mother by what "mothers" are supposed to be like? Even at my worst, though, I never said that my mother didn't treat me well. But I've heard about "bad mothering" from daughters and sons all my life: "smothering," self-absorption; withdrawal or neglect (the result of alcoholism or mental illness). I've read charges I've never heard first hand—battering, sexual assault. Bad mothering has become so immense a backdrop, so vast a glowering sky, that "good mothering" scarcely seems possible, not to mention something that a daughter here and there might actually have experienced and want to talk about publicly. Meanwhile, "bad daughtering"/"bad sonning"/"bad childing" is so vacant a concept that words don't exist for it.

Angry adult "daughters" in our age class have extended the definition of bad mothering temporally—it now covers the whole of a woman's child-rearing, at the very least a twenty-year span of life. At one time a mother's failure was limited to the "pre-Oedipal" period, when she might be unable to give the right kind and amount of love to her baby. That naming only sticks when everything is looked at, as usual, from the *child's* point of view. When "the pre-Oedipal mother" is looked at in terms of her *own* development, she is likely to be a young woman partially caught in her own adolescent narcissism, discovering inequalities in her heterosexual partnership, and numbed by the shock of primary responsibility for the precarious new life. As the post-Sixties sexual "revolution" progressed, the mother's inability to explain the next requirements of heterosexuality properly to her pubertal daughter extended bad mothering longer into the mother's life course.

On top of that, since the Seventies bad mothering refers to failures coming later yet in the life course of mother and child, when the now-adolescent daughter sees her now-midlife mother as a parental/social/economic model to be either imitated or avoided. And now there are or seem to be more such mothers to be avoided: they weren't strong enough. Mother-blaming by women probably expands during feminist eras. It starts as a historical by-product of the revolt against sexist conditioning. As Adrienne Rich has said, the mother figure "stands for the victim in ourselves, the unfree woman, the martyr." Women who identify as "the daughters" publicize bad mothering as a way of repudiating maternal complicity and exhorting same-age sisters to be braver. (Publicizing good mothering, as I am doing, can accomplish similar goals.) At first, it's only a writer like Doris Lessing who risks attacking the mother, as in her semiautobiographical series of novels about Martha Quest.[11] But as time passes larger cohorts who have absorbed feminism reach midlife. They don't need to have read novels or feminist theory to look back beyond the encounter with work, to revise past family scenes of conflict or silence.

Perhaps the mother didn't stand up to the father in those years when the social, economic, or educational decisions to be made for the daughter would determine what she would be able to become. Perhaps the mother favored giving benefits to a son, or assumed the daughter's life would inevitably be like her own. As I knew, daughters depend on their mothers during the mothers' middle years.

Later they view them *then* as middle-aged women passing on subordination. The mother is seen not as she saw herself or as she sees herself now, but from outside, by a daughter who may currently possess much greater midlife power. In this retrospect, her mother's inferior place in the family power structure now seems ignominious, her own early girlish vulnerability more pathetic. Now she sees this: in a family where the mother didn't earn money or didn't control it, a woman could be forty years old and of no account. At the same time, the adult daughter can imagine a better outcome: her mother could have argued and made a scene, so that even if the two women lost, they would have been on the same side; the daughter would have heard her needs defended.

Age autobiography would ask us to separate out of any bad history the share that is *not* the mother's. To think again of young adulthood—economic helplessness, psychic fantasies of being protected from the harsh world of work; soul-deadening, everyday solipsism, scapegoating; internalized classist/middle-ageist indifference or scorn; generalizations about "mothers" or one's own mother based on the worst cases. Later, in midlife, enraged reinterpretation of the past on behalf of the past youthful self. In short, in our "memories," the private and the social have been inextricably mixed up, confusing judgment, muddying the issues for decades. The least of these confusions could interpose formidable barriers between an actual woman and her actual mother and contribute to the pitiless personal outcome of the lost decade.

Literary daughters—some themselves no longer young—have rendered the verdict. They have chosen to represent dangerous mothers, in fiction, nonfiction, magazine articles and full-length books, in pulp and high pop and in now-classic bildungsromane. Our contemporary portrait gallery of midlife women has huge blanks, another form of bias. What is hard to find at full length are leading characters like the Mama in Alice Walker's much anthologized story "Everyday Use" (1973)—a first-person narrator who is the moral center of the tale. And even she only defends one daughter against the other. There are some strong midlife mothers in major contemporary novels, and some of them have daughters. But their strength does not operate especially on behalf of their daughters. In the spectrum, some are detached (Nadine Gordimer's in *None to Accompany Me,* Anne Tyler's in *Breathing Lessons*); others need the daughter's help more than the daughter needs theirs (Paule Marshall's in *Praisesong for the Widow*); some need to break free from guilt over what they did to the daughter (Toni Morrison's in *Beloved*). Larry McMurtry's *Terms of Endearment,* book and movie, was a hit because its sentimentality drew on some latent longings on both sides of the age gap for this reconciliation put so far out of reach by "experience" and culture. Do so many women really feel either that they would have to die to get their midlife mother's protective attention, or that if they were dying she alone would be there for them? Or both?

Frankly, speaking now as a mother who is living intensely through her middle years, I don't believe I deserve to be fantasized, ignored, or scorned—by young feminists, by women writers, or by the culture. If the system required our son to blame his parents instead of its power, I would want him to let us help him confront the system. I don't want to be aged up prematurely by art. Let my life-retold end at some other less arbitrary, brief, and incidental point than death. Let me be remembered in vigorous midlife, shaking a fist at a devil. For the sake of all midlife women, in the past, now and in the future, let's write more about the Betty Morganroths, the mother-as-her-daughter's defender and friend. Let's write about the mothers, including me and mine, who marched on Washington in 1989 to save fertile young women from back-alley abortions. And about the Russian mothers who went into Chechnya in 1995 to rescue their sons from the cursed stupidities of state power. This is the Nineties, thirty years into a widespread feminist revolution. There must be many vigorous women who have raised children and wielded their share of interpersonal, economic, social, and moral power decently. My mother shows they always existed. Now, for sure, they are no longer rare. Is there a good reason why fiction cannot sometimes portray midlife women who have realistic amounts of power and whose relationship with their adult children is benign? When will we start explaining to our children, in good time, how their first adult encounter with the ideology may reduce them to rage, passivity, matrophobia, and middle-ageism, and in the process delay or destroy the foundation-building of our adult friendship? When will they join us in explaining all this from their own experience? And when will fiction and nonfiction show this friendship coming into being?

Justice across the Generations

Even if your mother damaged you, that may not need to be the final story you tell about her and you. Everyone who has read *A Woman Warrior* knows how the mother serves as a primary teacher of female insignificance. It was her mother who told the narrator the exemplary story of the "No Name Woman" who was forced to give birth in a pigsty and drown herself and her illegitimate baby in the well. Speaking as an older woman, the narrator tells us about the long-term harm that the sexist system did her: her whispery voice, her timidity, her long struggle to prove herself. When I met Maxine Hong Kingston (in 1990), we talked a little about the girl-belittling forces of her childhood, and then I asked, "But where did your strength come from?" Because clearly there had been strength. Hong Kingston does not now have a whispery voice, and she looks straight at her interlocutor in a calm, interested way. "No one has ever asked me that," she said, and then went on without hesitation, as if the answer were obvious, "It was my mother, and her talk-stories."

Several unexpected conclusions can be drawn from this conversation. The first is that even a well-indoctrinated, docile mother who is cruel to her daughter may transmit an important, potentially liberating power. This conclusion could in fact have been drawn from the novel by a reader motivated to look for it. Critic Leslie Rabine saw it: "In repeatedly enjoining her daughter from telling this story . . . is the mother not also seeking her own release from silence and giving Maxine the means and material to break the injunction?"—including a sense that the mother takes pleasure in telling it secretly.[12] But the mother's rebellious pleasures and the daughter's later-life ability to learn is not what Hong Kingston chose to dramatize in *A Woman Warrior*. She had an angrier, more heroic, and more dramatic story of bad mothering to tell—the right story for 1976 and the right story for any woman who is desperately struggling to survive what she feels is mother-transmitted self-depreciation. It's the story about how hard your obstacles are and how tough you need to be to survive.

But let me suggest other ways in which an injured daughter might come at midlife to retell her relationship with her mother. For the sake of justice. If I had had a father who injured me and a mother who had not protested, I too might still be magnifying bad mothering and using my mother as an example of female cowardice. But perhaps not—perhaps eventually I would have had the sense of justice to indict the father who actually held the power. Incest survivor Rose Stone acknowledges poignantly, "I realize how much more difficult it is for me to forgive my mother than some of the other people (men) whose sexual mistreatment of me was far more unambiguous."[13] Mother-blaming would be lessened throughout the culture if daughters recognized that in midlife some men try, in different ways, to reach for patriarchal powers.

Maybe when she knows she is no longer only a victim, unfree, a martyr, a midlife daughter can also separate her mother part way from whatever harm her mother did, as Jill Ker Conway does in *The Road from Coorain*. She distinguishes between the mother of her childhood, from whom she got some of her grit, and the mother of her college years, a lost widow. Ker Conway understands that no woman's life is of a piece. Finally, feminist age studies also explains that there is a system looming over your mother and standing behind your father: the impersonal enemy, the historical system that produced both.

The more history we learn, the more deeply we understand that beneath that system's sway many of our mothers were worse off in midlife then than we are now. Among my same-age friends, I don't know any—no matter how hard their lives—who would change midlives with their mothers. It makes an enormous difference—*or could*—that so many more of us have incomes and independence now at midlife. The expression "the prime of life" is not for women so great a mockery as it used to be. Individually, the most assured and independent midlife women were weaker in the past because they had fewer collective tools for resistance, and the system was stronger because it had fewer female warriors against it. And whatever hatred toward our mothers was righteous and survival-oriented and self-fashioning when we are twenty, it cannot be right to go on hating them because they had the misfortune to be forty or forty-five, *when we happened to need them most*, in a bad time. A woman who is a mother may rise heroically above her circumstances. But no magic operates here. The outer limits of freedom, when looked at retrospectively, turn out to be strict. Can any woman be better than the best of her time? How much better than her time can we fairly expect her to be? How much better am I? Or you?

Justice requires that daughters (whether twenty years old or sixty) mind their mothers' midlives, mining them for their constraints and for the undiscovered ore of good example; revising them as the story the mother would tell if she could tell it completely. Not only historicized justice, but generosity too demands it. As I want done to me by those younger I will try to do by others who are older. And progress requires that our daughters and our sons make these discoveries younger than we did, while they are still young enough to use the precedents in raising their own children and in getting along with us. For all these reasons at this time in our culture there need to be representations of midlife paladins. And we women currently living through our middle years need to act as if we were merely disguised in the garb of ordinary womanhood, while simultaneously armored to draw sword and change the world.

Part Three

Men: All Together Now?

8

The New Gender Politics of Midlife Bodies

OVER AT LEAST the past decade, the experience of aging into the middle years has been changing, for men and for women, in separate, dramatic, unprecedented ways. For their part, many men have begun to worry more obviously and anxiously about aging. The signs of this are all around, but I began to hear this news in most detail and with most poignancy from women. As a student of the history of the middle years, I feel men should be warned that they are in danger of falling into the same cultural traps laid for "aging women."[1]

At all ages, the male "body" (like the female) experiences itself through the mesh of culture. What a midlife man sees in the mirror, like what a woman sees, has long been overlaid by youthist comparisons—images from movies, current magazines, old photos of himself, chance personal remarks he's overheard—associations so dangerous that men too may look away. Even while making love, which seems so private, what we do and say has been influenced by advice (maybe even manuals), yet more images, borrowed fantasies—by culturally shared ways of living in a body of a particular age and gender and sexual orientation. Ways of interpreting living in a body are not eternally fixed; as we age they are changed; history can startle us.[2] At the end of the twentieth century we find ourselves entering a new cultural situation. Where the body intersects the middle years, traditional norms are being crossed, stereotypes of midlife aging are sliding around with alarming looseness. As the changes in midlife men's relations to their bodies become more visible, within heterosexual life (my subject here), midlife women have a new perception of men to assimilate and a choice to make, of how to respond. At the same time, men have to respond to women's new attitudes and behavior, and so on, interactively, without forseeable end.

In this transition period, there is bound to be confusion—possibly wrenching but potentially liberating confusion. I discern one distinct trend: coming from very different levels of age privilege, women and men are converging in their middle years. Different groups and individuals are moving at different rates; as with all social developments, this one is uneven. But powerful forces are moving middle-ageism toward being a unisex problem. For good or ill, for however long it lasts . . . we're all together now in a new era of sex, age, and gender politics.

"My brother went to the hospital to have his love-handles removed. Well, he wanted to get it over with, so he didn't tell them he had a cold, and he wound up spending a week in there with pneumonia. And what did he do it for anyway? He's been married for years; he's only just turned fifty."

"He's thirty-eight years old, and he's suddenly started wearing his high-school class ring. He's starting to babble about his girlfriends from the Sixties."

"When he had his forty-fifth birthday, he decided he couldn't coach the basketball team anymore and he was giving up basketball for good. 'Why don't you start pickup games with people your own age?' I said to him. But no, if he can't play like a teenager, he can't play. Since then he's let himself go, he must have gained fifteen pounds."

"He comes in from tennis and he's beet-red, puffing, winded, bent over—looks like death. 'Don't you guys ever take a break? Whaddya trying to do, kill each other?' Is this for *health*?"

"He was interviewed by the newspaper—big spread about all his theatre work for the last ten years—and he lied about his age. He took off five years. Why, I don't know *women* who do that any more."

Women I know are worrying aloud about their same-age husbands and lovers and brother and friends. Since midlife aging is a concept an individual applies to himself, applying it personally depends less on birthdates than on a person's state of mind. As women interpret the signs, these men are in a bad state, giving up, acting out, succumbing to the cult of youth. No doubt these women are not telling me all they know about the feelings of these men. Men in their middle years should tell their own diverse stories; I would like them to consider *Declining to Decline* an invitation to do so. Women like me do not want to speak for the Other as men used speak for women during the ages of resentment. Behind the women's readings lies sorrowful speech: hints of misery in half sentences, "humorous" confessions, bedtime conversations in the dark. They come in murmurs because many men also conceal their fears of midlife aging. And perhaps these women erupted to me because codes of silence make it harder to speak plainly to their loved ones. As they and I break the code, men may react angrily.

In the funny pages, though, Garry Trudeau goes public with the subject.

Rick Redfern turning forty uses products supposed to prevent wrinkles, retain hair, prolong life; other midlife male characters in the strip are given stereotypical fantasies of seducing younger women. Rick's wife is advised to "lie"— presumably, about his changed looks. During the Eighties, cartoons joined many other genres in spotting and supporting the trend toward jocular self-deprecation and jokey self-pity. Like flypaper, they fixed the language and the ideology that still circulate elsewhere.

Ed Koren produces an image of a man floored at a cookout (p. 142). Whatever went wrong is due to age—or in some unspecified way, his reaction to age. The cartoon, mildly satirizing the label "midlife," nonetheless leaves it intact, reiterates and authorizes the associations with crisis. At least as far as the man is concerned. Like Rick's wife, the woman who speaks is presented as unaffected; in Koren she's not only unmoved but blithe, not to say gleeful. It's all done in light pencil, but these cartoonists fix a new gender binary: men as decked, women as immune. Like me, they want to point out some changes they've noticed—some changes they assume everyone has noticed. But they want to show them as a *total reversal* of cultural norms, men and women simply changing places. The actual, more complex situation doesn't fit into the cartoon weltanschauung: that some men now *share* the condition that women have been forced to live, that we have this intimate problem in common, that the genders are not once again opposed but in some freaky new way overlapping.

It's man against man, however, in Koren's Sunday in the Park, a dutiful herd jogging scene.[3] The runners are almost entirely male. In the foreground are two men. The one in jogging gear looks trim, "healthy." The male-male

"Well, there's mid-life."

binary pits the Jogger against an isolated figure: the thicker, padded, hirsute, bespectacled Pipe-smoker with a book under his arm, the intellectual zhlub. The caption reads, "I'm in various stages of deterioration." At first I assumed that the speaker had to be the Pipe-smoker, but age studies led me to intuit that it's just as likely to be the Jogger. Which one does the man reading the magazine identify with? (I know a few who ask: Are there really only and always two sides?)

One level of pop imagery, like some fiction, keeps implicitly proposing that midlife aging is a "problem" for men but that it's superficial, low-serious—a joke.[4] But the women involved know that whatever the problem, it isn't comical. They find themselves talking in unexpected ways about the bodies and intimate states of mind of men their own age. In some cases they're worried about depression; in some, they've hinted at the man's fears of work competitors—unknown others, younger men who do the same work. On the other hand, none assumes the situation will go on forever. They wouldn't want to call it "self-delusion," label it a "midlife crisis," say he's "high in denial" or (without other issues) urge the guy into therapy.

Women who are feminists, after all, recognize middle-ageism (even before they know the name) as a cultural problem that spares no woman. And they have practice fighting against the culture. Some respond with love and reassurance. The immediate way to fight is to go on admiring our loved ones and letting them know we do. This doesn't mean lying, but it does require us to reject unceasing pressure to continue using anachronistic youth standards for judging bodies and faces. It involves working our way into an appreciation of male midlife bodies and forms of beauty—or, falling short of that, disregarding features that we cannot succeed in finding attractive. "After all" (I imagine some women conveying), "I didn't marry you for your hair (waist, profile)." Or they convey instead, "Great legs! Great back! Great buns!" "Let me count the ways." But there are different ways to count. Some women really do want him to want to fit into the size 34 bikini underpants.

I hear in the voices of my friends, aside from concern and support, some anger and puzzlement and pity. Privately, they're irritated that men they know and influence can't deal with it better. They're mystified that the men are hit so hard. And they're astonished to be powerful enough to pity men. (Pity has a component of tenderness, but it also has a component of the condescension of power.) "Men! *They do age.*" Of course women know that women are scarcely exempt from worrying about decline, but they once thought that men would be. Men benefited sensationally from the "double standard of aging," as Susan Sontag described it in the early Seventies. She began her essay with a long explanation of the symbolic—and she believed widespread—phenomenon of *women* lying about their age.[5] Many women would swear the situation remains unchanged: at midlife, men can still take advantage of accrued male superiority, and women still learn to internalize female deficiency. But, if now some midlife men lie about their age it suggests that the supports for the double standard have been weakening. Over the last twenty years, many men in midlife are having the same problems women have, caught in the head-trap of having to figure out how to "stay young." Stay young or, in the prevailing binary, feel they've "given up" and "lost out" in a race that has tremendously high stakes. Beyond Central Park, in the culture at large, both the Pipe-smoker and the Jogger are caught in the trap.

For the historically minded who do age theory, the new situation marks the decline of a piece of male privilege that once seemed eternal. Even those who know how much the appearance of "the natural" depends on culture may find these particular changes in age/gender relations baffling. "What's happening?" a historian asked me. "It used to be that men didn't age: *they* just got 'distinguished' while women got 'dumpy.' It used to be that only women got called 'vain.' Now the opposite seems true. Is it just aerobics?"

It's a complex story. Several things have happened more or less simultaneously. The way many women *see* men is changing. Men see themselves differently. And the system that sells products based on fears of aging has turned its giant voracious maw toward that next great big juicy market, men. Theorist Roe Sybylla argues, "Although it will exploit sexual differences, capitalism is not primarily concerned with the biological sex of the body it utilizes." Historian Lawrence Birken describes ours as the era of the genderless consumer.[6] Age, not gender, is identifying the system's next market.

A market too is made, not born. A male body learns when young to take on the signs of male power through "mental body-images and fantasies . . . muscle tensions, posture, the feel and texture of the body." "My male body does not confer masculinity on me; it receives masculinity (or some fragment thereof) as its social definition," writes theorist R. W. Connell.[7] But age is crucial: later the male self can thus be taught that masculinity recedes. If they can get you to "feel your age"—to feel over-the-hill and wistful about youth because you think youth equals true masculinity—you are theirs.

There's profit in making midlife men anxious. "Boomers will grow increasingly affluent as they reach their peak earning years around age fifty," is the refrain, flattering only to that percentage in the middle-class, mostly white, male, and college educated, whose incomes are still rising as they approach fifty. The heading on one article in "the magazine of consumer change" reads, "Looking and feeling good will be a priority for aging baby boomers."[8] The age class being targeted is even vaster: potentially it includes older men as well as those born since the end of the boom who although chronologically young are aging into the American cultural situation at this time. Thus my son and his friends, now in their twenties, are at risk. The members of this vast group are all being battered with signs that they need or will need "help against aging." The market reasons the need. Competitive anxiety makes the most minute marginal advantage seem, first, "interesting," then no longer minute, then "desirable," "necessary" and finally, "indispensable." Middle-ageism includes noticing and disliking signs of age in one's peers, let alone the old. The fetishism of small differences, self-hatred, aversion—it's a potent interactive mixture.

Men show they are becoming increasingly vulnerable to the commercial packaging of youth. All across the country they're buying hair dye. They're self-conscious about balding and willing to buy remedies to grow thicker hair. (In *Iron John* Bly pushed good hair to holy prominence.)[9] Sy Sperling, the hair-insertion promotor, does over 10,000 male heads a year in a rapidly growing field. Designers are marketing perfumes and cosmetics for men; salons are doing facials. Men are buying exercycles, rowing machines, expensive athletic shoes, home gyms. Men are spending more than women on what are called "beauty aids" when women buy them. They're getting fashion-conscious. Fine, maybe; fun, maybe. But there's a change. Cultural critics who have been worrying about female consumption of youth products and practices would do well not to glide over this male trend. In one two-generational study, men of fifty are almost as self-conscious about being overweight and far from their ideal body as are midlife women and young women; more young men feel relatively closer to their ideal body form, but a full third of them feel they are overweight and diet. Midlife men's sweatsuits are often the same as those of the toned-up young. As with women, sharing youth's exhibitionistic clothing ups the ante, teaching everyone age-related difference. Another study, by Todd Heatherton, shows that ten years after graduation from an elite college, men's anxiety about their weight has gone up. "Males' distorted body imagery is as profound and obsessive as that of females," says David B. Gilmore, a researcher who interviewed men between thirty and fifty.[10] Thirty seems to be the age at which men may begin to internalize a falling off from their peak.

Men are the fastest growing market for plastic surgeries—dermabrasions to create smoother and younger skin, "coronal lifts" on the forehead to erase lines ("that make a man look angry or tired," said one publicist to me); alterations on noses, ears, chins, bellies, eyelids; total face-lifts. Men make up somewhere between 16 percent and 25 percent of the market.[11] "Love-handles" means extra flesh at the waist; excising it is part of the "body-sculpting" movement. The newest craze on the West Coast is silicone implants for calves and chests. Surgeons don't care whether that body part is male or female. Men are being taught to shop and chop their way to oblivion. "Men are proving a lucrative market for surgeons," according to a *Boston Globe* article on "The Male Makeover." One surgeon said, "Women must have reinforcement to give themselves permission to spend the money. But men always feel they deserve it."[12]

The next steps? Based on what we know of the ways women have been manipulated, we can fairly safely anticipate the moves to be made on men. To sell the concept of rejuvenation, the system needs to raise men's anxiety to unheard-of levels. On the way to the higher levels of stress, aging at midlife— shorn of its accompaniments of poise, sexual pleasure, accomplishment, wisdom, and the like—is reduced to a state of subtractions, compounded of many and varied losses, with an emphasis on the visible, physical ones. The marketeers and their media shills will smooth over the difference between fashion consumption that is considered "normal" and the products they're in the process of normalizing. One way they teach women not to refuse face-lifts is to say it's no different from lipstick. Age ideology will teach men to want to transform their body to match the way they feel "inside." "I want to look as young as I feel"—a standard line—creates an interior self that doesn't mature, at odds with a body defined as aging and disagreeable. (Maturity doesn't exist anywhere, in this scheme.) They'll tell men that a jowl-nip is just the next thing to buy after your exercycle, your new briefcase, your thousand-dollar suit; that knowing more about your field is no substitute for looking young; that "everyone" is doing it. The media no longer can be counted upon to protect midlife men: some recent magazine articles about implant surgery for men voice an antique gung-ho spirit. (There are more articles about women's surgeries, but by contrast they almost all contain warnings.)[13] "He's so vain," one newspaper title fluted, constructing male vanity while mocking and soothing it through the allusion to Carly Simon's hit.[14]

These approaches work. One man said that "his wife's appearance motivated him to have a face-lift, as he did not want his wife 'to look much younger.'" Because double-standard language lingers, reminding men that they can't afford to sound as if they care how they look, "some men may deliberately misrepresent [their concern for appearance] . . . complaining that they 'can't breathe' to cover up their wishes for a better-looking nose."[15] The ads also target the older man afraid of downgrading or unemployment, who badly wants to look as if he's able to make it; they hold out the promise of maintaining middle-class status.

If men behave the way women have done, the most vulnerable in terms of practices will be in the higher income brackets, where not only are the codes of perfection strict, the competition keen, the fear of failing great, the marginal advantages of "youthfulness" high, but also the money is available for expensive procedures, from workouts with massage to spas and surgery. Like women, midlife men want to "take control" of aging. But lower-income men, like lower-income women, may wind up psychologically worse off, with new desires for cultural goods, and age anxieties they can't allay in any of the fashionable ways.

In a story of midlife helplessness, the climacteric will loom much larger. They'll teach men that *their* aging too results from a hormone-deficiency disease and that it can be cured by buying chemicals or implants. Prostate cancer—mainly a slow-growing disease of old age—is presented as if it were the next thing that happens after your fiftieth birthday.[16] Already men with hot flashes and "dysfunction" are being given testosterone injections; the pattern is to make the use broader and more frequent. A pharmaceutical company is researching a daily under-the-tongue testosterone-replacement product.[17] According to researcher John McKinlay, over sixty clinical trials are underway for a wide array of products—drugs, prostheses—targeted for the next market.[18] What man has not heard about the eight-hour erection? Already there have been scandals because scientists have been promoting for rejuvenation purposes unapproved products like Retin A and collagen after having received grants from the pharmaceutical companies that produce them.[19]

The system will teach men that "midlife crisis," which has been viewable as an interesting self-reorientation available to some especially perceptive and future-looking individuals, is somehow both pathological and universal, linked to self-loathing and sexual "dysfunction." (Here sex therapists, writers of self-help guides, and publishers add themselves to the commercial enforcers). Victims of the crisis are meant to age "badly, increasingly obsessed with penile tumescence, increasingly estranged from any other life, from any other flesh," in the words of ethicist John Stoltenberg.[20] They're meant to feel emotionally helpless without the practices and products being promoted. Films still offer the solution of seeking (and sometimes marrying) young female flesh, the solution-by-sympathetic-magic. This narrative often involves disprizing, if not abandoning, same-age women. In solemn psychological tones, it constructs a hero tormented by his behavior—guilty, but somehow helpless to do otherwise. Theorists do no good by attacking these feelings without explaining how they get constructed.

The long decline in real wages over the course of the Eighties (affecting 90 percent of Americans in some way), and the Nineties recession, unemployment, and job insecurity, have softened up the market. People in the middle class as well as the working class have been hit—by downsizing, deindustrialization, the expansion of the "contingent" workforce, reduced value of pensions, the flight of jobs and capital abroad. Those who might have relied on their economic security or professional achievements or seniority to maintain their age identity have been weakened in their work lives—this core area in which they had been comparatively strong. Forced to expect less satisfaction from the job sphere, they back into private life looking for affective compensations—again, just as women did for so long. In that ever more crucial encounter, women are both the prize of achievement and the judges of failure. And it is precisely there in the world of love and sexuality that the system exacerbates their "problem," offers men an explanation and a solution: "aging" and its alleged antidotes. Little in mainstream discourse now warns men and women that national economic weakness raises their stress levels, makes them feel old, and raises their mortality.[21] Instead, all of us are encouraged to believe that our problem, although natural, inevitable, and awful, is controllable. We're supposed to concentrate on the private sector of body control.

It will be fascinating as well as horrifying to watch how the system uses all men's vulnerabilities to get them to accept all this. When looking in the mirror, they have to be brought to see themselves as older-than-young and thereby deficient. In another Koren illustration a man does just that, fingering

"In the last few months, Matthew has gone on twenty-four-hour alert for signs of aging."

his under-eye area. Again, this cartoon places women as spectators of male distress and commentators on it, exempt. One continuous form of preparation for the Mirror Scene is effected by ads—all those unsmiling young men in the national glossies, selling their young kissers as the only true allure. That niche market is alleged to be very fashion conscious, having achieved "equality with women" in this realm. Generation X "is teaching the baby-boom generation new tricks." The sly old dogs can learn! And this is the way they prove it. No doubt we can expect a blockbuster book for men called *Masculine Forever* that makes men's sexual problems more public and humiliating and trumpets a medical magic bullet for male aging.[22]

For a long time I didn't even know there was a commerce in male aging. And if I had been told, I might have denied it or said it was trivial, because for a long time—and not alone—I believed that men manage capitalism to their own advantage. But eventually we may look back and ask, "How come they didn't move sooner? The market was just sitting there, aging quietly, privately, and (relatively speaking) happily."

I, of course—speaking for a second as that supposedly essential figure, "a woman"—had nothing to do with all this. I try to dissuade women from getting anxious about aging, so I'm not about to encourage men to follow suit. I've never sold a man an "antiaging" product either directly or indirectly, either by innuendo, deprecation, or by admiring other men. I have been married for decades to a man my age, and he reciprocates: he doesn't produce my "aging" for me either. In many ways we share my project, which he thinks of as emancipatory. The worst I could be charged with as the years have passed is urging him on the rare occasions when he needs something new toward sexier and handsomer clothes. In general men's clothes are becoming more visually interesting, textured, patterned, colorful. Men can wear velour, chenille, silk; soft sweaters, more lavish scarves, larger coats with more swing to them. Inside these clothes they can disport a more expressive body. Feminist and queer theory and one part of youth culture can take some credit for this, insofar as they support crossing gendered boundaries. But my own kind of antiageism advocates that men as well as women—including younger people—think critically about "androgyny". Age, not gender, will be the crucial variable. Fashion practices, as chapter 10 shows, accelerate the life course. Men too need to try to distinguish between forces permitting them new pleasures and forces coercing them into new anguish and new expenditures, while labeling them pleasures.

I discovered that I didn't see men's bodies the way I was supposed to when I went to my twenty-fifth college reunion, that institution for cohort-gazing and cohort-comparisons. I noticed that the women looked better than the men—and I was surprised to notice it. It wasn't that many were stooped, waistless, jowly, or inappropriately "youthful." It was also the way some talked. "They bore themselves," one woman said sagely; "they're tired of being them. We're not." I tried to move beyond my first impression, a combination of shock and—I dare say—some relief. I was not displeased, at first, to notice that I noticed that men aged. But I soon came to other more firmly held and politically useful feelings, to which I'll return. Of course there are also men in my cohort who can transfix the eye. Some men look their very best in their middle years (unless they go on improving, of course): they've filled out the hollow chests and thin arms they had at twenty. I like the silky skin under their eyes, their laugh-lines, and the way some look at me now when I'm talking, no longer mesmerized by something in my face I never could see. Now they're seeing *me*, the once invisible me behind the young-female flesh. Others are well-kept shrines to boyhood. The joggers looked drawn. The unmarried didn't look as if they felt self-confident and lucky; they looked dispirited. There was a lot of joshing about age.

There was more pleasure to be got from the women. This too was a surprise, proving to my dismay that I had retained some of the poisonous expectation that women decline by midlife. (I hadn't yet taught that Radcliffe seminar on "Midlife Heroines.") The women were larger and more lined than twenty-five years ago but they looked womanly, and some were beautiful. In all, what mattered to me was their expressiveness. They didn't hide sorrow—we have always had remarkably intimate reunions. But they broadcast vitality; there was so much individuality to be deciphered. "We've grown into our faces," said Connie Wilson Higginson, a friend of three decades, "we've earned them." Our college favored a low-maintenance "natural" style, which became a habit for most of us sooner or later, and which serves most women at any age very well. Many women swim, jog, or dance—they've discovered their bodies as sources of pleasure and pride in midlife, and they are trying to stay on the safe side of that line I mentioned, away from commercial coercion calling itself pleasure. In Margaret Drabble's novel *The Radiant Way*, the heroine dressing for a party opens her makeup kit to "put on her face" (as people used to say) and then closes it. When I came back from that reunion I started to see the new spirit elsewhere: knowing you look fine *as is*. The relatively unretouched face and body tell a new story about being female in the middle years. A lot of the old formulas about women's aging demand revision. "A woman of about fifty strikes us as a youthful, even unformed individual, whom we expect to make powerful use of the possibilities for development opened up for her. . . . A man of the same age, sadly, often frightens us by his physical rigidity and unchangeability. . . . There seem to be no paths open to future development." This is the way Freud could rewrite "Femininity" if he were writing it today and had replaced ageist misogyny with ageist female-chauvinism.[23]

The future depends on men too recognizing that they are subject to culture. Until recently, midlife men have not thought of themselves as a gendered and aged category. Although that is usually spoken of as a piece of their privilege, in many contexts it marks their lack: it makes each man an isolated individual, vulnerable to commercial manipulation, unable to resist. The popular men's movement is fueled at least in part by unhappiness about aging: Bly's *Iron John* tells a historical narrative whose outcome is that "the father-table, the groundwater" and "the salt" of life, "get no respect" from their sons.[24] But Bly doesn't recognize how contemporary constructions of aging and generational difference may contribute. Although many men of mature years are leaders in critical theory and dominate feminist men's studies, age is rarely theorized as a historical product there either. Meanwhile, women who wanted resistance to the youth cult and to the denigration of the midlife have had feminism. Its antiageism may be inconsistent or perfunctory, but (as the articles warning women against plastic surgery suggest) most of the theoretical resistance and effective rhetorical opposition that makes its way into the mainstream comes from that source.

Among a million other things feminism made possible for me was that I aged past thirty under its friendly gaze. My professional interest in age as a cultural construction thickened the padding I needed to resist the culture's constant age assaults. I take hits (like the movie *Death Becomes Her*, which tried to reinstate the double standard by glorifying Bruce Willis as an aging cosmetic surgeon who'd literally rather die than join women in their female aging frenzy). But after painful experience I've taught myself how to recover. I've said how unhappy I was as a youthful sex object. Another reason I was mad at my gender was because I thought (oh how mistakenly) that boys didn't worry about their body parts. Now at midlife I look to like. A few years ago, I caught myself admiring my feet, my "broad, peasant feet," for the first time. Some of the parts I once disliked—or prided myself on—could now conceivably be viewed as problems, but they simply don't disturb me in the young way. If my appearance now saddens my husband, my friends, or my mother, they haven't been letting me know. I earned my workers' hands and those keen lines around the eyes. I *waited* to get that silver streak that says, "This is a woman whose experience you can trust; listen to her. Pay her well."

Women who see the way I do turn to each other in wonder. "*That men didn't age, while women did*—we made men magical by repeating this preposterous idea over and over."

Another sign of the new era is that it has become much harder to believe that men were "really" at one time more "distinguished" in their middle years than women, or that women "aged" sooner. Was it an age/gender ideology that made everyone see differently then? It has to have been. Discourse about male/female bodies is always (although not only) the surface of the lopsided power struggle. Women were taught to feel older but not to notice men feeling older, and rather than critiquing the difference they were pushed into explaining it. Why did they accept the explanation, "Men don't age as fast"? Compared to women, men have always had more access to money, security, comfort, power, and fame, and they often controlled even more of these good things as they aged. No wonder they continued to look desirable. And from desirable it's a short step to handsome. Understanding the mechanism, Proust once said wryly, "All duchesses are beautiful." I recovered early from a brief participation in American mythmaking about "glamorous" middle-aged men. In my family, all the women but one worked, and some earned more than their husbands. Maybe it was just a coincidence that when I was growing up I never heard anyone glorifying my uncles' midlife attractions and denigrating my aunts'?

Understandably, some wives were complicit in the interactive process that produced their husbands as "younger" than they were. Caroline Cross Chinlund, a friend who is a psychoanalyst, says, "I think Barbara Bush had definitely done this for George. Her accepting the burden of overweight and white hair allowed George to seem/feel by contrast young and possessed of more horizons. Maybe 'good wives' always agree (tacitly/preconsciously) to speak up on behalf of both by making *a contrast between* wherein the man could feel superior.[25] Some women let themselves lapse into the forms of "aging" that are culturally prescribed. But in contrast to Bruce Willis, heroic natural man, they do so in silence, without receiving gratitude. And they experience public shame, because to perform their valuable emotional service, they have to eschew the other cultural imperative for "older" women: looking young. Women are sold the-need-to-buy-youth—and when they dutifully do so can be mocked for visibly trying to simulate youth. Now men may find themselves caught in this mocking viewfinder: it's where Garry Trudeau places Rick. He's been found out in his simulations, and needing to simulate is ipso facto failure.

In the bad old days for women, when few had incomes and almost all were commodities, inevitably women felt intense pressure to package themselves for the male-dominated marriage market. Naturally, distinctions had to be invented to connote marketability. And "youth" was part of what older male buyers were taught to seek. The longing to be marketable still grips many women. But more and more, women in my cohort refuse to identify themselves as either poor or dependent. They've mostly finished raising their children, and if they did that—the hardest part—alone, they're not going to get desperate now. They're sliding or striding into the new age where "What I want" prevails over what the culture made us need, and "What I see" prevails over what the culture wanted us to see. Now *our* eyes judge. (If 65 percent of income equality can achieve this, what's next?) Feminism helped narrow that wage differential, and is responsible for telling women over and over that their eyes judge.

The gender gap remains. Midlife men have not become commodified in the same way women were; they haven't lost their economic edge or the personal power that can be borrowed from the larger context of inequality. But they are losing prerogatives. One of them may be easy access to young women. Educated women in their twenties now are less likely to marry older men out of fear of failing in the economic system; they can make it on their own—and it may be the midlife men who fail. Demography is also against the midlife man who wants to marry a younger woman: the cohort is too small. In general, men's "prospects for marriage are declining. . . . Among men under 45, the remarriage rate has dropped by nearly half, to 58 percent of its 1970 level."[24] Divorced or widowed, independent midlife women I know are not hastening back into matrimony (even though the culture keeps shouting

"Men are scarce" to frighten us). We may want male companionship and am-
orousness and love, but more are refusing to pay the old high wages of female
subservience. If some marry younger men, it's partly because younger men
are likelier to be feminists: likelier to listen, to see a midlife woman as irresistible, to appreciate *Thelma and Louise*. The ads imply that what women like in
men is pecs and baby skin. Let me tell you, it would be more useful for a man
to say he supported human and sexual rights for women than to have silicone
implanted in his chest.

The culture handed men—all men—the double standard of aging. Older
men traded on it: many ignored same-age women, called us ugly, told jokes
about our alleged frigidity, left the Peter Arno cartoons lying around, foisted
on us those stereotypes we're still trying to lift off. Husbands out walking with
their wives may shop younger women, point out their appetizing characteristics, imply unflattering contrasts. At parties, flirting, some flaunt their potential mobility. They can flash superiority through pornography, trophy brides,
and sex practices that enhance their sense of dominance. Cultural power
makes them mean.

Female independence across the life course teaches men a whole lot faster
than argumentation or fashion photos of gorgeous fifty-year-olds that same-
age women can be desirable. Women aren't automatically knocking women
any more, or knocking them over on the way to the nearest man. Unless they
love the man and he's good to them, they don't have to overlook male paunch-
iness and rename gray hair "distinguished" when it appears on male heads. If
now we decide that life's lines and silver streaks have beauty and "character,"
it may be because they look good on women we like. And *we* will decide, out
of a better use of midlife power than men have made, whether it's only fair to
like on the second sex what we like on our own.

Men may read this and say, "Double whammy." And then, as the bad news
brought to them by capital and commerce gets worse, some may blame "feminists." Or all women. Let me summarize why they shouldn't.

Men have known they aged, of course. There's an individual life, after all,
modest and scared, that goes on beneath all the hype of the culture circus and
the gender war. Looking in the mirror, how many midlife men see Johnny
Depp? Do they even see a midlife star—Robert Redford or Clint Eastwood
(who are now touched up less in their movies and who announce this as a
sign that they "accept" aging)? Ordinary men see themselves creased under
the eyes, with deeper squints, a little dry fold under the chin, "hacked," as
Saul Bellow has said, across the back of the neck, flabby-armed, lean-shanked,

high-hipped. Human, like us. But men need to understand that what they see
and feel about their bodies also depends on training. From the opening decades of the twentieth century, various discourses have aged them in ways
that biology alone never can. Every trick that is being used by commerce now
was active earlier in the century. The male climacteric was moved back from
old age into the midlife. The generation gap, the cult of swinging youth, the
desexualizing of midlife women and long-term marriage, began then. The
later life of men was collapsed by heart-attack discourse, and, as Barbara
Ehrenreich as shown in some wonderful chapters on *The Hearts of* (Midlife)
Men, in the Fifties, Sixties, and Seventies they were sold "creative divorce" and
Playboy lifestyles under the rubric of personal "growth."[27] Once age ideology
has made men frantic about their aging, it borrows from gender ideology
to offer palliatives that involve objectifying and dominating and rejecting
women, creating competition between young and midlife women—in short,
carrying generic male socioeconomic power into private life in cruel and unjust ways. The manipulation of men was once less visible only because the
subordination of *women* to age-grading was so vast, so prevalent, so dis-
cussable, so easily made public and ridiculous. The anger of women as they
came to understand this history has frightened men. In being offered tyran-
nies as modes of compensation for imagined aging and its real economic
causes and consequences, older men were victims too. Culture gives power—
like a line of credit—even to men who don't use it. And culture can also take
it away. All men need to see this in order to free one another and their victims.

So here we are together—more or less together, if we can dispassionately consider the idea—in the human condition. Both being aged by culture, and now
in more similar ways. My sober final assessment, however, is that this is not a
cause for rejoicing for anyone. This isn't a trend toward "age equality" between men and women. Generally, it is a most dangerous moment for everyone, of all ages. The painful irony is that just as women in greater numbers
might be breaking free of decline thinking, men are sinking deeper into it.
Women may be dragged back down with them. What is perilous is that *both*
genders are now wide open to decline thinking, with all the psychological,
moral, and political consequences that I began this book by describing. Both
are exploitable medically and commercially. And *both* are vulnerable to
romantic and economic blackmail: "The younger-looking person will be
the one who gets the lover/spouse/job." As I detail in the final chapter, this
pressure already comes from the job market, mediated by opportunistic

agents like surgeons and pharmaceutical companies that use fear of youth-competition as their marketing tool, and by the media, naively passing along the cultural messages without querying their effects. If the economy slows further, it could get much worse much faster. In any case, markets and profits need to grow. So my message to men is—as the kids say—"If you're dissin' the sisters, you ain't fightin' the power."

Whether the pressure on men to feel old and pay to get young will also start coming from women in private life remains to be seen. In the unknown days to come, what's going to matter is what men do, say, and choose, how they act in the streets, at parties, on dates, at the breakfast table, in bed—all the places beside the workplace where behavior has political and ethical consequences. The women I quoted initially weren't mocking men for being in the fix they're in, nor were they demanding that men try harder to mimic youth; on the contrary. They want men to liberate themselves. But not all women are liberated. The evil done by the era of the double standard lives on, as *The First Wives' Club* shows. The kind of woman (or, for that matter, man) who has bought into the aging crisis is going to take it for granted that you'll buy in too; if you get a hair transplant, he or she can feel free to get a face-lift. Such people are not acting to harm, but to *help* you, out of simple blitheness: "It's a product you want, buy it." Think twice. Anxiety about aging is not a simple purchase.

As for women who think consciously as antiageists (feminists, in short)—who knows how each one will react? Women don't feel in control in their middle years; they're wary about becoming victims of male power; they'll wait to see whether this alleged trend toward male vulnerability will lead any given individual man to reciprocities—or to retaliations. "How sweet revenge could be . . ." I envision some wanting to get even—thinking it would leave a good taste in the mouth. Here and there in this essay I've left traces of its preliminary savor. Yet maybe it is a new situation. There are other sweet emotions too. Fighting ageism in alliance with men might be one of them.

As far as I'm concerned, losing midlife men to American ageism would be a disaster—for men of all ages, for the women who care for them, for women of all ages, and (not least) for the future of any antiageist movement. The way men were imagined to age—carelessly, unthinkingly, contented in their changed bodies—was to me a utopian image, one proof that such an attitude could make a space for itself. I thought that feminism could make a related attitude possible for women, with the advantage that feminist women would be conscious of all the complex relations between culture and economic power that had once made men the sole repositories of that image. *Then* there might be an era of age equality. This is written out of deep sadness at the waning of that good hope.

Can we reinstate contentment in the midlife body for men—or perhaps, cultivate it for the first time? Can we make it possible for women, and extend it to more women? Are these the right goals? As a first step, can age studies succeed in clarifying the issues, denaturalizing "midlife aging" and fixing it more explicitly as a product of pressures that can be resisted?

Will men resist? And resist in alliance with women? I'm not always sanguine on either question. When they need to evade age consciousness, people learn to be ingenious. Some men say there's nothing to resist; they're not buying the products, they say . . . Well, they're not buying many. And what would be wrong with buying the products, or telling jokes about urination and impotence, or even having a midlife crisis—as long as they're not putting women down? If I suggest they're internalizing the discourses, they respond like the woman in Alta's poem. "Let me be anxious and unhappy, let me try to buy my way out, let me stay me."

Men who come from ethnic or religious backgrounds in which aging is positively valued as access to wisdom and authority, sometimes say they feel less vulnerable. Some men in academe, who in their middle years usually have tenure, have told me they don't feel vulnerable at all. I take them at their word, although I sometimes wonder whether self-reflection might bring out further, more complicated, more interesting truths.

Men who deny cultural aging spare themselves work whose results we need: the introspective task of picking out what in culture needles them, the emotional tasks of admitting that they are in any way like women their age or in any way in competition with the young, who include their sons and daughters; the intellectual tasks of describing male midlife culture and locating sources of resistance. These are brave and altruistic projects. Men in this group certainly postpone taking a share in liberating other men (including warning the young). So when academics explain that it would be a travesty of oppression/liberation discourse for them to "play victim," I demur. (Even tenure doesn't provide complete inoculation against midlife aging. Making or inheriting millions doesn't provide it.) Their attitude makes it less likely that age can soon be added to the historical and theoretical fields that need it, and (as age studies is establishing itself) postpones vital discussions about differences among men—the ways in which age and gender intersect with race/ethnicity, class, and sexual orientation.

And looking ahead I wonder whether by the start of the next century even the most privileged men in America are going to be able to feel immune.

Some men believe they have a personal interest in asserting immunity: by doing so they might maintain the double standard a little longer—and "get away with being less sensitive, less reliable, less analytic about human relations," in the words of Stephen Chinlund, a friend and a minister.[28] Denial comes in many forms. Men may find themselves arguing in the old positivistic way that they're simply aging biologically, that deterioration is not a cultural label with a complicated history. There's some deep fatalism around—an attitude meant to be stoical. Within its limiting context, it is admirable—but helplessly naive. A gendered variant argues (as the cartoons do) that *women* don't age but men do. Resentment and self-pity fuel this mystified reading of the cultural situation. Men need to think more introspectively and deconstructively about all these issues, act in accordance with their findings, and move their discourses onto a plane beyond.

A complicated assignment. How much more complicated, the next chapter begins to show. Yet there are signs that some men have been taking it on. And when we strategize about change—as opposed to when we describe the culture—we should concentrate on the spots where the system is breaking down rather than the ferocious remnants of the double standard. The past twenty years have been revolutionary for some men too. In the Seventies a new concept of adulthood arose in feminism and developmental psychology that explicitly included men. It was sold as "gender cross-over" (not an entirely felicitous marketing strategy), with men seen as tending toward "greater nurturance, passivity, dependence, or contemplativeness" in their middle years. Now we'd be likely to use such terms as interdependence. Psychologist Bert Brim described such men as early as 1975, as "more diffusely sensual, more sensitive to the incidental pleasures and plains, less aggressive, more affiliative, more interested in love than conquest or power, more present than future-oriented."[29]

In this context, what might have been perceived by men as coercion to behave differently, to be different, was absorbed by them as part of their ego ideal. (Both gay and straight men could take it to heart.) Some heterosexual men set out to create more just gender relationships: they actively supported her goals, shared in child-rearing. They set out to marry a feminist, even unconsciously, intuiting that adulthood would be easier with a partner. Over the past twenty years, some men have absorbed into their emerging concept of (midlife) masculinity new self-images, language, sexual behavior. In the arena of second marriage, where so much bitterness can be engendered by the double standard of aging, some men have learned to reinterpret their best interests. The increasing economic independence of women means that at remarriage, a man can feel better assured that the woman can't be said to have been bought. People have been inventive about relational changes in the longer postparental period, a period that, in Janet Z. Giele's words, "traditional age-sex roles no longer easily 'handle.'"[30] In such versions, couples have lived their way toward midlife equality—not without tension, but with affection, relief, and faith in the future.

Many men have lived with women who appreciated all this and gave in return a less grudging, wary, and self-protective love than would have been possible earlier. In such relationships, men risk telling secrets, even scary secrets that might have humiliating consequences—like the murmurs I mentioned at the beginning. And then, the conversation is open for women to talk about how they suffer from—and resist—menopause discourse or the "empty-nest syndrome" or Oil of Olay promotions. In an equal relationship, men see that the culture condemns women to age unequally, yet don't feel exempt and don't need to exaggerate the gender difference. I want to hold out the possibility—the undocumented actuality—that men and women who bring more confidence and trust into their intimate lives can admit their degrees of age vulnerability, compare notes, and practice resistance together. What do *these* midlife conversations sound like? What forces have kept them from being represented? These narratives need to be made public and accessible to everyone.

In the long run, for men, it simply makes good sense to join forces with like-minded women in this cause at this decisive moment. Good sense and personal happiness. Culture ages me less because feminism and age studies helped me walk past those shopwindows. It's time for men to learn what women know about cultural resistance to age constructions, and share whatever they know. We'd all benefit from inventing the next strategies together.

9

From the Master Narrative of the Life Course: The Entrance into (Male) Midlife Decline

I knew then, at that inexorable moment, that I had become, finally and forever, middle-aged.

—Gerald Early, "Black Men and Middle Age"

WHEN I GIVE talks on "the midlife," I am often asked with some trepidation, "When do the middle years *begin*?" The trepidation confirms that decline is felt to be backing down the life course. A startling phenomenon in a nation that prides itself, misleadingly, on living so much longer than its Victorian predecessors. (In fact, in 1910 a man who was fifty could expect to live 20.2 more years; a woman 22.4—not so different from today as we are led to boast.)[1] The answer, in any event, is not a particular date. The middle years begin *when the culture gets you to say they do.* It now says even to men: "Young, and getting younger."

Age theory reminds us that the very concept of a "beginning" depends on accepting the positivist claim of age ideology: that there's a real category of being there, separable from earlier stages or age classes and distinguishable from continuous processes as well. The midlife now is localizable. Through familiar spatial metaphors like "transition" or "entrance," time becomes a space; the midlife, a bad space. In this chapter, I want to show how much of this happens through the trope of entrance.

The existence of such a temporal/spatial category as "the midlife" is what makes difference possible, and with difference comes inferiority. If the binary for gender is male *versus* other; for race, white *versus* other; then for age it is young *versus* other. Theory posits that the first figure of each binary (male, white) is considered superior to the other and that this ideological superiority is supported by power. But when youth superiority is investigated, do the young really have similar powers—wealth, better access to goods, direct control over the discourses that maintain the binary? Not in any obvious way. Nevertheless, age inferiority at midlife is accepted as plausible, human,—even profoundly true. Tom McGuane, successful and affluent, volunteers in an interview: "When you hit fifty or fifty-two like me, losing it is becoming the state of being."[2] In the male midlife decline imaginary only the younger have "it.": members of Generation X are never poor, never unattractive, never unhappy about losing or frightened of the future. The privileging of youth harms anyone older-than-young while doing younger people at best only a little temporary good. The young grow up to grow older.

Actual young people learn this: that they will someday fall out of being "young." That moment is something the ideology prefers we be too twitchy to settle on. Twenty-five? Receding Hair? Thirty-something? The first laugh-lines? Forty? The first gray hair? Fifty-five? Do the ages matter more than the signs, or are the signs all that matter? In a 1990 *Esquire* article entitled "How Old Are You *Really*?" the authors announced, "You'll be encouraged to examine rather closely your hairline, and to keep an accurate account of the number of orgasms you experience in a week."[3] The middle years, that mysterious land of loss, is like a foreign country without a definite border. The border keeps shifting. ("Your heart is forty, your knees are sixty, your hairline is thirty-five" shouts the *Esquire* outtake.) Undecidability gives some people the illusion of exemption. Others become more desperate as they suspect they're approaching enemy territory.

Of course fear of midlife aging appears *before* any signs appear—long before—to keep us on guard, examining ourselves closely. But viewed from a different angle, fear of aging is what *produces* the signs. The Koren cartoon implies the stages: First you're on alert. Then you're on twenty-four-hour alert. How long after will it be before the anxious eye sees and names "the first wrinkle" or calls thirty the end of the world?

Age theory might say that for each person midlife aging "begins" whenever he or she comes to fear that not-young, a condition that has been lurking about since late adolescence, has finally and undeniably manifested itself. It is whatever you fear you can't postpone. The feelings of dislike and apprehension that used to be transmitted about the older now have a midlife target, yourself. Entrance stories—even those about declines you haven't experienced, don't expect to, and can't imagine feeling so terrible about—begin to make sense. You begin having your own soliloquies of age anxiety. The admiration that used to be transmitted about the older doesn't stick as well to you. We're back where this book began.

Cultural critics have not looked hard enough at *how* resocialization into midlife aging occurs—how it manifests itself in a particular subject or in circulating discourses, or in interactions between the subject and his social texts. Much goes on through narrative, written and oral. We are used to congratulating ourselves for this "human" storytelling capacity, but we have it for better or for worse. "Aging" too is learned, and narrative teaches it.

Declining to Decline began with the strong claim that our culture provides subjects with a master narrative of aging—something like the master narrative of gender or race: popularly disseminated, semiconscious, so familiar and acceptable that it can be told automatically.[4] The plot of this one is peak, entry, and decline, with acceleration on the downslope. Anyone exposed to it can take decline to heart: now that men have to be included, it's a universalizable plot. "My Private Midlife" began with two of the more unisex emotion/ knowledge constructs: nostalgia about the youthful past and fear of bodily decay.

The "universal" plot comes in men's versions and women's versions. My gender self-assignment determines what messages will be aimed at me; which I "choose" to accept; above all, how intensely I attend to them. Identifying as boy and man, men read or hear or view certain texts as having special reference to them. "Menopause as magic marker" is one complex entry narrative that is told about women, addressed mainly to women, and only *overheard* by men. Likewise, prostate discourse is heard by men as intensely relevant to them, and is overheard by women. Gender is probably the most important determinant of the details that give plausibility to the master narrative. But women listening in on male discourses that seem universal risk identifying with them. That's why chapters like this concern women.

Eventually we'll have an inventory of all of decline's literary devices. Meanwhile, the story of the Entrance into Midlife Aging seems to be crucial. Without entry stories dividing the indivisible life course there could be no midlife category to which to attach detraction. All of the entry-into-decline stories analyzed here are about men. In the last chapter I suggested that many overlapping factors were reducing male immunity to midlife aging, bringing men psychologically closer to the situation that women are supposed to experience at midlife. Discursively, if not in other ways, the situation of men seems even worse. Midlife men are now writing fragments of the master narrative of decline with surprising alacrity. Men's access to print publication and writing awards (two of the articles I cite have been singled out for their literary excellence) may encourage the retelling of male decline stories. Features of male midlife culture may now make it difficult for men *not* to write decline. When many men in our culture tell such stories, and when such stories can plausibly be told about men as a group, these circumstances must change our notions of maleness, of midlife, and of narrative.

Male midlife decline used to be located mainly in dissolute classes or individuals who orchestrated for themselves spectacular descents. Consider how they saturated prized works in the canon: F. Scott Fitzgerald's "Babylon Revisited"—which I first read in grade 7–8210; Waugh's *Brideshead Revisited,* Lowry's *Under the Volcano,* Nabokov's *Lolita*—works recommended to me by prestigious older professors. That literature is still circulating, taught in colleges and translated into film and video. Nowadays, the male characters represented in the texts I quote are in ordinary walks of life, middle class or above, mostly white, heterosexual, with good life expectancy, and relatively young. The youngest are thirty-five and thirty-seven. Entrance stories can collapse men into "later life" earlier than menopause discourse does it to women.

Some Entrance accounts can be found in so-called fiction, others in nonfiction—interviews or autobiography. Some are chipper, some matter-of-fact, some stoic, some anguished. (Decline has many tones, being wisdom, and being wisdom, is licensed to repeat itself.) I used to be snagged by these expressive variations, lost in empathy. To attend to both individual modes of expression and ideological frames remains a constant problem for cultural critics. But, as Kaja Silverman says, there are contexts where "it is a mistake to think in insistently individualizing ways about the psyche."[5] Ultimately, I emphasize the unifying pattern.[6] Wherever found, the Entrance story is brief but culturally reverberant—an anecdote with a restricted wallop, like a karate chop. Beneath all the esthetic diversity, if we look hard enough, we can see the bare knuckles of the master narrative.

Constructing an Epiphany

If men now "know" they age, and how, it's partly because representations of altered appearance have become not only ubiquitous but minutely circumstantial. Frederick Exley's narrator in *Last Notes from Home* addresses the aging of TV's Matt Dillon with a kind of relish of disgust: "Your puss, old boy, is drawn with lines and wrinkles. There is melancholy in your blue eyes. Your jowls, Big Jim, are drooping like cows' udders. That girth of yours appears to be held in by a corset. . . . Excuse me for laughing, marshal." Like the *Esquire* article, fiction also tells men when the droops occur. Writer Norman Lavers begins a mini aging autobiography by describing two "events" that occurred at fifty and fifty-five: "My own muscular forearms fell into wrinkles" and "wrinkles [were] forming in the middle of my cheeks." Lavers's essay, cited as notable in *Best American Essays 1992,* measures one bodily deterioration before another—at forty, at thirty-one. He locates an age-graded physical peak early in life (at twenty-five, when he was "as strong and fit as I would ever be in my life"). Even a one-liner can do the trick. "The paunchy side of thirty-five," quips the first page of an older John Leonard novel.[7] In novels about midlife men, the first physical description is often telling. I'm finding more of the cruelty or self-deprecation that used to color midlife women characters.

Men, like women, tell Mirror Scenes that teach listeners or readers how shocking entry is. Thomas Mann's scene of Aschenbach having makeup put on in *Death in Venice* was one of the landmarks of early construction of male decline. No one is surprised to find repeated, even in the *New York Review of Books,* lines from a play of Luigi Pirandello's about the horror of a male midlife character at seeing his own face. "One sees oneself in a mirror—quite accidentally—and each time the desolation of seeing what one sees is stronger than the amazement of having forgotten it. . . . It's like an obscenity for a person who looks so old to feel so young and ardent."[8] (Reprinting this without comment is itself a way of carrying the perilous mirror around in the world, as the wicked demon's pupils do in Andersen's fairy tale "The Snow Queen.") How many readers think to wonder, "*Every* time? 'Desolation'? Isn't that melodramatic?" Scorched by literary intensity, sentences like Pirandello's disown the need for explicit context or reasoning. By now, midlife horror can be captured in a poem, a scene, a single sentence—even a phrase. One of the best proofs that decline is dominant is that its most truncated shorthand is now meaningful.

Entrance can also occur in the absence of physical alteration, which means that men (as yet) exempt from drastic bodily self-critique find other causes to show themselves falling into midlife aging suddenly.

> A few years ago, in my late thirties, I began to play basketball with under-graduates at Boston College. After a few months I became "a regular" on the court and imagined that I was just "one of the guys." One day as I was walking off the court, feeling particularly good about a well-played game, a teammate turned to me and said, "Nice game, *sir.*" That one communication disabused me of the "one of the guys" self-image. Everyone experiences similar moments during which age-related self-conceptions are called into question.[9]

Professor Karp—a sociologist whose topic in this essay is "the fifties"—concludes this anecdote in a reasonable and confiding tone, with a static social-science reminder that "*everyone* experiences similar moments," as if "experience" were obligatory and had no cultural component. This anecdote is apparently not told out of deep pain; it's only rueful. But it teaches the lesson of communal resignation all the better.

Actually, the anecdote can be reframed resistantly. Critical age theory notes how this anecdote is structured as a "scene of discovery"—an epiphany. "That one communication" connotes suddenness; authoritative formality; one sole meaning. The pupil says he won't need to be told twice. On the scene, an apparently untutored subject learns (here, at a mere thirty-seven years of age) to "accept" being not-young. His body is not at fault: it has "well-played" its part. But "feeling particularly good" about it in this setting has a hubristic quality. (Midlife) punishment swiftly follows his (age-inappropriate) confidence. Everything about this miniature modernist lesson hides the local and specific ways in which culture ages an individual. Athletes have their identity concentrated on their bodies in youth just as the photogenic do; all become vulnerable to premature entry-into-decline stories. Maleness and occupational superiority, which particularize this encounter, are occluded behind the "everyone." Boston College is full of students from parochial schools trained to say "sir." Karp says he must query his own "self-conception," which amounts to his having felt "still young." In fact, he does not ask himself where his decline conceptions came from, or in what sense they are "his."

An age-conscious therapist (if there were such training) might ask a man who feels this way how he could better protect himself against such situations. Traditional (youth-oriented) academic settings and sports encounters provoke age-graded contrasts that enlarge generation gaps and create inferiority in "older" men. What if he had responded, pleasantly, "Call me Dave"? Perhaps the young men had been waiting for him to say "Call me Dave," while he deferred, enjoying a pleasant sense of lèse-majesté. Some privileged attributes (status and authority) may also be lost on becoming merely one of the guys. Karp might have told a more interesting story—and it would not have normalized male midlife decline—had he reported that he had some share in producing as well as interpreting this exchange.

Ethnomethodologically speaking, this man was not untutored and unprepared. He was a postwar American male closing in on forty in the Eighties, a scholar wide open to social influences, and a jock. Expecting such a scene, young as he was, he in fact constructed a perverse rite in which, on a sacred site—the basketball court—he expelled himself from guyness by interpreting a single syllable as an expulsion order from the entire dominant group.

An epiphany transforms a mere fleeting chance encounter into a significant life-course narrative. Richard Powers, in his highly praised *Galatea 2.2: A Novel,* independently tells a more wised-up, epigrammatic version of the fatal "sir-story." A frat boy collides with the narrator, age thirty-five. " 'Sorry, sir,' he placated."

> The word was a slap in the face, the young's coded self-righteousness. People under twenty-one needed to work that fact into the conversation,

even if the conversation consisted of two words. In this country, youth was a socially acceptable form of bragging.

A horrible mistake coming here, to this college bar, to this college town. These were the same people who had gotten tanked every night, while I broke my neck studying. They had stayed twenty, while I'd dissolved into middle age.[10]

Karp, in the late Eighties, represents the young male as well mannered; Powers, in the Nineties, as arrogant. Anger grows fast as the generation gaps grow more vicious. But sensationalism has a role too: novelists compete, escalating midlife emotions. Neither man queries the belief that all status-superior "guys" are young, that they have the power to confer (or withhold) guyness, and that once they have denied it, the "older" man has permanently lost his ability to be comfortable on other terms with the members of the group or in himself.

The long-expected, long-avoided Entrance into middle life is diversely anecdotalized. In the North American master narrative for men, culture does not clearly name a cause for automatic entry (cf. menopause, or puberty), nor provide a legal definition and date (cf. majority) nor a rite (cf. the sixtieth birthday party in Chinese culture). Instead, it provides an endless array of normal occasions that can be used for epiphanies: New Year's Eve, reunions, children's weddings, the birth of a grandchild, going to a bar, eating (or not eating) a peach. (One reason the Entrance story has not been noticed, perhaps, is that it is so diffused, so normalized.) Some occasions that used to be "women's material," although being revised more positively or complexly by women are being taken up by men as occasions for discovering and expressing grief and loss. Taking a child to college in "Empty Nest Blues," Charles McGrath writes, "I had a momentary and depressing vision of myself and my roommates of thirty years ago reunited in the old suite. There we are, four middle-aged guys without a clue."[11] Although humorous about youth's pleasures and touching about paternal loss, this fantasy of failure and failure of fantasy fixes midlife men as techno-illiterate, inept at joy, and childishly lonely. A man's midlife epiphany, however light in tone, turns out to be an emotional application of the cultural script to his own single life. Meanwhile, it confirms the script for others.

In sum, the middle years of life are now often seen to begin with something like an extorted confession of an internal event: that moment when a subject is forced to "recognize" simultaneously that he has suffered a loss and that this is what "no-longer-being-young" means. However trivial the loss, it links up with the decline anticipated in the master narrative. Once ushered in, implicitly the now-"aging" man will neither recover anything that has been lost nor acquire anything of equal value. The first moment of recognition matters so much because the subject finds himself installed in a permanent new state of losing. Thus the title of Norman Lavers's essay, mocking and convinced, borrowed from a song that millions have known for decades, "Yours Sincerely, Wasting Away."

The "Terrible Conflict" about Midlife Narrative

In conversation as in writing, men too have some choice about how they will represent their aging. Male midlife progress novels are being published; there are even midlife progress poems. But the current range of choice can feel quite limited. One remarkable recognition of such limitations comes from a 1930s novella by Rebecca West, "There Is No Conversation." The encounter once again pits a male midlife character against the young. The social currency or decline-measure in this class fraction is not athletic ability but conversational distinction. The man in question, an aristocrat named Etienne de Sévenac, "is fifty and an inveterate beauty," who seeks out people who are "beautiful and gay and young, who obviously would not bore themselves for one moment with the society of anybody who was old." When, however "the talk began to stream past him" as if he were "outmoded," Rebecca West's narrator tells us, "an expedient for laying hold of the attention that was rushing past him would occur to him. . . . He was impaled on a choice that to him, poor fellow, was a really horrible necessity." He could entertain the young with stories of the prestigious people he has known intimately. "Young people will listen if one speaks of twenty, of thirty—oh, the little brutes—of forty years ago. But to have such memories is to admit that one is old," Etienne thinks to himself. So sometimes he finds a pretence to leave, and sometimes he begins, "That reminds me of the first time Marcel Proust ever came to see my mother." The narrator comments coolly, "Then victory had been gained, but at what a price. It interests me to watch such conflicts."[12]

As West realized, such conflicts can be horrible. Within the narrow scripts of midlife aging, either choice involves being "impaled." On the one hand, a person can tell his own autobiography, which will unavoidably include his real niche in historical time and his personal events and interpretations. In short, he can refer to his full age identity through bits and pieces that are personally important. But that is precisely a "too old" story. It is also, currently, a "too long" story. How would I summarize "Ordinary Pain" or "Face-Off" so that they don't sound defensive or boastful to someone who doesn't know me? Decline has control of the public sound bite.

The alternative to decline is silence, distortion, self-suppression. Silence confirms Etienne as a boring old man, but silence is a verbal form of "passing" for younger. Passing, as Barbara Macdonald has said, is "one of the most serious threats to selfhood"—"except as a consciously political tactic for carefully limited purposes."[13] The practices of passing, even if "successful" from the point of view of onlookers, may be devastating to the self. When Etienne is forced to leave the room, speechless, West shows us the cost of even tiny invisible modes of passing. There are narratives that are supposed to promote passing—disguising one's chronological age, for example, or one's college class—that can scarcely be uttered without reminding the speaker of his age, of his subterfuge, and thus of his neediness. As in the case of men or women who get liposuction or face-lifts, the social benefit may be negligible, the internal damage substantial.

In fact, I observe that most people at midlife, men or women, do *not* conversationally try very much to pass as younger-than-midlife subjects. What actually happens is that we are invisibly taught to accept decline in order to speak *as* "honest" midlife subjects. We may have to lie to do so. Women and feminists do it too. A friend with high school age children, talking with another mother about forthcoming departures to college, found herself saying, "Me too. I don't know what I'll do without them." "Actually," she commented to me, "that wasn't true at all. I have plenty of plans. I'm looking forward to being postmaternal."[14] She wasn't being hypocritical; it was a sympathetic white lie. But suppose the other woman was also partially misrepresenting her experience, out of fidelity to gendered age expectations? Both lost the chance of hearing an alternative truth.

Changing the meaning of passing, I'll say that in the realm of age, men too pass by learning to tell some pithy midlife decline story—a Mirror Scene, a joke about eyes, hair, muscles, or memory, a sardonic comment about the younger that actually puts *us* in our place. Like Lavers, Karp, McGrath, and my friend, many of us pass as appropriately aging subjects.

Some in the midlife age class may feel that in telling an Entrance story they're sharing the hard lot of same-age women, "being-their-age." But in the Nineties, pushing traditional midlife unhappiness into print is not *per se* a feminist goal; discovering the enemies of well-being at any age is the point. In a book about feminist mothering, Judy Remington, reacting to her son's announcement of his engagement, plunks in the middle of her personal essay one of those memorable decline sentences that can reverberate dangerously far beyond the text. "It felt like having cement poured over me."[15] But Remington, a divorced lesbian, opens and closes "The Reconstruction" with her dancing "joyously" at her son's wedding. It's a delicate, multilayered counter-entrance story.

Passing as appropriately aging is a discursive pressure in our culture. What is toxic is that subjects expect to "experience" decline or expect others to do so, expect to report decline as real or expect to hear it reported as real. Telling life-course autobiography is a necessary "ongoing accomplishment" in culture, as Harold Garfinkel puts it—"known, used, and taken for granted" by adult members.[16] When people succeed as speakers of their midlife aging, is when they learn to speak a personalized version of the obligatory, and inevitably falsifying, master narrative of decline.

Learning to Speak the Master Narrative

People are socialized into telling false midlife narrative and feeling it must be true by a "secret apprenticeship." One of the most remarkable accounts of a secret apprenticeship that occurred in adulthood concerns a woman who had been raised as a boy, had always felt "like" a girl, and went through a sex-change operation at the age of twenty, in 1959. Afterwards, she was preparing to marry her boyfriend. Agnes had watched women being women, of course; now, as Harold Garfinkel, the sociologist who interviewed her, explains, she had to act on this passive knowledge: practice acting and feeling and *speaking* like a woman. Much of this she learned from the boyfriend. He did this "[for example] by angrily analyzing the failings of a companion's date who had insisted . . . on offering her opinions when she should have been retiring, on being sharp in her manner when she should have been sweet, on . . . demanding services instead of looking to give the man she was with pleasure and comfort." Listening to him, "not only did [Agnes] adopt the pose of passive acceptance of instructions, but she learned as well the value of passive acceptance as a desirable feminine character trait." At times, she too (like Etienne) had to be silent because she didn't have the right autobiography. She hadn't "been" a girl in her childhood and adolescence, and she lacked, in Garfinkel's formulation of her unspoken ideals, a "natural, normal" past.[17]

Studying Agnes's speech and silence, anyone (especially feminists) can see ways in which Agnes's narrative and the sense of identity it gave her to tell it were both real and false. We see how eager Agnes was to get her statements of "feelings, motives, and aspirations" right—that is, consistent with those of other speakers whom she considers "natural, normal." She was like a five-year-old who carries a Klan banner; she was gaining a "commitment to compliance."[18] Eventually, if Agnes were "followed longitudinally"—if she lived as a woman long enough under her boyfriend's thumb—her gender identity would probably slide smoothly into her normal narrative of age identity.

Lacking contact with feminist social constructionists, she might never question it. The false would become true.

Likewise, more slowly and unselfconsciously, those lacking a strong habit or concept of age resistance gain a commitment to compliance with an obligatory informal education in learning how to be a "natural, normal" midlife person, an unwitting speaker of one's own autobiography of "aging," and an unwitting biographer of others' "aging." We even have to change our "body" conformably, not by undergoing surgery but by learning appropriate practices and a set of knowledges guiding the age gaze. That gaze sweeps over our imperceptibly changing anatomy and decides *when* to speak, negatively, of "changed" looks.

We know a little about how men, Agnes-like in the Nineties, are prepped to tell narratives of aging. Part of the background is a standard of perfection that comes from the conjoined cults of masculinity and youth. Thirty years ago Erving Goffman explained why "youth was a socially acceptable form of bragging"; this North American system certainly influenced all the men raised under it. It hasn't changed enough since.

> There is only one complete unblushing male in America: a young, married, white, urban, northern, heterosexual Protestant father of college education, fully employed, of good complexion, weight, and height, and a recent record in sports. Every American male tends to look out upon the world from this perspective, this constituting one sense in which one can speak of a common value system in America. Any male who fails to qualify is likely to view himself—during moments at least—as unworthy, incomplete, and inferior.[19]

The *first* attribute on Goffman's depressingly restrictive list is "young." And this was in 1963, before the youth revolutions of the Sixties started a new wave of generational divergences, which has subsequently been consolidated by the reciprocal construction of Generation X and the Baby Boomers.

At some early point in the life course, both boys and girls begin to learn the decline narrative. As Goffman says, we are "trained first of all in others' views" of what normal/abnormal means. In the Doonesbury cartoon shown in the last chapter, Rick Redfern's son is learning (not from his mother but from his panicky father) how to pass-as-younger, what items serve to measure decline, the emotions connected with fear of aging. Children are being exposed to "an accelerated development narrative."[20] "Are you going to die, Daddy?" Parents are passing on the contemporary slide (midlife = aging = mortality). Through all this, a child learns that he or she is "just a body" and "just another body." Philosopher Paul Ricoeur calls this "impersonal description" and puts it in opposition to "mineness."[21] Over time, the practice of impersonal description is going to coincide perilously with postmodern discontinuity, as the adolescent and young-adult self changes selves to match the needs of consumerism and employers. The habit of obediently replacing self with newer self converges on middle-ageism with devastating effects. It prepares us to override whatever we know about our own development through our multileveled ongoing age identity and to substitute for it the decline story of our time.

The struggle between the two perspectives takes place in a historically specific literary/cultural setting. In North America in the Nineties, the perspectives are not equally powerful. The impersonal-description perspective has dominated "serious" writing about midlife aging and is now becoming more visible in popular and semiserious writing and conversational self-presentation. The epiphany of Entrance is facilitating these trends—unless indeed it marks their triumph. A person subject to a rule of autobiography like telling entry epiphanies is implicitly only one among others, however vivid and idiosyncratic his or her style. Even in theoretical writing, until quite recently "*the* body" implied one sole kind (it occluded gender, sexual orientation, class, race). It still implies the same aging "fate."

Insofar as they are less well instructed in social construction of the emotions, unpersuaded of the degree to which the personal is ideological, men are likelier to be mystified by universalism. When men tell a male life-course narrative they often make universalism dogmatically explicit: "losing it is a state of being," "everyone experiences similar moments," "that inexorable moment," "what one invariably feels" (Orwell). They assume and assert one fate. For a long time I believed them. Under humanism, I read male midlife Entrance stories with a shivering trust that they were the curt hieroglyphic of my own future.

Now it occurs to me that all that male assertion may imply a doubt, or even a prayer, "Prove me wrong." But whatever the hesitations, the outcome (after learning the master narrative by heart, repressing doubt or hope or other mixed experiences) is that at crisis moments—when, as Ricoeur says, we should in "the most radical confrontation place face to face" the two perspectives and, I add, fight on behalf of the personal narrative of age identity—men (and women influenced by their master narrative) may find themselves with poor weapons.[22]

The gradualness of the psychosocial-literary learning mechanisms and the fact that those who appropriate decline narrative do so in a separate, solitary, apparently *individual* process of resocialization and self-narration are factors that mask the inauthenticity of the "normal, natural" "human" decline story—its subservience to history and commerce and literary form, its common tropes, its ontological impersonality, and, I'm sorry to say, its stifling sameness.

The Epiphany Anchors the Midlife Crisis

The point at which a given person applies the aging label to himself is critical—the point when impersonal and other-directed decline narrative becomes real by taking on autobiographical specificity. The crucial period comes after the master narrative loses its vague applicability first to Mommy and Daddy and then to others in my age class, and gradually becomes self-referential—a story about *me*. We should hypothesize considerable resistance to losing so much previously accumulated identity. After all, each "I" must learn to refer a story of decline to himself rather than reserving it, in self-preservation, for everybody else. ("Doing Age Theory" returns to the problematic of resistance. "The Other End of the Fashion Cycle" begins to unwind the mystery of how deep internalizations go. And the final chapter ties these learning mechanisms and literary forms to economic insecurity and status apprehension.)

The Entrance epiphany in its brief, comic and semiserious forms would not have the power to reinforce decline if literature in longer forms had not already made it portentous. In the nineteenth century, people could be found in fiction whose hair had turned white overnight because of grief. In the twentieth, that kind of sudden writing on the body became coded as implausible. But no longer *feeling* young became itself a separate cause of grief, a specifically midlife moment, invested with the conventions of suddenness, shock, and loss. Many of the narrative parameters of the representation of that new age, the middle years, were established in the first third of this century. In a 1934 novel called *The Folks* by Ruth Suckow, a married father of two sons with a very good future ahead of him (a new job in a bigger city, a possible affair with an up-to-date woman named Gladys) comes upon his wife as she is trying to kill herself out of jealousy and a sense of inadequacy. To save her, he decides not to take the job and not to pursue the adultery. He then makes some discoveries. "Carl recognized in wonder that he was not the same. The brightness of his easy, superficial confidence had been turned into an essential caution that came from a deep wound. He could look back at his old self as eager, youthful, hopeful, radiantly blind. . . . the need for Gladys was as if beaten out of him. He had aged beyond that at a stroke. His youth was gone." The decisions that could be interpreted as psychosocial (moral development, say, or cowardice in the face of guilt-tripping), he decides are simply irreversible signs of bad aging. Later, he plays with his boys in the garden. "As he felt their small hands depending upon his clasp, he realized that he had crossed the entrance to middle age. That sense of expectancy had imperceptibly passed out of his own life into the lives of his children."[23]

Suckow provides the metaphor ("entrance") and the forms: a private moment of confession, an elegiac mini aging autobiography. Always preposterously, one-sidedly "innocent" and eager, youth retrospectively becomes the place where hopes of material gain and luscious infidelity resided—and there are no further hopes in unexpectant middle age. After the 1960s, many people reading *The Folks* would have a newer label for Carl's experience. A "midlife crisis" in fiction or life often connotes a turn away from hated responsibility. But it also links "middle age" to *any* crisis—any work-related setback, any health problem, any marital problem, any defeat that happens during the long middle of adulthood.

Lavers's essay on "wasting away," for example, turns out to be an account of *accidents* that occurred to him at different ages. From boyhood on, he overstressed his body, risking injury even when he knew he could have avoided doing so ("Once more I found . . . that I was slightly out of position, but decided to go ahead and muscle it up"). Nevertheless, told after his wrinkle stories, the accidents too appear universal and connected with aging.[24] In another notable recent essay, a forty-year-old writer and professor of English, Gerald Early, connects his entry into middle age with a moment of hospitalization, pain, humiliating infantilization, and excruciating race consciousness. After a gallstone operation, he found himself in the recovery room. He describes himself as "a black man, sick and drugged upon a table, his wounded body being cleaned and examined by a white nurse. I knew then, at that inexorable moment, that I had become, finally and forever, middle-aged."[25] This slow, dramatic periodic sentence—the crux of the essay—epitomizes every Entrance epiphany. Readers can see that Early had a terrible moment, but it's hard to explain why he wants to call this "middle age" (it could have happened at any age)—except that the master narrative of aging brings such pressure to bear.

In time Early returned to health, teaching, and a prestigious writing career. Although he doesn't mention such things, he goes on to show that he did not remain utterly despairing.[26] He says that at twenty he hadn't even been sure he'd live to middle age, given the male violence around him. In light of his sense of survivorship, it would probably have been truer for him to write, "I *felt*, for that agonizing moment, that middle age was going to be a tragedy forever. I was wrong." Instead, the decline view of aging writes for him, "I knew then." This is alleged to be a general kind of event: the essay is called "Black Men and Middle Age." Why might we not eventually expect "Asian Men and Middle Age," "Chicanos and Middle Age"—male writers of a certain age and status making contingent connections between a nightmarish fifteen minutes of their life, their race or ethnicity, and the "onset" of the middle years? As the titles get more specific, the condition becomes more "universal." Once midlife decline is written into the life course and circulates through conversation and literature, being *human* may require telling an entry story.

One of the best sociologists of emotion, Steven Gordon, says that "social construction is most evident in . . . situational definitions of emotion-relevant meanings."[27] In my view, the genre "epiphany of Entrance into the middle years," provides a situation in which painful emotions are defined as age-specific and coded as relevant and valid and important (and emotions that are *not* age-specific are not), certain negative ideas of aging count as "truth" (and others do not), certain masochistic age-related vocabularies are appropriate (and other more affirming ones are not).

"Finally and forever middle-aged." Whether an exact age is mentioned or not, the period of decline/recognition of decline/anticipation of decline, is now understood to be "the middle years." A man, a mirror, the desolation of seeing what one sees—such words (cursory, vague, oblique) now simply imply midlife deterioration. We needn't know the age of the man; who ever knew Prufrock's age? Any negative age reference can pull up a chain of signifiers, confusedly multiplying bad things and linking them to "the midlife." The master narrative runs on synechdochic muddle. Because historically an epiphany anchors a grave midlife crisis, any Entrance story now drags a long chain.

In 1995 Ann Beattie published a novel called *Another You* about a male midlife Wanderkind who tries for a while fleeing far from home, self, and midlife aging. He winds up at the end with a dry but useful conclusion. "Quite possibly, this would be the most ludicrous place on earth to come if you were looking for an epiphany."[28]

Resisting the Master Narrative of Decline

Decline narrative has, I believe, the standing of a default position. Culturally, default standing means that the subject feels an internal pressure to speak in decline's terms, even when resistant experience or theory intervenes. In the default position, people do think the thoughts, do feel the feelings that go with the words, do use the labels, do consider themselves in the age class ("aging Baby Boomers"), do apply the language to other people, sincerely. They judge what they read by its conformity to such truths. Alternative narrative doesn't feel as real. They may utter the fragments of the master narrative jocularly (as stating what everyone knows) penitentially (as revealing a partial fault), conspiratorially (as seeking confession from their interlocutor), intimately (as revealing truths admitted only between friends), interrogatively (as seeking denial from their interlocutor that they belong in the age class or assurance as to their degree), preemptively (as warding off an accusation that they are in denial) or assertively (as declaring a terrible truth that others lack courage to admit). These are mere stylistic differences. Humanly, of course, the tone in which each one starts to tell decline narrative matters enormously, and it may even affect one's power to resist.

The master narrative of decline has benefits for able tellers, whether novelists or speakers, just like knowledge of any "truth" or "discipline." As feminist theorist Sandra Lee Bartky says, "Whatever its ultimate effect, discipline can provide the individual upon whom it is imposed with a sense of mastery as well as a secure sense of identity. There is a certain contradiction here: while its imposition may promote a larger disempowerment, discipline may bring with it a certain development of a person's powers."[29] Bartky is explaining why women trained in femininity may resist feminism. Likewise, the practice of age resistance might threaten able decline narrators with a temporary *loss* of identity, an absence of story. If telling an entry story is a normal accomplishment, giving it up may mean feeling, at least for a while, less human.

Ultimately, I am moving toward the conclusion that the master narrative of midlife aging, as long as it remains dominant, needs to be treated with suspicion as a pressure on us to tell unreliable and misleading or even false narrative. I recognize all too well that people tell decline narrative as if it were personally true, with the fidelity to detail and the emotional tone that come from believing that they are describing their "own" experience. They *are*. This makes it hurtful to say of any single account by another person, "This is false."

But I can say it feelingly of any of my own prior accounts. Having written enough of my age autobiography, what I write now is "true"—as true as I know how to be at this moment. In other words, a preferred fiction. At the same time, like George C. Rosenwald, "I propose to look at any given life story as provisional, poised to antiquate itself."[30] This attitude—my story is a provisional truth—is especially useful for people living through their middle years during the current crisis of narrativity. Even before people have widely shared their personal counternarratives, we can speak as if the cultural script on which epiphanies of decline now draw is questionable. Not just because it is a decline narrative (although its masochism by itself might be—but has not proved to be—a strong argument against it).[31] Not just because it topples over so often into cliche, bathos, melodrama.

No, the basic script is "false" because it is automatic, repetitive, and coercive, and excludes and conceals so much. Insofar as it refuses to confront alternative causality or alternative interpretation, its intensity is unearned. It is simply stunned by middle-ageism. The unchallenged priority of decline distorts whatever happens to us and denies us the possibility of a free creative process in which each subject might reinvent her or his own age narrative throughout life.

Narratives of decline might come to be judged authentic if they did not so rigidly preclude fun, or gain, or reason. Or sheer joy, like that I knew after my nightmare of bounding immobility, when I woke feeling utter relief. That is told as a counterepiphany, an entry into the emotions of midlife *progress*. I believe that the period when we begin to go "Am I winning or losing?" and begin to tell Entrance stories is "stressful in the extreme"—just as, Garfinkel says, Agnes's acceptance of her gender locutions was, even though she had taken on her new identity voluntarily and actively.[32] I would judge our speaking and writing more authentic if we were given the concept of choosing among age identities—if, to begin with, women and men versed in age critique assured us, as *Declining to Decline* does, that what decline ideology is teaching is not the only way of being human in that category (middle-aged). There can be no stable personal or collective solutions to this situation until normal speakers can tell alternative narratives *as alternative*. Moreover, we need to keep in mind, as the late Glenda Laws usefully said, "Just as we are not always gendered, so we are not always aged either. Identity as an aging person is intermittent."[33]

Here are some of the other cognitive projects that might help us move forward as we work toward a narrative with midlife figures in it that anyone could speak with more freedom, flexibility, achieved sense of authenticity, and thus, conceivably, pleasure. We have to deny the reality of the terms we currently use: No one should think that "Boomers" is a serious, stable category of being. Or even that "the midlife" does us any good, except used (if this were possible) in a strictly denotative way. We need to expose the entire repertory of the narrative of decline. Simultaneously, we need to urge that progress narrative (in the definition expanded in "Midlife Heroines") be considered a priori authentic and authoritative. That is, unlike now, progress narrative would not be dismissable as a "feel-good" rhetoric for chumps, or women, narcissists, the rich or the smug, who cannot accept "the truth" of aging.

At the same time—everything always needs to happen at the same time— we need to disaggregate the other decline forces that are dangerously confused with "midlife aging." Perhaps there is something hurtful in, say, successful black male life at forty that cannot yet be uttered directly but whose misery can be expressed under cover of "middle age." No doubt many social harms can be extricated from the confusion: the fixity of economic conditions, so that class standings are in fact unlikely to improve after a certain age; the health consequences of enduring homophobia or racism or overwork for decades; the veiled condescension of the young; the deaths of teenage children; the inability to find a loving partner; forced early retirement. Once we get that far in clarity, people could write tragedies or what they will about these conditions—they cry out for adequate expression. But midlife aging would not be the culprit. How would decline appear? No longer tainted as default or scapegoating narrative.

I hear someone objecting to the very idea of a master narrative of aging on the grounds that "there's no such dominance. There are too many counter-narratives around, women's and men's." Or "Even within a single decline narrative, deconstructive possibilities lurk." I don't deny validity to these points of view. But I have tried to suggest how, given the culture in which our age class came to midlife, alternative reading or writing of experience is foreclosed or hampered or marginalized.

And I would remind objectors also that the hypotheses of master narratives of gender and of race have been extremely fruitful. To posit "a" master narrative with differentiated "versions" may have many benefits in the current phase of age theory and the historicizing of the life course. Certainly we need further evidence of the operations of the master narrative of aging. I have speculated that we go through an active developmental process—imitating adults, practicing a secret age apprenticeship, learning to personalize impersonal narration—in which ordinary conversation and published writing are deeply implicated. I feel there is much more to discover. As people learn to tell retrospectively the autobiographies of their ageism, and investigators study prospectively the ways children, adolescents, and young adults learn about aging, and critics investigate contemporaneously the ways culture pumps out midlife meanings, the evidence should thicken.

As we look for decline stories in fragments and at full-length, and begin to find them whereever we look, we will certainly find ourselves living in a culture more saturated than we had thought. And the harder we try to refute, replace, or ignore them, the more we will find ourselves put on the defensive. The more we search around for smarter weapons—"Don't refute, deride"; "Don't proliferate progress stories without deconstructing decline"—the harder it will be to deny decline's mastery of print, its mastery of speech, its mastery over our own ability to think about life. A little theory is necessary;

counterdiscourse is essential. And faith that we can blow away some of the toxic air simply with our warm breath. Eventually, it may be true that "there's no such dominance." Whether we are speaking of men or of women, that time seems very far away.

Part Four

Combat Positions

10

The Other End of the Fashion Cycle: Practicing Loss, Learning Decline

Age Studies Looks at the Fashion Cycle

M Y MOTHER still buys almost all my clothes. After college, when she might have stopped, she really didn't want to. Even after I married, had a baby, got my first leg up in academe, published my first book . . . even after she retired, she continued to dress us all up at her expense. She likes shopping, has excellent taste, and wants us to be well-dressed. I still get most of my clothes when we visit in our respective cities, twice a year. Shopping together, we are two well-dressed women, obviously chromosomally related, getting along, mildly disagreeing about what is in, what is "right for me." When we come out with some useful items, we share a tired satisfied glance; we say, "We did well." Other times of year, surprise packages arrive. If at first as a young, wannabe-independent woman I went along grudgingly, in time I found myself relieved and grateful.

This arrangement is unusual. It has saving touches of excess—the very fact that my mother continued her loving, generous practice into my middle years provided one.[1] That ongoing practice surfeited my level of need at a time of life—early mid-adulthood—when overextended working parents can vaguely feel undercherished, giving more than they're getting; they may be individuating but they're feeling orphaned. Moreover, my attractive wardrobe comes free. Recognizing the cultural oddity of our whole arrangement helped me wrench the practice of clothes shopping out of the class of thoughtless habits and lift it into the realm of the theorizable. This partial detachment was crucial in enabling me to bring to bear on fashion my work in feminist age studies.

In the long run, I was freed to see involvement in fashion as a practice that demands of the participant not just money to buy new objects but an experience, driven by the object's "life cycle." A chilling metaphor.[2] It's the product, not the human being buying it, whose life is attended to—and only a limited part of its cycle at that. The known life of an object moves from purchase, through consumption (public display of possession), to the decline (going out of fashion) necessary to start the cycle again. Even when the psychology of the human purchaser is in question, the investigators (whether marketeers, sociologists, economists, or cultural critics) use a metaphor that privileges the beginning, "point of purchase." The youth part of the cycle. Youth! Again, yanking this chain of signifiers out into cleaner air, we find decline ideology.

I see the experience of undergoing the cycle—especially the final stage of discarding—as a core experience of consciousness. Analyzing it shows, first of all, how emotional self-manipulation and continuing education go on throughout our human life course. Every fashion change you perform, in whatever your zone of alleged expertise, requires new learning, conscious and unconscious. The conscious knowledges (e.g., brand names) may become obsolete. Yet there are always millions who master them, and not just once and for all, but after a punctuated interval, again, many times. People become "knowledgeable," "smart shoppers," "educated consumers." (Praise for market learning uses the vocabulary of academic success.) I'm not interested in the *content* of what each individual learns in order to begin the cycle again, but in the unconscious experience, especially the continual unlearning that marks the end of the cycle. "Who loses and who wins, who's in, who's out . . . packs and sects of great ones, That ebb and flow by th' moon"—King Lear rightly begins with those who lose.

All our lives long, we—the entire population of the country—do remarkably well at these repeated educational and emotional examinations, including the forgetting required at the ebb. Gaping at the culture, critics notice prodigious acquisitions of new knowledge and feelings, and equally precipitous deaccessions. Running up to a war, for example, a nation learns geography, history, current events: the names of the enemy, the issues to be passionate about and those to ignore. Unlearning never comes without emotion; having learned to feel strongly, we are encouraged to let those feelings go. It may be painful.

In all fashion, the pattern we learn by going through the entire cycle is freighted with emotion. Purchase involves learning and wanting and spending money; possession involves some affective relationship with the object over time; going out of fashion (the end of one cycle) involves some yet-to-be-measured degree of rejection and loss. Wanting, getting, living with, losing, and—the phase omitted—discarding. Going through such a cognitive/emotional cycle unconsciously can be considered a process of socialization. It may seem like a "unique," "individual" experience, but it is structured into everyday life in such a way that participants experience the same cycle, time after time. Social practices can score—scar—the psyche. Feminist theorists like Thorsten Veblen, Sandra Bartky, and Naomi Wolf have shown how dangerous fashion can be in constructing aspects of gender identity: shame and narcissism, "femininity," the sense of being an object of display, a devalued commodity.[3]

But the fashion cycle has never previously been considered a practice through which American culture constructs our age identity and our sense of the meaning of "aging." What I propose here is that going through market cycles affects *our* experience of the life course. Our one and only life course. The fashion system promotes a specific "knowledge": what befalls the self in time. If purchasing-and-display make troubling demands on the psyche, discarding—in part because it is an unrepresented experience, an untheorized practice—can be far more dangerous. Over time, the routine involves constant relearning and altered emotions about such identity issues as durability versus transitoriness, investment of self versus withdrawal of self, and the most basic question about temporality: whether time can be relied upon to provide us with gain or loss. Discarding teaches us that the self can expect to *lose* from living in time—lose selfhood. And we learn this not just exceptionally but as a routine of everyday life, over and over. Under the rubrics of need and pleasure, people are taught that obeying the cyle is coterminous with life. Ninety is not too old to shop.[4]

The zone of my story is clothing, and my story is dense with specificity— I'm a woman of a certain class, historical era, region, and age, with her own family dynamics, personal psychology, access to theory. Why then do I want to posit some degree of broadly shared vulnerability to the fashion cycle? First, because the market's reach changes. In North America at the turn of the century, the rise of the department store, mass production, and advertising went along with the expansion of consumption-dedicated classes: middle- and upper-class women were the designated shoppers. Theorizing about fashion is often still based on models appropriate to that era. Men too still assume that men are never "docile bodies," never adversely affected by fashion.[5]

Now postmodern capitalism is making those older gender and class binaries anachronistic. The imperializing tendencies of the transnational apparel industry are sweeping up new male consumers, and swooping down the class ladder. In many countries men above the ideal age grow steadily more vulnerable to the cycle, but so do youthful male mall-goers. With "the mass production of cheap smart clothes," George Orwell pointed out during the Depression, even the unemployed in First World countries invest in the cycle.[6] Now the employed in Third World countries have been lured in. I see this in postrevolutionary Nicaragua every year. There too fashion is connected, via jeans, donated T-shirts, children's paintbox colors, and TV, with North

America/youth/vitality/pleasure. Everywhere higher status tends to mean more intense and repetitious involvement in the front end of the cycle, more rapid and frequent discards. Do people with that experience have *less* protection against decline narratives? And what of the increasing number of Americans who at midlife are downwardly mobile? These correlations are unstudied.

Moreover, "fashion" might include all cycles that comprise practices-with-objects. Perhaps they all make participants more vulnerable to decline narratives. Any semidurable objects that you must later replace may let you in for the basic experience of unwilling loss: music systems, cars, boats. The object need not be made of heavy metal. It can be furniture or houses, vacation spots. The object can "as easily take the form of a person or a person's time"; as Rachel Bowlby says, "anything at all" can be commodified.[7] Affective relations with the object are the key. Sports are one (once primarily male) version of the lifelong experience: there people voluntarily learn prominent names, facts, relationships, winners and losers, just the way in the clothing zone people learn the "new" and the "old-fashioned." Politics, film, popular music have also become zones of human discard: the prematurely declining careers of people with whom we have deeply identified teach related emotions. Language is a another powerful zone of loss, as expressions that made us feel "with it" become kitsch. Philosophies go out of fashion, and moral ideas. There are attempts to make whole political theories extinct. Through pressure to be "on the new" some degree of relearning, self-manipulation, and loss can be a part of any life.

Innocently going through normalized routines that appear to concern "things" softens up our psyches to accept other narratives of necessary loss personally and prematurely. The fashion cycle is only one of the mysterious ways both men and women learn, early in life in American culture and certainly no later than the middle years, that we are no-longer-young, no-longer-new. I can't speak *for* anyone but myself, but I speak here *to* all participants in any cycle who are willing to examine the degree to which they have been trained and aged by culture in ways they cannot yet imagine.[8] And—tactics again—whenever a true antiageist movement begins, women and men will need to be allies, and the elite too will need to see they have multiple stakes in the outcome.

Early Learning and Long Loves

My mother started taking me shopping with her, to Brooklyn's baroque and gilded discount store, Loehmann's, in the Bedford-Stuyvesant district, not far from Ebbett's Field, when I was only about six years old. Amid the grandeur of Jacobean-style benches and sculpted-figure torchères, I didn't yet care about clothes. The marble lion on the landing up to the second floor served as my mount from which to regard incuriously the "ladies" changing on the floor below. My mother wasn't then working, but she had worked at Macy's as a clerk and was still dreaming of being a buyer. By the time I was ten she had her teaching job and her checkbook.[9] Shopping was a pleasure for her for many reasons.

As a teenager, I was driven to Loehmann's by my mother regularly. By then I had moved into the next and ghastliest role in the history of my lifelong involvement with the garment industry. The clotheshorse. My mother had a connoisseur's eye for designer fashion and a Jeeves-like sensibility for correctness. By my college years, the combination gave me a wardrobe of a small number of perfect garments and a habit of minute attention to details: the cleanliness of cuffs, the absence of loose threads, the evenness of hems—a perfectionist's stance. Away from home, a scholarship student from a family trying to settle permanently in the middle class, I served as my own Jeeves. Bertie Wooster was not more meticulously turned out every day. Before dates, I fretted over matching hats and shoes and gloves. When I was asked to give a makeup demonstration girls crowded in, looking at a "New Yorker" applying eyeliner, mascara, eye shadow, blush (never lipstick). That era included French existential fashion associations (Vogue: "the unforgettable Juliette Greco")—pallor and doe eyes and some intellectual man like Sartre in the background. My favorite models, Suzy Parker and Dovima, broke through pre-pill restraint with sophisticated sultriness. I'm dropping these names and sense-of-the-era to demonstrate what a good student I was, how effective the training. My husband remembers the heavy boots he wore at that age, borrowed iconographicly from Marlon Brando in *The Wild One*. Almost everyone has this kind of recall about their first teenage learning experiences with "fashion." It was so intense, so sexualized, that it laid down the conditions for later-life nostalgia—as well as later-life purchasing habits.

As a college freshman, nota bene, I was already not just a student but teaching the lore. My students were prepped to learn (especially the private-school kids, previously sheltered from boys and lore and thrust in timidity into the college sex and marriage market). I didn't do any more to emphasize the importance of the subject than to appear during orientation week in broad daylight in my green eye-shadow and black turtleneck in front of eyes that had been looking at shirtwaists and white blouses and saddle shoes for a decade. In my appearance, foreign and yet tailored, "exotic" (that was Jewishness seen from outside) and meticulous, they may have seen a way of being both sexy and rebellious at relatively low social cost. I don't want to mock me or them. All steps toward rebellion can lead on to more interesting and subversive rebellions.

Retrospection, sharpened by the right questions, can demonstrate the construction of emotions and demystify "experience." I want to emphasize the cognitive/emotional functions of the little rite we were accomplishing in the bathroom of Comstock Hall during the postwar economic boom. Disregard the tiny style differences between us that loomed so large: some would go on buying shirtwaists and a few would buy turtlenecks. Disregard even the vast economic differences: some would buy gemstones and others have modest budgets for clothes and shoes. Whatever style we affected, from the point of view of lifelong learning and emotional baggage, every one of us attended boot camp for American culture, just like the kids who didn't go to college. The commitment to conforming to local norms is never so strong and credulous as in the teen years. In the Nineties fashion learning starts earlier yet, with preschoolers being inducted via toys and sneakers. Although one's relationship to fashion can and often does become more alienated over time, the process of involvement is "continuing education" in that it goes on outside of formal settings and continues forever. Nothing I say is likely to stop any of these behaviors. But theory can skew the meanings of this activity in slightly subversive ways, to make more conscious resistance possible.

I dislike shopping, even with my mother's help and high spirits. But there were many pleasures in the system my mother set up for turning me out in style. This is important, as no learning goes on without affect, and intense affect makes learning memorable. I shared some of the pleasures she got. Inducted into the fashion system in filial ways, we associate shopping with the way we bonded with the parent investing in us—usually a mother?—who provided the desire for the objects, the guidance, and the cash. Even leaving aside the factitious desire conferred by advertising, in any practice of cathecting an object can be found, thickly layered from childhood on, pleasure and serious misery, money power and symbolic love, class aspirations, competition in the sexual sweepstakes, "taste," and (for women), gender identity and female bonding. Were my own layers especially thick?

I also loved the clothes. Loving the clothes was so overdetermined and is now so transparent in my case that it strikes me as almost laughable. I had one little black dress, long and sleeveless and buttoned from top to bottom with two-dozen tiny cloth-covered buttons, that I felt made me look like Audrey Hepburn, who managed to give a slightly foreign and risqué air to looking boneless and cool. We were trained to find a model and try to transform ourselves in that direction. All my clothes were beautifully made: in the textures and cut of clothes, the love of beauty ("esthetics") can find an everyday outlet. Influenced by my mother, I appreciated the craft that went into them, the ingenuity of the design, the skill that set up the looms, the pains-taking that produced the final material item. When profit margins were lower, even "affordable" clothes were lined, some seams were finished; and in more expensive clothes, fabrics were matched across pockets and openings and finishing (seams, embroidery, sequins) was done by hand. "We don't see workmanship like that any more"—except in a garment that costs what a Nicaraguan family spends to survive for a year. I won't knock esthetics or appreciation for skill, but that's all the space they'll get here, because from the point of view of continuous education these values just give a fillip to learning what "taste" is and demonstrating expensively that you have it, and they provide the subordinate emotions that, added up together, overproduce "loving the objects."

I "loved" the clothes more than we are supposed to. And that was another saving touch of excess—perhaps the crucial one—for the cycle to snag on. My good feelings toward an object take a form fashion must frown on: I go in for long possession. I have clothes for comfort and show that I go on wearing year after year. I have a house-painting outfit flecked with as much paint as a Jackson Pollack. I had a bathrobe that I wore to write in every day for years, until it fell into tatters at unrepairable places. Two party dresses, as the second-hand furniture dealers say, "have age on them."

I harp on this subversive affection because it is relevant to the emotional swings of the cycle. No possession without its levy of feeling. No intense initial relationship with objects, without some perilous aftermath pinned into its side. The bad side of loving the objects now emerges. Leaving them. As long as one is growing physically, discarding is necessary not optional; it has its own name, "outgrowing." Childhood is (or was) the innocent time of the cycle: relatively little cathexis at the beginning, no coercion to discard, no sorrow at the end. It's after one has outgrown outgrowing that people can unconsciously feel coerced when forced to discard. And some enact their resistance.

I keep a drawer full of fabrics, from clothes whose styles or patterns were made obsolete. Fabrics with Renaissance or art nouveau designs, a scrap of silk velvet I bought a yard of in Paris in the Seventies, a cotton piqué dress that I was led to cut too short in one of the recurrent miniphases. I regret many that I didn't—couldn't—save. If that verb sounds human, that's close to how I felt. I look regretfully as each favorite faultlessly becomes "unfashionable." Stubborn but unable to break out of the system, I have my bottom drawer, a small permanent private museum of my sensualities and esthetic tastes and semiotic intentions and economic ambitions that have publicly been made "passé." They may be *shmattes*—a Yiddish word for old clothes that nicely combines contempt and affection—but I didn't make them rags. The drawer is a mausoleum in which are housed the relics of objects I learned to love and then learned to relinquish publicly. I'm not nostalgic about them; I don't yearn to be the self that wore them. By itself my sweet museum of schmattes doesn't take us far. But it's telling, a bit of the "micropolitics" of everyday life, a bit of filial synthesis of my parents' values. It expresses my originally intuitive resistance to the required second half of the fashion process: the death of the loved object, the making of the current into "the past"— the emotional production of the passé and every other dire outcome that is thus foretold—in short, the shedding of pieces of the self.

Some Possible Sources of Resistance

Do other people have museums? How would we know how widespread clinging to old objects is when next to nothing is spoken or written about this end of the cycle? I was astonished and charmed to find, in Ann Beattie's *Another You,* a midlife woman who hangs onto her clothes. When she turns embroidered free-flowing dresses into summer nightgowns, she does it as a semiconscious resister: "Maybe . . . it wasn't judiciousness so much as a desire to make the past fit in with the present."[10] Beattie senses the mute urge to undo the binary that savages "the past." "The past" is something we learned to love and assumed we'd long possess. Indeed, I like to believe that everyone reading this essay has devised some ways in which they resist mandatory obsolescence.[11]

In my own case, the exceptional conditions of my arrangement provided private sources of detachment. To start with, my mother writes the checks. My husband doesn't come on these trips and he invariably likes what I bring home. His kind of noninvestment maintains and supports some of my estrangement from the system, the reach of its economic, psychosexual, heterosexist, tentacles. For most of my life, most of the time, I have not paid and do not pay much at all for having a relationship to fashion. It's amazing what a difference it makes. Since I also frequently wear what my mother sends, including her hand-me-downs, I wear clothes without any fetishizing of my "unique" taste and choice and semiotic intentions. I can wear something without any delusion that getting it was the fun part. A garment suffices if it marks me—when a mark is needed—as a just sufficiently fashionable New England woman of the middle class of an academic/bohemian type who has pretensions to shoulders, legs, etcetera.

Therefore, other explanations are needed for why I am so loathe to relinquish the clothes. Certainly they represented my mother's continuing good will, which didn't let me down when I was no longer "young" but follows me through my middle years. They represented her money, which she earned—with pleasure, to be sure, because she enjoyed being a first-grade teacher, an educator, a Deweyite, and, of course, an independent woman. My mother's own complex psychological, feminist, and class relationship to clothes—which I have known since childhood—is a set of facts material to my narrative of resistance. I knew the values of a woman-earned dollar.

And those of a dollar earned by a man. My father, who died in 1974, was a leftist with a lifelong, eloquent, proselytizing and aggressive allegiance to the working class. A man marked by the Depression, who worked long hours in all weathers, he never forgot how hard it could be to make a living under capitalism. During his forties, from being a working man with skills he turned himself into a small businessman who owned and drove his own truck and later owned and worked his small parking lot. All this time the clothes he wore were a kind of uniform: khaki pants over a union suit, heavy plaid work shirts, layered one over the other in the winter so his arms would be free, a watch cap. He never wore a tie; he didn't own a middle-class jacket until many years later. I've known only one person more alienated from the American fashion cycle. (This was my mother's brother, my Uncle Charlie. In adulthood, he never owned more than two pairs of pants. When the other pair was stolen, and my mother expressed sympathy, he shrugged, "One less thing to worry about.") My father bought good tools and saved them and over time gave them to me. My shop is not a museum; I use these tools frequently. He repaired things—not just (as a young man) professionally but lifelong as an instinct and a form of identity. He was not only frugal in practice but anti-bourgeois in theory. My mother and I went shopping, he kept to a different standard. In my teens, I experienced that contrast of personalities and ideologies with pain, but now I see it as part of the excess that saved me.

My mausoleum was a result of already being partly detached from cold-hearted fashion even before I knew how to theorize it. Later I discovered that modern capitalism needs to train us all to perform the cycle. Those who can see that they are part of the system feel somewhat degraded by their powerlessness to resist it much, or to exit entirely; somewhat sheepish about showing off the latest item they've purchased even though it proves what they've learned about technology or style or whatever "the new" proves; somewhat embarrassed about conspicuous consumption even though their class situations may require it as condition and reward; and defensive enough to harp on pleasure.[12] So far, we are vulnerable to these self-criticisms without (even on the left) having found sufficient justification for inventing collective resistance.

There is a justification. I believe that everyone caught up in the cycle potentially has a grave emotional grievance against it. We are emotionally manipulated by being required to give up allegiances, and deprived when we succumb and do give them up. Muriel Spark has a poem about seeing "one sad shoe" thrown out on the highway. Perhaps the owner kept the other because he was afraid "to hurt its feelings?" She too speaks of "my awe and my sad pity."[13]

Like the old shoe, our objects may be trivial in themselves—I'll say here that for my argument they *are* trivial, *pace* my dear, loyal, working-class-identified father, who saw them as equivalents of hard labor. *Pace* my dear, generous, middle-class-identified mother, who sees them as objects of beauty and skill and signs of achieved status. Their points of view are both right, within their contexts. She will forgive me, and he would, once I make my theoretical point clear, because together, jointly and severally, they freed me to learn what I needed in order to make it. As things, clothes are rags and heavy metals are scrap. What counts is how we feel about them—the amount of self we use up in the fashion cycle, and what we are forced to learn by loving and losing, again and again, bits of self. Awe and sad pity can be reserved for ourselves.

Maybe resistance to the fashion cycle is connected with a kind of positive or Kohutian narcissism, the kind of self-preservation that in extremis rescues us from thoughts of suicide, that nerves us to survive torture—the power that not only keeps us from succumbing to staggering onslaughts on selfhood like these but also helps against the minute, repetitive, incremental, and invisible onslaughts that culture exposes us to.

The Scream Came from the Dressing Room

A kind of resistance actually may begin early in the cycle, in the relationship between the fashion we buy and the putative "self" that buys it. This happens at point of purchase, the cynosure of anecdote and theory. Young, participants develop the habit ("shopping") of providing moments when they are supposed to cathect an object. Marketeers and economists talk about the point of purchase as the moment of the self's greatest "pleasure," not just to sell goods but also because they have an interest in representing the object as gradually becoming less satisfactory—another simple decline narrative. Obviously, point of purchase has to be made into an intense moment. Here the culture succeeds one way or another, because intensity can as easily be made out of pain as pleasure. More easily. The fashion side of my age autobiography began with my being driven as an adolescent toward that moment, in order to provide a context in which to analyze all the unpleasures, especially those of the unregarded end.

Everyone who tries on "looks"—whether in clothes or cars or houses or vacation spots—believes that she/he has a relationship to that look which seems pretty important. "The self chooses its look." In my lifetime, I have moved from a girlhood spent in the working/lower middle classes to a mid-adulthood in the academic/middle upper classes, and I have not known a woman who did not speak as if she had a special relationship with the front end of the cycle—meaning, "her" look. We sidle up to any "choice" we make and think of it, naively, as an "expression" of self. There's flattery in this mar-keteers' view: the buyer is made to seem creative, individual, intentional, potent. When semiotic approaches to fashion privilege "expressivity" and expand discourse about "meanings," they too effectively enhance the intensity of the transactions around the point of purchase.

There's mystification too: it implies free choice, and an original uninflu-enced self, and an "infinite" array of looks, provided by the astonishing American "free-market" system, the envy of all the world. But in fact there's only a limited array of looks (rigidly determined by the market despite all the talk of "choices"); the self is strongly influenced to change by the multiple discourses elaborating the purported differences among looks past and present; and the idea of "selecting" among current looks (perfectly accurate within the most constrained view of the procedure) hides the prior condition of selection, which is money. Most of shopping is not-buying, because you can't afford to. Each time you back away from a purchase you relearn your class standing, as based on disposable income. This we're not supposed to mention, since in a class hierarchy it's humiliating to admit we can't afford something.

Despite knowing at some level that "free" choice is a joke, everyone in the culture who can afford to buy semidurable, obsolescing goods participates in some part of the mystification that goes with a vocabulary of choosing. *Later,* suppressing any prior misery, we say, "I chose the little black one with buttons."

The self in consumption studies (as in marketing) is the self that wants to buy, gets enjoyment, "appropriates" the object. The self in age studies (as in feminism) can not be considered just a mystified victim; it is also a source of resistance. But neither is it a perfectly free and delighted elector of its plea-sures. This complex self is a necessary assumption for antiessentialism—for an age theory that sees the life course both historically and developmentally, as, ideally, an uncoerced narrative of being and becoming.

The consumption self is belied by pain we know we are having. Say I'm in a dressing room and I shuck off a dress. I've divested myself of a look. I'm still well within the system. I'll try on another, discard that, and so on, maybe for hours; then I get fraught, fret, conclude "nothing looks good on me," leave the store depressed and discouraged and even truly grieving. Every woman I know says this happens to her. Going into the dressing room might always result in an inner scream. For women, clothing comes with too many competing images, too many confusing discourses, too much coercion to be in the system, too much fear of failure. Moreover, while some looks might be better than others for the majority of the population, we in the majority don't get them. The average American woman is not quite 5'4" tall and weighs 143 pounds.[14] So any look that emphasizes slenderness, or height, or perfect muscle tone—qualities also falsely associated with "youth"—is going to be wrong in the dressing room. Most of the time, then, the majority must feel wrong about itself while trying on clothes, doesn't want to buy them, and leaves the place of defeat in dejection. Feminist theory has provided saving explanations for this phenomenon. The feminist self knows itself always about-to-be-grieved by fashion.

Maybe all selves are grieved. Economist Albert O. Hirschman, a rare analyst of disappointment within the cycle, thinks that "disappointment with oneself" might be the result of "any purchase that requires discrimination on the part of the buyer."[15] With young men overwhelmingly featured in ads, what protects midlife men in the dressing room? Perhaps disappointment with oneself comes from any purchase that requires more money than you have, or more "taste" (class-based learning) than you think you have, or a different body. In fact, isn't it possible that the point of purchase brings about a net lowering of self-esteem in one way or another? This must be denied in many ways so that treadmill of cycling can go on.

Subjects might want to calculate how much at point of purchase they are avoiding pain, how much denying pain, and how much finding pleasure. One of the compromises a woman often describes conversationally to a friend involves maintaining some unstated continuity with the way she likes to dress. I can always find basic black, one friend wears eccentric belts, another handwoven cloth. The shopper has succeeded, as my mother and I did in my first paragraph, in buying *something*. In describing this as a success, she hides the scream and reveals her semiparticipation in the system, constrained but mildly subversive of the automatism of changed selfhood. No one I know shucks her wardrobe annually; people postpone getting into another new look; they slow down the cycle. At some level, by my age most women are not "seduced" by fashion. If they get a little anticipatory lift when, say, the previews of the fall collection come out, that rather complicated feeling does not actually translate into joy or wholehearted expectation in the stores. "The triumph of hope over experience" ought to be torn away from its current demeaning locus (second marriage) and put squarely where/wear it belongs: attached to *fashion* in all its forms.

As a relationship with a chosen object continues, however, it may become genuinely personal—not necessarily happier—because of the life we lived in it. I remember the evening I first wore that little black dress—the first freshman "mixer"—and the way even though *it* was perfect, I didn't make a hit. I didn't blame the dress. Even now I can think of it and immediately recall the lonely, shy girl who wore it. There was another great dress later on that the hostile age gaze declared "too young." A wool suit that I felt wonderfully competent in, that I still keep hanging in my closet. The scarf I wore at my father's funeral. However slightly, identity is bound up in some definite way with the events associated with the item, the historical era or time of life. There's a whole range of ways in which we *put* self into a chosen object.

Despite the buyer's feelings of relationship, reserve, and reluctance, she/he eventually goes on to make a replacement purchase. An inexhaustible will-to-believe in the system? As a life of consumption goes on, the misery accrues, and hesitation builds up. I doubt that by midlife many believe the implied promises of the manufacturers (that we'll advance our status or beauty or youth or superiority, or acquire someone else credulous enough to believe in our representation). Middle-ageism too raises doubts about the connection between a delivery and a surge of happiness. That is why the guy driving the red convertible seems such an ingenu. The will-to-believe is not exactly robust. The tantalizing resources of advertising must be constantly at work so that the no-longer-deluded self can hide from itself its grudging enforced relationship to the system.

If we return to the scene in the dressing room, then, your dejections fit into the fashion cycle. The cycle survives them. It doesn't care one way or another if you go out into the harsh world of observers feeling anxious. But might you buy more if you didn't get dejected? If, say, you yearned to fall in love with the fall line and then the fall line turned out to fit you in some delicious way that actually fed and satisfied some modest fantasy of improved life chances? But then you might keep using the magic garment rather than discarding it. For built-in obsolescence to work, you need to buy not once but many times. You need not only to fall in love, but to fall out of love. "Dissatisfaction is our most important product." And discarding actually comes more readily if you feel unhappy and unexpectant as early as the first stage of the cycle—like so many women, and now, midlife men. On our way to estimating our deeper grievance against the system, it is worth noting why point-of-purchase dejection—low self-esteem, anxiety, premonition of failure (whatever you record it as)—is not incidental to the system but useful. As long as you locate failure in the object and in your self, rather than in the cycle, the system remains untouched by your misery.

Get Rid of/Reject/Lose/Grieve

The moment we're not supposed to acknowledge is the moment of getting rid of a now-unfashionable object that we once identified with. In neither marketing nor consumption theory is there a name that matches "point of purchase" to describe the end of the relationship with that object. Call it "the point of losing." We're supposed to get it over with, and get over it, rather silently. The ideological label we learn to apply is that discarding is, once again, free choice. To express this, we are trained to welcome the new enthusiastically and mock the old. Men look in disbelief at their old ties, narrow pants, tennis sneakers. Women: "How did we ever wear those psychedelic pastels, those shoulder pads, those . . . ?" Such language makes relinquishment seem voluntary. Men boast that they keep clothes long, but the system half-permits men to do that; so keeping things, for men, doesn't prove they exercise more will within the fashion cycle or have more detachment from it. (My father could have provided arguments against "commodified desire" on behalf of the real needs of the world.)

For clothes, structures are provided to assure good riddance. Goodwill, the Sister City project, and now, as the middle class diminishes, the consignment store. Clothes used to go as hand-me-downs to younger siblings or cousins. Now they go mostly to strangers. Isn't it lucky for the market that the poor ye shall have always with ye? Rules are provided for relinquishing. "If that tired old skirt has been in your closet for more than two years, now is the time to get rid of it." (Apparently, many people keep clothes hanging in the closet for *years* after fashion says no.) Since it is practical and virtuous to give away clothes, this makes any painful feelings we may have about discarding irrational, preventing hostility toward the entire cycle. The concept of "recycling" enrolls our once-valued objects in the lists along with plastic, green glass, newspapers, and other waste.

The unhappiness involved in change—even when it's upwardly mobile (supposedly desired) change—doesn't often come into print in advanced industrial societies. But in a 1935 novel by Margaret Ayer Barnes, about a successful man whose conspicuous consumption keeps leaping ahead of his submissive wife's, the misery of the wife about moving on wells up in pages of soft-voiced objection. "I love this house and I love Oakwood Terrace. I like the neighborhood and I like the neighbors and I'm perfectly devoted to Susan and Elmer. . . . If we moved we'd never see them." Her husband devalues these feelings along with the other current satisfactions Edna has: the friends the children have made, the class status they already possess, the love they have shared in that place. He tells a future story he calls progress: headier friends, handsomer goods, higher status. "She raised her head a little to look around the den at the beloved household objects that surrounded them. She could not see them clearly because of the tears in her eyes."[16] She is never happy with their (his) possessions again.

When sorrow about the new is given to a character, it's given someone who isn't quite with the program. Edna has to be represented as not only humanly conservative (which can be read as touching) but also as slow to add new skills, interest, and knowledge. She's affectionate but boring. She's also unfashionably plump and no longer young. The idea of progress that her husband lives has been a model from early in the era of conglomerate capitalism, as Thorstein Veblen explained in *The Theory of the Leisure Class*. People with increasing incomes are led to believe that if you are rich, you're smart; if both, you should readily pick up new social class cues and change your consumption patterns. Early in the century, a term from the clothing industry began to designate *people* as back "numbers." In F. Scott Fitzgerald's *Tender Is the Night*, a midlife woman thinks young people are saying it of her and her husband, even though they are rich and fashionable.[17] Suddenly people were as discardable as clothes. Visual images of men or women clinging to "past" styles are still a metaphor for not keeping up. Back numbers can be the poor, the rural, the elderly, or the dowdy. Barbara Ehrenreich said once that the working classes had been "assigned the symbolic burden of [representing] the past."[18] Now anyone in midlife, however style-conscious, is also liable to carry that load. Those whose being is less important that their ability to bear a product appropriately: this is beginning to look like a majority category. Only the younger—and a tiny part of that age class—will be left to represent the future.

Given our eyes' reliance on the semiotics of dress and appearance, midlife people who wear older hair or dress styles do look retrograde—even if we know that men can be stupid in Armani suits and that we ourselves can think just as well in a bathrobe as in a Chanel. Ayer Barnes was writing during the Depression, when people forced into downward mobility did not just know but passionately felt all the flaws in the dogma that we choose our fashions and that our fashions "represent" us. Edna gets to utter one mildly subversive query as she succumbs to her husband's constructed desires. "Oh, dear . . .

why not be satisfied?" (235). If being satisfied over the long term with what you already have is constructed in mainstream discourse as something that only the dim-witted or the unsuccessful or the middle-aged feel, then we'll never get people to acknowledge that there are significant human problems at the end of the fashion cycle, as there are at the beginning, not to mention something disturbing about the entire cycle itself.

The Fashion Cycle and the Life Course

The fashion cycle constructs our emotions to teach us, unconsciously, a normal pattern of feelings over time, about time. As I have suggested, this begins with some degree of wanting/desiring, and, however qualified, some level of self-identification with our "choice" that could be called (self-) loving. This phase is complexly associated with "youth." Then the middle of our relationship contains some degree of affect (comfort, loyalty, esthetic enjoyment, eventfulness)—a continuity of self-investment. And then comes the need to enter the allegedly more progressive next cycle: (self-) rejection. Obedience sooner or later follows. As it does, the self learns it *will* lose the object into which it has genuinely put a part of itself. The part may be tiny—that wouldn't obviate some sense of loss. Compulsory repetition brands the lesson as experience. That's the point of losing. Over time, the self learns its relationship to passing time: loss from within. The social name given to this biographical movement is "decline." The social name given to the process is "aging." The item in question is "old" and having feeling for it labels you as old.

Roland Barthes has described the workings of fashion in his own emotional, resistant way as "a vengeful present which each year sacrifices the signs of the preceding year, it is only *today* that . . . 'Prints are winning at the races.'" "Each year it reverses entirely and at a single stroke collapses into the nothingness of the past. . . . [Fashion] disavows the past with violence." I admire Barthes's vengeful language. But we need to go beyond projecting emotions on to the fashion system in order to talk directly about the effects on us—on our sense of self over the life course—of participating in its cycle. It isn't just that "fashion is systematically unfaithful" but that it makes us unfaithful to parts of ourselves. We don't in fact disavow the past "with violence" or glee, as a more rigid system might ordain. (Sorrow or regret; wry amusement; silent oblivion are also possible.) But we do disavow the past in whatever mode we relinquish the prior object. It's not that the past is shameful, it is we who incur shame if we ally ourselves with the past, the unwanted, the "old."[19]

It is essential to the market system that we be constructed, by consumerism, to live the cycle even though the cycle implicitly devalues our prior selfhood. Into the foreseeable future, then, people will go on learning to downgrade old knowledge, dispraise past objects of affection, discard them, and identify the renewed self with the newly accepted values that despise the old. If we were to start explicitly opposing fashion on these philosophical grounds, the system would insist we were just losing competence in another locus of control and trying to hide the loss. Since midlife aging—being not-young—is now almost synonymous with being unfashionable, this would be plausible to many people. They would displace their rage onto what they think of as natural aging, where rage appears to be futile.

In such overdetermined circumstances, it is naive to think that "aging Baby Boomers" with nothing but financial power are going to be able to reen-gineer American culture and save their cohort from middle-ageism. They can't expunge their own internalizations and displacements before they un-derstand the mysterious condition of being (re)socialized into midlife aging.

Aging-as-Loss at Midlife

Of all the emotional learning we endure, the very oddest acquisition in this historical era is an individual's internal acceptance of a lesser identifi-cation with an "aging" and "declining" self, occurring long before debility at some unspecified time in the middle years. As male superiority in age identity is being diminished, men as well as women are likely to accept a new self-image as a being who fails on certain already-specified and essentially desir-able measures. At first these may be read as piecemeal moments of random failure—the soliloquy of age anxiety works to hold on to this idea of ran-domness. But eventually (as we saw in the Entrance story), the incidents are fit into a master narrative of aging. The middle years can be recognized, al-though that is far too definite a verb, as the stage when one's worth has sud-denly become shaky. We are aged by culture through a process of accepting "Time" as ensuring losses to prior achieved identity.

The analysis of the market cycle begins to answer the question of why people accept any of this in midlife (especially when they are otherwise as healthy, well-employed, loved, as before). This is a strange phenomenon; let's estrange it. Accepting decline counters the instinct for maintaining self-esteem and for preserving identity. Psychologists tell us (or used to tell us) that people tend to have rather stable traits over the life course, and post-Freudian therapists and theorists speak of developmental processes going on through midlife and beyond, so the notion of midlife decline counters both our own intuitions and many contemporary theories about self.[20]

Identity-stripping via aging also requires the self to reject or consider in-consequential all the counternarratives that emphasize aging into wisdom or maturity or any valued progress. True, we don't all read development literature, high or pop, or feminist midlife progress fiction. But we have all been taught from childhood on through everyday practices and celebratory occasions that we relinquish a past self only to come into a same-but-better one. We happily gave up the self that carried a blanket and sucked its thumb, that didn't know how to gargle, skip, or read, and in that process we learned to look forward to growing older in order to get better attributes. In other words, in the early crucial decades we learn, without benefit of purchases, one way to see the life course as a progress. Suddenly, not much farther along, through a kind of enforced progress march symbolized by relinquishing objects, we have to begin to unlearn that, and learn that it's a decline.

The specific mechanisms by which this form of masochistic knowledge gets installed—even in those with what I would consider excellent defenses (in their different ways, Alpha males, older feminists, minority-empowerment advocates, those emerging into the middle class at midlife)—need to be detailed. The installation involves a long, silent resocialization. Other resocialization processes that sociologists talk about concern incarcerated prisoners getting therapy or immigrants becoming naturalized as citizens—all groups of people in institutional programs that cost someone else real money, that require the subjects to participate consciously and voluntarily, and that offer positive outcomes as the reward for change. While learning aging, on the other hand, each of us is responsible for our own internalizations. We rarely know it's happening, we don't known what it's costing us, and it hurts. "Mechanisms similar to those found in the mourning of loved ones must be set in motion, if change is to occur. Since these of necessity involve anguish and fear, resocialization is not tranquil."[21] But discovering our unconscious pain may be difficult.

With so much personal pain and even some cognitive dissonance involved, it seems even odder that belief in midlife decline is so entrenched. This happens at a time in history when the life course has been extended even further than at the turn of the century, for men as well as women, when many of us believe we look better and feel healthier than our parents did at the same age, and when antiageist thinking is seeping slowly into some subcultures. If the culture must have decline-via-aging, why isn't it getting located ever later in the life course?

Midlife decline is a side of culture that needs a lot of explaining.

Age Consciousness and Resistance

There's no standard explanation for how men and women learn around midlife to feel we are losing and to blame ourselves for aging. I'm building narrative and theory here, hoping others will want to continue with the project. *Declining to Decline* has mainly emphasized the level of discourse, to show how subtly and continually age "knowledge" is being diffused through culture. Yet people do not become resocialized in mid-adulthood simply by being told we're declining. Discourse cannot by itself explain how midlife identity-stripping occurs.

If it did, all (all!) we would need do, once united into a pressure group, is reform mainstream culture. We could pressure the mainstream to eliminate the malign stereotyping of Boomers, and for experts on "aging" turn to novelists producing midlife heroines and heroes, to humanistic gerontologists, midlife development specialists, age theorists and critics and historians. We could offer an age-conscious conceptual framework in which to do textual, autobiographical, and social analysis. Putting discourse on the defensive cannot be accomplished as long as only a few people do it. We few can be attacked as querulous, as if we were asking for a special dispensation of the laws of the universe for ourselves. With enough creative reinforcement and conceptual backing, with numbers of people in crucial discursive sites, however, I think we could have some successes at this level of the enterprise, and that they would be important. Chains of age-graded decline metaphors might appear in print not casually, as now, as if they were accepted truths, but as hesitant (declining) opinions that needed to be explicitly defended and reasserted. And because of the lively, persuasive, and frequent repetitions of antiageist ideas, young people might learn *them* by rote and tell them with creative conviction.

My earlier writings were organized to abet these strategies. I not only tried to put decline on the defensive; I also tried to shoehorn a more plausible idea of progress into the unreceptive mainstream, offering readers options for recognizing the falsities of the narrative of decline and renarrativizing their age autobiography. People have let me see them working through these ideas.

But such reasoned invitations and examples might prove inadequate in an atmosphere so toxic. Even if we were to change discourse considerably, we could still find ourselves stymied. Decline feels true to many people because it *enacts* itself. *Practices* constrain us to translate "messages" into feelings, meanings, and habits. The important fact about practices, in Ian Hunter's terms, is "that the use of such and such a procedure becomes compulsory: that a particular technique has been installed, that . . . individuals master a particular technology for identifying colors or confessing their sins or finding their conscience reflected in literary characters, and so on."[22] My discussion of the fashion cycle suggests that as we master a technology of remaining fashionable, within the current discursive climate, we practice identity stripping and learn decline unconsciously.

The fashion cycle teaches losing as fate through its own cumulative emotional effects, but other practices, cyclings, and stories of losing deepen the unconscious lesson: discontinuities in work life (where your "old" skills or knowledge become useless, or your "old" job disappears). Bodybuilding, whether through aerobics or weight training, is another practice that, in the words of Margaret Morse, teaches its participants "constant effort without redemption," "a continuous awareness of the shortfall," a kind of "'slow death.'"[23] Like the fashion cycle, body building promises a staving-off of decline but no exit from the cycle. There must be many other sources of invisible, insidious aging practices. Resocialization-into-midlife-aging is bound to have a curious, thick, overdetermined story. This chapter's analysis of a particular practice, added to previous analyses of specific midlife discourses, can help us comprehend how little of midlife pain is natural; how much it depends on reiterated stresses and patterns. Age studies is vitally interested in these issues and in encouraging the other cultural studies to address them.

In the current culture it would be pointless to instruct numbed participants to stop shopping, give up aerobics, never look in mirrors. As early antifashion feminists realized, the answer cannot be to end harmful practices mechanically. But it might snap shoppers into mindfulness to warn them that they'll reach the point of losing whenever they get into the cycle.

In general, once we recognize our location in a cultural war centered on age, we need to experience ourselves as both targets and resisters. "The contradictions . . . must be intensified," as Sandra Bartky reminds us in a related context.[24] If "aging practices" happen, so can creative alternatives to aging practices. If you can't wait to find out what would happen to your relationship to shopping under this regime of wariness, good. (And let us all know.) With practice and collective reinforcement, just like antiracism, antisexism, antihomophobia, age consciousness becomes automatic, permanent, freed from the cycle. It becomes a piece of self you need never lose.

11

Doing Age Theory

What is this science which only holds good when its subjects
stand still?

—Martin Nicolaus

AGE remains an impoverished concept in much of the theorizing about
discourse that has made American intellectual life so exciting in the last
twenty years. Where age studies should be, there are gaps—really (to use a
metaphor from the spatial realm favored by theory), a landscape of crevasses.[1]
And since each crevasse, covered with untouched snow, looks like ordinary
terrain, theorists march across unwarily. One definition of theorizing could be
"to problematize the ordinary"—including categories of the self that remain
stubbornly ordinary. Theory plants red flags in discursive fields that look innocently (but are ominously) blank.

As someone who has been teaching myself an age-conscious perspective
over many years in part by applying existing cultural theory, I want to set up
red flags to mark places where theoretical work on age and aging might begin.
In the process, I need to point more precisely to some of the harms that come
from neglecting age as a construct and as an aspect of identity, and some of
the benefits that might accrue from doing age theory in the humanities. It is
too soon to list and order the conditions that have prevented age from receiving the scrutiny it warrants, but we might pause to wonder why the respect,
sensitivity, skills, and urgency that go into analyzing gender, race/ethnicity,
sexual orientation, class, nation, or geographic place (and sometimes politics,
handicap, and religion), have not been transferred to age. In the academy
failures of transfer must have powerful inhibiting causes. Steady reinforcement of other "identity" issues has made many theorists conscious of their
multiple subject positionings. Coming to consciousness has transformed their
writing and their lives. That in turn is changing the university, the society.

Similar startling changes might come from theorizing age. Kathleen
Woodward, who has advanced age theory at her juncture of feminism, literature, psychoanalysis, and philosophy, has written, "I want to insist that we

take a person's age and experience into critical account when we entertain their formulations of life's events."[2] Before we can insist on any such thing, of course, literary and cultural critics and theorists need to take into account their own conceptions of age and their relation to the cultural system organized around age. At present, few do. Meanwhile we are offering "formulations of life's events" in a vast array of contexts: to begin with, whenever we talk about subjectivity or identity—or temporality, narrative and character, generations or "waves," youth culture, and of course old age; when writing biography or autobiography; and when using age tropes to talk about a vaster array of topics. I will focus mainly on autobiography and biography, broadly understood as the age-graded life-course narratives that each of us tells about self and others, whether for archival purposes or informally in conversation.

I argue that age-inflected discourses draw upon the assumptions of contemporary American age ideology and are constrained even in details by the master narrative of decline. Many formulators alert to other constructions implicitly keep in circulation the sleepy illusion that age and aging are ahistorical, prediscursive—natural. And this can happen because age is still at the stage where gender and race used to be: hidden by its supposed foundation in "the body." Because the master narrative of decline biases our personal narratives of aging, it—like the master narratives of race and gender—threatens our being. Because becoming is linked to being, the neglect of age is a comprehensive threat.

"Doing Age Theory" might be called an informal prolegomenon to age theory. If we can understand the so-called *aging body* as a discursive construction, that outcome could change the way we tell our autobiographies and the biographies of others. In the study of narrative, where temporality can now be wrenched away from aging only with difficulty, it would give us a conceptual tool. It should strengthen theorizing about gendered and racialized bodies, about "the body" in culture. Here, toward the end of the book, I try to encourage readers directly—or perhaps incite them—to engage in age work freely and creatively in tandem with their existing interests. Can we now recognize common interests in the emerging discourse of age? Not because we all have bodies or because we all have the "same midlife" (whatever that would be), but because in different ways human subjects in North America are exposed to ageism and middle-ageism and don't know it. Other "essentialist boundaries" are being used to divide the body politic and the labor force and make coalition politics difficult.[3] "Middle age" is being added to these, sharpening the divisions into ever smaller competitive fractions. Although the stakes may not be identical for all, all have a great stake in revising age ideology.

No Riddle: A Digression on Method

There are moments when the most dramatic and efficient way to teach is to pick out deficiencies in common ways of thinking—because the eagerness to learn comes from yearning to transcend one's blindness. This yearning has come over me several times. With feminism, it happened in an instant in the early Seventies. A riddle was going around the country: "A father and son are driving in a car; there's an accident in which the two are terribly injured. They are taken to two different hospitals. A surgeon coming into the operating room where the boy lies stops short, exclaiming, 'I can't operate. This is my son!' How could this be?"

I didn't get it.

My failure was a revelation. I had to learn why I, not only a member of the class of women, but a progressive, a woman getting a Ph.D., the daughter of a career woman and the mother of a son, should have missed grasping that the surgeon is a woman. The acknowledgment that even the well-positioned sometimes miss the riddle must justify my use of exempla taken from current writing by people in literary and cultural studies.[4] Any particular example I chose could be matched by dozens of others. As so often in the close encounters of the academy, the critic winds up, with a groan, appearing to single out for criticism the very people who might with one deft turn transfer their acumen to the subject of age and join an age-oriented critical culture. For all these reasons, I offered a dialogue to those whose work I used at greater length.[5]

It would have been elegant to provide a single riddle. Actually, one useful riddle might be: "How old am I [the author of this book]?" Given the pressure to think age-specifically some readers may have been trying to figure this out from clues found in my age autobiography. Some part of their response to this book may be based on the age they imagine me to have.[6]

As more instances accumulated—as I learned I was in fact uncovering a master narrative whose grip over discourse was staggeringly tenacious—I had to create principles for selection. At first I thought everyone would notice and object to ostentatiously sexist and ageist comments, like the following, without my intervention. A cultural critic, Rob Shields, attacking previous writers on consumption, quotes Alan Tomlinson, who "in his introduction to consumer cultures, has called the critiques, 'sad, dislocated, elitist, perhaps menopausal.'" Shields continues his argument without a moment's pause over that final adjective. Like Tomlinson, he too wants to persuade us that consumer culture "can be exciting, novel, convenient, and fun." In order to personally possess all these glittering adjectives associated with youth, Tomlinson (then forty-one) used "menopausal" as a male pejorative. Shields (thirty-two) endorses all this. Readers are interpellated by age: younger ones are casually socialized into the idea of midlife aging as "loss and dislocation," emotions appropriate to their future age class; people "in" their middle years are reminded; potential resistance, if any, is weakened. Both sets of readers learn that the coded opposite to "young" in contemporary culture is not "old" but "middle-aged." In such binaries the midlife is to all intents essentialized—reified—as a category of being. In a Duke University Press catalog, Bruce Robbins's blurb for a book describes it as "a young, lively, street-wise, culturally cool reappropriation of a tradition of thought often associated with graying white male modernists."[7] Doing cultural studies in this age-unconscious way offers many opportunities for signing "I'm not middle-aged" to others in the academy.

The examples that follow survived my cuts. None could be as egregious as those just cited. Each appeared in a prestigious setting. Each, although subtle in its own terms, illustrates a fragment of the master narrative that is troubling, representative, or crucial to age theory at the present time. They could not be so obscure as to require an extended reading on my part. Let's start by calling age theory an educated sensitivity to age-related cultural cues.

A Thirteen-Year-Old Makes a Joke

A theorist writing the afterword to a book of terms for literary study begins by telling an anecdote. To do so, he defines an "anecdote" as something that "stands for . . . a socially pivotal and pervasive biography"; its effect is "to trigger a narrative sense of community that the anecdote evokes by evoking the master biography."[8] This is initially promising for an age theorist, because biography almost invariably obfuscates the biographer's dependence on the age constructs of his or her own era, and if the biographical subject lived under a different age system, ignores the influence of that system. Foregrounding "biography" and "community" together holds out hope that something more original might happen here. If an age theorist were using the term *master biography,* it would refer to the master narrative of aging, the integrated life-course plot that makes sense of the fragments. It would mean what subjects, at a minimum, share—such as the names and attributes of the ages, the differences between privileged stages and subordinated ones, the features of the emplotment (the approximate location of an age-related peak, the signs of entry), and the parameters of possible feelings and debate on all these matters.

In fact, Frank Lentricchia goes on to tell an anecdote that, precisely, depends on such a shared master biography. But he doesn't know it. In fact, he declares that this story is unsupported "by a single myth" and thus without "rhetorical power." It concerns his grandfather, specified exactly as "age seventy-nine," who is being observed by his grandson, specified, less exactly, as "about thirteen." Red flags go up at this vast age division between subject and object, combined with the unlikely implication that any subject ever knew his grandfather's age more exactly than his own. The risks ahead are already clear. Some youthful misconception is likely to get textualized and thus be reinforced even if the teller were ultimately to refute it explicitly. The likeliest youthful misconception is that the grandfather represents "Old Age."

> One day my grandfather, my mother's father, at age seventy-nine, while rocking and smoking (but not inhaling) on his front porch in Utica, New York, in mid-August heat (which he disrecognized by wearing his long johns), directed his grandson's attention (who was then about thirteen) to the man sitting on *his* front porch across the street: not rocking or smoking but huddled into himself, as if it were cold, age eighty. Gesturing with cigarette in hand toward "this American," as he called him . . . all the while nodding, and in a tone that I recognized only much later as much crafted, he said: *La vecchiaia è 'na carogna.*[9]

To translate, as the theorist does not, "Being old is a bitch."[10] ("For sure funny if you can translate the Italian," Lentricchia asserts). For me, however, the anecdote possesses the sadness of all jokes at the expense of constructed classes. Humor is so often dying ideology. To the grandson, the vast difference the grandfather wishes to create between seventy-nine (himself) and age eighty (when old age will be a bitch), is the point of the joke. To the theorist in his middle years, it is still a joke worth telling. He still identifies with the self that at thirteen lumped all old men together.

I would want people in midlife, who have had some further experience with aging, to deconstruct "old age," or any age, as in fact not a homogeneous age class, either in body or in mind, but as made up of vastly different experiences—*just as his grandfather thinks*. The grandfather *is* better off: he has energy and pleasure-in-the-body. He has a personal sense of his age that does not conform to common North American stereotypes. Why should adult readers be asked to agree, with a thirteen-year-old, that the grandfather is only "one year away" from the reduced state of the other man? No subject feels so comically certain about the precariousness of her or his *own* health. I'm healthy right now; and despite many grievous warnings from the culture about cancer and heart disease—directed at my age-and-gender class—I do not sit here reminding myself that next year I might be sick or dead. If I'm healthy at seventy-nine, I suspect my attitude will be quite similar. What keeps us from ascribing to older others a body orientation—a sense of age identity—like our own?

The grandfather's sense of disparity between two men who are around eighty does not conform to the North American stereotype, but it is not preposterous. Historically, before mandatory retirement was invented, some societies differentiated between "the aged" and "the infirm" (as in the institution of the English poor law). Infirmity, economic dependence or social uselessness, not chronological age, served as decisive markers of old age. If the grandfather held this traditional view, his remark could have been said about a neighbor of sixty. He may have been expressing repugnance for illness. Perhaps he wanted to teach his grandson that seventy-nine, in *their* (immigrant) family, could be triumphantly healthy. But we don't need to know this much to agree that the grandfather's self-congratulatory sense of having a self free from the age category could have some warrant.

The word *carogna*, which I translated as "bitch," literally means "carrion." The anecdote would end maliciously, and grimly, if the punch line were translated as "old age is carrion." Yet many age theorists would agree that the saying "old age is carrion" is one Ur-meaning of age-related jokes and anecdotes, one subtext of the master life-course biography to which the stories all refer.

Gerontophobia, we might say, infects the grandson of thirteen, the grandson grown older, and the culture in which the joke is meaningful.[11] What else causes midlife readers to tell me that the grandfather made the joke ironically: "Of course he saw himself equally involved as carrion"? (How could he not? "Old age equals sickness equals death." Everyone gets the joke.) One common way to position oneself as far as possible from elderly carrion (or the Jew/the black/other Others) is to see "them" as "all alike." Gerontophobia is another form of impersonal narration. Even where difference among "them" is obvious it amounts to the difference between seventy-nine and eighty—it's nothing. Because of this slide, people in their middle years try to relegate age and the study of age to some later point in the life course. Many are not far from believing that middle age is carrion too. The anecdote reinforces the idea that gerontophobia too is a set of feelings, beliefs, interpretations, and formulas learned young. Age theory can collect such instances of normal socialization-into-aging, using them to contest the theory of innate gerontophobia and the naturalness of middle-ageism.

The collective, constructed, North American master narrative of decline must be powerful and ubiquitous if even through jokes it can contrive so that an affectionate man ignores his grandfather's private sense of self rather than privileging it, so that a practiced trope-user uses metaphors ("master biography") taken from the life course and narratology without feeling any need for reflexivity. If "ideology" can be defined, most simply, as any dominant system that produces and maintains consciousness through discourses, institutions, and practices, so completely that its effects then become invisible to this extent, then twentieth-century North America certainly has its own age ideology. The first task of an age-oriented criticism is to make the textual effects visible.

Toward Full Age Autobiography

Let me move from a youthful joke to a death scene, to suggest ways in which the whole life course is tongue-lashed by the master narrative. But I don't want to proceed without warning the reader again that age studies is not synonymous with gerontology and that its object is not specifically "old age" or (old) "women" or even the links between gerontophobia and middle-ageism but the vast inclusive topics of age and aging.

Intentionally, then, age theory must comprehend subjects of all ages. At the same time it should declare that although it privileges age over other categories at least initially, it does so only for specific purposes—history, analysis, and resistance—without making a foundational claim for age. Any category "will in its turn show up as a sub-system in accounts that are concerned primarily with the system of gender or of race or of age."[12]

Rewriting biography and autobiography to include socialization-into-aging is one of many promising projects for an age-conscious cultural criticism. The analyses of the Mirror Scene and the epiphany of Entrance into Midlife Aging suggested that we must not stop at the acquired self-distrust or self-disgust of middle age; now we know to look backwards for their origins.

We know a good deal about how children are socialized into gendered and racialized identities, different from the dominant "normal." Proper socialization also requires that one learn preparatory age lore young.[13] By thirteen in our precocious culture, some subjects have apparently already been inducted into the age system of their era (which is unlikely to be the same as their grandparents'). How youngsters come to remember for a lifetime particular sentences that relatives or authorities pronounce is a topic for the sociology of the emotions, one of the most valuable tools age theory has. When do children first use the fragments in speech, practice verbal formulas that are gender and age appropriate, first unlearn the progress narrative of childhood? Do some milieux endow children with antidotes to age ideology, as some do to racism and sexism? With children linking aging to "the" body in vast chains of signifiers so young, it's easier to see why adults defend themselves ineptly later on.

The social history of the life course in the twentieth century in North America, when it is written, must begin with a study of the culture's methods for teaching children that they will be "aging" and for teaching older subjects when to start applying the lore personally. Clever experiments and age-sensitive interviewing can teach us if the most vulnerable periods differ by gender, race, class, sexual orientation. Direct questioning could never have elicited Lentricchia's precious recollection of age-socialization. But now people can try to remember such material. Age-wise autobiographies can reveal both how obedience is practiced and how to recognize resistance, if any, retroactively. As these specific accounts emerge, "aging" will have less and less to do with the body as such.

To counter these tendencies, children, starting very young indeed, need to be taught optimal resistance to age ideology.[14] As soon as they are old enough, deconstructing age should be as much a part of their curriculum, in and out of school, as any other cultural analysis. That curriculum too needs to be invented, with the same cautions against reinscription that good antisexist and antiracist curricula use. There must be all kinds of alternative social materials that have not yet been spoken because of dominant discourse, which will seem ridiculous and inconceivable as long as we remain within it.

Power and Age Hierarchies

A critic and theorist who has taken on the subject of referentiality "in a journal of opinion about and for the modern language profession" focuses on autobiography, and then more closely on "memoirs of a dying other," and then on parental memoirs, and finally, at the end of her brief essay, on Simone de Beauvoir's *Une mort très douce* (*A Very Easy Death*), about the illness and death of her mother. Nancy K. Miller is interested in circumstances in which "the self of autobiography may [not] be simply autonomous and separate."[15] She chooses one paradigmatic case in which the self can allegedly transcend separateness: "In the continuum of identification between parent and child, between beloved others, 'I' sometimes *is* someone else."[15]

The self alleged sometimes to have the power to get beyond autonomy and separateness is not the parent, but the healthy adult child in the prime of life who will be a survivor of the Other and who will inscribe the experience. I call this memoir "filial" to distinguish it from a memoir written from a parent's viewpoint. In this kind of filial memoir the Other is not necessarily old but rather terminally ill, and the two states are collapsed together, so that the parent is described as an "aging body, wounded and devastated." Beauvoir herself, in *The Second Sex,* set up many red flags that should be transferable to this terrain, including the language of "othering" that has been so fruitful in unmasking gendered and other unconscious oppressions. And antiageist work from Beauvoir's *La Vieillesse* (*The Coming of Age*) on, has warned theorists of pitfalls in representing the "old." So it is troubling to have a theorist endorse a "task" that focuses on the "unnerving" sight of the dying body: "The task of autobiographers entails representing this sight—already consigned to notes and diaries—to themselves but also to the reader." The autobiographer needs to represent this because "memoirs are relentless in their commitment to exactness."[16] Surely in this context an injunction to represent any "*sight*" of the Other with "exactness" would have to be ironic? To make the case that the self "is" ever the Other, what would be needed is not more of the self's own consciousness, however "exactly" recorded, but some proof that the Other too—not just the privileged survivor-to-be—no longer felt "autonomous and separate."

To make her case, Miller selects these words of Beauvoir: "I had put Maman's mouth on my own face, and in spite of myself, I copied its movements. Her whole person, her whole being, was concentrated there, and compassion wrung my heart." Had Beauvoir been writing exactly, she would have asserted, as she did elsewhere, "It was impossible to enter her suffering."[17] She would have had to accept her mother's separateness. "I found myself copying the movements of her mouth, trying to feel just a little of what she felt. Yes, compassion wrung my heart, but whatever Maman felt at that moment, it could not have been 'compassion'—that was what *I* was feeling. Whatever *she* was doing with her mouth, it could not express her 'whole being.' I intimate that *she* was unnerved at the sight of her own body. Failing to know what she felt about dying, I had only her external body to report on." I would find such an account not only more "exact" but also, in its unflinching recognition of difference, touching.

But Beauvoir was not then attempting to prove anything more than her personal compassion. What the dying of others seems to produce in loving bystanders is a desperate will-to-be-the-Other momentarily, an attempted refusal of the privilege of surviving, a sense of frustration and despair at one's own helplessness, and pity for the greater helplessness and suffering of the other. All these loving emotions are in fact proofs of separateness. In a filial memoir, when an adult child apparently denies separateness, it only makes her emotions more vivid: it gives the effect of someone wrenched out of "rationality" by suffering. It's a trick of representation. But the survivor/writer might later understand this—that it was not an attempt to overlook the difference between the dying and the surviving. I know something about the discovery of difference, because about a year after my father died, I felt compelled to write a book about "the" experience—his and my mother's, as well as mine. I just assumed that was possible. I called the book *Determinations.*

Undeniably powerful, *Une mort très douce* nevertheless colonizes the body of the (older, female, once-rejected) m/other for Beauvoir's own therapeutic and writerly purposes.[18] How we think we "own" our mothers or fathers, and refuse to relinquish this ownership in writing about them even at midlife, is a grave problem for some people that may be connected in many ways to age unconciousness. Deciding not to publish *Determinations* was an important step for me away from owning my parents. Writing it had brought me to understand that I did not have good access to my father's experience. That was a hard, hurtful discovery, but eventually it gave me space to conceive of something enormously different from our culture's filial accounts. A parent's memoir.

Parental accounts would start from the subjectivity of the parent. If ailing parents told their own stories, we might learn how burdensome the loving gaze of the survivor can feel. Maya Angelou writes in the voice of a dying woman, "My children's concerns are tiring me. . . . I'd rather give up listening." I accept this as possible because a neighbor said almost the same thing to me when she had been diagnosed with an operable cancer. If we were dying, we'd quickly realize how we wanted our *own* "wounded and devastated" bodies treated in narrative. We'd feel how much we prefer to be remembered as living. We'd see in a flash that the so-called "memoir" is actually a sliver of a genre, the "last illness and dying" account. Roth in *Patrimony* summarizes the caution that I believe should hedge both fictional and critical writing about the older, dying Other, when he has his father accuse him in a posthumous dream. The charge? "I had dressed him for eternity in the wrong clothes."[19]

Adult children can of course write as if their parents might read the book. Blake Morrison ends his 1995 book about his father not with his death but with his cheerfully finishing a repair job with his son. The book is titled *And When Did You Last See Your Father?* He picked a time when his father could equally well see him. The issue is discursive power, conferred through age hierarchies. The risk of appropriating the life course of an Other rises in situations of considerable inequality. F. Scott Fitzgerald is said to have objected to Zelda using stories from the life that he and she shared, saying, "This is *my* material." A person living through dying suffers from a loss of power that encompasses power over *her* or *his* material. It is the nature of the growing genre of filial illness-and-dying accounts that the adult child records the parent's losses; the sight of the wasting—often naked—suffering body (as the beloved Other fights for the best possible death inside it) becomes "the" material. It's not the motives but the age effects that concern me: these texts can erase the idea of old age as "normal," obscure the subjectivity of the old, and mar the readers' anticipations of our own aging, old age, and dying. They may hide the fact that _we_ may eventually suffer the unchallenged power of an objectifying—younger—gaze.

Who takes the material? Writers, critics, theorists (and everyone else) are currently likelier to overlook relevant affective, moral, epistemological, and cultural problems in two contingencies. Specifically, when the Other is older or aged (rather than younger or the same age). And generally, all across the life course, when power differences related to age have been suppressed through the absence of age theory. We should be passionate about this and urgent in rectifying it, because long before we are dying, we suffer as if we had been silenced: the master narrative takes _our_ material and tells _our_ life story.

Age Theory in Its Infancy

Midlife decline becomes visible and speakable not because a body ages by nature (although in some yet-to-be-defined ways it presumably does), but because our culture finds it necessary for subjects that young to be seen and be said to be aging. So expanding our ability to describe the discursive production of midlife aging is a significant immediate and ongoing task of age theory. Time for some green flags. As we amplify the concept "aged by culture" to cover all the sources—the discursive formations, the economic and political forces, and the practices—age studies needs the work of myriad disciplines: social epidemiologists, environmentalists, left economic and political analysts, psychological anthropologists, critical social scientists, therapists and psychoanalytic theorists, and of course, literary and cultural critics and historians. Out of its multi-, or even antidisciplinary project, it focuses all of them on undermining age ideology.

I believe the first tasks are to cast in doubt the authority of the master narrative and build alternative theories and stories that compel assent. The one-two punch. Practice cannot change meaningfully before consciousness does, and consciousness must evolve considerably before people are willing to expend the energy required to modify structures. _Declining to Decline_ has taken swipes at practices and turns in the final chapter to the politics and the economics of the midlife. But it has inevitably concentrated on the discursive conveyors of the master narrative. It has shown decline's lore blowing down on high and low, gritted into jokes and science news and daily clichés ("You're only as old as you feel") and silting up the most elaborated age anecdotes of realist fiction. It has shown how decline knowledge circulates in our heads, weakening our age identity and tormenting us into scenes of confessional ranking, the Entrance into Midlife Aging, and the Mirror Scene. These discourses make us "experience" aging as if decline were, at one and the same time, a given, a merely personal process (an effect that ignores the falsely universalizing features of the narrative and its constructions of difference and sameness) and a universal wholly biological process (an effect that erases culture altogether: group differences, competing discourses, my right to name its individual dimensions).

We are *infants* in theory, almost speechless, at this stage. We lack a basic common vocabulary. Two words—*age* and *aging*—cover and blur too many separable ideas. *Aging* (when it doesn't refer to the Boomers) is just a euphemism for "old age." This means first that we lack a term to identify the entire cultural process we endure. I have called that process "being aged by culture," or "'aging' in quotation marks" and picked out the crucial effect on the relevant age class as "midlife aging" or aging-into-the-midlife. In thus wrenching the signifer "aging" conceptually farther away from "old" age, I am also trying to show up its constant quick slide back toward the ideologized nexus: "age" equals "aging" equals "old age" equals "sickness" equals "death."[20] Whenever we use "aging" indiscriminately for "older" people we shrink all of life-after-youth—a lengthening span—into a foreshortened space, as it exists (we are told) in the imagination of the young. I have used "socialization into aging," for the early stages of linguistic indoctrination and psychological preparation for being aged by culture. "Resocialization" names the long self-alienating process through which we internalize midlife decline through personalized impersonal narrative. We lack a concept like "gender" or "race" to identify the system that keeps a regime of age knowledge circulating. We have no word like "patriarchy" that permits us to conceive of age as another field of power and hierarchy, politics and narrative, demystification and resistance. I use "age ideology."

Some of these terms may initially have had a useful oddity (useful for distancing the reader from the system). I hope that over the course of the book they have become naturalized, as the botanists say of foreign flowers that are now happy to live in your garden. The confusion is multiplied when we want to name the object of study: if "gender" names the concepts through which we study "woman" and "man," "age" (again) names the concepts by which we study the categories of being clumped as the "ages" of life. Sexism names the forms of discrimination related to gender, while "ageism" (again!) is all we have for the equivalent. I had to invent "middle-ageism."[21] Before I had coined it I simply could not see clearly the historical, cultural, psychological phenomena the term covers. And although we have words like "gendering" and "racializing," we have no separate word for "cultural aging." Positivism glued our tongue to those two poor words. Did either of the other body-based ideologies hide behind a more successful muddle?

Let's ask that central question: If the ideology pervades discourse and discourse suggests that almost all subjects internalize decline to some degree, why do you believe we can have success breaking that circuit? Where will resistance to the master narrative come from? We can't begin to answer before demolishing the ideology's current definition of "resistance." In the general population, which includes the academic world, resistance often amounts to little more than mouthing—signing discreetly, in as many ways as possible— "_I'm_ not aging" or "_I'm_ not middle-aged yet." As Baby Boomers age in front of Pirandello's Mirror, they are likely to multiply such mouthings. This is not resistance. In general, age theory needs to shatter the regime of knowledge in which decline is "truth" and resistance is called (borrowing from psychoanalysis at its most hegemonic) "denial." The effects of this binary are: (1) to constitute aging as a biological "truth" (only truths can be "denied"); (2) to build failure into acceptance too (you confess your aging faults, laugh at ageist jokes, groan at the mention of birthdays); (3) to structure rejuvenation as the only egress and consumption (of goods, practices, medications) as the only means. Perhaps we can advance the entire project, both deconstructing age ideology and constructing optimal resistance to its narratives, by clarifying the concept that came closest to my heart while writing this book: age identity.

Age Identity and Identity-Stripping

Identity is a life story, a long tale in the telling.[22] In autobiography, it stands (at any chosen moment) as a sense of an achieved portmanteau "me"—made up, for each subject, of all its multiple, changeable, and self-defined selves together—an intrasubjective agglomeration. My identity is first of all what I know it is when talking to no one but me. My traits and special history, facts that have no objective interest for the world but that I hold dear, like where the Mouse Kingdom was, what my father told me in the basement when I was twelve, what I told my son when he reached his majority. Even what I have forgotten with regret was mine alone to forget. This secret history grows every day.

Identity also includes personalized versions of the supposedly body-based and socially overloaded identities, gender and race.[23] We learn "who" we "are" according to these publicly shared attributes very young. However degrading

and stereotypical some of these are (for women and minorities), by reimpos-
ing their own meanings on these identities, subjects can privately experience
them as real, positive, necessary, even cherished possessions.[24] These are of
course later-life interpretations that may have survived earlier miserable periods of self-hatred and wishing-to-have-another-body. Freshman year in college, for example, asked to write on the topic, "I Wish I Were a . . ." I wrote,
"I Wish I Were a Man." At that time, wanting-not-to-be-a-woman was a per-
cipient and perfectly reasonable—and terrible—wish. But I no longer wish
it. Recognizing that we can voluntarily discard identities that have come to
seem false can be made a part of the immense project of revising age ideology.

Much of age identity depends on knowing whether, for each aspect of
identity, one has aged in a favoring or devastating historical moment. For
gender identity, I give credit to the collective provided by feminism. Over
twenty years I learned not to reject the "female" me by extirpating some of
the mainstream definitions of "woman" that had been imposed on me. I
gained—in some sense, saved—a more privately meaningful and positive female identity. Anti-anti-Semitism helped me do the same for my Jewish identity. Black psychologists have described a model in which African Americans
discard younger/given identities and develop later-life identities with difficulty, relief, even exultation.[25] Gay pride, and the Native American rights
movement, to mention only two, have made this development possible for
others. For members of the relevant communities, this history could become
part of the meaning of the concept "progress narrative." Not everyone who
could, will live such change as progress or be able to revisit it at every moment
as a progress narrative. But whatever the self-meanings of gender, race, ethnicity, class, or sexual orientation, aging (like history) is implied in every account, always there already.

And finally, my identity is what has emerged from the confrontation between me and age ideology over the events that it linked with (bad) "aging"
but that I took over for my own: how I dealt with my vanishing spine, re-
guarded my face, raised a child who at twenty said to me, "Safe at last, out of
adolescence," rescued my mother and me from a piratical culture that would
have kept us sundered. What was crucial was that I started to write against
the master narrative; at first, not knowing what I was doing. Although I fell
into decline mode at times, in print I never lifted a column from that jocund
journal *Middle Age: The Magazine for You—Yeah, You!* I never lip-synched a
simple sound bite from the Age Channel. Just as I could not manage to tell a
simple Failed Body story in "Ordinary Pain," I refused to confess to a Repulsive Face in "Face-Off." I now believe that I was influenced first and foremost
by the directionality of my intense, private, founding age myth, which I dis-

covered and wrote about in "A Good Girl." And I was influenced by the midlife women's progress novel, as it is and as I wish it were ideally. The autobiography of my aging and of my ageism is a new, ongoing acquisition of my age identity. For each of us, the Annals of Developing Age Identity could be part of the treasure chest of me-ness.

At any chosen moment, in telling our state-of-being (tied to one corporeal body), we find some co-identities disliked but accepted; some discarded; some improved; some in conflict and flux (is this to be me or not-me?). Some exist only as fugitive desires—selves we admire and will try to become. Others we condemn and will try to doom. But all in all, the portmanteau identity, however unfinished and imperfect, feels self-chosen. Even if we need to admit that parts are unchosen—weaknesses, errors—we might not want to disown them entirely. Even containing some unwanted parts, the whole deeply and rightly matters to people.

We may be able to estimate how much, if we can tease out why people might resist the idea of having identity stripped from them. Although when I wrote "I Wish I were a Man" at seventeen, I meant it, I would now be deeply shocked to wake up one morning in a male body. I would fight to get back that self-defined aspect of my being that is called "woman." I would fight the same way if I woke up in the body of another woman, even if I knew how superior she was to me.

I would fight almost the same way if I woke up recognizably "myself" but younger—say about ten years. What could I gain that was worth the losses? Of course I might undo the deaths of loved ones and a series of reactionary administrations. But this is not a thought experiment about undoing history. What about income? What if the younger self earned more money a decade ago? (In fact, she did.) Perhaps me-ness is tightly tied to what a person earns only when a fall or rise brings with it a perceived change in status or expectation large enough to distort identity. And I would look somewhat younger, and thus possibly get a job I might not be able to get now. Ah, no scapegoating. Age theory reminds me not to blame "my aging" when I should blame the economy or age discrimination or some other cause. Losses have certainly occurred in my "midlife" (if I still find any use for that term). Such losses must no doubt be part of my age identity, because any story can be included in my age identity. But they are no longer (I want to underline this important distinction) *automatically* age-specific and thus cannot fit the scenario of irreversible doom and be used by age ideology to make my life time prematurely crepuscular.

If I were forced into being younger I would also lose all the secret history I've accumulated between then and now, and all the co-identities that feel more true. I don't want to know less, have felt less, have accomplished less, have fewer friends—have fewer or different *stories*. (Which of the midlife stories that I've told here would I want to drop?) I don't want to lose practices I have embraced—parenting, political activism—that have helped to give me an enhanced sense of selfhood. I shudder at the idea of going backwards toward wanting knives. Even as a thought experiment, youthening quickly becomes dismaying. In short, if I felt that *any* of my important identities could be threatened by an ideological project, I'd fight.

I discover through this experiment, *pace* poststructuralism, that my "I" wants to feel relatively stable, an outcome of my life to that moment. Not inert (no, "change" is a widely shared cultural value, and I share it), but within my own control, narratable first of all and most authoritatively by me. I imagine most people who have lived in their adult selves for decades would feel similarly resistant to an imposed switch. We need to wake up every day securely still "me." My native body—as is, keeping my smells, my quirky pinky, my laugh lines, my scars—I find works for me here as a sign of the continuity and integration of all the rest, everything I currently consider me-ness. Subjects do not have to love every aspect of their "me" to value their identity, to follow my argument, or to do age studies. In fact, the people likely to gain most are those who dislike the parts of self that have come to them labeled as "bodily" and "aging."

Age has mattered a lot in this account: "decades," "long-known," "eventually self-chosen," "continuity" have been crucial terms. So have "reinterpretation," "re-formation"—terms that emphasize how narrating our selfhood changes over time. As *Declining to Decline* keeps emphasizing: if co-identities change, if the subject is not unitary, this is because of temporality.[26] Identities are personal and reportable outcomes of living through the life course to a given period—of aging. Long-lived-in identity—intimate, rarely spoken but narratable, *achieved*—constitutes our being. Did I possess an age identity in the period before I invented the term? Before I had started writing age autobiography? Whenever I got it, here it is. Once we have consciously added (life) time to our sense of being, we can call the accumulated, comprehensive self each of us wakes up with our age identity.

"Age" again. The alternatives in our pauky age dictionary do not captivate me. "Maturing" could be resuscitated for some contexts, but a term like "maturing identity" implies that everything that happens in time has a civilized, rational, "adult" quality. "Age identity" makes room even for flimsy, negative, self-deluded bits, for continuities as well as changes, and, of course, for non-ideologically-induced decline narratives. (It even makes a space for intermittence.) *After age theory*, people will know better what degree of decline, if any, they're experiencing. They will have considered the propositions that midlife aging is a destructive ideology and that the master narrative is its discursive vehicle. Ultimately, after thinking about narrative through age theory, each of us could better decide what "aging" means, what changes, if any, result from it and what to say about them. Decline, as I said, would not be default narrative. Changes or continuities whose meanings now come solely from the master narrative would not have to be excluded from my sense of age identity as long as I were conscious of their source and my role in interpreting them and had some warrant for believing that I do not interpret out of direct cultural compulsion. (After regaining control of the narrative, I am willing to call some changes "mine" in a more tranquil frame of mind. Gray hair, "me"; arthritis, "me.") I might or might not rank my self higher on many measures; I might or might not tell a progress story about it. Telling a progress story and valuing one's age identity are theoretically separable. For that matter, people who now tell simple progress stories as a matter of subcultural compulsion might find themselves freer.

Age identity is never writable in its entirety; it's too comprehensive. But even in fragments, critical age autobiography has the thrill of a new genre. Contemplating its mysteries is a continuous entertainment, and pondering its nature could be a new puzzle for literature and philosophy.

"Age-" prefixed to "identity" is intended to be subversive in our current cultural conjuncture. As a category of difference, age has neutrality and possibly prestige. Using it, we reclaim power and positivity for its allied term *aging,* as the process that gives us whatever identity we currently possess or are ever going to possess.

Once we adjust our view of the self to take into account the loyalty we feel toward what, on examination over time, we find we consider "me," we realize how tenaciously we might hold on to age identity. This loyalty is important. Indeed, it is what we have to motivate us to save ourselves, once we recognize that there *is* an actual and fearfully powerful, public, ideological project that can undo us. As I slowly write my age autobiography and simultaneously piece together an age theory, the gap has been widening for me between a person's private sense of self-in-time and the stripped and distorted version of age identity being forced on us. Following on my account of age identity, by midlife (barring the kind of disaster that shakes the most solid identity), people who understood it could value the accumulated self. When some currently fail to do so, we want to ask how, in detail, identity-stripping causes us to lose the being we had or might have had.

This is an altogether different view of the forces constructing aging from the one that pitted "progress" against "decline" as implicitly equal antagonists on page 1. This is not about which story is "truer" or closer to "nature," a binary that is naively positivist and false and makes us crazy. The concept of age identity has precious consequences for dealing with age ideology. It pits against that invasive cultural power something close to our whole being and our prospects of becoming. Once conscious of itself, convinced of its right to its meanings, being must will the defeat of antagonistic powers.

To fend off the master narrative, we need to have more careful and vivid descriptions of how it harms and how much harm it does. Its repertory is vast, sly; its power overdetermined. Some people will want to resist it because they see it adding a depressive clincher to the weight of other cumulative oppressions, like racism and sexism and economic immiseration. Some people will feel that it affronts their individuality. They abhor anything that smacks of "institutional identities" or totalizing systems. Others dislike the "bodilyness" of being just "one body among others." I hate universalized decline as well because it spoils the suspense of life. Whatever I am complexly doing with my multiple identities, decline's tight script requires me to confess that I am "really" losing, predominantly, precociously, and permanently. Whatever metaphors I want, it chains me to its synecdoches. Especially when people have suffered massive losses, decline reduces the possible meanings of their life events. However seductive other people find it as a literary form, I feel it imposed on me, powerful, narrow, coercive, terrifying in its ubiquity, sometimes grandiose and exclusive, ultimately repetitious, tedious, banal. To the degree that we learn it well, each of us loses power doubly—to create our own unfolding narrative of age identity and to share it publicly. It makes the culture deaf. Decline narrative used to make me helpless. Now that I see it as narrative, it offends me. As many will be, I am appalled by the intellectual confusions it creates and the grief it displaces onto "aging" and away from reformable agents. Yes, the anger some people direct at their own "aging" would be better directed at the culture that produces daily doses of narrative indoctrination for all of us.

In our culture, because men as well as women have been taught to consider identity-stripping via aging "natural," even after individuals find their motives for resistance, many won't know what methods are appropriate for them. Cultural influences can never be homogeneous; there is complicated work ahead. But dismaying conclusions emerge from the fact that age has not been theorized the way other categories of difference have been. We are far more ignorant about middle-ageism than about sexism or racism or homophobia. Probably more of us are vulnerable to cultural aging than to any other kind of cultural imposition and assault.

Where age is concerned, both the privileged and the apolitical should be wary of assuming that it is the politics of *some Others* that they are invited to attend to (although they are certainly invited to attend to others once the first shock of coming to age consciousness is past). It is not the politics of the elderly (although age theory also embraces the politics of old age). The politics of the midlife are likely to require the building of large coalitions; we want to prevent anyone from saying, too rapidly, either "My midlife is okay, I'm exempt" or "*Their* midlife is okay, they won't help." This is *my* cause, and it is my brother's; everyone's; it is theory for myself-with-others—theory with, let's hope, mass relevance.

Conclusion: Getting On with Age Theory

In cultural theory circles, many are still developing concepts, respect, sensitivity, urgency by working through the "And Lists": "race and class and gender and . . ." Innumerable lists omit age or include it perfunctorily. These lists are not merely gestures of inclusiveness, important as that would be for age studies. They are in themselves theoretical statements. A simple omission can imply an ideological position.[27] Lists contain assertions of relevance and importance, and state or imply relationships between and among variables known not to be perfectly homologous. In using gender and race as "body-based" analogues to age, for example, I purposefully referred to concepts with a history of success in inserting their concerns and strategies into theory, practical criticism, book indexes, university reading lists, and mainstream culture. I have argued that unlearning the master narrative of aging may in some ways be like extirpating racist and sexist narratives. I made the implicit claim that age theory deserves to join materialist feminist, African-American, queer, postcolonial, and cultural theory as a powerful tool of cultural and historical analysis, and a liberatory discourse. But age is also sui generis.

Age theory would certainly be enriched if there were a more general attempt to add age to the lists. And often work would need to be developed considerably (possibly with startling results) to make it possible to "add" age honestly. In writing about "Ideology," for example, one theorist produced a longer than usual list of the systems of difference "that affect how ideology works up a 'lived' relation to the real." He left out age ideology.[28] Narratologists uncovering master narratives would help by naming the other parts of decline. Feminist and race theorists could ask whether devices that keep those binaries in place function analoguously within age ideology. What now counts as undeniable in speaking about age comes to be fixed very narrowly. To put age and aging into the *tones* of theory (logical, comparative, wry, amazed, angry, utopian—interrogative or alternative) would be to deprive them of automatic recourse to the master plot (decline) and show them up as language constructs within ideology. Trying to integrate age within existing theory will raise perplexing questions, leading well beyond the confines of this prolegomenon.

In general, how can we better theorize "aging"? As we tie it more and more to culture, how fast can we change our speech? Can we write about it without recourse to the master narrative's assumptions that "changes" are natural, prediscursive, and unwanted, and without falling into positive aging's simplicities?[29] Before age theory has done much work, this is hard to conceptualize. But I would suggest that one major theoretical and psychological weapon lies in developing the concept of age autobiography that I began with, the story of the portmanteau self, which at any given moment of the life course is what I possess as my known being and holds my true prospect of becoming. In conclusion, I want to emphasize that age identity too is always already another narrative, which means that it can become explicit about its workings. I am proposing an active concept of aging as self-narrated experience, the conscious, ongoing story of one's age identity. Once we can firmly distinguish between the culture's aging narrative and our own versions (particularly if we do so within a collective formed for that purpose), we learn that its threats to being and becoming are resistible. The most radical hypotheses of the social construction of aging are truly radical.

At best, we will all be recovering ageists for a very long time. But people have much to gain. One early consequence of age theory is that we will be building a community within which, when we defy the age-graded practices and discourses and institutions that now appear indestructible, we will be understood and appreciated. That community should try to include children, people outside the academy, people who watch TV more than they read, people without institutions and other means to support their progress narratives, people of any age who now believe without question that aging is just *natural*. Within that community, we would be able to mock the harmful banalities that injure us. We can try anything. Eventually we'll invent riddles.[30] If as a result of my repudiating the Mirror Scene and the scenes of confession and Entrance into Midlife Aging, other people bit their tongues before automatically launching into decline stories, and then felt wickedly liberated, and went on to bad-mouth another compulsory practice . . . the community would already be alive.

All the intensity and the techniques we have discovered developing other kinds of theory will be necessary for undoing age ideology. We'll need self-love to get through the scary process of expunging the internalizations we want to discard. We'll need compassion as other people go on reproducing the dominant narrative. We'll need aggression to finger the commerce in aging that supports the cult of youth, the generation gaps, the life stages that turn out to be demographic markets. But what might be hard work if it were purely intrapsychic changes when a collective forms around us. Perhaps when "the body" intersects with age we never can be entirely free of cultural impositions, but even now we can imagine a good deal more freedom and pleasure and narrative control in having an age identity than we currently experience.

Selves are sometimes said to have four dimensions, three spatial and one temporal. That is the modern self in twentieth-century North America—lopsided, body-heavy. With time having been reduced by the dominant narrative of the life course to an oppressive and masochistic, biological and universal decline story, the "three-dimensional" body looms overblown, with grotesquely gendered, racialized, sexualized, and age-graded features. Perhaps a truly described postmodern self will *not*, after all, have so much body. If postmodern selves, in a gigantic cultural shift, begin to redescribe *life* time (in innumerable age-conscious narratives), the culture may finally find itself moving toward a more minimal "body" and an automatic shift within the controversies over mind/body and culture/nature. "Age" is now the laggard. When "age" joins "race" and "gender," all the body-based categories and constructs will make sense only if read within quotation marks. Adding age theory will change theory; and it might give us a better chance at the equality and expressiveness that all the master narratives deny.

12

The Politics of Middle-Ageism in the Postmodern Economy

The Wonderful Woman on the Pavement

IN 1994 a handsome woman appeared on TV news in the Boston area: poised, energetic, well groomed, with healthy body language—the kind of midlife woman who looks competent simply walking across a street. She said she was forty-five. In feminist eras like our own when ages over forty can be broadly represented as "wonderful," she was instantly recognizable as one of the wonderful midlife women. There are millions. Telling her story on TV, Patricia was articulate even though her self-confidence had been badly shaken. She was hired by the Massachusetts Commission Against Discrimination (MCAD) in a sting operation to test whether a woman her age could get a job in retailing at $6.00 an hour in competition with a younger woman. She and Becky, aged twenty-two, composed one set of four all-white teams matched for education, personal qualities, and (limited) work experience. Patricia and Becky happen to look alike, and they dressed similarly on the test days. By the end, Patricia had been told there were no jobs or turned down by retailer after retailer about three times a week for a month; some didn't even take her résumé. The twenty-two-year-olds had frequently been offered full-time permanent jobs with benefits and ladders. The testers over forty-five had been offered a few jobs, but they were the new service jobs: seasonal and without benefits.

The midlife woman told me later that she was shocked and humiliated and had become more anxious about beginning her own real job search. I expect readers share her shock—but perhaps we are not surprised. Age discrimination at midlife is becoming a silent given in America. It now concerns more groups and classes and individuals than anyone has imagined. Aside from its terrible effects on individuals and their families, it proletarianizes the workforce, reduces the expectations of the young, hampers the exercise of midlife powers. I hope to show how it threatens deeply held social value, an ideal image of the life course. It is an urgent issue.

"Fifty"

In describing the economic situation of Americans, I start with the Wonderful Midlife Woman on the Pavement, the canary in the coal mine. She is at risk of age discrimination even if she has a solid résumé behind her; women are dropping from high places. Lotus fired business manager Carol Moskowitz, one of the highest-paid people in her department, after she turned fifty; the personnel manager admitted circling her age on the list. Moskowitz sued Lotus for discrimination and won money.[1] But not enough people turn to civil law remedies; when they win they can be gagged, and the press doesn't publicize the victories enough.

Economically, the midlife can be the most critical part of the life course. Some women find themselves newly divorced, with no alimony and no work history. Many are single heads-of-households. Even in a two-income family, their income is necessary. Many need to care for older relatives, get kids through college, or help their adult children breaking into a difficult economy. Some in "two-income families" are married to midlife men whose incomes have dropped or vanished. Having earned less than men all their lives, most women also know they had better bolster their Social Security, pensions, and savings before it's too late. They are able to work full-time because they are postmaternal. They need full-time jobs at higher wages. Projections are that they will constitute a growing percentage of the workforce. Fifty-four percent of women aged fifty-five to sixty-four are expected to be working by 2005, some 9 percent more than in 1990.[2] Will midlife discrimination preclude this? It's crucial to know what's happening to women in the forty to forty-nine slot, a conjuncture of readiness, ability, and need. The percentage of women working in that decade is now higher than for any age above thirty. Free of child-care conflicts, with long-term work histories, they should be desirable employees.

The reality, however, is grim. At forty-five, women's earnings have already peaked—sometime in the decade after thirty-five. The male wage advantage, visible since one's twenties, looms enormously at midlife: as we saw in chapter 1, at the median, women earn about half what men earn. The devastating change in the economy is that full-time work is becoming a privilege denied to midlife women, and to men as well. Fifty seems to be a turning point in one large and important study that disaggregated the workforce simultaneously by age, gender, race, and education.[3] Sixty-nine percent of black women in the five years after forty-five are employed full-time; only 44 percent of those in the lustrum after that—a drop of twenty-five points, the biggest five-year drop for any group, male or female. Seventy-nine percent of women college graduates have full-time work between forty-five and forty-nine; only 60 percent of those five years older do—a nineteen-point drop in the group of the most privileged.

Fifty is a drastic downward turning point for full employment for men too. Ninety percent of white men in this sample are employed between forty-five to forty-nine; of the group five years older, only 77 percent are—a surprising thirteen-point drop. College-educated men suffer less—still, a drop of eight points. African-American men as a whole don't drop then but suffer a drastic drop, of twenty-two points, five years older. And the data come from 1987–88, before the recession, downsizings, capital flights, technological displacements, and wage declines of the Nineties. In one year, October 1991 to October 1992, "the increase in the rate of unemployment for people 55 and over was seven times that of people 16 through 54."[4] Commentators have noticed these victims of job loss, but not understood what their losses as a group portend.

The magnitude of these descents is astonishing. Having even a few studies of this kind certifies a phenomenon that many in the midlife cohort suspect. If we haven't suffered personally, we know someone who had substantial seniority who has lost that once-secure job at good wages with benefits, has searched fruitlessly even for lateral mobility, and settled silently into subemployment. Many of us know—and we're right—that people do not recover their original economic standing. When you look over the cliff at the food pantries in the suburbs, the seasoned neighbors "displaced" with so many good years before them, the children dropping out of college or running up big debt, the humiliating makeshifts, it makes sense when scholars say that the middle classes, "whether blue-collar, white collar, middle-level manager or professional," are "disappearing." The median earnings of one elite group—men with four years of college (most of these are white) fell in constant dollars from $55,000 in 1972 to $41,899 in 1992.[5]

Why is *midlife* subemployment—especially that of white middle-class men—not a major, continuing mainstream story, complete with punditry, outrage, and action plans? Federal employment data are not graded to provide access to comparable information.[6] This suggests that midlife information is not in demand. The reasons for that, when we are provided with other particulars in the bad news about the economy, are likely to be ideological. Male privilege at midlife has been a given, and false cohort universalism has touted the Baby Boomers' wealth. And conceivably, declines for men at the prime of life, especially middle-class and white men, are too embarrassing, too serious, too damning to the system, to be confronted by the mainstream.

Middle-ageism had power to engineer these drops and help to hide them.[7] Their magnitude suggests that "middle-age" status should be considered with race, class, and gender, as conjoined discriminations.

The Lead Ceiling; or, Breaking the Rungs on the Ladder

These data suggest ominous trends. Midlife free falls in full employment should be alarming even before we know exactly why different people leave full-time work or what they find to do for a living afterwards. (Most observers believe that the rate of involuntary part-time employment is high and that self-employment—a growing category—covers a variety of diminished situations.) Some, particularly the poor, have to leave work because they contract the socioeconomic disabilities or diseases described earlier; some die prematurely. But healthy, vigorous people lose jobs. The less skilled do, but so do the skilled and well-trained experts. (In some studies, the percentage of people who think they might lose their jobs within the next year rises as high as one-third.) Many who think of themselves as rising hit the "glass ceiling" prematurely. Perhaps we should call it the lead ceiling, because with age discrimination there's no way back up. People are pressured to "retire" prematurely—but only if they're privileged, because that is the face-saving way to be let go. One way or another, at around fifty women and men are being forced out—out and down, into economic decline.

Being out in the job market in the Nineties is a special hell for "older" people. A sting organized by the American Association of Retired Persons (AARP) used résumés of women and men whose age could be inferred as fifty-seven, versus people of thirty-two. "Older [*sic*] job applicants are likely to confront age discrimination one of every four times they apply for available jobs," estimates AARP lawyer Cathy Ventrell-Monsees.[8] The ratio for women is probably worse than one in four. I ran into Lydia (not her real name) on the street. She's fifty-six, divorced, white, college-educated, strikingly good-looking, precariously employed, and furious. "Don't let them say the word 'retirement' to me. I can't retire. I've been working all my adult life and I can't afford to stop. I might live to be eighty—ninety. I'm not *middle-aged!* I'm scarcely into my middle years. Of course I've been age-harassed, who hasn't." In one interview where the Man asked illegal questions, he was *her own age.*

Men shouldn't be fooled by telling themselves they are doing less badly than some women; they're doing badly enough. The personnel director who lays them off and the CEO who discriminates against them are probably other men. Whatever capitalism can do to midlife women is a rehearsal for expanding those practices to include more men. The middle class cannot count on exemption. Whatever can be done to lots of midlife men holding only high school diplomas and to some men with college degrees and higher degrees can eventually be done to more men in the privileged classes. Already "among men wages have fallen more"; high-wage workers have experienced some of the largest declines.[9] "The global drive to the bottom" is expanding.

There are underlying structural causes for our age quandary. One of the facts of late capitalism in the slow-growing North American Empire is that the national labor market is failing to create enough good jobs—possibly not enough jobs at all (economists debate this)—for the available workforce.[10] Corporations now act as if the fastest way to raise profitability and enhance productivity were to cut the wage base and overwork the remaining employees. The new unemployable are not being thanked for opening up jobs for others. They have to be demonized or marginalized so victim-blaming can occur. The first visible victims were young black working-class men, who in a vital unionized manufacturing economy would be a backbone of industry. Unskilled workers generally, the lower white-collar classes, and now middle management are in crisis. As corporations and sectors shrink good jobs, other categories will be marginalized, by whatever discriminations lie at hand. Few analysts have brought home to us the full horrors of a postindustrial, transnational economy. One of them is premature superannuation. Suddenly, it appears to make more sense to cut the most expensive employees rather than the cheapest. Middle-ageism may be the most efficient way of pushing wages toward the bottom, because it cuts off the top of a person's economic life curve.[11]

Aging into the midlife is supposed to mean a curve of earnings rising with age. Up to a point. Men's salaries peak between forty-five and fifty-four, women's during the decade earlier; the lower classes' earlier than those of the middle/upper strata.[12] Wage-peaking over fifty-four is the utmost privilege of the culture, available only to a small percentage. Wage-peaking between forty-five and fifty-four could be limited to fewer. This would be one inevitable effect of widening midlife subemployment.

A rising age-wage curve, however modest, has been the unspoken foundation of the American Dream: it makes possible buying a home, getting the kids more education, helping them get started, saving, securing one's old age. And the economic rise accompanies and anchors elevations into responsibility and into new social roles as "authorities," as parents, teachers and coaches, informal advisors or managers, mentors. Any slight rise over time may carry with it the benefits of feeling oneself the protagonist of a progress story. (Nostalgia isn't necessary, or is harmless, when enough of the values of youth continue and the gains of midlife aging are palpable.) Respect in America as one becomes middle-aged partly depends on these curves, these peaks; so too the value of one's opinions, the power to act on those judgments, the ability to help others beyond the family. Actually being able to run the store depends on the relative security and prosperity of midlife. "Seniority"—a word resonant with values from an older time—sums up the unstated psychological, social, economic, ethical, and political aspects of the Dream.

Union seniority is a life-course model: the rules meant job security, chances for upward mobility (within blue-collar limits), greater job satisfaction and responsibility, bonuses for continued service—a recognition of workers' "investment of work, health, safety, and life." The working class's investment "is entitled to some sort of security, as much as that of the banker," declared a major AFL-railroad agreement of 1921. The implicit goal was a life course that approached the bourgeois standard. The agreement asserted that "the rule tends to place the burden of insecurity of employment where it can best be borne, namely, on the younger men recently employed. It is thus fairer than any other system."[13] Fairness depended on young people understanding that the life course plus the seniority system would help them in their turn. Fairness meant they understood that if there was no age-wage rise for their elders, there would be none for them when their turn came.

It's still true, and it's true at all class levels. Without a seniority system, either legal or customary, the first wage a young person earns could be the highest wage she or he ever earns.

The Dream of later, higher peaks has been shared more widely in the last thirty years by African-Americans and immigrants, women of all races and ethnicities. The expansion of seniority depends on the continued existence of rising curves and high peaks. Seniority breakthroughs were fought to assure that the curve kept lifting for the new entrants too. Before unions established seniority rights, management frequently laid off older women and put prettier/younger/cheaper women in their jobs.[14] Senior African-American women wanted plantwide single seniority systems, so they could move into a different department rather than being laid off. The establishment in 1966 of the single seniority list made affirmative action operational and opened midlife perks to all. And now that job turnover is a more common expectation, seniority needs to be portable, attached to a long résumé and a face with some good age on it.

Many economic facts announce or portend the weakening of seniority, broadly understood, at all class levels. Seniority now can consist of very slight material or status advantages: in manual trades, earning a few dollars more than the young, or getting the chance to choose first among work conditions all of which are more onerous than they used to be. As unions weakened, not just wage levels but security, regular raises, and protections against arbitrary dismissal for older employees disappeared. (Seniority may actually mean "first hired, first retired.")[15] All that too was a rehearsal.

Now the unorganized middle class is losing out to market forces combined with middle-ageism. The middle class was always vulnerable: "still only a *middle* class," in the words of Barbara Ehrenreich. "Its only 'capital' is knowledge and skill, or at least the credentials imputing skill and knowledge. And unlike real capital, these cannot be hoarded against hard times. . . . The 'capital' belonging to the middle class is far more evanescent than wealth, and must be renewed in each individual through fresh effort and commitment." Throughout the entire midlife, I would add. When defense contracts disappeared, a firm in Massachusetts I was told about laid off every one of its computer consultants over fifty—more than 25 percent of its workforce, many of whom supervised men of lesser expertise. None of them sued. In the medical profession, senior physicians perform under the supervision of accountants. Stanley Aronowitz and William DeFazio warn that "low and middle-range scientists and engineers may not look forward to occupying a privileged place in the corporate order." Tenure is under attack in universities, not just discursively but in the silent practices of the two-tier system (part-time versus full-time), as fewer young people are invited to enter on tenure tracks; as the Boomers retire, the ratio of part-timers will increase. Tenure may vanish without ever having been debated. And "tenure" (whether in the academy or government service) is the model of lifetime security and modest age-wage increases over a person's entire working life—an ideal to be cherished, fought for, and expanded to other groups and classes.[16] In short, those climbing the ladder as well as those beginning to move their feet up, often find the rungs broken.

Creeping "proletarianization," as the labor theorists call it, has discovered middle-ageism. Middle-ageism is useful: it imputes losses of ability (slower reflexes, technoretardation, memory loss, general cluelessness), so that the layoffs or downgrading have some show of justification. The ontological reality of the "age class" turns out to be an effective mediator, because it provides a box into which to toss decline attributes. Under this assault, the old patriarchal combination by which whiteness, maleness, and middle-age added up to top wage-peaks at midlife is unlikely to go on buffering even the formerly protected classes.

We seem to be in an era when capitalism and patriarchy are silently clashing over seniority. Why should capitalism let patriarchal midlife privilege endure if it gets in its way? Why should it extend midlife privilege to the clamoring others? When the most privileged groups (save the top 10 percent) are vulnerable, what can stop the drive to the bottom? If anyone—if almost everyone—is at risk after forty-five, then all our expectations of what management can do to labor in America, with the acquiescence of the state, have to be changed.

Any value that depends on the age-wage curve is at risk. Age identity, insofar as it is connected with earnings and expectations, is imperiled. The human costs, as the new system is lowered into place, are likely to be staggering. In the broadest senses of well-being, in the broadest intergenerational perspective, the current or future well-being of 90 percent of the workforce is at stake. This is a "midlife crisis" that is simultaneously a national crisis. And since everything that happens in the U.S. can be exported, it should be a matter of international concern as well.

Demoralization Is Useful to the System

> Middle age doesn't exist, Fast Eddie. It's an invention of the media, like halitosis. It's something they tame people with.
>
> —Walter Tevis, *The Color of Money*

We always need to move quickly beyond the hard demoralizing facts into explanations and on to the politics of resistance. The midlife, like all age classes (or "life stages") is an ongoing invention of culture, and in the Nineties the invention is getting grimmer. It would be obvious from the sting stories alone that in North American mainstream culture, "aging" has crept down into the middle years. That "aging" connotes "old people" is now a clear mystification, implying as it does that nobody of working age is subject to pejorative age hierarchies, stereotyping, status losses, and job bias. Everywhere "the midlife" is deployed, or midlife "aging" is the subtext, these terms should be in scare quotes for as long as it takes until we get the point. Recognizing the lead ceiling makes it impossible to ignore the invention's other disconcerting skids and slides; makes it imperative to search out its other unnamed manifestations.

The weakening of the Dream puts decline discourse under a white-hot light. Representation does real work: that insight chains together our dumb birthday cards and our 2:00 A.M. soliloquies and the loss of another part of the American Dream worth struggling for. This must change the tones in which discussions of the midlife are couched. In North American culture at the present time economic forces multiply representational forces to make any subject liable to be labeled "aging" or "too old" at ages that in a century of longevity in a First World country should be the prime of life. Middle-ageism (including the master narrative of decline) prepares subjects to expect their own economic decline while believing that "Boomers are rich" and to scapegoat "aging" when it happens to them. The people who suffer directly from it may know "It's the economy, stupid"—a slogan every midlifer ought to have emblazoned on a sign—but that doesn't necessarily protect them from feeling ashamed of having failed to reach, or maintain, the American Dream. The economic facts are unlikely to go away and will probably spread. That means that the pressures on representation to age us all at midlife will also increase. The invisible hand—that trope of irresponsibility[17]—will pump decline narrative faster into our already bad air.

The system that disciplines the workforce needs age anxiety and middle-ageism more than at any earlier time in the century. The postwar workforce has been covertly nurturing a potential sense of entitlement. It has gotten more heavily white collar and middle class over the last thirty years: since about 1960 "the knowledge-producing" workers have outnumbered manual workers, and the percentage continues to go up.[18] White-collar managers and professional and technical personnel are accustomed to ladders with seniority and expect perks that come with age. As educating children becomes more expensive, even in public colleges, economic need makes even two-income families at midlife less willing to settle for what they know are stagnant in-comes. An "aging" workforce now threatens to ask for more in wages and fringe benefits: seniority, sick time and health insurance, family leave to take care of dying parents and dying children. Some of their needs have gotten translated into legislation; others such as national health insurance perch like Poe's raven, obstinately. There is always the chance of political union from a midlife generation that has watched other coalitions work. An overthrow of our decline relationship to aging would have many dramatic effects on politics and the economy, way beyond the industries we could put out of business if we stopped buying youth products.

The economy has managed to find numerous ways to contain the threat arising from all these human needs and expectations: in the Eighties real wages flattened or actually dropped for all but the top 10 percent, and hours worked went up for many who still had full-time employment. I would like to know whether the age-wage profile has also flattened in these decades. To the degree that midlife people feel they're in an irreversible decline that merits less pay, consideration, and leisure, they may simply struggle harder to be individually "deserving." Age anxiety keeps many on their toes, whether they're galloping to fulfill their life projects before it's too late or beginning wistfully to think about smelling the roses. Midlife women and midlife men of color, falling farther behind same-age white men in wages every year, are supposed to know they need to look younger and work twice as hard to boost *their* final run to the finish line. The pervasive ideology of aging disempowers everyone. The most effective way to disempower people—even those who have money and education—is to create the conditions in which they do it to themselves without knowing it.

Any person's life in "the middle years" has a reality outside of the dominant fictions. But the social fictions are powerfully determining—like the one that told so many personnel directors that Patricia and Carol and the defense computer consultants were "too old." Patricia wasn't going to cost those companies more than Becky. On the contrary. At midlife people work harder and more efficiently, have less absenteeism, and are loyal. (I shiver as I assert this, because such assertions used to be required only of gerontologists.) Not hiring Patricia was a cultural decision. Carol and the computer consultants were relatively expensive, but given their competence and networks, it's at least as relevant that in cyberjobs youth is king (the average age at Lotus is thirty-four).

"Too old" is a code that justifies middle-ageism. It is given meaning by infatuation with youth, enforced by the generation "gap"—an abyss being deepened by high-tech, the construction of glamorous and unreal Generation X culture, images of Boomer wealth and greediness, and double-sided resentment. The "Invaders from the Planet of the Recent College Graduates," as R. Chast portrays them, say they are "willing to do your job at *half your salary!*"[19] ("Willing" is cruelly misleading—as if they had a choice.) Youth's competitive advantages are being manipulated to undermine the age-wage peak and justify every midlife loss as deserved or unavoidable. Even jokes reinforce age competition; cumulatively, even trivial cultural clichés have savage power.

Now everyone on the life course desperately needs cultural criticism, a politics, and a future.

Changing the Midlife Subject

Declining to Decline started with the positivism of people assuming there was "truth" in decline discourse and that the problem for them as individuals was deciding when and how to apply it fairly to the self—meanwhile believing the source itself unalterable. After I've replaced midlife aging with economics and representation, they may still. An exchange of despair for despair? No, I think we gain a vantage point from which to work our way free.

For the sake of resistance, let us imagine a series of cognitive/emotional states that could erupt out of . . . simply no longer accepting the naturalness of decline. The moment of refusal may well bring the chills and revelations of disappointment. Describing women's unnatural lot, near the beginning of the first women's movement in 1855, Lucy Stone said, "It shall be the business of my life to deepen this disappointment in every woman's heart, until she bows to it no longer." Disappointment can be a ferment, as that wise woman realized: it leads to the recognition that the oppression one feels is unjust and unnecessary. William Blake is the poet of this phase. "Reading that indignant page"—brooding on the injustice of having rightful expectations frustrated—can lead at least two ways. One anger edges toward vengefulness: wrong targets, wasted energy, self-pity, frenzied efforts to defeat or destroy those seen as competitors, ignorant subservience to irrelevant ideologies. The militias and the "angry white males" include "disproportionately displaced white male industrial workers in their forties and fifties."[20] The commentators who think that a great mass of Americans identify with these groups have gotten something right. It's not their goals, their hopeless malevolence. What unites us is the sense that a powerful enemy without a name is doing *me* down, and I above all am helpless and alone to combat it. This is true on both counts: it *is*, and, alone and mystified, I am. This sense is sometimes called "paranoia," without any acknowledgment that pain this deep can go somewhere. It has been one business of this chapter to deepen the "paranoia" of the allegedly privileged midlife classes.

The next stage requires a giant leap into analysis. Here we name the enemies. By identifying the discursive system and the economic practices that construct midlife aging, we demystify and judge them. Emotional/cognitive resistance becomes pro-active. Practicing counterautobiography, a resistant subject twists and wrenches decline ideas out of the self. As externalization sheds automatic decline elements, age identity is left with a greater ratio of what feels like innate richnesses, relieved of the inner conflicts of the binary and free to tell more complex and meaningful life-course stories. As people exercise narrative freedom, their practices change, or the meanings they put to them change—in ways that could not have been prescribed beforehand, and accompanied by a feeling of rightness.

The higher anger that accompanies liberation has an honorable impersonal element: it is felt on behalf of all kindred sufferers. Some people leap to it directly from disappointment. These are already collective emotions. The higher anger estimates the broadest possible human collective, takes the measure of the ideology and its components, envisions slightly more than reasonable goals, operationalizes procedures. At this phase age identity has filled the personal narrative the way the body fills its corporeal envelope. The next move carries us off the pavement.

Midlife Muscle

"If [people now in midlife] were to organize as an interest group . . . it would be political suicide for anyone in Washington to ignore them."[21] Would that we could take for granted the struggle of the workforce to resist devaluation of their labor power and their economic product. To the economic motive (which we know does not always galvanize the exploited into looking for collective solutions) *Declining to Decline* has added a profound psychological struggle: to resist identity-stripping. These two motives combine irresistibly, not because they are "midlife interests," although they are assuredly that, but because only by twining them does the contemporary American life course make sense. Being and becoming: both depend on age identity, and the age-wage curve and seniority (along with many other measures) are implicated in that self-narrative. This sense of the life course goes so deep in the acculturated psyche of Americans that we scarcely begin to have words for it.

Learning simultaneously that these things are integral and fragile could motivate people to construct a "crisis" for age ideology. Together, these causes might differentially activate people at different subject locations. The "march" I envision could embrace new multitudes. No one will anticipate that the 90 percent of the American workforce that is vulnerable will resist. But I'll let others say why coalitions, like the one I envision, have so often in the past failed to coalesce.[22] When coalitions occur, it is not because everyone gains equally but because everyone gains, or hopes to gain, something compelling. My hope is ad hoc, historical and particular: that *this* midlife crisis can be perceived as critical enough to bridge, if not heal, class, race, and gender antagonisms. And in the vast spectrum of active resistance, from mocking old jokes to devising new movement strategy, each will contribute according to their ability at the time.

The first into the street are those who have been there all along: union members and their allies in politics and the academy. A couple who are both railway conductors summed it up for me, simply: "Seniority is all we have." (That could go on a second sign.) The unions have been acting on this. Everyone needs to know what national and international unionism is accomplishing in a time when mass unemployment is a major social and political problem throughout the deindustrialized world. When the Swedish social democrats returned to power, they reversed seniority deregulation. European unions are demanding and getting shorter work weeks, eliminating one source of job scarcity. In America we need a Bill of Economic Rights based on a just Age Compact. The Act for the American Dream could refer to the Middle-Aged and Older Workers Full Employment Act of 1968, and launch a complete census of necessary labor law reforms, full-employment projects, and legislative constraints on multinationals. Whether the census is adequately considerate of working-class, nonwhite, and women's midlife needs will determine whether the necessary groups find sufficient incentives to coalesce into lobbies and parties.

Those next into the street come from the millions in this country who are underemployed and unemployed. Those who felt shame have overcome it, and they're carrying the signs. Here the working class and the middle class, people of color and whites, find themselves together, and women and men, and our children, and our parents. Among them are the millions in civil society who have literally been in the street before for the sake of social justice, equality, food, health, education, peace, here and abroad. Here too the veterans are a Rainbow Coalition. The last time my family marched together, there were twenty-one of us, including my mother, my husband, our son, my cousins and their children as young as eleven, my aunt and uncle in their eighties. We were marching then for young women; it was the pro-choice march in Washington. Our multigenerational rainbow will come out for this cause too. I envision a national lobbying group also linked to the Gray Panthers and a reformed AARP turned advocacy group. The concept of an age coalition has been astonishingly effective for postretirement Americans. Its history should enable us to reimagine (as I have started to do here) the unifying potential of a midlife mobilization.

These developments would propel age studies, critical life-course development and critical gerontology, materialist feminist theory, cultural studies, history, anthropology, clinical psychology and psychoanalytic theory, left economics and political science, religion and philosophy, into a phase in which they are connected on unexpected ground, intensely closer. The interdisciplinary conversation should be a basis for intellectual coalition-building and curricular changes.

The stir in the street is going to bring new writers to the windows and the curbs and send them back to the word processor. Men writing male midlife novels almost never treat the economy as an actor; when they do, they write about it the way a branding iron marks a hide: it doesn't know what seized it, heated it, or forged its mark, it just leaves a deep smoking imprint. Challenged, men writers may rapidly cover the ground between Dreiser's Hurstwood to Steinbeck's Ma Joad, move out of the History of Increasing Humiliation to the History of Increasing Empowerment (where the women's midlife progress novel lives), leaving along the way the stupid modernist binary between "politics" and "art." Together women and men can invent the next midlife genres.

Two groups that will provide marchers need to be looked at separately: "midlife men" and "midlife women," those imaginary categories that may yet be made to function usefully. Some midlife women may prove to be a stubborn and difficult target of postmodern America. Many of us—valorized by the historic accident of maturing within movement subcultures—are the products of empowering pro-female fictions: that a female collective can bring personal and social change, that justice is worth working for, that the future ought to be better than the past, and, therefore, that it should be better to be older than younger. These fictions, touched with antiageism, have over time *made* many of us midlife progressives—in two ways: they helped us counter hegemonic sexist ageism and grow into activism. Surveys show that many women are in synch with these empowering images: they have good self-esteem; they're not afraid of aging. Although the surveys are sometimes dubiously motivated, I believe them. "Hope is a muscle," in the title of a recent book; and that muscle has gotten stronger with exercise and done some real work in the world. The multicultural movements have been learning one by one to add up the reasons why forcing changes in representation matters. If these groups have better integrated "cultural" concerns into their other interests than the academy in general, or the male left, as some of us feel, perhaps this is why.

In the postmodern economy, however, whatever the wonderful woman has achieved of inner strength and midlife wisdom, not to mention work experience, may not avail her at the painful moment of the job search or at other crucial moments, such as deciding whether to join a protest or a strike. In mainstream culture at this time, everyone is receiving mixed and contradictory messages about what midlife women are *worth* and what we can do. "In this postmodern era, economic, political and cultural relations are not [always] synchronous."[23] There is a war going on within the culture about the representation of midlife women, between feminist-inspired fictions producing wonderful women, and antifemale fictions that justify curtailed laborforce participation by updating twentieth-century stereotypes of female midlife decline. And there's a war going on in midlife women's psyches, between an achieved sense of confidence and improved status and a fearful sense of danger and decline.

This is the postmodern quandary of women. Does this make us crazy or enraged, passive-depressives or outraged activists? There's no way to say how it will end. But I can bring some news from the front. In the spring of 1993 I studied both wars with my seminars participants at Radcliffe. The fourteen women were mostly in their forties and fifties, with two in their sixties, two in their thirties, and one, an undergraduate, of twenty.[24] We read journalism focused on "the midlife woman" as well as midlife women's progress novels. Our age-focused close reading of fiction brought out personal anecdotes about the social construction of age. Over the semester, I watched the women move easily into more sophisticated theory. They emerged not only with new motives for talking up "the midlife" but also with raised expectations about public discourse, fictional and journalistic—in short, a more aggressive anti-middle-ageism.

If not for these developments, it could have been dismaying to turn to mainstream so-called nonfictional discourses. Each participant clipped out everything she found about "midlife women" (defined any way she wanted) in the course of her normal reading. Normal reading was a crucial component of the assignment. I wanted to find out what "information" each reader would have absorbed just by casually perusing whatever newspapers and magazines and journals she ordinarily received, and what the overlaps in "knowledge" would be within the group. By the end of the semester most were freely exercising the idea that midlife discourse has its own foci around which contests of images and facts cohere. The election year 1992–93 should have been an upper, if the media had only noticed as we did, that it was the Year of the Successful Midlife Woman, the Star. But a number also noticed that the women doing well had prestigious careers and that they weren't finding news about the work lives of ordinary women like us. Of course, anonymous women in news stories are mostly presented as passive victims of male events: mothers of fighting men in little wars far away, crying over their sons' coffins.

Domestically, most of the negative images came in the health news. "What was the popular culture story that most shocked you?" I asked. Many had been outraged by the discovery of how discrepant care for heart disease was, with men getting better attention before heart attacks and better treatment afterward. That was important news—and it was coming to us, of course, because of feminist activism in women's health care, political pressure on the NIH. The menoboom was in full sway in 1992–93, making menopause so public that no one of a certain age could blush anymore without knowing that others had received a signal about her bodily fluids, her dangerous age, and her fearful future. We dissected the article that ended with the gruesome anecdote of the older woman who lost eight inches in height. We had a good time in that session, putting together the pieces of the implicit "midlife woman." Only one participant, who had done brilliant work on the novels, didn't get it. "You're paranoid," she said. That was the undergraduate.

No midlife woman is untouched by feminist representation and social change; none is totally immune to sexist ageism. Working from those I know, let me describe a woman—not that "average woman" journalists imagine, but an average made by Patricia, Lydia and Carol. This woman is armored against bad midlife culture (although not as well as she thinks). She decodes the morning paper. She's a good-natured person but she hates the man who laid her off. She's ideology-alert and self-protective in censoring her moviegoing: that year she didn't bother going to *Mr. and Mrs. Bridge,* to *Waterland* (midlife woman crazed by missing out on maternity) or *Indochine* (gorgeous midlife woman loses lover to own daughter), or *Death Becomes Her.* She saw *Fried Green Tomatoes* twice. If her partner is a man, she's been explaining to him why these movies have bad effects personally, interpersonally, and culturally, and if he's one of the men I describe next, he doesn't go to them either.[25] She belongs to NARAL, gives money to battered-women's shelters; she hasn't yet joined OWL, the Older Women's League. (That's a touch of internalized youthism she has overlooked.) That middle-ageism reaches into the culture everywhere, she gets more convinced every day. This woman will be in the march, and she'll bring her partner and her family and friends.

Midlife women need to take their postmodern quandary seriously, and ponder it collectively. The power of the feminist movement has been implicitly grounded on having women achieve economic gains; if this begins to slow further, or if advances turn out to benefit only younger women, what will happen to feminism? It is not true, and never was, that the movement can focus on gains for younger women on the understanding that they automatically translate into gains *for the same women as they age.* To the extent that women believe in our value at midlife, we are likely to resent any attempts—discursive or economic—to reduce our status or economic participation or level of gender equality or any other of our hard-won gains. Feeling entitled is one of the strengths we can count on. But we don't know how it will survive the present crisis.

Many midlife men too—of color and white, gay and straight, liberal and left—have participated in liberatory movements since the sixties. Men who spent ten or more years in America before their movement(s) began, experiencing Jim Crow, McCarthyism, or the closet, could also thank history and aging for how far they've come, if such movements generally nourished that kind of thinking. But valorizing aging was not only off those screens; in some movements, the cult of youth was implicit and powerful—initially a source of vitality, detrimental in the long run. Am I correct in fearing that the men who believe similar messages about life-course empowerment are few? Unprotected by a collective movement, each will discover the malice of the lead ceiling and decline ideology alone. Some may have to discover the fundamental concepts of the social construction of maleness and of the midlife simultaneously.

What will protect men from the "historical trauma" of these combined discoveries? Kaja Silverman describes historical trauma as an "event, whether socially engineered or of natural occurrence, which brings a large group of male subjects into such an intimate relation with lack that they are at least for the moment unable to sustain an imaginary relation" with the primary sources of their referred power, which I would define as patriarchy for all men, capitalism for the higher classes, racism for white men.[26] Wars create such introjections of lack; but so can economic or representational catastrophes.

Some midlife men are already ambivalent about power: partially conscious that they have too little within capitalism, uncomfortably conscious that they have too much in other contexts. They are also uncertain about what life-course narrative to tell—and who would listen. Some men's fiction (including novels, films, TV) suggests that in relation to self and women men believe and crave redemption stories; guilty and regretful for youthful abuses of conferred power, they have overcome a lot of bad shit. We have changed, they say. But not even the "men's movement" gives them enough credit for making progress, and Alcoholics Anonymous and Christian fundamentalism revive men for a second chance only under certain narrow conditions. All are told that as leading men they're being swept off the historical stage: "too old." This combination only begins to explain the self-pity and lack of faith in growth found in so much fiction by white men in their middle years.[27] Their protagonists lack the resoluteness and heroism that midlife women characters are being endowed with. It may be that there is also a war going on in men's psyches, between the representations they intuit and long for and the paralyzing ones they find. The war going on in the culture is between the hype of male youth and the complementary decline narrative, and images (like that of midlife men seducing or marrying or torturing or rescuing young women) that are supposed to compensate in fantasy for men's other losses and explain the male "psyche." This is the postmodern quandary of midlife men. How will midlife men respond?

Clarity about the high stakes of "aging"—specifically, about the (male and female) midlife under postmodern conditions—could produce faster changes. Those on the left might be partly protected by prior analysis. Men savvier about the social construction of midlife masculinity and less dismissive of midlife qualities could rewrite their age autobiographies, figuratively or literally, perhaps more openly and easily than in fiction. There would be room for modest progress accounts about male struggles to end micro and macro age-inequalities: his humiliating jokes about himself and her, his-and-her body surgery, her lower-wage ceilings, his gay-bashing, status-quo values in the bedroom, the barroom, the boardroom, the personnel office, the law courts, the PACs, and the councils of state. They could include images of the cooperation that goes on in real midlife: women helping women and men to think their ways out of decline miasma, and men helping others as well. These accounts could deal with the competitive success that is supposed to accompany male midlife, the aggravated chances of failure and its hideous compensations. If men who are white grow to understand whiteness, racializing practices might diminish, and progress narratives could report more friendship and more equal distributions of health and wealth at midlife. If men who are intellectually influential change, the level of mainstream analysis with regard to social problems including middle-ageism would rise, and so would the ability to imagine altering institutions. Ordinary heroism might increase—the kind of heroism that already surfaces in labor struggles, rights movements, long-term commitments to reform and writing and publishing liberating texts. Theoretical savvy; egalitarian ethics; activism (personal, discursive, institutional, political). We need more discursive space for noticing ordinary heroism, male as well as female, and more encouragement for the emergence of new midlife subjects.

The man who looks for conceptual precedents, models of psychological externalization and age valorization, and social supports for his demystification project could find some of them in feminism or the cutting-edge side of feminist men's studies. The inspiration for a historical and theorized men's studies, practitioners like Victor Seidler are very ready to say, came from feminism: "It is crucial to keep in mind that it has been the challenges of feminism that have made the dominant conceptions of masculinity problematic." Male feminists have made good use of "the transformation of resistance into a liberation project addressed to the whole gender order" and other aspects of feminist analysis.[28] Yet men's studies has produced next to nothing about men at midlife. One of decline's strategic political effects has been to make "age" seem like a dreary and inert topic, fit only for positivists and gerontologists; middle-ageism and machismo have made aging seem like a soft issue. The aversions have kept most male intellectuals away from theorizing age.

If midlife men join the march, finally convinced of their own interests, what would convince the young that aging in our culture should unite them with the midlife generation in solidarity? Already, the young have been told that Social Security will enrich their parents and pauperize them, and that the Medicare system will be bankrupt when it is their turn to benefit from it. Both untrue. The short-term interest of the young lies in getting the jobs that senior workers are being ejected from. Under conditions of middle-ageism and artificial scarcity, young adults joining the workforce are put in the position of white men who want to end programs that "put" blacks and women into "their" jobs. Doug Coupland's 1995 novel, *Microserfs,* has a plot that furthers a midlife decline narrative. "Soon enough, for ours are *not* ordinary times, Dad is working under his son in Michael's hardscrabble video-game startup, a fiftysomething (Generation L?) reduced through computer illiteracy to childish impotence in a contracting economy."[29]

The invention of Generation X has not been trivial. It has darkened midlife nightmares. It has justified not just generational competition but youthful arrogance (also a reflex of economic insecurity). It has divided the Xers themselves, into "slackers" and the overworked. Through economic pressure and ideology, the young are being prepared to fight, of course unwittingly, against seniority and the American Dream.

The concept of life-course continuity—that as the young grow older, their interests change and long-term values begin to matter—has been a difficult idea for parents to convey to their children in this America. This national cultural failure is not a natural condition of "generations" but an effect of middle-ageism impinging on family life. The fact that parents are being proletarianized as midlife producers weakens their authority to speak with confidence about such basic values as reciprocal roles, binding ties, love, and the human and economic logic of seniority. Whatever success parents achieve in creating family solidarity and age equality with adult children is additionally weakened by the dominant culture's animosity to these unspoken ideals. How many parents can say to their adult children, "Youth is being used to make midlifers settle for misery in everyday life and hopelessness in economic life," or, "If 'we' lose midlife economic power now, do you understand why it won't be there for you when your turn is supposed to come?" And we have to be prepared for them to respond, initially, "You're paranoid." Dismantling middle-ageism, in short, is an agenda for midlifers as parents too: they need to invent an intergenerational language in their own words and live it through. What the young can do to help depends first on their comprehension of what is at stake.

Adding age is an immense challenge—psychological, theoretical, political. What about the relations between the economic, the political, and the representational: how can we explain the sometimes screwy lack of synchrony? How can we try to counter popular media representations of midlife women and men? And how can we make improved images matter, if solid representational advances bring personal empowerment but not necessarily economic gains? One prior question unsettles all others. Given that the midlife members of many of these constituencies for the time being feel secured from threatened disasters by "seniority"—the ownership of tenure or apparently unassailable professional standing or the equivalents—will the conversation even begin? Before seniority crumbles across the board, who will begin to publish or broadcast these issues, frame the questions in the right way—at least let the conversations start? And if we overcome this difficulty, how, within the rightward politics of the state and the increasing power of global enterprises, can even the widest collectives with an antiageist agenda make change? We won't know until we try.

When contemporary pressure feels too strong, a resister can look back and ask indignantly, "Where did this come from?" (the historian's release), and look forward to speculate about what's coming (the prophet's release). The historical irony we want to dwell on is that, since 1900, the life narrative should have altered dramatically with the effect of *youthening* people of forty and up, since great improvements in the material facts of health and longevity and the birthrate have become apparent. But this didn't happen.[30] It was precisely as these facts were becoming known that the new century reinvented its own canonical stories about midlife decline, fitted for an industrialized, individualized, standardized, sexualized, medicalized, gender-conscious, class-based, age-graded, politically contested epoch, quite a lot like our own.

All of us, plain selves, always still caught up in getting by, may doubt—not the urgency of the anti-middle-ageist endeavor but our strength and readiness to fight. It will take enormous effort. But the gains in energy from self-transformation will also be immense. A demystified midlife man, or woman, knows from experience what it means to be a midlife subject with agency, not just an obsolescing object wrapped in a "Boomer power" label. They have figured out that they are supposed to think that "aging" is innocent of politico-socioeconomic connections, the last unideological *res*. They know how decline creates self-involvement, atomization, resignation, and pain; they know why a nation governed by such people might be dangerous to itself and others. They're getting a kick out of putting decline ideology on the defensive. They never never ask when the middle years begin.

Off the Pavement and into the Street

In theory, it's not chic to be optimistic.[31] But in theory, all can change rapidly. If age were to catch on as a category of analysis, the way gender, ethnicity, class, race, and sexual orientation once had to be caught on to; if age studies pervaded the human and social and medical sciences; if we all pooled our verbal cleverness and rhetorical strategies to counter the massive mainstream decline story, if it led to cohort solidarity between women and men, between men and men, and all the other betweens; if we could teach the young, form new unions, start a lobby, pressure the political parties . . . Does this convey the savor of the doable, the idealism of the Utopian, the thrill of a Cause? Initially, perhaps, new exponents of this Cause might ironize themselves, as befits victims unsure of how much harm the new conditions can do to *them,* and how major the damages are compared to the other ideological toxins we breathe in all the time. But as damage and resistance stories proliferate—drawing on the density of fiction and the detachment of cultural analysis—deconstructing age could quickly attain for all of us the earnestness that marks moral urgency.

I want to end with the tone of cautious, realistic looking-to-the-future that characterizes, and facilitates, political progress narratives. The life course goes in only one direction for all of us, toward being older; and if that direction, at this historical moment in American age consciousness, might make available a greater number of cultural goods, especially discursive reinforcement of our best ideas and collective action of behalf of *all* of us who are passing or will pass through the middle years, well then, "Let it come."

Notes

Chapter 1: Vulnerability and Resistance

Andrea Petersen and I talked out the major issues of this introduction on a memorable beach walk in the summer of 1995. Suzy Scarff Webster and Carl Brandt gave helpful advice at earlier stages, and Mike Brown, Sean Gullette, Andrea Schumann, and Nancy Essig at later ones.

1. I have found no study of "internal conversation," as Ariel Phillips calls it ("Inner Voices, Inner Selves"), that also explicitly deals with age. Phillips's point about her (young adult) subjects is that stress precipitates internal debate. In general, the concern with personal narrative as shaping identity "has for some time been bringing psychology, sociology, anthropology and literary studies closer together" (Rosenwald and Ochberg, Introduction: "Life Stories," 1). Howe, "Tis of Thee."

2. The "rebuttal" comes from Brody and Osborne, *Twenty-Year Phenomenon*, 56. The second is paraphrased from an interview John McLeish conducted in the early Seventies. He commented, "To my astonishment, a number of men distinguished in their professions, including a physician, a priest, a publisher, and an economist, referred to 'withering of the brain cells' or 'daily loss of neurons'" (*Ulyssean Adult*, 2).

3. American Board of Family Practice Report; Hunter and Sundel, *Midlife Myths*, 8–21. A popular summary is provided by Gallagher, "Myths." For data on psychological well-being, linked to gender, race, and education (class), see Bumpass and Aquilino, "A Social Map of Midlife."

4. Sherman, *Meaning*, 16. Notice the untheorized use of the word "entrance."

5. I first used the formulation "aged by culture" in "What, Menopause *Again?*" 37.

A brief history of the sociology of knowledge is given in Berger and Luckmann, *The Social Construction of Reality*. Contemporary readers may have different entries to the idea through work by feminists, antiracists, Foucault, neohistoricists, neomarxists. The first prominent history of the social construction of (a part of) the life course was by Philippe Ariès, *Centuries of Childhood*.

6. I argue elsewhere that the middle years was invented in Anglo-American culture between 1900 and 1935 ("Midlife Fictions: The Invention of Male Midlife Sexual Decline," in progress). This use of "culture" is like Raymond Williams's rather anthropological view. Using the term *ideology* here is heuristic. At the present stage of age studies, the term serves as an alarum and a sign of work-to-be-done. For a general defense, see Eagleton, *Ideology*, especially chaps. 1 and 7.

7. Luther, "Questions of Style," 113. *Middle Age: The Magazine* is a Roz Chast invention, *The New Yorker*, 103.

8. An age class such as "aging Baby Boomers" (first used by the *New York Times* in 1982) is broader and vaguer than either an age category like "childhood" or a *cohort*, the term for a group of people born in the same era or allegedly marked by the same event or united by a single politics (e.g., "Depression Babies" or "the Class of '68").

9. Epstein, *With My Trousers Rolled,* 110.

10. Cards by Boynton, 1986. My private collection. Although Alex Comfort coined the term *sociogenic aging* in the 1970s, he applied it only to those in the postretirement stage of life (*A Good Age,* 9).

11. Everyday life as described here is not a *habitus,* as it is often conceived (following Pierre Bourdieu), in spatial terms. It is a sequence in time, defined through the life-course constructions of a particular society and era.

12. Earnest, "Ideology Criticism and Life-History Research," 252.

13. Because the North American life course is universalized, everyone exposed to dominant culture grows up into the age class.

14. Goodman, "Just keep thinking, with hope, about tomorrow," 23.

15. Sociologists and historians have begun to study the social construction and history of emotions. The assumption is that although people are born with the capacity for certain feelings, "emotional culture" is deeply influenced by social structures, especially language. "'Emotional culture,' as I term it, includes emotion vocabularies (words for emotions), norms (regulating expression and feeling) and beliefs about emotions (e.g., the idea that 'repressed' emotion is disturbing)" (Gordon, "Social Structural Effects," 146, 148).

16. As reported by Gallagher, "Myths of Middle Age," several researchers associated with the MacArthur Research Network on Successful Midlife Development see people who score low on tests of introspection and high in denials as prone to midlife crisis (34). Some therapists too explain *true* midlife crisis as the property of people who have trouble dealing with "reality," adjusting expectations down, etc.

17. In psychology, *identity-stripping* refers to behaviors that intentionally denigrate and de-individualize a group of human subjects, as in a concentration camp (Brim, *Ambition,* 25). In sociology, *status degradation* refers to more invisible forces present in everyday social life. See also chap. 11.

18. McMurtry, *Texasville,* 51. See Billig et al., *Ideological Dilemmas,* 2. *Declining to Decline* is intended to encourage readers to see the ideological aspects of the midlife, "the dilemmatic aspects of ideology and of thinking generally" (2), and to move beyond the current midlife binary between progress and decline.

19. Barlow, Translator's Introduction, xi; emphasis in original. The book was first published in 1968 in a context of youth revolutions.

20. Although some adults living in subcultures do not know the terms *midlife* or *middle years,* that does not by itself mean that they are exempt from middle-ageism.

21. Collecting stories from "midlife minorities," with attention to class, place, and historical experience, is beginning. Katherine S. Newman, interviewing Harlem dwellers, and Thomas S. Weisner and Lucinda P. Bernheimer interviewing Sixties counterculturists, are consciously working with midlife disjunctures in mind (both in Shweder, *Middle Age*). Critical age studies would require of interviewers that they also be aware of midlife narrative, and perhaps ask subjects questions that elicit their relationship to it (without nudging them toward a particular genre).

22. For example, some middle-class African-Americans whose careers lag behind those of whites of the same class may know that racism is their problem: see Ellis Cose, *The Rage of a Privileged Class,* 84, and the midlife accounts in Joe R. Feagin and Melvin P. Sykes, *Living with Racism.*

23. Malamud, *Dubin's Lives,* 11.

24. See Gullette, "Perilous Parenting," on the deaths of children. On the prestige of decline, see "In Defense of Midlife Progress Novels," in my *Safe at Last.* (I would add that

accepting decline can be conceived by men as a macho trait. The topic deserves more extended gender analysis.)

25. In the words of Francis Barker, "I have preferred [initially] the situated use of a critical lexicon over formal introductions and definitions. Terms emerge. . . . eventually, I trust, they deepen their theoretical purchase somewhat" (*Culture of Violence,* ix). On "good theory," see Narr, "Prophetic Radicalism."

26. This narrative, called by Robert Butler "the life review," was supposed to be told first in old age. Now, however, it seems useful to assume that in North American culture, everyone begins to tell life-course narrative rather early in life. See Gullette, *Safe at Last.*

27. Rosenwald, Conclusion: "Reflections on Narrative Self-Understanding," 270.

28. See Kathleen Woodward's "Tribute to the Older Woman" and the essays in *Aging and Its Discontents.*

29. Even feminist theory has been weak on using age as a concept. See Gullette, "Age (Aging)" and "One Necessary Future." Alta, "Pretty," 227. In Ferguson's context, this prose poem can be read as muted cry for help getting out of sexist ageist ideology.

30. Williams, *Modern Tragedy,* 100.

31. Brantlinger, *Crusoe's Footprints,* 103–4, 106, 112, 116.

32. Moore, "Beautiful Grade," 122.

33. Remy, "Patriarchy," 45. See Sontag, "The Double Standard of Aging," and chapter 8 for a historical updating of the gender situation.

34. A perceptibly healthier midlife and increased longevity have not, historically (as at the turn of the century) prevented discourses of midlife decline from being installed in the culture. Culturally constructed diseases, like menopause and the male climacteric, overwhelm the demographic advances; and the attitude that such advances are trivial (see Epstein quotation, above) is becoming more widespread as middle-ageism deepens.

35. The median income for white women was $15,701; for black women, $13,656. The 1991 medians come from the U. S. Department of Commerce, *Money Income,* Table 26.

36. On age-wage profiles, see Edwards, *Contested Terrain,* 170–73. On gendered wage peaks, see Rayman et al. "Resiliency and Inequality," 140.

37. "MAAD" quotation from the *Los Angeles Times,* in Kevin Phillips, *The Politics of Rich and Poor,* 22; see also 126.

38. Gail Sheehy's 1995 book uses a basic idea from *Safe at Last*—the "midlife progress narrative" (*New Passages,* 170 and passim)—without developing the context of power and ideology in which such a narrative is received, evaluated, contested, used or discarded. On the weaknesses of positive aging at midlife, see Gullette, "Declining to Decline." On positive aging in general, see Featherstone and Hepworth, "Images of Positive Aging," 29–33.

39. A pamphlet prepared by the Consumer Research Center (1985). Numerous publications hype the wealth of the age class, although the distribution of income within it is, of course, tremendously unequal.

A search of one database reveals that "middle age" appeared in only one title out of sixty-four about "the midlife." Although anti-middle-ageism produced the written change, without politics and theory such local improvements have little effect.

40. On age as a category more resistant to "the erosion of ascription," see Giele, "'Deceptive Distinctions,'" 13.

41. The first use of "age studies" occurs in Gullette, "Creativity, Gender, Aging," 45–46. See also Wyatt-Brown, "Aging, Gender, Creativity," 5; and Gullette, "Age (Aging)."

42. I would like to be at a point equivalent to that argued by Judith Butler in *Gender*

Trouble, interrogating aging as a "natural process" altogether, but I think that the most age studies can do now is to urge a radical social constructionism that pushes "the natural" out of context after context.

43. For the phrase "natural weight," see Gilday's video, "The Famine Within."

44. Eagleton, *Ideology,* xiv.

Chapter 2: A Good Girl

1. And "*because* it stands at the confluence of many theories that . . . continue to shape postmodern thought" (Steedman, "Difficult Stories," 323).

2. Heinz Kohut has developed this position; the formulation is Jessica Benjamin's ("Oedipal Riddle," 204).

3. They asked for a more patriotic "upbeat" conclusion, and, if Wright made the "improvement," held out the promise of best-sellerdom, which it in fact achieved: it ranked fourth among nonfiction sales in 1945 (Thaddeus, "The Metamorphosis of Richard Wright's *Black Boy*").

4. As *Midlife Fictions* and *The Invention of Male Midlife Sexual Decline* will argue, "the middle years" was invented in a period of debate (1900–1935) about whether that phase of life should be considered a decline or a progress. Fred Davis, *Yearning for Yesterday,* 55; see the entire chapter "Nostalgia and the Life Cycle." I am historicizing Davis's account.

5. Jessica Benjamin says that this conservative view is challenged by post-Freudians ("Oedipal Riddle," 203). But unless developmentalists ask themselves constructionist questions—like, what "new satisfactions" are made available and which are withheld?—their analysis of the life course will still remain overessentialized, ahistorical.

6. This is the ending Orwell used when he put together *Such, Such Were the Joys* for Harcourt, Brace in 1953. Most editors reprint this ending, in middle-ageist fashion, although another version ends with several demystifying sentences about adult detachment from childhood misery.

Chapter 3: Ordinary Pain

1. Baltes, "The Many Faces of Human Aging," 29.

2. Brim, *Ambition,* 1–2. The man was his father.

3. In conversation. Behind my thinking about the economic and social causes of disease lie many conversations with my cousin Peter Schnall, author of major papers on the social etiology of hypertension, now the director of the Center for Social Epidemiology at the University of California at Irvine. See his "Job Strain."

4. Medical anthropologists, humanistic gerontologists—colleagues like Tom Cole and Byron Good—are listening.

Chapter 4: Face-Off

This essay is particularly dedicated to my husband David, because he isn't afflicted with the fatal age gaze.

1. See Fred Davis's *Yearning for Yesterday.*

2. One chronological marker of the positive midlife in the mainstream: my "Hers" article on "midlife exhilaration" appeared in January 1989.

3. Douglas, *Where the Girls Are,* Introduction, esp. 20; also 27; see also Breines, *Young, White, and Miserable.*

4. In psychoanalytic terminology, the "soft" is first of all the realm of the young mother as seen by her (pre-Oedipal) child. I see those values resummoned by older bodies, male or female, but then invalidated (through, for example, the negativity of "weight gain") by the ways we name and notice aging. "Youth," by contrast, is now the realm of the "tough"—synecdochally, the chic, the technologically able, the financially successful. This is why today's young too have to try to look young.

5. Kathy Davis, *Reshaping,* 24.

6. I limit my focus to those plastic surgeries implicated in middle-ageism.

7. Kathy Davis, "Remaking the She-Devil," 21.

8. Davis thinks feminism "undermines" the women who "opt" for surgery. She says feminists see them as "cultural dope[s]" ("Remaking the She-Devil," 29). This attack has become a standard move in popular culture studies: alleging elitist motives for doing cultural analysis. My response: with an age ideology this smart "dope" is a huge category. If I were to use that label, I'd have to put it around myself.

Chapter 5: Midlife Heroines, "Older and Freer"

The advice of David Lynn and Andrea Petersen was crucial in developing this essay.

1. Perry, *Women Writers Talking,* 38.

2. Some of the observations I make here may be relevant to men's midlife novels, but the meanings of "progress" and "hero," the values that the endings support, the representation of the opposite gender, and many other features seem to me quite different.

3. See Palmer, *Contemporary Women's Fiction,* 7. Palmer was not discussing the midlife.

4. Drabble, *The Middle Ground,* 229. When novels are quoted more than once, subsequent page numbers appear in the text.

5. This trend frees a critic from the patriarchal pressure to call a genre focussed on women a 'feminized genre.'

6. Ebert, "Gender and the Everyday," 93, emphasis in original. Armstrong, Book Reviews, 437–38. Altieri, *Canons and Consequences,* 16.

7. Lessing, *If the Old Could,* 285–86.

8. Drabble, *A Natural Curiosity,* 22; Drabble, *The Radiant Way,* 300–301; Walker, *The Color Purple,* 220.

9. Sarton, *Education of Harriet Hatfield,* 158; Lurie, *Foreign Affairs,* 11.

10. Kingsolver, *Pigs in Heaven,* 8.

11. For an expanded account of recovery in midlife fiction, see Gullette, "Perilous Parenting."

12. Alther, *Other Women,* 230.

13. Ford, *Independence Day,* 14. By my evaluation of these balances, Ford grants Bascombe as a kind of surprise (for a character who deserves it) a cautious progress ending.

14. For a brilliant attack on the use of the term *progress* in history, see Wallerstein, *Historical Capitalism,* final chapter.

15. Nolan, "Gays in San Francisco," 1, 16.

16. In nineteenth-century autobiographies written by working-class men and women, a progress plot was nearly inconceivable, according to Regenia Gagnier. Progress was a bourgeois emplotment. "The bourgeois climax-and-resolution/action-and-interaction

model presupposed an active and reactive world not always accessible to working-class writers, who often felt themselves passive victims of economic determinism" ("The Literary Standard," 104).

17. Amis, *The Information*, 128.

18. Russo's *Nobody's Fool* (1994), movie or novel, is probably influenced by the self-forgiveness and second chances of the adjacent midlife women's progress novel. Anne Tyler's novels about midlife men may have helped: e.g., *The Accidental Tourist, Saint Maybe*.

19. Ryan and Kellner, *Camera Politica*, 160.

20. Lesley Hazleton uses "applied feminist" more narrowly to mean "entering previously male-dominated . . . fields" ("Power Politics," 1).

21. This motto is also the title of a newsletter put out by the Women's Commission of the Democratic Socialists of America.

22. Based on a sentence in Aronowitz that has nothing to do with fiction but is about utopian thought in general ("Postmodernism and Politics," 55).

23. Associated Press, "Women aren't making Page 1 much," 20.

24. Weldon, *Praxis*, 25.

25. Lessing, *Diary of a Good Neighbor*, 26, 11, 30.

26. Gerontologists who regard middle-ageism as trivial in comparison to old-ageism need to reconsider in light of this problem.

27. See Gullette, "Letting a Son Become His Own Man" and "The Postmaternal Phenomenon."

28. Shulman made sections of this work available to me in manuscript. The passage appears in *Drinking the Rain* (6) in a slightly different form.

29. Sarton, *Education of Harriet Hatfield*, 213.

Chapter 6: Menopause as Magic Marker

I am grateful to editor Jeanne Daly for asking hard conceptual questions. My thanks to Dr. Alice Rothchild and others who discussed an earlier version at Harvard's Center for Literary and Cultural Studies, and to Andrea Walsh for inviting me.

1. "Menoboom" initially comes from Linda Roach, an editor at the *Los Angeles Times*, according to Barbre, "Meno-Boomers and Moral Guardians," 23.

2. I know of no single history of the menopause in the twentieth century. But we know enough about the Twenties and Thirties to say that reconsolidations after feminist disruptions have occurred. For a brief overview, see Banner, *In Full Flower*, 273–310; for the premodern era, see Formanek, "Continuity and Change," 3–41. Other periodizations can also be useful: post-*Feminine Forever*, post-ERT (moment when ERT is linked to endometrial cancer).

Vanity Fair published an article by Gail Sheehy in October of 1991; because of its location and prominence, I take it to be the first item in the new consolidation.

3. See Gullette, "Brief Golden Summer."

4. The U.S. Department of Health and Human Services concludes, "Menopause is natural and takes place smoothly for most women" (5).

Mainstream culture anachronistically tries to link puberty and menopause, "menopause, puberty's dark twin," in the words of Tony Cappasso (*Seasons*, 17). *Seasons* is published by Wyeth-Ayerst Laboratories, which as a major producer of hormones has a stake in discourse that reproduces pronatalism and related younger women/older women distinctions by emphasizing "the passing of fertility." There are cultures in which "menopause may not be recognized as a concept, . . . nor is it usually considered a difficult time" (Lock, "Menopause," 307). "Local biology" can distinguish subcultures as well. For the term, see Lock, "Cultivating the Body," 146.

5. On flushing, Ginsburg and Hardiman, "What Do We Know . . . ?" 41. The collection in which this essay appears (Sitruk-Ware and Utian) exemplifies the medical model. One chapter actually says, "Cessation of estrogen can be considered a medical oophorectomy" (60). I've cited it often because the assertions, hesitations, and admissions in its own discourse make it useful. It would not be a good starter book. Poovey, "Figures of Arithmetic," 275.

6. By 1890 the average woman had stopped having children at thirty-two (Gullette, "Inventing the 'Postmaternal' Woman," 226 and n. 17).

Postmenstrual women who wanted children but had infertility problems sometimes feel that the social-constructionist approach to menopause excludes them.

7. See Gullette, "Eliza Farnham." I believe that many women prefer continuities to the concept of a great Change. But a woman can enjoy the ceremony, welcome the novels, and agree that it would be better for mainstream discourse to downplay negative change.

8. Taylor and Sumrall, *Women of the Fourteenth Moon,* n.p.

9. The other full-length book, by Germaine Greer, uses this as its title.

10. The value of the market before the consolidation was $750 million. Premarin got 80% of it (Gross, "Aging Baby Boomers," 30). Premarin now estimates 1996 sales at $1 billion.

11. On the percentage taking HR"T," see Knox, "They're starting to take women's heart disease seriously," 28. Source: Wyeth-Ayerst Laboratories.

In Harris's study of mostly white affluent women, 40.6% of women ages 50–54 were taking hormones, as compared to only 23.1% of women aged 60–65. "Younger women reached menopause at a time physicians were increasing their postmenopausal hormone prescribing" ("Are Women Using Postmenopausal Estrogens?" 1267).

12. For *Modern Maturity,* John Walters writes about his discovery at age 72 that he has lost height. He told his wife. The following dialogue ensues: "'A touch of osteoporosis, I'd say,' she offered helpfully. 'Osteo-what?'" Nevertheless, this article ("Humor," 92), in the major magazine for the over-fifties, is the first time I'd seen any mention, not to mention a first-person account, of male bone-mass loss in a mainstream publication.

13. Suzanne Phillips, "Reflections of Self and Other," 290.

14. "Even 'asymptomatic menopause' may initiate silent, progressive, and ultimately lethal sequelae" (Wulf Utian, the High Priest of hormone replacement, quoted in Callahan, *Menopause,* 32). Greer links menopause and "death" in emphatic ways several times in her opening pages.

15. Waye, "Menopause."

16. On percentage of fractures, see Lindsay and Cosman, "The Risk of Osteoporosis," 54. On reducing risk, Eagen, "Reconsidering Hormone Replacement Therapy," 5.

17. The study, produced by Lyonnais researchers at INSERM, was published in the *New England Journal of Medicine,* Dec. 3, 1992. Their intervention showed fewer fractures in the treated population. The dosage was 800 milligrams of calcium daily.

18. Even when articles about midlife men and women are "paired," disparities are glar-

ing. See Angier, "A Male Menopause?" versus, on the same page, Jane Brody, "Personal Health" (both in the *New York Times*). The article on men carefully keeps reminding readers about how "gradual" the (alleged) slump in testosterone production is.

19. MacPherson, "Menopause as Disease"; see also McCrea, "The Politics of Menopause." I value *The Meanings of Menopause*, edited by Formanek, and *Changing Perspectives on Menopause*, edited by Voda et al., and the chapter on menopause in Betty Friedan's *The Fountain of Age*. Voda, MacPherson, and others can be found in the new anthology *Menopause*, ed. Callahan. Margaret Lock's cross-cultural work is consistently illuminating. In all the popular writing, only one brief article seemed to me sufficiently debunking: Pollitt, "Hot Flash."

20. Worcester and Whatley, "The Selling of HRT," 2.

21. Cole and Rothblum, "Commentary," 510.

22. Ginsburg and Hardiman, "What Do We Know . . . ?" 41.

23. Diczfalusy, "Demographic Aspects," 8.

24. One study of "all the articles on this topic in the magazines most regularly read by US women" in 1985–88 found that "three-quarters were clearly pro-hormones: fully half . . . did not mention any risks with oestrogen use" (Nancy Pearson, cited in Worcester and Whatley, "The Selling of HRT," 7).

25. Norma Swenson's warning, cited in Lehman, "Cultural anthropologist says," 29.

26. In these interviews, "a surprisingly large number" of [Radcliffe College] alumnae mentioned vaginal dryness or sex problems they assumed were related to menopause, and some were angry at feminist discourse for not addressing this need (Cushman, "The Hormone Replacement Therapy Decision," 79).

27. See Gullette, "Brief Golden Summer."

28. "Vaginal lubrication . . . may take 10–30 seconds in the younger woman, it can take from 1 to 3 minutes in women over 60." The author of this article labels this statistic a case of diminution "to an obvious degree" (McCoy, "Menopause and Sexuality," 78). This is a painful example of a woman taking on the hostile male subject position I call "begrudging the time."

29. Leiblum, "Sexuality and the Midlife Woman," 498.

30. Exercise is the only remedy that can increase bone mass (Gannon, "The Potential Role of Exercise," 118). On calcitonin, see Lindsay and Cosman, "The Risk of Osteoporosis," 62. Although diet, exercise, and healthy lifestyles make sense at any age, for older women alone they are sometimes named "alternative therapies"—which suggests how medicalization and HR "Therapy" dominate discourse.

31. Sitruk-Ware and Utian, "Risks and Benefits," 287; Hunt and Vessey, "Use of Hormone Replacement Therapy," 151; Sitruk-Ware and Utian, "Risks and Benefits," 287.

If women taking estrogen have lower mortality rates than women not on estrogen, is this (in part? what part?) because women given estrogen are richer, more used to getting medical care, able to afford better care, and for these reasons healthier?

32. Gannon "Endocrinology of Menopause," 222.

33. Kaufert and McKinlay make this point ("Estrogen Replacement Therapy," 132).

34. Harris, "Are Women Using Postmenopausal Estrogens?" 1266. "McKinlay, McKinlay and Brambilla found that menopause status per se was less associated with physical complaints than was a prior health history marked by a tendency to utilize health services" (Cole and Rothblum "Community," 497). One feminist gynecologist I spoke to thought

that the automatic taking of birth-control pills had prepared the current midlife cohort to think of medication as the answer to all "reproductive problems."

35. Olesen, "Sociological Observations," 356.

36. Rickie Solinger, reviewing *The Selling of Contraception: The Dalkon Shield Case, Sexuality, and Women's Autonomy,* by Nicole J. Grant, says that Grant found that "these women had faith in the concept of 'choice,' believed in the 'value of information and education as insurance against injury,' and trusted in the rectitude of the experts, a set of attitudes that may have deepened their risk" ("A Cautionary Tale," 19).

37. Cushman, "The Hormone Replacement Therapy Decision," 92, 64–65.

38. J. McKinlay, "Some Contributions," 20.

39. Williams, *Marxism and Literature,* 130.

Chapter 7: My Mother at Midlife

My mother's main comment on this chapter, characteristically, is that I give her too much credit.

Although the chapter does not specifically discuss fathers and sons, a critic interested in developing the connections between patrophobia, middle-ageism against men, psychological development, and midlife fiction might find it useful.

1. I am grateful for E. Ann Kaplan's distinction between "psychical" and "social" mothers (*Motherhood,* 31–32; also 6–7). Benjamin, "Oedipal Riddle," 214. Benjamin's work since then—*The Bonds of Love* and *Like Subjects, Love Objects*—continues to emphasize the importance of recognizing one's mother as an independently existing person.

2. What Daly and Reddy call "daughter-centricity" means that "few fictional or theoretical works *begin* with the mother in her own right . . . and those that do seldom hold fast to a maternal perspective" (*Narrating Mothers,* 2, 3).

3. Benjamin, "Omnipotent Mother," 139.

4. On additional benefits that might come from expanding "maternal discourse," see Marianne Hirsch (*Mother/Daughter Plot,* 164–67).

5. Oldham describes a process of "intrapsychic structural change that centrally relate[s] to the involution and death of one's parents" that he calls "the third individuation" ("Third Individuation," 89).

6. In the 1970s, according to Schweitzer and Hirsch, "Feminism . . . suffered from so-called matrophobia" ("Mothers and Daughters," 584). Matrophobia (a term I don't like) still exists, arising from many cultural causes that are still inadequately theorized and historicized.

7. Many women of the relevant age internalized the mainstream culture's worry that by working, women would neglect mothering (Suleiman, *Risking,* chaps. 2 and 3); at the same time, our children were told by the media to consider themselves, retrospectively, "latch-key children."

8. Benjamin seems to feel that girls learn the same male (Oedipal) split between "infantilism" and "autonomy" ("Oedipal Riddle," 202). Boys are made to feel effeminized as well.

9. Chancer, *Sadomasochism,* 115, 114; Heller, *Something Happened,* 15.

10. Lebe is quoted in Abramson, *Mothermania,* 10, 105; 104.

11. Adrienne Rich, *Of Woman Born,* 236. According to Alkalay-Gut, *matrophobia* was

first used in a 1973 article about Doris Lessing by Lynn Sukenick ("Learning to Love Mother," 31).

In every feminist era, too, patriarchal backlash against midlife women who are attempting to improve their status can be inadvertently abetted by the discourses of the angry daughters. On these confusions and overlappings, see Gullette, "Inventing the 'Postmaternal' Woman."

12. Rabine, "No Lost Paradise," 155.

13. Rose Stone, "Night Song," 241.

Chapter 8: The New Gender Politics of Midlife Bodies

1. There is remarkably little ethnography of midlife male aging and a dearth of firsthand reports from men. Private conversations have informed all of this book, but especially part 3. The approach I begin with—using the reports of heterosexual women—arises precisely from the dearth of written materials. The gay midlife seems to me even less well recorded (but see Martin Duberman's *Midlife Queer*). It's possible that the impact of midlife aging is even greater on gay men. One of my friends who came out at forty said to me, "I aged ten years."

2. This has been shown in the lives of men by many writers, including Stephen Heath in *The Sexual Fix* (1982) and George Chauncey in *Gay New York* (1994).

3. Koren, "I'm in various stages of deterioration," 27.

4. The role of fiction and the relation of fiction to popular and mass images of midlife men would require separate discussions. Novels with midlife male protagonists assume readers who accept decline plots and decline tropes. John Updike, for example, could plausibly kill off the protagonist of his tetralogy—whom many men identify with—at age fifty-seven. Updike made Harry a Deteriorating Man beforehand: overweight, a compulsive nibbler. (He also made Harry's wife in her middle years newly fit and athletic.) On the difficulties Updike and Saul Bellow had writing an alternative genre, see my *Safe at Last*.

5. Sontag, "The Double Standard of Aging," 462–78. This now reads as a chilling account of the way things were before any breaks in male superiority could be imagined. Many relationships continue to reproduce that model, of course.

6. Sybylla, "Situating Menopause," 18. Birken, *Consuming Desire*, vii, 68, 89. Historians link twentieth-century changes in gender relations, the transition from a "productivist" to a "consumer" society, and new sexological discourses. My contribution is to focus on the middle years as a zone where such forces intersect with increasing intensity over this century, for men as well as women.

7. Connell, *Gender and Power*, 85, 83. Although Connell uses the passive voice, in the next chapter I describe the "activity" involved in accepting midlife aging and demasculinization.

8. Thompson, "Baby Boom's Mid-Life Crisis," 3; Ostroff, "Targeting the Prime-Life Consumer," 30.

9. In this binary, hairiness marks masculinity in later life. Bly insists that "what the psyche is asking for now is a new figure . . . a religious figure but a hairy one"—as opposed to "bald, ascetic" (*Iron John*, 249, 248).

10. In Rozin and Fallon's study, 59 percent of the fathers, 60 percent of the daughters,

and 67 percent of the mothers thought themselves overweight, and roughly the same percentages diet ("Body Image," 342–47); Gilmore, "The Beauty of the Beast," 211–12; see also 207–8; Heatherton, private communication; see also his "A Ten-Year Longitudinal Study."

11. As of 1986, men were getting 95 percent of the hair transplants, 44 percent of the ear "revisions", 27 percent of the dermabrasions, 25 percent of the nose reshapings, 10 percent of the face-lifts (Camp, *Plastic Surgery*," 224–25). See also Dull and West, "Accounting for Cosmetic Surgery," 55 and 54 n. 2).

12. Stocker, "The Male Makeover," 63.

13. Articles about men in the Academic Index for 1986–91 carried titles like "Want a Lift?" "More Males Having Aesthetic Surgery," "Now men too pumped to pump iron can turn up the volume with a set of pectoral implants." The articles about women, influenced by feminism, have titles about the dangers of silicone, the "Colonization of Women's Bodies," "Liposuction under Federal Review."

14. Reynolds, "Style," 90.

15. Dull and West, "Accounting for Plastic Surgery," 66, 65.

16. An ad in the *Guardian,* a British paper, for a brochure called *Your Prostate: What Every Man over 40 Needs to Know Now* suggests that the age of anxiety can be begun even younger.

17. Beck, "The New Middle Age," 54.

18. J. McKinlay, private communication.

19. Foreman, "Drawing the fine line on Retin A," 13, 15. The study linking balding and heart attacks was "financed by Upjohn Co., which makes minoxidil" (Hohler, "Medical News Taxes Patience," 1).

20. Stoltenberg, *Refusing to Be a Man,* 99.

21. Studies that appeared in 1992 estimate that bad economic times raise mortality rates from major diseases from 3 to 6 percent. Gosselin, "Studies: Recession Bad for Health, Too," 83. See also Catalano, "The Health Effects of Economic Insecurity."

22. Reynolds, "Style," 90. One of the landmark documents in the effort to sell women their midlife aging was Robert A. Wilson's *Feminine Forever* (1966), about the magic of estrogen-replacement "therapy." To its credit, at the time the medical profession reacted strongly against the hyperbolic promotion. It has since weakened.

23. Readers of "Femininity" may recall that it was actually "a man of about thirty" whom Freud stationed in the lucky developmental slot ("Femininity," 134–35).

24. Bly, *Iron John,* 93, 92.

25. Caroline Cross Chinlund, private communication.

26. "The decline in the male remarriage rate has typically been overlooked, because the rate is so much higher than that for women" (Goldscheider, "The Aging of the Gender Revolution," 542, 538). Goldscheider compares remarriage rates in 1970 and 1980.

27. My next book is titled *The Invention of Male Midlife Sexual Decline, 1900–1930;* for excerpts, see my "Male Midlife Sexuality," and "Midlife Discourse." A chapter in *Midlife Fictions* is called "Sex-Starved and Doomed to Disappointment; or, The Post-sexual Woman." Ehrenreich, *Hearts of Men,* 97, Chaps. 6, 7, 8.

28. Stephen Chinlund, private communication.

29. Quoted in Giele, "Adulthood as Transcendence," 166.

30. Ibid. 167.

Chapter 9: From the Master Narrative of the Life Course

I am grateful to Michael Brown for bringing to my attention in this context the work of Harold Garfinkel and Erving Goffman. I thank Ken Pobo; Mary Berg; Rick Shweder and Tom Shaw for inviting me to present this work at, respectively, the Northeast Modern Language Association, the Society of Institute Fellows (Bunting Institute of Radcliffe), and the Society for Psychological Anthropology.

1. Laslett, *Fresh Map of Life,* 84 (table 6.2). Statistics about life-expectancy changes in the twentieth century also incorrectly imply that the advances reflected changes at the end of life, whereas the big improvements occurred mainly between birth and five.

2. McGuane is quoted in Muro, "Tom McGuane Grows Up," 37.

3. Bechtel and Waggoner, "How Old Are You *Really?*" 127.

4. Postmodern theory has taken as one of its goals the uncovering of master narratives. As far as I know, this is the first recognition of a master narrative of aging.

5. Silverman, citing Althussser, *Male Subjectivity,* 23.

6. Critics argue, on behalf of narrative analysis like this, that its "strength lies in [its] applicability to a series of cases. They are directed to the comparative analysis of patterns" (Mishler, "Missing Persons," 28).

7. Exley, *Last Notes from Home,* 19; Lavers, "Yours Sincerely, Wasting Away," 4; Leonard, *Naked Martini,* first page.

8. Quoted in Annan, "When One Is A Somebody," 47.

9. Karp, "A Decade of Reminders," 727; emphasis in original.

10. Powers, *Galatea 2. 2,* 37.

11. McGrath, "Empty Nest Blues," 112.

12. West, "There Is No Conversation," 69, 70, 71.

13. Cynthia Rich, "Aging, Ageism and Feminist Avoidance," 55.

14. In using the word *postmaternal,* my friend was alluding to my essay "The Postmaternal Phenomenon" and to many conversations we have had about the subject.

15. Remington, "The Reconstruction," 248.

16. Garfinkel, *Studies in Ethnomethodology,* vii.

17. Ibid., 147, 146, 147, 121.

18. Ibid., 149.

19. Goffman, *Stigma,* 128.

20. Ibid., 134. The idea of accelerated development comes from Ted Schwartz, in conversation. This expert in early childhood suggested that researchers look into the "enhanced sense of discontinuity" he believes very young children are learning from their parents. Researchers might look too at the pressures on these twenty- and thirty-something parents.

21. Ricoeur, *Oneself as Another,* 132. I am adding to Ricoeur's binary literary/cultural thickness (by linking "impersonal description" to a dominant age narrative), and psychological/phenomenological duration (by inserting midlife aging into a developmental story).

22. Ibid., 132.

23. Suckow, *The Folks,* 236, 251. To make the "entrance" passages more akin to contemporary ones, I have left out two of Suckow's contextualizations. "If he, Carl, had actually failed as a husband and father! . . . He could no longer hold up Lillian's lacks when he felt

so deeply his own defects and inconsistencies" (251). "And yet he felt a kind of firmness—not wholly cynical—underlying the future" (250).

24. Lavers, "Yours Sincerely, Wasting Away," 12, 8.

25. Early, "Black Men and Middle Age," 26. This too was cited as notable in *Best Short Essays 1994.*

26. Early ends by recounting a meeting with Mohammed Ali, whose career ended because of injuries caused by boxing. Early calls this "not so much meet[ing] his middle age as crash[ing] into it with a suddenness, a recklessness, that pulled us all up short" (28). What happened to Ali had nothing to do with middle age. But "acceptance" comes to Early when he realizes, in the final sentence, that Ali is "another middle-aged black man" (29). He seems to be considering middle age—like death—a great equalizer.

27. Gordon, "Social Structural Effects on Emotions," 147.

28. Beattie, *Another You,* 296.

29. Bartky, *Femininity and Domination,* 77. The context is about learning gender identity.

30. Rosenwald, Conclusion: "Reflections on Narrative Self-Understanding," 270.

31. Gullette, *Safe at Last in the Middle Years,* chap. 7, for some preliminary account of why people do not feel justified in denying a decline narrative of aging—even when it doesn't suit their own life story.

32. Garfinkel, *Studies in Ethnomethodology,* 149.

33. Laws, "Tabloid Bodies," n.p.

Chapter 10: The Other End of the Fashion Cycle

The catalyst for this essay was David Gullette's and Daphne Kenyon's innovative course "The Construction of Economic Desire." I benefited from the readings of Michael Brown, Alix Kates Shulman, Penelope Sales Cordish, Sarah LeVine, and from discussions with Ellen Rosen.

1. My mother sees nothing marvelous about our arrangement. She believes parents who can afford to should continue to give gifts to their adult children.

2. George B. Sproles is given credit for identifying the fashion "life cycle" (McCracken, "Trickle-Down Theory, 43). Its phases span a product's existence "from invention to decline" (Simon-Miller, "Commentary," 71). Stuart Hall and Richard Johnson appropriated the metaphor for "the passage of cultural forms through the moments of production—circulation—consumption" (Nixon, "Looking for the Holy Grail," 466).

3. Veblen and Bartky do not write about age. Wolf has index entries on age and several examples of practices that can be reread as affecting women's age identity (*Beauty Myth,* 35, 83).

4. A *New York Times Magazine* fashion spread for Sunday, September 12, 1993, featured models over ninety, men as well as women.

5. Middle-ageism and modern patterns of consumption emerged simultaneously at the turn of the century. For "saturated" markets, "more efficient factory techniques," and the rise of advertising, see Wicke, *Advertising Fictions,* 104. On prior history, see Fred Davis, *Fashion:* "The fashion cycle [is] exclusively a product of Western civilization" (16 n. 8)." On the nineteenth-century origins of the "presumed connection of women and shopping," see Bowlby, "Modes of Modern Shopping." "Docile bodies," comes from Deveaux ("Femi-

nism and Empowerment"). Kidwell and Steele (*Men and Women*) assume that men are docile, but argue that they are satisfied.

6. Orwell, *Wigan Pier,* 88.

7. Bowlby, quoted in Williamson, "Storyville North," 228.

8. A distinction between speaking "to" and "for" comes from Schweickart, "In Defense of Femininity."

9. Her subsequent career was a distinguished one, but she still sometimes says that she could have had a very happy life as a buyer. And of course in a way she has. A buyer for a select clientele, of one sole family.

10. Beattie, *Another You,* 41.

11. In the Simmons' course on economic desire, students are asked to write on the topic "Where I Shop, What I Shop For, and What I Think About When I Shop." (Again we note the standard emphasis on point of purchase.) But many women write about disliking the fashion cycle and about alternative shopping practices. A number mention their reluctance to discard.

12. Many current ways of writing about consumption minimize the profit orientation of the market system. One, identifying itself as "postmodern," distracts attention from the profit orientation by emphasizing the "fun," "agentic," or "carnivalesque" elements of markets.

13. Spark, "That Lonely Shoe," 82.

14. Gilday, *The Famine Within.*

15. Hirschman, *Shifting Involvements,* 43.

16. Barnes, *Edna His Wife,* 233, 235.

17. Fitzgerald, *Tender Is the Night* (1934), bk. 3, chap. 7, the water-skiing scene.

18. Ehrenreich, *Fear,* 119.

19. Barthes, *Fashion System,* 289 and nn. 10 and 17.

20. See Oldham and Liebert's edited collection, *The Middle Years.*

21. Fein, *Role Change,* ix. Feminists more than others are conscious of this kind of resocialization. Sociologist Ellen Rosen (private communication) suggests that what Carol Gilligan discovered about eleven-year-old girls losing their self-confidence could be considered a study of resocialization in my sense.

22. Hunter, "After Representation," 193.

23. Morse, quoting Baudrillard ("Artemis Aging," 34).

24. Bartky, *Femininity and Domination,* 43.

Chapter 11: Doing Age Theory

This essay has benefited enormously from the appreciations and suggestions and reflections of Charles Altieri, Michael Brown, Penelope Sales Cordish, David Gullette, Nancy K. Miller, Alix Kates Shulman, Werner Sollers, Kathleen Woodward, the members of the Northeastern University Women's Studies Colloquium present on April 28, 1994, and the members of the Simmons Feminist Theory group present on November 30, 1995.

Epigraph: Martin Nicolaus, quoted in Stuart Hall, "Cultural Studies," 26. Both men refer to the subject in history.

1. On lack of age consciousness in (postmodern) theory, connected to the prevalence of the spatial, see Altieri, "Temporality"; on "bracket[ing] the diachronic," see Fraser, "Uses and Abuses," 55; on neglect of modernist "durée," see Jameson, "*Ulysses*," 146. Spatial meta-

phors can ignore, displace, or minimize the diachronic: not necessarily historical time but personal time—the life course and narrativity's constructions of the life course.

2. Woodward, "Late Theory, Late Style," 30.

3. Brown and Martin, "Left Futures," 63.

4. One model for this section was a paper by Peggy McIntosh on the omission of race in discourses that should have been conscious of it ("How White-Skin Privilege Commonly Frames U.S. Academic Writing").

Some age-studies work has also been published under the rubric "literary gerontology." See Nuessel's bibliography.

5. Both Frank Lentricchia and Nancy K. Miller accepted and were sent a draft; Miller wrote back at considerable length. That exchange has been valuable to me.

6. If you believe that my resistance to identity stripping is unjustified denial, is that judgment based on the meanings you attach to the age you imagine me to have?

7. Shields, "Spaces for the Subject," 2. Tomlinson, *Consumption,* 17. "Male menopause" is becoming used more frequently in the United States. Bruce Robbins on *The Jamesonian Unconscious* is quoted in Duke University Press's Literary and Cultural Studies catalog for 1995, 5.

8. Lentricchia, "In Place of an Afterword," 321.

9. Ibid., 322.

10. "La carogna" (a feminine noun) can also be used to mean "slut" or "old hag." "La vecchiaia è una carogna" is a female personification, almost an allegorical figure. Like "menopausal," above, this is another example of sexist ageism used by a man to diminish another man or men.

11. See Woodward, "Gerontophobia."

12. Frow, *Cultural Studies,* 109.

13. See also the section entitled "Socialization into Aging: Exposure," in Gullette, "Midlife Discourse."

14. "Optimal resistance" as a term and program comes from Jernryd, *Optimal Resistance.*

15. I learned the term *age hierarchies* from Dickerson-Putman and Brown, *Women's Age Hierarchies.* Age issues, of course, matter in all phases of the academic humanities, including laws about when faculty retire, rhetoric about tenure and "making room for the young," the age of students (traditional undergraduate or "continuing"), curricular choices based on their age-related needs (or what are taken to be such), the teaching of works as if they did not have age-related contents.

Miller's entire sentence: "These memoirs of the other suggest that the self of autobiography may well be neither simply autonomous and separate, as canonically (Gusdorfian) based theory has made 'him' out to be, nor terminally fragmented and dispersed, as fans of the postmodern have claimed" ("Facts, Pacts, Acts," 13).

16. Ibid., 12.

17. In a beautiful longer essay, "Autobiographical Deaths," Miller provides considerable evidence of the separation Beauvoir experienced between herself and her mother during the mother's last illness: she even quotes this sentence (41; see also 36, 47).

18. Woodward speaks of Beauvoir's miming activity as "an unconscious act of reparation in the Kleinian sense" from a daughter who had "resisted identification with her mother" and had always seen herself as a son ("Simone de Beauvoir," 102, 103).

19. Angelou "The Last Decision," 149; Roth, *Patrimony,* 237.

20. Copper has called "the age/death connection" "that virulent stereotype." "The assumption that death is a preoccupation, or subject of expertise, of midlife or old women is ageist." "Death has become a private buzzword for me, warning me of the shoals of ageism before me" ("Voices," 55). "Death" here, as in many other discursive situations, should be in quotation marks.

21. I was slow to see the need for the term *middle-ageism* partly because of loyalty to the elderly: why should I imply distance from them (which I myself would regret soon enough)?

22. Some theorists prefer "subjectivity" to "identity." Using "identity" of course makes possible the contrast with "identity-stripping."

23. Many other group identifications based, however crudely, on the body, could be added to this list: sexual orientation, physical handicap, ethnicity.

24. The sociology of knowledge distinguishes between private "identity" and "identity" that is socially ascribed. Werner Sollors' terms about ethnicity—descent and consent—are roughly analoguous (*Beyond Ethnicity*); see also Appiah, "Identity, Authenticity, Survival," 150–56.

25. Like Charles Taylor in *Multiculturalism,* I want to see some self-identifications as importantly based on "recognition" rather than primarily the result of imposition. For a review of the literature on the formation of an African-American age identity, see Mama, *Beyond the Masks,* 57–63.

26. According to Paul Ricoeur, "Narrativity [is] the language structure that has temporality as its ultimate referent" ("Narrative Time," 169).

27. For example, Molly Hite paraphrases Paula Caplan: "Academia in general emerges as a citadel of entrenched attitudes about women, especially older women or racialized women. Caplan's intelligent choice of adjective emphasizes the way 'race' as a marker of social otherness is bestowed by dominant ethnic groups on other ethnic groups" ("First the Bad News," 19). Although aware that people can be "racialized," both writers leave "older" unmarked, unbestowed—naturalized.

28. Kavanagh, "Ideology," 311.

29. "Decline" and "change," for reasons I cannot go into here, make another problematic binary. Thomas Cole observes a similar problem in gerontology between ageism and "activism" (*Journey,* 123).

30. The answer to mine: as of this writing, fifty-four.

Chapter 12: The Politics of Middle-Ageism

Venturing onto the terrain of economics and public policy, I owe particular thanks to Michael Brown, John McDermott, Richard Parker, and Ellen Rosen. For information on current union attitudes toward seniority, I am indebted to many people, including John Murphy of Teamsters Local 122, who is involved in his second multiyear battle over seniority issues.

1. Lewis, "Lotus defends layoff," 51; "Lotus loses age bias case," 47.

2. Rayman et al., "Resiliency amidst Inequality," 134.

3. Bumpass and Aquilino, "A Social Map of Midlife," table 55. A recent study in Britain found similar steep declines (Ginn and Arber, "Exploring Mid-Life Women's Employ-

ment," 73–91). They too say there has been little research on the factors influencing midlife women's employment participation.

4. Linda Stern, "How to Find a Job," 25.

5. Jacobson et al., "Long-Term Earnings Losses." After five years, the high seniority workers he followed had lost about 25% of their prior earnings. Barlett and Steele, *America: What Went Wrong?*" xi. Barnet, "Lords of the Global Economy," 755.

6. The Department of Labor's data by age omit education, which means differences between subgroups are obscured. "Black women" drop 8.1% from 45–50 to 50–55; "white women" 7%; "white men" 4.5%, "black men" 3.8% *Employment and Earnings,* 164–66).

7. Discrimination can be hard to prove to skeptics, as everyone following the debate about "affirmative action" knows. It will be interesting to see whether the reality of midlife discrimination is called into question, and by what groups or interests.

8. Robert Lewis, "Tests Find Age Bias in Hiring," p. 2.

9. Mishel and Bernstein, *The State of Working America,* 143, 141.

10. Sheak, "U.S. Capitalism," 36; see also Aronowitz and DiFazio, *Jobless Future.*

11. On the concept of an "age/earnings profile" see Mark F. Stern, "Poverty and the Life-Cycle," 529.

12. In Rayman ("Resilience amidst Inequality," 140), citing Deborah Figart. The earlier peak of the age-wave curve for people in the working and lower middle classes may be one reason why so many feel that "middle age" begins earlier than people in middle and upper strata say it does.

13. Lauck, "Seniority Rules of the National Agreement," 3.

14. Fehn, "'Chickens come Home,'" 328–29.

15. See Cornfield's study, "Ethnic Inequality," 131; see also 132.

16. Ehrenreich, *Fear of Falling,* 15. Aronowitz and DiFazio, *Jobless Future,* 38. Hamer-mesh, "A Ray of Sunshine?" 13 and n. 8. On why minorities and women should fight to retain tenure systems, see Kolodny, "Why Feminists Need Tenure."

17. David Gullette, in conversation.

18. Frow, *Cultural Studies,* 94. The trends are clear even if the exact figures are debatable.

19. Chast, "Coming Soon to an Office Near You," 58.

20. Lucy Stone, "Disappointment Is the Lot of Women," 106. Joseph M. Schwartz, "A New Solidarity," 7.

21. Newman, *Declining Fortunes,* 200.

22. For a short annotated bibliography, see Sheak, "U.S. Capitalism," 54.

23. Aronowitz, "Postmodernism and Politics," 57.

24. Almost all the participants had worked or were working out of the home. Some had college degrees from ten, twenty or more years before; one was getting a Ph.D. at Brandeis. Most were white. All would probably have said they were somewhere in the middle class.

I started the course, "Midlife Heroines," with only a few concepts briefly defined but underlined as crucial: the midlife age class, social/economic/political construction of aging, midlife as key to "aging," genres of aging (decline and progress), discursive characters ("postmaternal woman"), age ideology.

25. On the interpersonal renegotiations caused by watching demeaning films, see Gullette, "'The Piano': imperfect pitch."

26. For Silverman, the symbol of power is the phallus (*Male Subjectivity at the Margins,* 55).

27. Few studies have attempted to measure men's change or resistance to change. One is Thomas's "The Significance of Gender Politics."

28. Nomenclature has been a vexed question. Some suggested names: Pro-feminist Men's Studies, Critical Studies of Masculinity. In any case, as an antisexist movement it frequently distinguishes itself from the "men's movement" and the men's rights and fathers' rights movements.

Seidler, "Men, Feminism, and Power, 218. Carrigan et al., "Hard and Heavy," 186. Recent historical and theoretical work on age by Mike Featherstone, Mike Hepworth, and Stephen Katz is changing men's studies.

29. Perlstein, "Reality Bytes Cybergeek," 934.

30. My works in progress, *Midlife Fictions* and *The Invention of Male Midlife Sexual Decline,* will try to explain how this paradoxical situation came about.

31. In writing this section on activism I am mindful simultaneously of left warnings about cultural pessimism and Anthony Gidden's reminder about "the reluctance of most progressivist thinkers since the Enlightenment to think in utopian terms" ("The Emergence of Life Politics," 213).

Works Quoted

Abramson, Jane B. *Mothermania: A Psychological Study of Mother-Daughter Conflict.* Lexington Mass.: Lexington Books, 1987.

Agger, Ben. "Marxism, Feminism, Deconstruction." In Gailey, 427–50.

Alkalay-Gut, Karen. "Learning to Love Mother: Candace Flynt's *Mother Love.*" In *Mother Puzzles: Daughters and Mothers in Contemporary American Literature,* ed. Mickey Pearlman. New York: Greenwood Press, 1989: 23–34.

Alta. "Pretty." In *Images of Women in Literature,* ed. Mary Anne Ferguson. Boston: Houghton Mifflin, 1991: 227.

Alther, Lisa. *Other Women.* New York: Knopf, 1984.

Altieri, Charles. *Canons and Consequences: Reflections on the Ethical Force of Imaginative Ideals.* Evanston: Northwestern Univ. Press, 1990.

———— "Temporality and the Necessity of Dialectic: The Missing Dimension of Contemporary Theory." Paper delivered at the Humanities Center, University of California, Santa Barbara, fall 1990.

American Board of Family Practice Report II, conducted by DYG, Inc. *The Physicians' View of Middle Age.* Lexington, Ky.: The Board, 1990.

Amis, Martin. *The Information.* New York: Harmony Books, 1995.

Angelou, Maya. "The Last Decision." In *Trials, Tribulations, and Celebrations,* ed. Marian Gray Secundy and Lois LaCivita Nixon. Yarmouth, Maine: Intercultural Press, 1992: 149.

Angier, Natalie. "A Male Menopause? Jury is still out." *New York Times,* May 20, 1992: C14.

Annan, Gabrielle. "When One Is a Somebody." *New York Review of Books,* May 12, 1994: 46–47.

Appiah, K. Anthony. "Identity, Authenticity, Survival: Multicultural Societies and Social Reproduction." In Charles Taylor et al.: 149–63.

Ariès, Philippe. *Centuries of Childhood: A Social History of Family Life.* Tr. Robert Baldick. New York: Knopf, 1962.

Armstrong, Nancy. Book Reviews. *Signs* 18, no. 2 (1993): 433–38.

Aronowitz, Stanley. "Postmodernism and Politics." In *Universal Abandon? The Politics of Postmodernism,* ed. Andrew Ross. Minneapolis: Univ. of Minnesota Press, 1988: 46–62.

Aronowitz, Stanley, and William DiFazio. *The Jobless Future: Sci-Tech and the Dogma of Work.* Minneapolis: Univ. of Minnesota Press, 1994.

Associated Press. "Women aren't making Page 1 much, a survey finds." *Boston Globe,* June 1, 1996: 20.

Banner, Lois W. *In Full Flower: Aging Women, Power, and Sexuality: A History.* New York: Knopf, 1992.

Barbre, Joy Webster. "Meno-Boomers and Moral Guardians: An Exploration of the Cultural Construction of Menopause." In Callahan: 23–35.

Barker, Francis. *The Culture of Violence: Tragedy and History.* Chicago: Univ. of Chicago Press, 1993.

Barlett, Donald L., and James B. Steele. *America: What Went Wrong?* Kansas City: Andrews and McMeel, 1992.

Barlow, John. Translator's Introduction. *On Aging. Revolt and Resignation,* by Jean Amery. Bloomington: Indiana Univ. Press, 1994: x–xviii.

Barnes, Margaret Ayer. *Edna, His Wife: An American Idyll.* Boston, New York: Houghton Mifflin, 1935.

Barnet, Richard J. "Lords of the Global Economy." *The Nation,* Dec. 19, 1994: 754–57.

Barthes, Roland. *The Fashion System.* Tr. Matthew Ward and Richard Howard. New York: Hill and Wang, 1983.

Bartky, Sandra Lee. *Femininity and Domination: Studies in the Phenomenology of Oppression.* New York: Routledge, 1990.

Beattie, Ann. *Another You.* New York: Knopf, 1995.

Bechtel, Stefan, and Glenn Waggoner. "How Old Are You *Really?*" *Esquire,* May 1990: 127–36.

Beck, Melinda. "The New Middle Age." *Newsweek,* December 7, 1992: 54.

Benjamin, Jessica. "The Oedipal Riddle: Authority, Autonomy, and the New Narcissism." In *The Prob-*

lem of Authority in America, ed. John P. Diggins and Mark E. Kann. Philadelphia: Temple Univ. Press, 1981: 195–224.

———— "The Omnipotent Mother: A Psychoanalytic Study of Fantasy and Reality." In *Representations of Motherhood*, ed. Donna Bassin, Margaret Honey, and Meryle Mahrer Kaplan. New Haven: Yale Univ. Press, 1994: 129–45.

Berger, Peter L., and Thomas Luckmann, *The Social Construction of Reality: A Treatise in the Sociology of Knowledge*. Garden City, N.Y. Doubleday, 1966.

Billig, Michael, et al. *Ideological Dilemmas: A Social Psychology of Everyday Thinking*. London: Sage, 1988.

Birken, Lawrence. *Consuming Desire: Sexual Science and the Emergence of a Culture of Abundance, 1871–1914*. Ithaca: Cornell Univ. Press, 1988.

Bly, Robert. *Iron John: A Book about Men*. Reading, Mass.: Addison-Wesley, 1990.

Bordo, Susan. *Unbearable Weight: Feminism, Western Culture, and the Body*. Berkeley: Univ. of California Press, 1993.

Bowlby, Rachel. "Modes of modern shopping: Mallarmé at the *Bon Marché*." In *The Ideology of Conduct: Essays on Literature and the History of Sexuality*, ed. Nancy Armstong and Leonard Tennenhouse. New York and London: Methuen, 1987: 185–205.

Brantlinger, Patrick. *Crusoe's Footprints: Cultural Studies in Britain and America*. New York: Routledge, 1990.

Breines, Wini. *Young, White, and Miserable: Growing Up Female in the Fifties*. Boston: Beacon, 1992.

Brim, Gilbert. *Ambition: How We Manage Success and Failure throughout Our Lives*. New York: Basic Books, 1992.

Brody, Jane. "Personal Health." *New York Times*, May 20, 1992: C14.

Brody, Jean, and Gail Beswick Osborne. *The Twenty-Year Phenomenon: Men and Women Talk about the Breakup of Their Long-Term Marriages*. New York: Simon and Schuster, 1980.

Brown, Michael E., and Randy Martin. "Left Futures." *Socialism and Democracy* 9, no. 1 (1995): 59–90.

Buchmann, Marlis. *The Script of Life in Modern Society: Entry into Adulthood in a Changing World*. Chicago and London: Univ. of Chicago Press, 1989.

Bumpass, Larry L., and William S. Aquilino. *A Social Map of Midlife*. MacArthur Research Network on Successful Midlife Development, March 1994.

Callahan, Joan C., ed. *Menopause: A Midlife Passage*. Bloomington: Indiana Univ. Press, 1993.

Camp, John. *Plastic Surgery: The Kindest Cut*. New York: Henry Holt, 1989.

Cappasso, Tony. "For Him: What the Passing Of Fertility Means to Women." *Seasons* 2, no. 3 (1992): 17.

Carr, Glynis, ed. *"Turning the Century": Feminist Theory in the 1990s*. Lewisburg, Pa.: Bucknell Univ. Press, 1992.

Carrigan, Tim, Bob Connell, and John Lee. "Hard and Heavy: Toward a New Sociology of Masculinity." In *Beyond Patriarchy: Essays by Men on Pleasure, Power, and Change*, ed. Michael Kaufman. Toronto: Oxford Univ. Press, 1987: 139–92.

Catalano, Ralph. "The Health Effects of Economic Insecurity." *American Journal of Public Health* 81, no. 9 (1991): 1148–151.

Chancer, Lynn S. *Sadomasochism in Everyday Life: The Dynamics of Power and Powerlessness*. New Brunswick, N.J.: Rutgers Univ. Press, 1992.

Chast, R. "Coming Soon to an Office Near You . . . " *New Yorker*, April 11, 1994: 58.

———— "Middle Age: The Magazine for You—Yeah, You!" *New Yorker*, October 24, 1994: 103.

Cole, Ellen, and Esther Rothblum. "Commentary on 'Sexuality and the Midlife Woman.'" *Psychology of Women Quarterly* 14, no. 4 (1990): 509–12.

Cole, Thomas R. "The 'Enlightened' View of Aging: Victorian Morality in a New Key." In *What Does It Mean to Grow Old? Reflections from the Humanities*, ed. Cole and Sally Gadow. Durham: Duke Univ. Press, 1986: 117–30.

———— *The Journey of Life: A Cultural History of Aging in America*. Cambridge: Cambridge Univ. Press, 1991.

Comfort, Alex. *A Good Age*. New York: Crown, 1976.

Connell, R. W. *Gender and Power: Society, the Person and Sexual Politics*. Stanford: Stanford Univ. Press, 1987.

Copper, Baba. "Voices: On Becoming Old Women." In *Women and Aging: An Anthology by Women*, ed. Jo Alexander et al. Corvallis, Ore.: Calyx Books, 1986: 47–57.

Cornfield, Daniel B. "Ethnic Inequality in Layoff Chances: The Impact of Unionisation in Layoff Procedure." In *Redundancy, Layoffs and Plant Closures: Their Character, Causes and Consequences,* ed. Raymond Lee. London: Croom Helm, 1987: 116–40.

Cose, Ellis. *The Rage of a Privileged Class.* New York: HarperCollins, 1993.

Cushman, Phoebe. "The Hormone Replacement Therapy Decision: Women at the Crossroads of Women's Health." B.A. thesis, Harvard University, 1994 [1995].

Daly, Brenda, and Maureen T. Reddy, eds. *Narrating Mothers: Theorizing Maternal Subjectivities.* Knoxville: Univ. of Tennessee Press, 1991.

Davis, Fred. *Fashion, Culture, and Identity.* Chicago: Univ. of Chicago Press, 1992.

———. *Yearning for Yesterday: The Sociology of Nostalgia.* New York: Free Press, 1979.

Davis, Kathy. "Remarking the She-Devil: A Critical Look at Feminist Approaches to Beauty." *Hypatia* 6, no. 2 (1991): 21–43.

———. *Reshaping the Female Body: The Dilemma of Cosmetic Surgery.* New York and London: Routledge, 1995.

Deveaux, Monique. "Feminism and Empowerment: A Cultural Reading of Foucault." *Feminist Studies* 20, no. 2 (1994): 223–48.

Dickerson-Putman, Jeanette, and Judith K. Brown, eds. *Women's Age Hierarchies: Journal of Cross-Cultural Gerontology* 9, no. 2 (1994).

Diczfalusy, Egon. "Demographic Aspects: The Menopause in the Next Century." In Sitruk-Ware and Utian: 1–14.

Douglas, Susan J. *Where the Girls Are: Growing Up Female with the Mass Media.* New York: Times Press, 1994.

Drabble, Margaret. *The Middle Ground.* New York: Knopf, 1980.

———. *A Natural Curiosity.* New York: Viking, 1989.

———. *The Radiant Way.* New York: Ivy, 1987.

———. *The Realms of Gold.* New York: Knopf, 1975.

Dull, Diana, and Candace West. "Accounting for Cosmetic Surgery: The Accomplishment of Gender." *Social Problems* 38, no. 1 (1991): 54–70.

Eagen, Andrea Boroff. "Reconsidering Hormone Replacement Therapy." *Network News* 14, no. 3 (1989): 3–5.

Eagleton, Terry. *Ideology: An Introduction.* London: Verso, 1991.

Early, Gerald. "Black Men and Middle Age." *Hungry Mind Review,* spring 1993: 26–29.

Earnest, William R. "Ideology Criticism and Life-History Research." In Rosenwald and Ochberg: 250–64.

Ebert, Teresa L. "Gender and the Everyday: Toward a Postmodern Materialist Feminist Theory of Mimesis." In Carr: 90–122.

Edwards, Richard. *Contested Terrain: The Transformation of the Workplace in the Twentieth Century.* New York: Basic Books, 1979.

Ehrenreich, Barbara. *Fear of Falling: The Inner Life of the Middle Class.* New York: Harper Perennial, 1990.

———. *The Hearts of Men: American Dreams and the Flight from Commitment.* New York: Anchor, 1983.

Epstein, Joseph. *With My Trousers Rolled.* New York: Norton, 1995.

Exley, Frederick. *Last Notes from Home.* New York: Random House, 1988.

Feagin, Joe R., and Melvin P. Sikes. *Living with Racism.* Boston: Beacon Press, 1994.

Featherstone, Mike, and Mike Hepworth. "Images of Positive Aging." In *Images of Aging: Cultural Representations of Later Life,* ed. Featherstone and Andrew Wernick. London and New York, Routledge, 1995: 29–47.

Fehn, Bruce. "'Chickens Come Home to Roost': Industrial Reorganization, Seniority, and Gender Conflict in the United Packinghouse Workers of America, 1956–1966." *Labor History* 34, no. 2–3 (1993): 324–41.

Fein, Melvyn. *Role Change: A Resocialization Perspective.* New York: Praeger, 1990.

Fitzgerald, F. Scott. *Tender Is the Night.* New York: Scribners, 1933.

Ford, Richard. *Independence Day.* New York: Knopf, 1995.

Foreman, Judy. "Drawing the fine line on Retin A." *Boston Globe,* November 23, 1992: 13.

Formanek, Ruth. "Continuity and Change and 'The Change of Life': Premodern Views of the Menopause." In Formanek: 3–41.

Formanek, Ruth, ed. *The Meanings of Menopause: Historical, Medical, and Clinical Perspectives.* Hillsdale, N.J.: Analytic Press, 1990.

Fraser, Nancy. "The Uses and Abuses of French Discourse Theories for Feminist Politics." In *Cultural Theory and Cultural Change*, ed. Mike Featherstone. London: Sage, 1992: 51–71.

Freud, Sigmund. "Femininity." *Standard Edition of the Complete Psychological Works*, 22, ed. and tr. John Strachey. London: Hogarth; New York, Norton: 112–35.

Friedan, Betty. *The Fountain of Age*. New York: Simon and Schuster, 1993.

Frow, John. *Cultural Studies and Cultural Value*. Oxford: Oxford Univ. Press, 1995.

Gagnier, Regenia. "The Literary Standard, Working-Class Autobiography, and Gender." In *Revealing Lives: Autobiography, Biography, and Gender*, ed. Susan Groag Bell and Marilyn Yalom. Albany: SUNY Press, 1990: 93–114.

Gailey, Christine Ward, ed. *Dialectical Anthropology: Essays in Honor of Stanley Diamond*. vol. 2, *The Politics of Culture and Creativity: A Critique of Civilization*. Gainesville: Univ. of Florida Press, 1992.

Gallagher, Winifred. "Myths of Middle Age." *Atlantic*. May 1993: 51–65.

Gane, Mike, ed. *Ideological Representation and Power in Social Relations: Literary and Social Theory*. London and New York: Routledge, 1993.

Gannon, Linda. "The Endocrinology of Menopause." In Formanek: 179–238.

———. "The Potential Role of Exercise in the Alleviation of Menstrual Disorders and Menopausal Symptoms: A Theoretical Synthesis of Recent Research." *Women and Health* 14, no. 2 (1988): 105–28.

Gardiner, Judith Kegan. "Self-Psychology as Feminist Theory." *Signs* 12 (Summer 1987): 761–80.

Garfinkel, Harold. *Studies in Ethnomethodology*. Englewood Cliffs, N.J.: Prentice-Hall, 1967.

Giddens, Anthony. *Modernity and Self-Identity: Self and Society in the Late Modern Age*. Stanford: Stanford Univ. Press, 1991.

Giele, Janet Zollinger. "Adulthood as Transcendence of Age and Sex." In *Themes of Work and Love in Adulthood*, ed. Neil J. Smelser and Erik H. Erikson. Cambridge: Harvard Univ. Press, 1980: 151–73.

———. "Feminism, Conservatism, and 'Deceptive Distinctions' in Gender and Race." Paper delivered at the American Sociological Association, 1988.

Gilday, Katherine. *The Famine Within* (video). Kendor Productions and the National Film Board [Canada], 1990.

Gilmore, David B. "The Beauty of the Beast." In *The Good Body*, ed. Mary G. Winkler and Letha B. Cole. New Haven: Yale Univ. Press, 1994: 191–214.

Ginn, Jay, and Sara Arber. "Exploring Mid-Life Women's Employment." *Sociology* 29, no. 1 (1995): 73–91.

Ginsburg, Jean, and Paul Hardiman. "What Do We Know about the Pathogenesis of the Menopausal Hot Flush?" In Sitruk-Ware and Utian: 15–46.

Goffman, Erving. *Stigma: Notes on the Management of Spoiled Identity*. Englewood Cliffs, N.J.: Prentice-Hall, 1963.

Goldscheider, Frances. "The Aging of the Gender Revolution: What Do We Know and What Do We Need to Know?" *Research on Aging* 12, no. 4 (1990): 531–45.

Goodman, Ellen. "Just keep thinking, with hope, about tomorrow." *Boston Globe*, September 9, 1993: 21.

Gordimer, Nadine. *None to Accompany Me*. New York: Farrar, Straus and Giroux, 1994.

Gordon, Steven L. "Social Structural Effects on Emotions." In *Research Agendas in the Sociology of Emotions*, ed. Theodore Kemper. Albany: State Univ. of New York Press, 1990: 145–79.

Gosselin, Peter. "Studies: Recession bad for health, too." *Boston Globe*, October 16, 1992: 83.

Gross, Jane. "Aging Baby Boomers Take Fresh Look at a Milestone." *New York Times*, May 17, 1992: 1.

Grossberg, Lawrence, Cary Nelson, and Paula Treichler, eds. *Cultural Studies*. New York and London: Routledge, 1992.

Gullette, Margaret Morganroth. "Age (Aging)." In *Encyclopedia of Feminist Literary Theory* ed. Elizabeth Kowaleski-Wallace. New York: Garland, 1996.

——— "A Good Girl." *North American Review* 275, no. 3 (1990): 51–60.

———. "All Together Now: The New Sexual Politics of Midlife Bodies." *Michigan Quarterly Review*; rpt. *The Male Body*, ed. Laurence Goldstein. Ann Arbor: Univ. of Michigan Press, 1995: 221–47.

———. "Autumnal Face." *Lear's* 2, no. 10 (1990): 135.

———. "The Brief Golden Summer of the Woman of Forty, 1904–1918." In *Midlife Fictions: The Invention of the Middle Years of Life, 1900–1935*, in progress.

———. "Cultural Combat." *Women's Review of Books* 13, no. 12 (1996): 1.

———. "Eliza Farnham: Brief Life of a Visionary Woman." *Harvard Magazine,* November-December, 1991: 44.

———. "The Exile of Adulthood: Pedophilia and the Decline Novel." *Novel* 17, no. 3 (1984): 215–32.

———. "Face Lift Con." *Lear's* 3, no. 1 (1991): 91.

———. "Inventing the 'Postmaternal' Woman: Idle, Unwanted and Out of a Job." *Feminist Studies* 21, no. 2 (1995): 221–53.

———. "Letting a Son Become His Own Man." *Lear's* 3, no. 12 (1991): 36.

———. "Male Midlife Sexuality in a Gerontocratic Economy: The Privileged Stage of the Long Midlife in Nineteenth-Century Age Ideology." *Journal of the History of Sexuality* 5, no. 1 (1994): 58–89.

———. "Menopause as Magic Marker: Discursive Consolidation/Strategies for Cultural Combat." *Discourse* 17, no. 1 (1994): 93–122.

———. "Midlife Discourse in Twentieth-Century North America: An Essay on the Sexuality, Ideology and Politics of 'Midlife Aging.'" In Shweder.

———. "Midlife Exhilaration," *New York Times Magazine,* Jan 29, 1989: 18.

———. "My Mother at Midlife," *Ms.* forthcoming, 1997.

———. "One Necessary Future." *Re-Visioning Feminism.* New York: Feminist Press, 1995: 34.

———. "Ordinary Pain." *North American Review* 278, no. 3 (1993): 41–45.

———. " 'The Piano': imperfect pitch." *Boston Globe,* December 3, 1993: 51.

———. "Perilous Parenting: The Deaths of Children and the Construction of Aging in the Contemporary American Novel." *Michigan Quarterly Review* 31, no. 1 (1991–92): 56–72.

———. "The Postmaternal Phenomenon." In progress.

———. *Safe at Last in the Middle Years: The Invention of the Midlife Progress Novel.* Berkeley: Univ. of California Press, 1988.

———. "What, Menopause *Again?* A Guide to Cultural Combat." *Ms.,* Summer 1993: 34–38.

———. "The Wonderful Woman on the Pavement: Middle-Ageism in the Postmodern Economy." *Dissent,* fall 1995: 508–14.

Hall, Donald. "My Son My Executioner." *Old and New Poems.* New York: Ticknor and Fields, 1990: 19.

Hall, Stuart. "Cultural Studies and the Centre: Some Problematics and Problems." In *Culture, Media, Language,* ed. Hall, Dorothy Hobson, Andrew Lowe, and Paul Willis. London: Hutchinson, 1980: 15–47.

Hamermesh, Daniel S. "A Ray of Sunshine? The Annual Report on the Economic Status of the Profession, 1994–95." *Academe,* March-April 1995: 8–15.

Harris, Robin B., et al. "Are Women Using Postmenopausal Estrogens? A Community Survey." *American Journal of Public Health* 80, no. 10 (1990): 1265–68.

Hazleton, Lesley. "Power Politics." *Women's Review of Books* 11 no. 5 (1994): 1.

Hearn, Jeff, and David Morgan, eds. *Men, Masculinities and Social Theory.* London and Boston: Unwin Hyman, 1990.

Heatherton, Todd F., et al. "A Ten-Year Longitudinal Study of Body Weight, Dieting, and Eating Disorder Symptoms." In manuscript.

Heller, Joseph. *Something Happened.* New York: Ballantine Books, 1974.

Hirsch, Marianne. *The Mother/Daughter Plot: Narrative, Psychoanalysis, Feminism.* Bloomington: Indiana Univ. Press, 1989.

Hirschman, Albert O. *Shifting Involvements: Private Interest and Public Action.* Princeton: Princeton Univ. Press, 1982.

Hite, Molly. "First the Bad News." *Women's Review of Books* 11 no. 8 (1994): 19.

Hohler, Bob. "Medical News Taxes Patience of Many Doctors." *Boston Globe,* February 28, 1993: 1.

Hunt, Kate, and Martin Vessey. "Use of Hormone Replacement Therapy and Breast Cancer Risk." In Sitruk-Ware and Utian: 143–60.

Hunter, Ian. "After Representation: Recent Discussions of the Relation between Language and Literature." In Gane: 167–97.

Hunter, Ski, and Martin Sundel. *Midlife Myths: Issues, Findings and Practice Implications.* Newbury Park, Calif.: Sage, 1989.

Irving, John. *The World According to Garp.* New York: Pocket Books, 1978.

Jacobson, Louis S., Robert J. LaLonde, and Daniel G. Sullivan. "Long-Term Earnings Losses of High-Seniority Displaced Workers." *Economic Perspectives* 17, no. 6 (1993): 2–20.

Jameson, Fredric. "Notes on Period Theory." Paper delivered at Harvard's Center for Literary and Cultural Studies, November 1987.

———. "*Ulysses* in History." In *James Joyce: A Collection of Critical Essays,* ed. Mary T. Reynolds. Englewood Cliffs, N.J.: Prentice Hall, 1993: 145–58.

Jernryd, Elisabeth. *Optional Resistance to Authority and Propaganda: Measuring Instruments, Age Developments and Educational Influences.* Malmö: School of Education, 1973.

Kaplan, E. Ann. *Motherhood and Representation: The Mother in Popular Culture and Melodrama.* London and New York: Routledge, 1992.

Karp, David. "A Decade of Reminders: Changing Age Consciousness between Fifty and Sixty Years Old." *The Gerontologist* 28, no. 6 (1988): 727–38.

Kaufert, Patricia A., and Sonja M. McKinlay. "Estrogen Replacement Therapy: The Production of Medical Knowledge and the Emergence of Policy." *Women's Health and Healing: Toward a New Perspective,* ed. Ellen Lewin and Virginia Olesen. New York: Tavistock, 1985: 113–38.

Kavanagh, James H. "Ideology." In Lentricchia and McLaughlin: 306–20.

Kidwell, Claudia Brush, and Valerie Steele, eds. *Men and Women: Dressing the Part.* Washington, D.C.: Smithsonian Institution Press, 1989.

Kingsolver, Barbara. *Pigs in Heaven.* New York: Harper Perennial, 1993.

Knox, Richard. "They're starting to take women's heart disease seriously." *Boston Globe,* November 21, 1994: 25.

Kolodny, Annette. "Why Feminists Need Tenure: Combating the Right's Agenda." *Women's Review of Books* 13, no. 5 (1996): 23–24.

Koren, Ed. "I'm in various stages of deterioration." *New Yorker,* January 28, 1985: 27.

Kovel, Joel. *The Radical Spirit: Essays on Psychoanalysis and Society.* London: Free Association Books, 1988.

Laslett, Peter. *A Fresh Map of Life: The Emergence of the Third Age.* Cambridge: Harvard Univ. Press, 1991.

Lauck, William Jett. "Seniority Rules of the National Agreement." Chicago: Bureau of Research, Railway Employees Department, American Federation of Labor, [1921].

Lavers, Norman. "Yours Sincerely, Wasting Away." *North American Review* 277, no. 1 (1992): 4–15.

Laws, Glenda. "Tabloid Bodies: Aging, Beauty, and Health in Popular Discourse." Lecture given at the conference on "Women and Aging: Bodies, Cultures, Generations," held at the Center for Twentieth Century Studies, Univ. of Wisconsin-Milwaukee, April 18–20, 1996.

Lehman, Betsy. "Cultural anthropologist says menopause can be seen as 2nd adulthood." *Boston Globe,* April 29, 1993: 29.

Leiblum, S. R. "Sexuality and the Midlife Woman." *Psychology of Women Quarterly* 14, no. 4 (1990): 495–508.

Lentricchia, Frank. "In Place of an Afterword—Someone Reading." In Lentricchia and McLaughlin: 321–38.

Lentricchia, Frank, and Thomas McLaughlin, eds. *Critical Terms for Literary Study.* Chicago: Univ. of Chicago Press, 1990.

Leonard, John. *Naked Martini.* New York: Delacorte Press, 1964.

Lessing, Doris. *The Diary of a Good Neighbor* and *If the Old Could.* In *The Diaries of Jane Somers.* New York: Vintage, 1984.

Lewis, Diane E. "Lotus defends layoffs in age bias lawsuit." *Boston Globe,* November 10, 1994: 51.

———. "Lotus loses age bias case," *Boston Globe,* December 1, 1994: 47.

Lewis, Robert. "Tests Find Age Bias in Hiring," *AARP Bulletin,* February 1994: 1.

Lindsay, Robert, and Felicia Cosman. "The Risk of Osteoporosis in Aging Women." In Sitruk-Ware and Utian: 47–72.

Lock, Margaret. "Cultivating the Body: Anthropology and Epistemologies of Bodily Practice and Knowledge." *Annual Review of Anthropology* 22 (1993): 133–55.

———. "Menopause in Cultural Context." *Experimental Gerontology* 29, no. 3–4 (1994).

Lodge, David. *Therapy.* New York: Viking, 1995.

Lurie, Alison. *Foreign Affairs.* New York: Random House, 1984.

Luther, Marylou. "Questions of Style." *Hemispheres,* March 1996, 113.

Macdonald, Barbara, with Cynthia Rich. *Look Me in the Eye: Old Women, Aging and Ageism.* San Francisco: Spinsters Ink, 1983.

MacPherson, Kathleen I. "Menopause as Disease: The Social Construction of a Metaphor." *Advances in Nursing Science* 3, no. 2. (1981): 95–113.

Malamud, Bernard. *Dubin's Lives.* New York: Avon, 1980.

Mama, Amina. *Beyond the Masks: Race, Gender and Subjectivity.* London: Routledge, 1995.

Marshall, Paule. _Praisesong for the Widow._ New York: Dutton, 1983.

McCoy, Norma. "The Menopause and Sexuality." In Sitruk-Ware and Utian: 73–100.

McCracken, Grant D. "The Trickle-Down Theory Rehabilitated." In Solomon: 39–53.

McCrea, Frances B. "The Politics of Menopause: The 'Discovery' of a Deficiency Disease." In _The Sociology of Health and Illness: Critical Perspectives,_ ed. Peter Conrad and Rochelle Kern. New York: St. Martin's, 1986: 296–307.

McGrath, Charles. "Empty Nest Blues." _New Yorker,_ September 18, 1995: 112.

McIntosh, Peggy. "How White-Skin Privilege Commonly Frames U.S. Academic Writing: Examples to Consider from Five Disciplines." Wellesley Center Luncheon Seminar, September 18, 1989.

McKinlay, John B. "Some Contributions from the Social System to Gender Inequalities in Heart Disease." _Journal of Health and Social Behavior_ 37 (March 1996): 1–26.

McLeish, John A. B. _The Ulyssean Adult: Creativity in the Middle and Later Years._ Toronto: McGraw-Hill Ryerson, 1976.

McMurtry, Larry. _Texasville._ New York: Simon and Schuster, 1987.

Medical Post. "Cardiology Update: Job strain seen as a risk factor for hypertension." February 7, 1995.

Miller, Nancy K. "Autobiographical Deaths." _Massachusetts Review_ 33 (1992): 19–47.

———. "Facts, Pacts, Acts." _Profession 92:_ 10–14.

———. _Getting Personal: Feminist Occasions and Other Autobiographical Acts._ New York and London: Routledge, 1991.

Mishel, Lawrence, and Jared Bernstein. _The State of Working America, 1992–1993._ Armonk, N.Y.: M. E. Sharpe, 1993.

Mishler, Elliot G. "Missing Persons: Recovering Developmental Stories/Histories." In _Ethnography and Human Development: Context and Meaning in Social Inquiry,_ ed. Richard Jessor, Anne Colby, and Richard Shweder. Chicago: Univ. of Chicago Press, forthcoming: 73–100.

Moore, Lorrie. "Beautiful Grade." _New Yorker,_ December 25, 1995 / January 1, 1996: 116–31.

Morrison, Toni. _Beloved._ New York: Penguin Plume, 1987.

Morse, Margaret. "Artemis Aging: Exercise and the Female Body on Video." _Discourse_ 10, no. 1. (1987–88): 20–54.

Muro, Mark. "Tom McGuane Grows Up." _Boston Globe,_ October 19, 1992: 34.

Narr, Wolf-Dieter. "Toward a Prophetic Radicalism: Notes on a Necessary Theory of Domination." In Gailey: 451–86.

Newman, Katherine S. _Declining Fortunes: The Withering of the American Dream._ New York: Basic, 1993.

———. "Place and Race: Mid-Life Experience in Harlem." In Shweder.

Nixon, Sean. "Have You Got the Look? Masculinities and Shopping Spectacle." In Shields: 149–69.

———. "Looking for the Holy Grail: Publishing and Advertising Strategies and Contemporary Men's Magazines." _Cultural Studies_ 7, no. 3. (1993): 466–92.

Nolan, Martin, "Gays in San Francisco." _Boston Globe,_ December 21, 1995: 1.

Nuessel, Frank H. _The Image of Older Adults in the Media: An Annotated Bibliography._ Westport, Conn.: Greenwood Press, 1992.

Oldham, John. "The Third Individuation: Middle-Aged Children and Their Parents." In _The Middle Years: New Psychoanalytic Perspectives,_ ed. Oldham and Robert S. Liebert. New Haven: Yale, 1989: 89–104.

Olesen, Virginia. "Sociological Observations on Ethical Issues Implicated in Estrogen Replacement Therapy at Menopause." In Voda: 346–62.

Orwell, George. _Road to Wigan Pier._ 1937. Rpt. New York: Harcourt, Brace Jovanovich, 1958.

———. "Such, Such Were the Joys." _Orwell Reader._ New York: Harcourt, Brace Jovanovich 1961: 419–56.

Ostroff, Jeff. "Targeting the Prime-Life Consumer." _American Demographics_ 13, no. 1 (1991): 30.

Palmer, Paulina. _Contemporary Women's Fiction: Narrative Practice and Feminist Theory._ New York: Harvester Wheatsheaf, 1989.

Pearlman, Sarah F. "Late Mid-Life Astonishment: Disruptions to Identity and Self-Esteem." In _Faces of Women and Aging,_ ed. Nancy D. Davis, Ellen Cole, and Esther D. Rothblum. New York: Haworth Press, 1993.

Pearlstein, Rick. "Reality Bytes Cybergeek." _The Nation,_ June 26, 1995: 934–35.

Perry, Ruth. "Grace Paley." In _Women Writers Talking,_ ed. Janet Todd. New York: Holmes and Meier, 1983.

Pfeil, Fred. _Another Tale to Tell: Politics and Narrative in Postmodern Culture._ London and New York: Verso, 1990.

Phillips, Ariel Ingrid Aino. *Inner Voices, Inner Selves: A Study of Internal Conversation in Narrative.* Ph.D. diss., Harvard University, 1989.

Phillips, Kevin. *The Politics of Rich and Poor.* New York: Harper Perennial, 1991.

Phillips, Suzanne B. "Reflections of Self and Other: Men's Views of Menopausal Women." In Formanek: 281–95.

Pollitt, Katha. "Hot Flash." *The Nation,* June 15, 1992: 808–9.

Poovey, Mary. "Figures of Arithmetic, Figures of Speech: The Discourse of Statistics in the 1830s." *Critical Inquiry* 19, no. 2. (1993): 256–76.

Powers, Richard. *Galatea 2.2: A Novel.* New York: Farrar, Straus and Giroux, 1995.

Rabine, Leslie. "No Lost Paradise: Social Gender and Symbolic Gender in the Writings of Maxine Hong Kingston." In *Revising the Word and the World,* ed. VèVè A. Clark, Ruth-Ellen B. Joeres, and Madelon Sprengnether. Chicago: Univ. of Chicago Press, 1993: 143–64.

Rayman, Paula, Kimberly Allshouse, Jessie Allen. "Resiliency amidst Inequality: Older Women Workers in an Aging United States." In *Women on the Front Lines: Meeting the Challenge of an Aging America,* ed. Allen and Alan Pifer. Washington, D.C.: Urban Institute Press, 1993: 133–66.

Reddy, Maureen, Martha Roth, and Amy Sheldon, eds. *Feminists Write about Mothering.* Minneapolis: Spinsters Ink, 1994.

Remington, Judy. "The Reconstruction." In Reddy, Roth, and Sheldon: 245–53.

Remy, John. "Patriarchy and Fratriarchy as Forms of Androcracy." In Hearn and Morgan: 43–54.

Reynolds, Pamela. "Style: It's a Guy Thing." *Boston Globe,* June 14, 1995: 85.

Rich, Adrienne. *Of Woman Born: Motherhood as Experience and Institution.* New York: Norton, 1976.

Rich, Cynthia. "Aging, Ageism and Feminist Avoidance." In Macdonald with Rich.

Ricoeur, Paul. "Narrative Time." *Critical Inquiry* 7, no. 1 (1980): 169–90.

————. *Oneself as Another.* Tr. Kathleen Blamey. Chicago and London: Univ. of Chicago Press, 1994.

Robbins, Bruce. Advertising Copy for *The Jamesonian Unconscious.* Durham: Duke Univ. Press Literary and Cultural Studies Catalogue, 1995: 5.

Rosenwald, George C. Conclusion: "Reflections on Narrative Self-Understanding." In Rosenwald and Ochberg: 265–89.

Rosenwald, George C., and Richard L. Ochberg, eds. *Storied Lives: The Cultural Politics of Self-Understanding.* New Haven: Yale Univ. Press, 1992.

Roth, Philip. *Patrimony: A True Story.* New York: Simon and Schuster, 1991.

Rozin, Paul, and April Fallon. "Body Image, Attitudes to Weight, and Misperceptions of Figure Preferences of the Opposite Sex: A Comparison of Men and Women in Two Generations." *Journal of Abnormal Psychology* 97, no. 3. (1988): 342–45.

Russo, Richard. *Nobody's Fool.* New York: Vintage, 1994.

Ryan, Michael, and Douglas Kellner. *Camera Politica: The Politics and Ideology of Contemporary Hollywood Film.* Bloomington: Indiana Univ. Press, 1988.

Saltus, Richard. "Medical Notebook." *Boston Globe,* December 3, 1992: 3.

Sarton, May. *The Education of Harriet Hatfield.* New York: Norton, 1989.

Schnall, Peter L., ed. *The Job Stress Network.* www.serve.net/cse

Schnall, Peter L., Paul A. Landbergis, and Dean Baker. "Job Strain and Cardiovascular Disease." *Annual Review of Public Health* 15 (1994): 381–411.

Schwartz, Joseph M. "A New Solidarity: Strategies for the Gingrich Era." *Democratic Left* 23, no. 2 (1995): 3–8.

Schweickart, Patrocinio. "In Defense of Femininity: Commentary on Sandra Bartky's *Femininity.*" *Hypatia* 8 (1993): 178–91.

Schweitzer, Ivy, and Marianne Hirsch. "Mothers and Daughters." *Oxford Companion to Women's Writing in the United States.* New York: Oxford Univ. Press, 1995: 584.

Seidler, Victor. "Men, Feminism, and Power." In Hearn and Morgan, 215–28.

Sheak, Robert J. "U.S. Capitalism, 1972–1992: The Jobs Problem." *Critical Sociology* 21, no. 1. (1995): 33–57.

Sheehy, Gail. *New Passages: Mapping Your Life across Time.* New York: Random House, 1995.

Sherman, Edmund. *Meaning in Mid-life Transitions.* Albany: State Univ. of New York Press, 1987.

Shields, Rob. "Spaces for the Subject of Consumption." In Shields: 1–20.

Shields, Rob, ed. *Lifestyle Shopping: The Subject of Consumption.* London and New York: Routledge, 1992.

Shulman, Alix Kates. *Drinking the Rain.* New York: Farrar, Straus and Giroux, 1995.

Shweder, Richard, ed. *Middle Age and Other Cultural Fictions.* Chicago Univ. Press, forthcoming 1997.

Silverman, Kaja. *Male Subjectivity at the Margins.* New York and London: Routledge, 1992.

Simon-Miller, Françoise. "Commentary: Signs and Cycles in the Fashion System." In Solomon: 71–81.

Sitruk-Ware, Regine, and Wulf H. Utian. "Risks and Benefits of Hormone Replacement Therapy." In Sitruk-Ware and Utian: 283–87.

Sitruk-Ware, Regine, and Wulf H. Utian, eds. *The Menopause and Hormone Replacement Therapy: Facts and Controversies.* New York: Marcel Dekker, 1991.

Solinger, Rickie. "A Cautionary Tale." *Women's Review of Books* 10, no. 4 (1993): 19.

Sollors, Werner. *Beyond Ethnicity: Consent and Descent in American Culture.* New York: Oxford, 1986.

Solomon, Michael R., ed. *The Psychology of Fashion.* Lexington, Mass.: Lexington Books, 1985.

Sontag, Susan. "The Double Standard of Aging." In *Psychology of Women: Selected Readings,* ed. Juanita H. Williams. New York: Norton, 1979: 462–78.

Spark, Muriel. "That Lonely Shoe Lying on the Road." *New Yorker,* September 20, 1993: 82.

Steedman, Carolyn. "Difficult Stories: Feminist Auto/biography." *Gender and History* 7, no. 2 (1995): 321–26.

Stern, Linda. "How to Find a Job." *Modern Maturity,* June-July 1993: 25.

Stern, Mark J. "Poverty and the Life-Cycle, 1940–1960." *Journal of Social History* 24, no. 3 (1991): 521–40.

Stocker, Carol. "The Male Makeover." *Boston Globe,* October 30, 1991: 59.

Stoltenberg, John. *Refusing to Be a Man: Essays on Sex and Justice.* New York: Penguin, 1989.

Stone, Lucy. "Disappointment Is the Lot of Women." In *Feminism: The Essential Historical Writings,* ed. Miriam Schneir. New York: Random House, 1972: 106–9.

Stone, Rose. "Night Song for the Journey: A Self-Critical Prelude to Feminist Mothering." In Reddy, Roth, and Sheldon: 229–41.

Suckow, Ruth. *The Folks.* New York: Farrar and Rinehart, 1934.

Sukenick, Lynn. "Feeling and Reason in Doris Lessing's Fiction." *Contemporary Literature* 14, no. 4 (1993): 515–35.

Suleiman, Susan. *Risking Who One Is: Encounters with Contemporary Art and Literature.* Cambridge: Harvard Univ. Press, 1994.

Sybylla, Roe. "Situating Menopause within the Strategies of Power: A Genealogy." In *Reinterpeting the Menopause: Cultural and Philosophical Issues,* ed. Paul Komesaroff, Philipa Rothfield, and Jeanne Daly. New York: Routledge, forthcoming 1996.

Taylor, Charles. "The Politics of Recognition." In Charles Taylor et al.: 25–74.

Taylor, Charles, et al. *Multiculturalism: Examining the Politics of Recognition,* ed. Amy Gutmann. Princeton: Princeton Press, 1994.

Taylor, Dena, and Amber Coverdale Sumrall, eds. *Women of the 14th Moon: Writings on Menopause.* Freedom, Calif.: Crossing Press, 1991.

Tevis, Walter. *The Color of Money.* New York: Warner, 1984.

Thaddeus, Janice. "The Metamorphosis of Richard Wright's *Black Boy.*" *American Literature* 57, no. 2 (1985): 199–214.

Thomas, Alison. "The Significance of Gender Politics in Men's Accounts of Their Gender Identity." In Hearn and Morgan: 143–59.

Thompson, Roger. "Baby Boom's Mid-Life Crisis." *Editorial Research Reports* 1, no.1 (1988): 3.

Tomlinson, Alan. Introduction. In *Consumption, Identity, and Style: Marketing, Meanings, and the Packaging of Pleasure* ed. Tomlinson. London: Routledge, 1990.

Tyler, Anne. *Breathing Lessons.* New York: Knopf, 1988.

United States. Department of Commerce. Bureau of the Census. *Money Income of Households, Families, and Persons in the United States. 1991.* Series P60 Current Population Reports. 1992.

United States. Department of Health and Human Services. *The Menopause Time of Life.* N.d.

United States. Department of Labor. Bureau of Labor Statistics. *Employment and Earnings* 42, no.1 (1995).

Updike, John. *Rabbit Is Rich.* New York: Knopf, 1981.

Vedantam, Shankar. "New Boom is Looming." *Miami Herald,* December 30, 1995: 1A.

Veblen, Thorstein. *The Theory of the Leisure Class.* New York: Macmillan, 1899.

Voda, Ann M., Myra Dinnerstein, and Sheryl R. O'Donnell, eds. *Changing Perspectives on Menopause.* Austin: Univ. of Texas Press, 1982.

Waye, Robert. "Menopause." Medfax Sentinel, 1985.

Walker, Alice. "Everyday Use." In *In Love and Trouble.* New York: Harcourt Brace Jovanovich, 1973.

———. *The Color Purple.* New York: Harcourt Brace Jovanovich, 1982.

Wallerstein, Immanuel. *Historical Capitalism.* New York: Verso, 1983.

Walters, John. "Humor: The Incredulous Shrinking Man." *Modern Maturity,* October-November 1992: 92.

Weisner, Thomas S., and Lucinda P. Bernheimer. "Children of the 1960s at Midlife: Generational Identity and the Family Adaptive Project." In Shweder.

Weldon, Fay. *Praxis.* New York: Penguin, 1978.

West, Rebecca. "There Is No Conversation." In *The Harsh Voice.* Garden City, N.Y.: Doubleday, Doran, 1936.

Wicke, Jennifer. *Advertising Fictions: Literature, Advertisement and Social Reading.* New York: Columbia Univ. Press, 1988.

Williams, Raymond. *Marxism and Literature.* Oxford: Oxford Univ. Press, 1977.

———. *Modern Tragedy.* Stanford: Stanford Univ. Press, 1966.

Williamson, Janice. "Notes from Storyville North." In Shields: 216–32.

Wolf, Naomi. *The Beauty Myth: How Images of Beauty Are Used against Women.* New York: Morrow, 1991.

Woodward, Kathleen. *Aging and Its Discontents.* Bloomington: Indiana Univ. Press, 1991.

———. "Gerontophobia." In *Feminist Theory and Psychoanalysis,* ed. Elizabeth Wright. Cambridge: Basil Blackwell, 1992: 145–48.

———. *Invisible Women.* Bloomington: Indiana Univ. Press, forthcoming.

———. "Late Theory, Late Style: Loss and Renewal in Freud and Barthes." In Wyatt-Brown and Rossen: 82–101.

———. "Simone de Beauvoir: Aging and Its Discontents." In *The Private Self: Theory and Practice of Women's Autobiographical Writings,* ed. Shari Benstock. Chapel Hill: Univ. of North Carolina Press, 1988: 90–113.

———. "Tribute to the Older Woman: Psychoanalytic Geometry, Gender, and the Emotions." In *Psychoanalysis, Feminism, and the Future of Gender,* ed. Joseph H. Smith and Afaf M. Mahfouz. Baltimore: Johns Hopkins Univ. Press, 1990: 91–108.

Worcester, Nancy, and Marianne H. Whatley. "The Selling of HRT: Playing on the Fear Factor." *Feminist Review* no.41 (1992): 1–26.

Wright, Richard. *Black Boy.* 1945. Rpt. New York: Harper and Row, 1966.

Wyatt-Brown, Anne M. Introduction: "Aging, Gender, and Creativity." Wyatt-Brown and Rossen: 1–15.

Wyatt-Brown, Anne M., and Janice Rossen, eds. *Aging and Gender in Literature: Studies in Creativity.* Charlottesville: Univ. Press of Virginia, 1993.

Index of Keywords